1st pts   8⁵⁰

BAB
86289

THE PROUD POSSESSORS

THE PROUD
POSSESSORS

The lives, times and tastes
of some adventurous American
art collectors

ALINE B. SAARINEN

 RANDOM HOUSE · NEW YORK

First Printing
© Copyright, 1958, by Aline Saarinen
© Copyright, 1958, by The Condé Nast Publications, Inc.
All rights reserved under International and Pan-American Copyright
Conventions. Published in New York by Random House, Inc., and
simultaneously in Toronto, Canada, by Random House of Canada, Limited.
Library of Congress Catalog Card Number: 58-9890
Manufactured in the United States of America
by H. Wolff, New York

A condensation of the chapter on the Henry O. Havemeyers
appeared in *Vogue,* Oct. 1, 1958.

To Eero

Foreword

I am deeply grateful for the generosity, friendliness, trust and helpfulness of the many, many people on whom I have depended for assistance in doing the research for this book. I have indicated my indebtedness to them individually, chapter by chapter, in the Sources and Obligations at the end of the book. I hope, however, that each of them knows my gratitude is far greater than such apparently perfunctory acknowledgments indicate.

I would like to mention here particular thanks to those who showed their faith in me and this project from its beginnings: to Bernice Baumgarten; to Hiram Haydn; to those who sponsored me for a Guggenheim fellowship—Alfred H. Barr, Jr. (who, in addition, debated the choice of contemporary collectors with me); Alfred M. Frankfurter (who also discussed the selection and answered many questions during my research), Sir Philip Hendy,

Lester Markel (from whom I have learned very much), Daniel Catton Rich, James J. Rorimer, Paul Sachs and James Johnson Sweeney; and to the John Simon Guggenheim Foundation, whose fellowship award made possible the extensive research that kept me crisscrossing America and the Atlantic Ocean. Particular thanks also to Mr. Rorimer and R. Kirk Askew, who read the manuscript, but should not be held responsible for it. By dedicating the book to my husband I have chosen the best, but still inadequate, means of thanking him for his loving encouragement and remarkable patience.

Here, too, a special word of gratitude and appreciation for Bernard Berenson, who has had perhaps more influence on American taste and collecting than any other single person. He appears in this book as adviser and expert, where his influence is direct and calculable. But to think of Berenson only in these roles would be to underestimate the man and to overlook the perhaps greater significance of the less tangible influence of Berenson the writer and Berenson the presence.

His writings, from the earliest handbooks to the latest essays, are not only scholarly art history but also a rare summons to see and feel and understand the work of art as an event itself.

Now ninety-three, Berenson still lives and works in his villa outside Florence. Visitors stream to see him and even strangers address him as "B.B." He is wryly amused at having become, along with his villa and its gardens, his exquisite treasures and fabulous library, a three-star item for sightseers in Florence. Not so long ago he spoke ruefully of a young girl eying him "quizzically, like an overpraised ruin."

There is more at "I Tatti" than the palpable attractions and the sharp, brilliant conversation. Berenson has made a work of art of his way of life, following "the life of the mind . . . stimulated by a passion for the visible world." Berenson, the presence, opens the hearts and eyes of others to the spark of God in a painting and the immanent Tao in the olive trees of the Tuscan hills.

Only inadequately can I express my profound gratitude to him for his penetrating and illuminating comments on and remembrances of collectors and collecting, for his generosity in putting at my disposal the John G. Johnson correspondence and, above all, for the visits to "I Tatti."

A.B.S.

Bloomfield Hills,
Michigan
April, 1958

Contents

Illustrations

WITH THEIR SOURCES

Following page 200

Mrs. Potter Palmer, 1905
Photo by Steffens, courtesy of Mr. Gordon Palmer

Mrs. Potter Palmer, 1892
Courtesy of Mr. Gordon Palmer

Mr. Potter Palmer, 1892
Courtesy of Mr. Gordon Palmer

The Palmers' Castle, Chicago, 1882-85
Courtesy of The Ryerson Library, The Art Institute of Chicago

The Picture Gallery, 1892
Courtesy of The Ryerson Library, The Art Institute of Chicago

Pierre-Auguste Renoir: "Two Little Circus Girls"
Courtesy The Art Institute of Chicago, Potter Palmer Collection

Anders Zorn: "Mrs. Potter Palmer," 1893
Courtesy of The Art Institute of Chicago, Potter Palmer Collection

Anders Zorn: "Isabella Stewart Gardner," 1894
Courtesy of The Isabella Stewart Gardner Museum, Boston, Mass.

Mrs. John L. Gardner, 1888
Courtesy of The Isabella Stewart Gardner Museum, Boston, Mass.

Antonio Mancini: "Mr. John L. Gardner," 1895
Courtesy of The Isabella Stewart Gardner Museum, Boston, Mass.

John Singer Sargent: "Mrs. Gardner," 1922
Courtesy of The Isabella Stewart Gardner Museum, Boston, Mass.

Fenway Court, Boston, 1902: The Court, with Nasturtiums
Courtesy of The Isabella Stewart Gardner Museum, Boston, Mass.

Fenway Court, Boston, 1902: The Titian Room with Titian's "Rape of Europa"
Courtesy of The Isabella Stewart Gardner Museum, Boston, Mass.

John Singer Sargent: "Isabella Stewart Gardner," 1888
Courtesy of The Isabella Stewart Gardner Museum, Boston, Mass.

Grace and Edward Root, 1918
Courtesy of Mrs. Edward W. Root

Edward Root in Texas, 1906
Courtesy of Mrs. Edward W. Root

The Homestead, Clinton, N.Y., 1849
Courtesy of Mrs. Edward W. Root

Edward Wales Root
Courtesy of Mrs. Edward W. Root

Charles Burchfield: "Childhood's Garden," 1917
Courtesy of Munson-Williams-Proctor Institute, Utica, N.Y.

Theodore Stamos: "Monolith," 1947
Courtesy of Munson-Williams-Proctor Institute, Utica, N.Y.

Joseph Hirshhorn at Public School in New York, 1913
Courtesy of Mr. Joseph H. Hirshhorn

The Gallery of Joseph Hirshhorn, New York
Courtesy of Mr. Joseph H. Hirshhorn

Joseph H. Hirshhorn in his New York Office
Courtesy of Mr. Joseph H. Hirshhorn

View from Hirshhorn's Desk in his New York Office
Courtesy of Mr. Joseph H. Hirshhorn

Mrs. J. Watson Webb with Some Hunting Trophies in Samuel B.
    Webb's Trophy Room
Photo by Richard Meed for Sports Illustrated, *copyright, 1958, Time, Inc.*

Mr. J. Watson Webb at Westbury, Long Island, N.Y.
Reprinted from Vogue, *copyright 1956, The Condé Nast Publications Inc.*

Mary Cassatt: "Mrs. Havemeyer and Electra," 1896
Courtesy of Mrs. J. Watson Webb

The Shelburne Museum, Shelburne, Vt.
Courtesy of The Shelburne Museum, Shelburne, Vt.

Elizabeth Schumatoff: "Electra Havemeyer Webb," 1958, (detail)
Courtesy of Mrs. J. Watson Webb

"Mary O'Connor," Cigar Store Indian
Courtesy of Mr. J. Watson Webb, Jr.

The *"Ti"* and the Lighthouse, Shelburne Museum, Shelburne, Vt.
Courtesy of The Shelburne Museum, Shelburne, Vt.

Blanchette and John D. Rockefeller III
Courtesy of Mrs. John D. Rockefeller III

The Guest House, East 52nd Street, New York, by Philip C. Johnson
Photo by Gottscho-Schleisner, courtesy Philip C. Johnson Associates

Nelson A. Rockefeller
Courtesy of Mr. Nelson A. Rockefeller

Pablo Picasso: "Girl with Mandolin"
Courtesy of Mr. Nelson A. Rockefeller

Alexander Calder: "Mobile" on grounds of Nelson Rockefeller House,
Pocantico, N.Y.
Courtesy of Mr. Nelson A. Rockefeller

The Museum of Primitive Art, West 54th Street, New York
Courtesy of The Museum of Primitive Art

Introduction

Taste in America is a singular and fascinating phenomenon. It follows no conveniently straight path. It is many-layered, complex and contradictory. In exploring it, I have heeded Lytton Strachey. The wise explorer, he says, "will row out over [the] great ocean of material and lower down into it, here and there, a little bucket which will bring up to the light of day some characteristic specimen . . . to be examined with a careful curiosity."

The "characteristic specimens" here are art collectors. They were not objective spectators. By purchase and patronage, they declared their convictions and supported or shaped different levels and kinds of taste. One of what Russell Lynes called the "Taste-makers"—an architect, a decorator, a dealer, an expert, an artist—is present in the life of almost every collector. Sometimes he hovers like a gray eminence, sometimes he plays the bold role of guide. But the collector is no mere foolish pawn. He makes the ultimate moves and decisions and choices himself. He backs his taste with cold cash and proudly exposes it to view. Whether he makes taste or follows it, he is its eloquent witness.

The men and women in this book form a bizarre company. There are among them the only son of the richest man in the world and the son of a blacksmith; a lady who lived by the genteel precepts of the Edwardian era and another whose behavior is that of a Scott Fitzgerald heroine; a man whose ancestors were among the first to come to America and another whose heritage is Creek Indian; the greatest financier the world has ever known and a quiet philosopher. One of them was a fastidious bachelor who lived exquisitely in a preciously contrived setting, another was all but oblivious to a home of Collyer brothers-like clutter.

Their adventures in art were equally diverse. One of the collections was valued at $60,000,000, another was built for less than $150,000. One of the women re-created a Venetian palace in America and filled it with old masters, another bought a Venetian palace on the Grand Canal and filled it with abstract and surrealist art. One of them ventured into the interior of China to find ancient Oriental art, another stormed the artists' studios in Europe seeking out the newest of the new. Some were patrons, some propagandists. Some of them sought masterpieces, others bought because of faith in an artist or a movement.

Their overpowering common denominator is this: For each of them, the collecting of art was a primary means of expression. Interesting human beings, actively engaged in life on many levels, their involvement with art collecting was passionate and urgent. None of them bought just what he needed or could use. They were all zealots in whose lives this passionate pursuit had deep meaning. They were not only possessors: they were also possessed.

"It has become the mode to have taste," wrote James Jackson Jarves in the eighteen sixties. "Private galleries in New York are

becoming almost as common as private stables." There was, however, more of merit in the stables than in the galleries. The taste
which was modish was so deplorable that when three discriminating collectors did appear, their collections were received with massive indifference even by the so-called art-minded publics of the
three most culturally mature cities, Boston, Philadelphia and New
York.

These three predecessors—Luman Reed, Thomas Jefferson
Bryan and James Jackson Jarves—were not only collectors, but
also missionaries. They were dedicated to the proposition of con-
verting American taste from tear-jerking sentimentalities, frip-
peries and anecdotal atrocities to Art.

Luman Reed, a black-eyed, black-haired man with the square-
jawed look of a friendly Charlotte Brontë hero, was a retired
wholesale grocer who, in 1832, built in New York the first private
art gallery in America. It was filled with works by such of his
American contemporaries as Thomas Cole, whose grandiose alle-
gories of "The Course of Empire" prophesy Cecil B. De Mille
spectacles. When Reed died in 1836, his friends raised $13,000 to
buy the pictures, hoping to raise more so that they could establish
them as the nucleus of a permanent gallery of fine arts in New
York. They begged in vain and finally gave the collection to the
New York Historical Society.

Thomas Jefferson Bryan was a wealthy dilettante who hugely
enjoyed shopping in Europe for 381 old masters, mostly Flemish,
Dutch and French. Although the quality was uneven and many of
the Great Name attributions optimistic, he did rather well. But
when, in the eighteen fifties, he offered the collection to his native
Philadelphia, it was refused. Undaunted, he opened it in New
York as "Bryan's Gallery of Christian Art" on the second floor of
a Broadway building. Between 1853 and 1864, visitors who paid
twenty-five cents could have their taste elevated and could also
meet the ever present Bryan, a venerable old man, wrapped in a
red velvet cape, with precise little features framed by flowing white

hair and a Santa Claus beard. Shortly before his death in 1870, he gave his collection, too, to the New York Historical Society, which seems to have been a uniquely hospitable institution.

James Jackson Jarves, the most significant of the three (who has been ably presented in a biography by Francis Steegmuller), had the most advanced and discriminating taste and received the most chilling rebuffs. In the mid-century, he spent about ten years in Italy forming an incredible collection of completely unfashionable—and even despised—Italian primitives, or, as he called them, "gold-background pictures." They cost him $60,000, but in 1859 he was willing to let them go for a third that price to his native Boston as the nucleus of a museum there. Boston was not interested. Nor was New York. Eight years later, he gave the 119 paintings to Yale University as collateral for a loan of $20,000. Since he could not keep up the interest payments, in 1871 Yale put the collection up at auction. No interested buyers appeared. With the strongest reluctance, Yale made the single bid of $22,000 and, with masterpieces by Antonio Pollaiuolo, Sassetta and Gentile da Fabriano, got the greatest art bargain of our time.

Reed and Bryan helped make the *act* of art collecting fashionable for others, though the junk and dross that people collected was another matter. Jarves' pungent writings were widely published but hardly influential, and his paintings hung in New Haven unappreciated and almost completely unknown for about fifty years. These dedicated missionaries made no impact on American taste. Years later, Bernard Berenson told the stories of Bryan and Jarves to Edith Wharton, and, combining them in her hero, Lewis Raycie, she immortalized the hopelessness of their mission in *False Dawn*.

The strategic change in American collecting and taste came with the new economic era that began in the eighties. The increasing population, the exploitation of natural resources and the whole expanding economy created enormous fortunes and released men from physical labor into the pursuits and professions of a leisure class. Searching for a stage-set, or reacting against the new America, the new-very-rich looked naturally to Europe and began hankering to re-create Europe here.

Along with the still fashionable enameled nudes, morose cows and sentimental storytelling pictures, the collectors began—far in advance of Paris itself—to buy the "modern art" of France. These early collectors, some of whom would turn later in other directions, proudly displayed their possessions in a loan exhibition at the World's Columbian Exposition in Chicago in 1893.

This book begins with that setting and with its hostess, Mrs. Potter Palmer. Although she is the only major character in this book who was *not* caught in an insatiable passion for art collecting, she charmingly epitomizes the prologue period and its taste, albeit with a uniquely advanced twist. The great era of art collecting and the taste for old masters in America were born with Isabella Stewart Gardner. Soon great art, following as usual the flow of wealth, was moving westward at a rate that alarmed Europe.

As Royal Cortissoz said, American private collections "travelled with incredible celerity from the tenth-rate to the best." The proof of their excellence is the extraordinary wealth of American museums. In Europe, the origins of the museum treasures reach back to the "collecting" of the pharaohs and their growth is due to the mighty patrons and collectors of Church and State. In America, there were no Roman emperors collecting Greek antiquities, no Dukes of Berry or Burgundy, no German princelings, no Medicis or popes, no Hapsburgs, no Charles I or Arundel or Buckingham, no Valois and Bourbon kings, no Richelieus, Mazarins, Colberts or Napoleons. There were only men and women like those in this book, and the museums they have enriched with treasures often unrivaled in the world began their mushrooming growth only in the eighteen seventies. American museums continue, today, to develop and expand with the gifts of collectors, large and small, of art, new and old.

Everyone has a favorite art collector. "Aren't you going to include So-and-So?" was an inevitable question while I was working on this book. In almost every case, I could have. But my aim was no more to include *all* the interesting collectors than to imply that these are the "most interesting" or that their collections are the "most important."

I chose these particular "characteristic specimens" because they especially appealed to me. Interesting in themselves, they seemed also to make a varied, contrapuntal gathering. Their tastes illuminate kinds of tastes important to America; they have been adventurous in their art collecting in one way or another; their actions have influenced or made an impact on others. In so far as possible, they reflect the cultural attitudes of different sections of America. None of them are "crude collectors" whose motives are dollar investment or social climbing.

Why did they collect? Why did they choose art? The urge to collect is as old as man himself, but the incentives and the pleasures are as varied as the appeals of art. The motives that drove the men and women in this book to collect art, and the satisfactions they derived, could not, without distortion, be forced into a common mold. The life of each illuminates his own necessities, means and pleasures, and, I believe, adds a fragment to truth.

THE PROUD POSSESSORS

Provincial Princess

MRS. POTTER PALMER

Of the 27,539,521 people who visited the World's Columbian Exposition in Chicago in 1893, all "the best people" and all the illustrious guests of honor were received by Mrs. Potter Palmer in her battlemented castle on the wind-swept shores of Lake Michigan.

Their hostess, Berthe Honoré Palmer, was a poised and regal beauty in her early forties, with the tiniest waist in Chicago, delicately precise features and a perfectly groomed pompadour of shining, prematurely gray hair. A Kentuckian of distinguished French descent, she was a perfect lady down to the last of the 2,268 pearls in her seven-strand dog-collar. She was married to the owner of the Palmer House hotel, one of the richest, most powerful men in Chicago, who eyed her reverentially; she had triumphantly fulfilled her responsibilities as chairman of the Board of

Lady Managers of the Exposition and was now not only the undisputed queen of Chicago society but, as she put it, "the nation's hostess and the nation's head woman servant"; and she had recently built onto her castle a seventy-five-foot-long gallery to hold three tiers of her contemporary paintings.

The Palmer Castle and its art gallery epitomized the best fashionable taste. As such, it pleased Mrs. Palmer. All her life she was an attractive, simple worshiper of what she had been told was the best—the best society, the best individuals, the best standard of life with all its appurtenances, including clothes, jewels and works of art. She expected the best as her queenly right.

She was no supine, pliant female. She had a keen business mind, so keen that between her husband's death in 1902 and her own in 1918 she doubled his fortune to $16,000,000. She had so sure an organizational talent that she could weld even the most overwrought and aimless female volunteers into a functioning corps. She had a sense of social responsibility that was typically Chicagoan, but, as a lady lecturer said, she was not one of those who "wear bloomer costumes" to promote the cause of women. Everything she undertook was accomplished with such tact, such cordiality, such charm and quiet self-assurance that her foes fell painlessly. The writer Henry B. Fuller, in a searching novel of 1894, had his leading character, Mrs. Bates—for whom Mrs. Potter Palmer was prototype—explain: "Keep up with the procession is my motto, and head it if you can. I *do* head it, and I feel that I'm where I belong."

The castle from which Mrs. Palmer led the procession was begun in 1882. The modest statement which accompanied the issuance of the building permit for a three-story brick house to cost $90,000 gave no hint of what would eventually inspire one *Chicago Inter-Ocean* writer to exclaim that "the age of Pericles seems to be dawning" and another to declare that the Palmer mansion was "the largest, finest, costliest" ever.

Of its size there was no question. The house, of brown Wisconsin granite trimmed exuberantly with contrasting light sandstone and bulging with projecting windows, loomed up threateningly along eighty-two feet of lake front. Its turreted tower, with a spiral staircase, rose over eighty feet. Rivaling the Rhenish castles which Milwaukee brewers were nostalgically raising in Wisconsin, the mansion was variously described as "English battlemented style," "a Norman Gothic castle," "domestic castellated" and "English Gothic of the square-headed variety."

Nor was there any doubt that it was costly. The estimates jumped within a year from $90,000 to $200,000 to $250,000. Even Potter Palmer got cold feet as he saw both the costs and the monstrous structure rising, and in 1883 he tried to unload it at a sacrifice. Unsuccessful, he went gamely on. But when the costs mounted toward the ultimate sum of $700,000 he ordered his bookkeeper to enter no further charges against the building as he did not wish to know how much more it would cost.

Finest? It seemed so to Chicago, especially in 1885, when the luxuriously eclectic interiors could be seen. So eclectic were they, in fact, that the journalists were rather confused. Quick in certain rooms to recognize the Moorish and "East Indian" styles, with pierced lattice and stamped Cordovan leather, they were perplexed by the (mostly) Flemish Renaissance library, with its mantelpiece, held by six life-size oak figures, and its muraled ceiling. They called it "a medieval adaptation of the Greek" and said it was "fitted in the style of Cleopatra."

They went into ecstasies over the gold-and-white drawing room. It was the first Louis XVI salon in Chicago, and the journalists knew it was "Louis," although they differed on which one. They doted on the red velvet ballroom, the iridescent Tiffany glass chandeliers, the parquetry and marquetry floors and the octagonal two-story foyer. They rose in the first private elevator. It led to Mrs. Palmer's bedroom, "roomy enough," one of them explained, "for Hercules and his wife." In her bathroom they found a basin with an inlaid mother-of-pearl wreath and a sunken bathtub in the shape of a swan.

Mrs. Potter Palmer, securely receiving her guests as she stood on the elaborate staircase, banked by flowers from the sixty-foot conservatory, felt no inferiority about being a Middle Westerner. Chicago had never yearned toward the East. There had been, on the contrary, a rather chilly suspicion of New York. It reached a freezing point in 1893 when Ward McAllister, Mrs. Astor's social arbiter, offered Chicagoans gratuitous advice on how to be fitting hosts for New York visitors to the Exposition. They were somewhat resentful of his assurance that "the fact a man has been brought up in the West does not mean that he is not capable of becoming a society man." Nor did they take kindly to his advice "to import a number of French chefs" and not "to frappé their wine too much."

In the eighties and nineties—as perhaps still today—the Middle West by-passed New York and looked to Paris. Middle Western manufacturers entered their reapers, plows and wagons in the great international expositions in Paris, and went abroad to see them. When they got the coveted Prix de Paris, they stamped it in gold leaf on their machinery to impress farmers in Iowa and Indiana. Since the French drew no distinction between the millions made by residents of the Midwest and by those of the East, Chicagoans were received in French salons. Chicagoans bought French clothes, and they bought French art—so early and so much and so continuously that the Art Institute of Chicago today has the best representation of French nineteenth-century painting of any public museum in America. Not so long ago, the president of the Institute silenced a visitor who patronizingly remarked that a whole gallery of Renoirs must have cost the museum a pretty penny: "Not at all. In Chicago we don't buy Renoirs. We inherit them from our grandmothers."

Mrs. Potter Palmer's appointment in 1891 as chairman of the Board of Lady Managers of the Exposition was a passport whose visas allowed her to have audiences with Their Majesties the Queen of Belgium and the Queen of Italy, contact with other royalty from the Empress of Russia to the Queen of Siam, and the working cooperation of a board glittering with ladies, duchesses and princesses.

It was nice to hobnob with "the best people," but she was no mere figurehead chairman and no opportunist. She was, instead, the epitome of the able and conscientious lady volunteer who is as uniquely American as Coca-Cola.

Chicago was the cradle of social workers, producing women like the good Jane Addams. It was also a city where Society with a capital "S" had a strong sense of lower-case "s" social responsibility. Sometimes its gestures took on a somewhat comic-opera aspect. Mrs. Palmer, for instance, troubled by such violent outbursts of labor unrest in Chicago as the Haymarket riot and the Pullman strike, put great store in the National Civic Federation, an organization dedicated to mediation between management and labor. She showed her faith by offering her castle for a meeting, an invitation accepted without any reservation by management's August Belmont and by the union men with but one: that they "not be expected to wear dress-suits."

If good works for the public worked also for private benefit, so much the better. Ward McAllister might declare contemptuously that "howling swells never go to a Charity Ball," but Mrs. Potter Palmer made the Charity Ball in Chicago the supreme social event of the season. But lest the fine-feathered ladies and gentlemen should forget why they were there, the letters C-H-A-R-I-T-Y stood out in gold against a rising sun on a field of blue. Mrs. Palmer let nothing stand in the way of these occasions and no one wrest the scepter from her hands. As a newspaper once reported it, "In the midst of festivities in a European court, she said, 'Adieu, I must go back to Chicago to give the Charity Ball.' Napoleon, knowing full well the details of his next campaign, could have been no surer of his ground."

But there were no mixed motives in her concern for the welfare of women, and through the Women's Building of the Exposition she made a lasting contribution.

She worked indefatigably. She forced recognition of women's work on a par with men's and got women on prize juries. She charmed extra appropriations from House and Senate committees; managed a mountain of correspondence second in bulk only to that of the prolific publicity department; and stung into awareness of women's rights countries so unenlightened in this regard as Japan and the Sandwich Islands. In her low, well-bred voice she made dozens of addresses, in one of which she maintained that countries which advocated polygamy, burned widows with their husbands and drowned female children were more logical and less cruel than those which denied women the right to "improve their lot" by working.

She advocated a "baby-sitting" building at the Exposition. To raise $25,000 of the necessary funds, she allowed her castle to be crammed for three days and nights with a miniature world's fair. The 8,000 curious visitors took away an intimate glimpse of the queen at home and souvenir spoons with the castle in high relief on the bowl.

In her hands the Women's Building became more than a female-designed Neo-Ionic structure. It illuminated women's position throughout the world; it opened new avenues for their employment and new markets for their wares. Its exhibits ranged from needlework to the making of raspberry jam; from statues of Susan B. Anthony, who was dedicated to equal rights for women, to Psyche, who was not; from Italian lace to a Japanese boudoir; from Women's Suffrage to Women's Temperance. The latter group proudly showed a globe with cards of 4,000,000 persons who had taken the pledge of total abstinence. The ladies were not the least daunted by the fact that the pledgers were all children.

At the dedication, Mrs. Palmer, in a Parisian gown of heliotrope

and black crepe, studded with jet nailheads and gold passemen-
terie, was given a laurel wreath of silver to place above the
ostrich tips of her bonnet and a gold nail to hammer into the
building for "the golden touch." At the end of the ceremonies,
the nail was withdrawn and became the crossbar of a brooch
from the women of Montana, a brooch which encyclopedically
depicted in copper, silver and gold the Montana state seal, a
mountain, a waterfall, a farmer, a prospector, a rake and a pick.
This ambitious object remained thereafter in Mrs. Palmer's
jewel case, along with gems that were reputedly second only to
those of the Queen of Italy. So fabulous were her jewels that a
newspaper declared that when she appeared on the S. S. *Kaiser
Wilhelm der Grosse* with "a tiara of diamonds as large as lima
beans, a corsage panned with diamonds, a sunburst as big as a
baseball, a stomacher of diamonds and all her pearls around
her neck, Alois Burgskeller of the Metropolitan, who was singing
at the ship's concert, was stopped right in the middle of a high
note."

The auspicious dedication ceremonies of the Women's Building
were marred only by the fact that some of the Lady Managers
lost their heads in the proximity of royalty. Two of them tried to
bear a *Chicago Tribune* reporter to the platform thinking she
was a Russian princess and several of them made a nasty public
scene about the fact that Mrs. Potter Palmer herself rode in a
carriage with the Duchess of Veragua (whose husband, as a
direct descendant of Columbus, was the supreme guest of honor
at the Exposition). Their petulance was so public that Mrs.
Palmer had to call a meeting the next day and reprimand them
for this "pulling hair over an introduction to a Duchess." The
press reported that "her scorching words . . . cowed them into
respectful and humble attitude." Half the women were in tears,
and the meeting ended with emotional eulogies of Mrs. Palmer.

But later she found herself in a direct contretemps with royalty.
The Infanta Eulalia, representing the King of Spain, declined

to go to the reception being given for her by Mrs. Palmer, saying, "I prefer not to meet this inn-keeper's wife." After a private talk with the Spanish Ambassador, however, she appeared. While Mrs. Palmer remained smiling and gracious, the Infanta sat in sullen and unbending silence and left without touching her supper. The *Chicago Weekly* records that certain historians point out that five years later Spain had fallen from her haughty place. Some years after, when she was invited to a fete in Paris in honor of the Infanta, Mrs. Palmer regretted: "I cannot meet this bibulous representative of a degenerate monarchy."

The World's Columbian Exposition was Berthe Honoré Palmer's most spectacular opportunity. It was also Chicago's. The city was in the flush of the energetic expansion which changed it from a prairie town to what its promoters called "The Infant Municipal Prodigy of the World." As a center of inland shipping and a growing web of railroads, it was already a pulsing lumber, grain, livestock and produce market in the sixties, when such far-sighted gentlemen as Marshall Field, Cyrus McCormick, George Pullman and a spare, six-foot young Quaker named Potter Palmer, who had started out as a grocer's clerk in Albany County, N. Y., lucratively involved themselves with it.

It had boasted a "dry goods store in a marble palace" and a population of 340,000 before the night of October 8, 1871, when Mrs. Patrick O'Leary's cow kicked over a lamp and started the dreadful conflagration that ravaged an area of three and a half miles, leveled 17,450 buildings, rendered 100,000 people homeless and burned 1,500 to death. The holocaust spread its devastation for twenty-seven hours before it was finally extinguished by rain.

But neither rubble nor ashes had stifled the faith of men like Potter Palmer. He had been successfully selling shawls and gloves and sundry dry goods for fourteen years, before, in 1854, he realized that land and real estate were the golden security of

Chicago's golden future. At the time of the fire he was in the East attending his sister's funeral, but he sent word to his very recent bride not to despair and to aid the sufferers. Thirty-five of his buildings, bringing in $192,000 a year, were leveled. His hotel, the Palmer House, which had opened only thirteen days before the fire, was a ruin. But he knew the city would rise again, more splendid, more solid. It was alive with ambition.

Two years later, when the restless young architect Louis Sullivan arrived in Chicago, elevated wooden sidewalks threaded shabbily through acres of ashes in the business district. But building was booming. The output of "first-class front" was being measured by the mile. Sullivan found it "all magnificent and wild: a crude extravaganza, an intoxicating rawness, a sense of big things to be done."

The big things would be done, and Sullivan would be a part of them. Within a few years he was to build, with his partner Denkmar Adler, a structurally astonishing office-building-hotel-auditorium. Its tracery of gilt-plaster decoration, which he designed with the help of a lanky seventeen-year-old draftsman from Wisconsin called Frank Lloyd Wright, would spellbind such box-holders as the Potter Palmers while they sat on opening night listening to Adelina Patti sing "Home, Sweet Home."

But such strivings toward "modern architecture" were peripheral. Chicago, before the Columbian Exposition of 1893, was bristling instead with a gaudy style. It rivaled the pretensions of architecture in New York, where the architect Richard Morris Hunt, gauging the still undefined desires of the new tycoons, dreamed up a Fifth Avenue chateau for William Kissam Vanderbilt, grandson of the Commodore who made $90,000,000 in shipping and railroads, and son of William Henry Vanderbilt, who doubled his father's fortune. The house was in the late French Gothic style. It not only enabled the millionaire's socially ambitious wife to bring the socially aloof Mrs. Astor to her knees, but, more significantly, it set the fashion for magnificence. The pinnacles and turrets and steep gables, the marble and gold, the balconies and balustrades flourished from Newport to New York to North Carolina, where, in another Vanderbilt chateau, they reached a stupendous climax.

Potter Palmer contributed conspicuously to the even fancier stage-set that Chicago planned for itself after the fire. He built a palatial $3,500,000 new Palmer House, which opened just two years after the fire. The second hotel in America to be lit throughout with electric lights, its dining room imitated the salon of the Crown Prince of Potsdam, its parlor was Egyptian and its barber shop held 225 silver dollars embedded in the floor.

Potter Palmer was a reticent man, as his reserved, clean face with its neat little chin beard suggested, but he was moved to expansiveness on the subject of his hotel. He pitied the architects of old Renaissance palaces who knew so little of "luxury in appointments." The Palmer House, he said, was "a realization of an era of magnificence." Rudyard Kipling, however, took a somewhat less enthusiastic view of both the hostelry and its inhabitants: "They told me to go over to the Palmer House, which is a gilded rabbit-warren, and there I found a huge hall of tessellated marble, crammed with people talking about money and spitting about everywhere . . . A man who had drunk quite as much as was good for him told me this was 'the finest hotel in the finest city on God Almighty's earth.' " And so it was for generations of Middle Westerners.

Potter Palmer installed his wife in the handsomest suite. There, within eighteen months of each other in 1874 and 1875, their two sons, Honoré and Potter Palmer, Jr., were born. But even though it was the handsomest suite in "the palace hotel of the world," the Potter Palmers wanted a home of their own. Thus in 1882 they commissioned their much admired castle.

When the style for the Exposition was under discussion, however, it was neither the florid architecture of mansions like the Palmer castle nor the new, "organic" modern architecture of

Louis Sullivan that triumphed. The fashionable Eastern architects —among whom were Richard Hunt and McKim, Mead and White—argued for the Neo-Classical style. The Chicago architect Daniel H. Burnham, himself working progressively in the Sullivan direction, humbly acquiesced to their sophistication. An array of colonnaded, cold-cream-white plaster buildings rose along the reflecting lagoons. The "White City" dazzled its beholders, whose taste for grandeur was just emerging (in the Pullman Palace Car exhibit, cars had Louis XIV interiors). French critics singled out Sullivan's original Transportation Building, with its glistening "Golden Door." But the American public—and especially the tycoons who visualized themselves in a grandeur grander than Rome's—approved the official white architecture of the Exposition so thoroughly that within a few years such extravaganzas as the Palmer castle would seem a little bit passé and the emerging "modern architecture" of Chicago would be thrust temporarily into eclipse.

Mrs. Potter Palmer could frequently be found in the Fine Arts Palace at the Exposition, one of the largest and most imposing of the structures. Among the tons of sculptures and acres of paintings that filled it was a loan exhibition of "Foreign Masterpieces Owned By Americans." It gave a piercingly accurate picture of "the best taste" for contemporary and near-contemporary art in 1893.

The 126 paintings were almost entirely by French artists— "Men of 1830" like Delacroix and painters of the Barbizon forest like Corot, Millet, Diaz and Theodore Rousseau. The vogue for these painters had started in Boston in the mid-eighteen eighties—long before they were fully accepted in France—when wealthy, social Bostonians like S. D. Warren, Quincy Adams Shaw and Martin Brimmer bought their paintings. Their credentials had been presented by William Morris Hunt, a painter who had studied in Paris and was the brother of the taste-setting architect Richard Morris Hunt. He came from a well-to-do New England family and had a magnetic personality and a witty tongue. He had an even greater asset as an arbiter of taste in Boston. Married to the daughter of an important Boston banker and philanthropist, he was a member of the inner social circle.

By 1893, Boston intellectuals had begun to look backward to the Renaissance, but the vogue for the "modern French" still held there and had spread widely in America. The lenders to the loan exhibition, in which Corot and Millet had the edge four to one and two to one respectively over any other painters, included prominent New Yorkers—such as Cornelius Vanderbilt, Alfred Corning Clark, Charles T. Yerkes and the late Jay Gould —Philadelphians, including John G. Johnson, and Californians, including railway magnate William H. Crocker.

Everything "the best people" approved was here. For those who liked nature, not in the raw, but in the mild, there were the leafy Barbizon forests. For an age that liked its anecdote with a literary cast, there were such uplifting objects as Sir Alma-Tadema's "A Reading from Homer." Lent by the eccentric Jekyll-Hyde collector Henry Marquand, who gave Flemish old masters to the Metropolitan and crowded his Richard Morris Hunt-decorated house with fashionable contemporaries, this painting was so popular that even in 1910 reproductions of it still gave an elevating tone to thousands of American homes. For an age that also liked anecdote with a homey touch, there were several appropriate pictures in this loan section, although the record-breaking tear-jerker was in the American section: Hovenden's "Breaking the Home Ties," whose folksy sentiment was potent enough in mail-order reproductions to loose the tear ducts of many hundreds of American "moms" all over again when Uncle Sam broke home ties so forcibly in 1941.

There was much here also to satisfy an age that not only confused truth of detail with beauty but also morals with art. Nowhere were the moral feelings of the rich better placated than in paintings of the poor of Brittany and Holland. It was consoling to dismiss the anarchists' bombs, the railroad strikes and the agitation of the Wobblies as extremist expressions and to think of the true workingman as the unspoiled, noble peasant depicted in Breton's still-beloved "Song of the Lark" and Millet's "Man with the Hoe." Based on Edwin Markham's poem and sent from the Crockers' Pacific Slope castle, this oil was not only a hit at the Exposition but was also the painting that moved a chubby little San Francisco girl called Gertrude Stein to her first enthusiasm for art. (It was also a favorite of the Crockers' butler. At the time of the San Francisco earthquake and fire of 1906, the Crockers were away. Left with the responsibility of saving what he considered best and most valuable in the house, he grabbed the Millet painting, a Daubigny landscape and an anecdotal painting by Ziem, and left the Crockers' recently purchased Degas and Pissarro paintings to burn.)

There were, however, a few disturbing notes in this loan exhibition, particularly disturbing since they, too, had been lent by the right people. There were, for instance, according to a contemporary chronicler, a painting by the "yet little-known Courbet" lent by the eminently respectable H. O. Havemeyers of sugar-refining fortune; some garish Renoirs; some bluntly direct Manets; a sketchy Pissarro, a Sisley, and some canvases by Degas which were "of little value except as specimens of the Impressionist school, from a man who seldom completes a picture and yet is hailed by his brethren as one of the most talented and original artists of his day." The primary lenders of these pictures were Alexander Cassatt, who was soon to be president of the Pennsylvania Railway, and the Potter Palmers of Chicago.

They were the only volcanoes in the loan exhibition. But even the most run-of-the-mill Barbizon School pictures in that section were far superior to the acres of paint that filled the galleries of the various nations in the Fine Arts Palace. The Americans, Homer, Eakins, Sargent and Whistler, all won minor prizes, but the style of the French salon—against which the advanced French painters were rebelling—was in ascendency and the galleries had a stultifying sameness.

There were Biblical scenes in which the personages were identifiably religious because they had the big, watery eyes of bovines, and, conversely, paintings of dewy-eyed animals that looked tremulously devout. There were freebooting Cossacks, peasants at table and spicy duels painted in finicky detail on canvases as large as billboards. But most of all there were nudes, exclusively female nudes, nudes cavorting on the seashore, rising from champagne bubbles, peering at themselves in pools (Thumann's "Psyche" later became the White Rock lady), nudes reclining, kneeling, turning, stretching, nudes swarmed over by cupids; nudes archly, coyly, teasingly keeping modest by hiding their femaleness behind a sprig, a piece of gauze, a casually placed hand, a fluttering dove; nudes so precise, enameled and salaciously naked as to cause J. P. Morgan to remark, when he visited the Fine Arts Palace, that the French section looked as if it had been picked by a committee of chambermaids.

The Potter Palmers had bought *objets d'art* to decorate their castle. That was a matter of course. The Palmers' taste, which included austere T'ang figurines along with florid late Chinese porcelains, was, however (as objects in the Art Institute today attest), better than that of many of their neighbors. The perceptive dealer Dirkan Kelekian, who was later to promote modern art, got his start in America in 1893 when Stanford White and several other architects urged him to bring his sixteenth-century Persian rugs, early textiles and potteries to the Middle West. "In Chicago," he recalled later, "prospective buyers would hold up one of my rare rugs to the light to see if there were holes in it, and when there were—exit the thought of acquiring it."

Equally as a matter of course the Potter Palmers bought contemporary paintings for their contemporary castle, and in this pursuit Mrs. Palmer had two advisers. One was a Chicago lady, Sarah Hallowell, who busied herself for fifteen years at the Paris salons "skimming the cream," as she put it, of work by "our painters over the water" and, after 1894, sending them home for annual exhibition. The couturier Monsieur Worth's advice on gowns was no more up-to-the minute than Miss Hallowell's on fashionable art. The Palmers enthusiastically followed both.

They also bought a few American paintings. Mr. Palmer even bid $1,650 successfully for a George Inness "Morning" at a New York auction in 1889 where Bastien-Lepage's "Joan of Arc Listening to Voices" brought $23,400.

The Palmers spent almost as much that same year for a Corot. It was a good Corot, from the Demidoff Palace in Florence, and it was right that they bought it, for as Mrs. Batcs, Mrs. Palmer's literary counterpart, explained in Fuller's *With the Procession,* "people in our position would naturally be expected to have a Corot."

Mrs. Palmer's second adviser was a painter. Collectors' attitudes toward artists vary considerably. Some collectors, swollen with the pride of possession, become strong adherents of the theory that environment is more important than heredity. Thus they seem to feel personally responsible for the excellence of the work of art for which the artist gradually seems only to have been an incubator. Other collectors reluctantly admit the artist is a necessary sort of fellow, but a little beyond the pale, a little peculiar and usually more than a little dirty. One of the advantages of collecting old masters is that the masters are old enough to be safely dead. Still other collectors, more romantically inclined, use works of art as passports into the world of Bohemia, in which they enjoy slumming. A few rare collectors, who are usually also the real patrons, simply regard artists as rare and wonderful human beings endowed with God's highest gift to man.

Many collectors take a middle-ground position. They like to know *some* artists, especially those who do not wear beards and who do cut their hair. Such presentable artists are sometimes exhibited as lions, sometimes as lesser mammals. Many of them, having gotten one foot past the butler, play a strategic role in directing the collector's taste. Numerous, indeed, are splendid collections in America which were formed with just such guides as these.

Mrs. Potter Palmer had the easy, uncondescending manner of the well bred to all kinds of people, so that even artists did not throw her off balance. She rather enjoyed those few she knew. She visited Monet in 1891 and bought a painting from him, the first of a great many Monets—so many that she ultimately had enough to make a frieze around her ballroom. She made a more favorable impression on Whistler than the Eternal City did. In 1891, Whistler made his only visit to Rome, to attend a friend's wedding, and on his return he described Rome to his biographers, the Pennells, as "a bit of an old ruin alongside of a railway station where I saw Mrs. Potter Palmer."

The important artist in Mrs. Palmer's life was Mary Cassatt. This spirited young woman shocked her well-to-do Philadelphia family first by becoming an artist, and then in 1868, at the age of twenty-three, when she had tired of drawing casts in the Pennsylvania Academy, by announcing that she was going to Europe. "I would almost rather see you dead," her father told her. She went anyway, spent years in Italy and Spain absorbing old master paintings and settled in Paris in 1874. There one day, as she later wrote her friends the Havemeyers, she "flattened her nose" against a picture dealer's window in the Boulevard Haussmann to gaze at a Degas pastel. Soon she knew who were her "true masters. I admired Manet, Courbet and Degas. I hated conventional art. I began to live."

Three years later she met Degas. It was an ambiguous relationship, almost certainly platonic, despite the incendiary nature of its ups of profound sympathy and its downs of irritated spats. She acknowledged his superiority, yet tried to keep her pride;

he admired her, yet feared lest admiration weaken his almost misanthropic egocentricity. He would pay her his highest tribute, telling her the head of a child had "the quality of a Holbein," next prick her with a barb, saying a painting of a little boy was "the greatest painting of the nineteenth century. It is little Jesus and his English nurse."

Their friendship had its real meaning as an inextricable part of the bigger friendship of all the artists in Paris who were rebelling against "conventional art." Manet, Monet, Renoir, Morisot, Pissarro, Sisley, Signac were among those whose endless shop talk, maneuverings, reciprocal admiration and encouragement, backbiting and double-dealings, gossiping and philosophizing were carried on, charged with the excitement of defiance, around café tables, in studios and in the galleries of those very few courageous dealers like Durand-Ruel who risked near-ruin to back them.

Mary Cassatt was a lively part of it. She helped them all. She bought quantities of Degas' work for herself and her brother, Alexander. Never was there a more effective tout for culture. When her wealthy American friends came for tea, Pissarro canvases would be more in evidence than scones. Importunately she directed her rich friends to her painter friends' studios. She bought from Durand-Ruel and sent him clients like Mrs. Palmer. From time to time she lent him money, helping him, for instance, to send to New York in 1886 America's first exhibition of so-called impressionist art.

The painters had been having a hard struggle in Paris, where the omnipotent Academy had a stranglehold on exhibitions, public taste and a large part of the press. Partly because Durand-Ruel had a respectable reputation in America as a vendor of mild Barbizon School paintings; partly because the exhibition was cushioned with conservative art; partly because there was no such powerful adversary as the French Academy in America; and partly because the American press had unprejudiced curiosity, the show received surprisingly favorable notices.

There were some blasts, of course. One critic called it "communism incarnate, with the red flag and the Phrygian cap of lawless violence displayed." Most of the critics, however, were attentive; many were downright appreciative. Seven or eight paintings were sold. The show seemed, therefore, such a success that competitive dealers in conservative art scurried to Washington to try to complicate customs regulations against such invasions in the future. They need not have been so nervous quite yet. Success is relative and the success of the Durand-Ruel exhibition was a limited one. It stirred a mere ripple in prevailing American taste, so that when a collector like Mrs. Potter Palmer, on the advice of Mary Cassatt, began buying impressionist paintings in 1889 she was indeed still a pioneer.

Her bills from Durand-Ruel commence in that year (and include a fascinating Degas pastel, "On the Stage," for $500). But her big buying years were 1891 and 1892. It was hardly coincidental. As soon as she was appointed chairman of the Board of Lady Managers in 1891, she made plans for the roomy new wing to house the picture gallery and banquet hall.

The impressionist paintings that she bought to go among the three-tiered mélange on the marble and brocaded walls of a room furnished with leopard skins and whatnots were extraordinarily good. In 1892, Mrs. Palmer's purchases included four Renoirs. Among them were the boldly abstract "Wave" and "The Canoeist's Luncheon," and, for $1,750, the bewitching painting of "Two Little Circus Girls" that is today one of the most popular pictures in the Art Institute of Chicago. (The four, which cost Mrs. Palmer a total of $5,000, were valued at $87,000 in 1922, and the "Little Circus Girls" alone would bring $200,000 today.) At the time J. P. Morgan was absorbed in autograph manuscripts and rare books, Mrs. Palmer was buying such paintings as Monet's now renowned "Argenteuil sur Seine" ($1,500) and three Pissarros, including the poignant "Café au Lait" ($650).

They made quite a splash in the new picture gallery. Other

Chicagoans, like the gentle Martin A. Ryerson, would soon be adopting dozens of little Renoir girls to keep company with exquisite old masters, but Mrs. Palmer was among the first to bring impressionist painting to America and was the very first to introduce it to the Middle West. She was not pioneering in art to enhance her social position. On the contrary, because she believed it was an appropriate appurtenance to her well-entrenched social slot, the art itself was made acceptable.

Mary Cassatt had been helpful, but Mrs. Palmer did Miss Cassatt a good—and rather courageous—turn, too. There were two enormous spaces for murals in the Women's Building. Mrs. Palmer tactfully gave one to the wife of the admired Exposition sculptor, Frederick MacMonnies, who filled it with academically classical ladies whose coiffures looked like inverted pots. She awarded the other to Mary Cassatt. Her speech to the board justifying the choice of this artist "unknown among us" was an example par excellence of precise art appreciation and Machiavellian suavity. She took the ladies' minds off modern art by describing how this well-to-do artist had built a vast studio for this gigantic undertaking and had the ground excavated so the canvas could be lowered into it when she wanted to work on the upper part. In the end, Miss Cassatt's perhaps too-small-scale figures, flat as those in a Japanese print, innocently mingling with geese and apple trees, commemorated "Modern Woman" without offending anyone.

One might assume that at the close of the Exposition, Mrs. Palmer could have reclined snugly on the pinnacles of international social success. But what general has ever rested on his laurels, no matter how comfortable, when yet another frontier remains to be crossed? She was an international star, but Newport remained the acid test. No Middle Westerner had yet forced McAllister's stronghold.

Mrs. Palmer's first two seasons in a rented cottage at this socially inbred and closed Rhode Island resort were rather chilly.

One of the dowagers, for instance, asking her friends, "Who *is* this Mrs. Potter Palmer?" was told, "I think her husband keeps some sort of hotel," only to be interrupted by another who said, "Oh, no, she used to sell things at the Chicago Exposition."

Her Newport campaign was aided considerably when President McKinley appointed her as the only woman commissioner of the United States to the Paris Exposition of 1900. Her accomplishments won her such diverse accolades as Jane Addams' unqualified praise and the French Government's Legion of Honor. They also allowed her, in a glittering Paris salon, to nourish her friendships with European royalty. Newport was quiveringly susceptible to titles. When, as a society reporter breathlessly wrote, Mrs. Palmer was able to entertain "in rapid succession two princes of the blood royal"—Prince Albert of Belgium and His Royal Highness the Count of Turin—and to marry off her personally sponsored niece (who was a granddaughter of President Grant) to Russian Prince Michael Cantacuze, the Newport ramparts fell before her. Ward McAllister must have shuddered in his grave when in 1908 the press acknowledged this Middle Westerner as queen of Newport.

After her husband's death in 1902, however, she spent a large part of each year in Europe. She played golf with Edward VII; she was rumored to be marrying various distinguished Britishers as well as King Peter of Serbia; and she gave superlative entertainments in Paris. She gave a party at which Pavlova danced; another at which the whole Russian ballet entertained; another at which an unknown Australian singer called Nellie Melba sang. In 1907, she rented the Duke of Abercorn's house in London and gave her home for a performance of *Salomé*. The Richard Strauss-Oscar Wilde opera, performed once in Dresden and once in Paris, had roused the critics to cries of "Necrolatry" and had been placed under the censor's ban. She imported the entire cast from Paris, and King Edward, Queen Alexandra and United States Ambassador Whitelaw Reid were her guests of honor.

She returned to Chicago long enough each year, as *Hampton's Magazine* put it in 1911, to "set her kingdom in order" and to disappoint the dreams of such yearning contenders for her crown as Marshall Field's second wife and the formidable Mrs. Harold McCormick, daughter of John D. Rockefeller, who rode in a plum-colored Rolls-Royce with attendants in plum-colored livery.

Mrs. Palmer's interest in art waned, except for the purchase of a few mostly mediocre old masters as decoration for her Paris residence. In 1906 she had her fingers on a painting of Pope Innocent X attributed to Velásquez and owned by Prince Brancaccio, but Bernard Berenson spirited it away for Isabella Stewart Gardner for $96,501. Mrs. Gardner's was a Pyrrhic victory: the painting is today attributed to "an other hand, probably, than Velásquez'."

After 1910, Mrs. Palmer became more and more involved in a recently acquired estate at Sarasota, Florida. She maneuvered the railroad to run a line to it; she planted fruit orchards; she began developing rice. She died there on May 5, 1918, and her body, in an orchid-covered casket, was brought to Chicago for services and burial.

Berthe Honoré Palmer enjoyed the best things of life as she lived them. She had no ambitions for immortality. Thus she willingly—and wisely—left to others the disposition of her $400,000 bequest to charitable and educational institutions and to her son and officials of the Art Institute the selection of $100,-000 worth of her art for that institution. The latter chose, of course, in 1922, all the great impressionist paintings and two Delacroix. But, sagely, because the swing of taste will someday soon surely bring the Barbizon painters back into high fashion, they also chose some of the currently less popular paintings like Millet's splendid "Rail Splitters" and four Cazins. She also left in her son, Potter Palmer, Jr., a sensitive collector and a devoted, intelligent future president of the board of the Art Institute.

She was both a lady and an uncommonly important and interesting woman. Ironically, of all the triumphs she won as she led the procession, her art collecting is the one for which she is best remembered—and it was only an incidental in the course of the parade.

C'est Mon Plaisir

ISABELLA STEWART GARDNER

Both Berthe Honoré Palmer and Isabella Stewart Gardner, who was ten years her senior, knew the Swedish painter Anders Zorn. His fashionable, fluent style made him one of the most popular painters at the World's Columbian Exposition. Fifty-two-year-old Mrs. Gardner "discovered" him there in June of 1893. She noticed a painting of an interior of an omnibus. She also noticed a ruddy-cheeked, mustached, thirty-three-year-old man, who was provocatively attractive, wandering in the gallery. She asked him if he knew anything about the painter of the omnibus. He was, of course, Zorn. She bought his picture for $1,600 and their long, close friendship began.

Both the ladies commissioned Zorn to do their portraits. The paintings leave no doubt as to which of the subjects most engaged him. Mrs. Palmer's is a candy-box stereotype with a careless, unfinished look. Chicago newspapers accounted for this apparent incompleteness by reporting that the artist hurt his right wrist in a horseback fall and had to complete the painting with his left hand. Gossip had it that he made a "pass" at Mrs. Potter Palmer and she ordered him away.

He painted Mrs. Gardner three years later, one evening in Venice after they had spent hours languishing together in a gondola. Throbbing with vitality, the portrait shows her bursting exultantly into the room from a balcony of the Palazzo Barbaro. It is the best portrait Zorn ever painted, but as he himself admitted, "Alas, all my subjects are not Mrs. Gardner and the backgrounds not Canale Grande." It is the most expressive likeness of this remarkable and fascinating woman.

Isabella Stewart Gardner, like most interesting and rewarding people, was an egotist. Like all egotists, she was driven by vanity. Hers was no mean variety: it was cosmic and insatiable. The ceaseless pursuit of its gratification led her, as her friend Henry James remarked, to "a preposterously pleasant career," and it has enriched America.

The Fates were kind to Isabella Stewart Gardner. They did not make her beautiful. They made her plain. She had fine, widely set eyes, but her features were rather large, the face a little flat, the coloring somewhat nondescript. But, as if to make up for these minor injustices, the Fates gave her a greater gift than beauty: they made her seductive.

They did even more. They provided her with a nimble, curious mind and a sense of drama. They gave her a vitality to abet her enthusiasms and an energy to support her will. They presented her with John L. Gardner, an eminently respectable husband, indulgent of her whims, to whose Gibraltar-like stability she could return when she had ventured as far as she wished. Nor was she denied the comforts of a generous income.

Then, even more magnanimously, the Fates granted her a perfect opportunity. They provided as her stage Boston in the eighteen eighties and nineties. Against no other setting would her caprices have seemed incongruous enough to put her in the coveted spotlight. Nowhere else could she have found admirers so desirably intellectual and cultivated nor have been stimulated to try to gratify her vanity by following such "a preposterously pleasant career."

In its pursuit, she became the intimate companion of a score of her period's most brilliant writers, musicians and artists. She concocted a fabulous Venetian palace—Fenway Court—on the marshy lands of the Boston Fens and filled it with treasures, including masterpieces by the great Italian painters from Giotto to Guardi, a few Rembrandts, a Vermeer, two Holbeins and other delectable items for good measure. In her will, she directed that nothing be changed, so that from the flaring orange nasturtiums, hanging like banners from the second-story balconies of the garden court, to the brocade beneath the most ravishing Titian in America, Fenway Court remains forever intact, the personal expression of a woman whose motto—engraved along with a symbol of immortality on Fenway Court—was *"C'est mon plaisir."*

Newspaper reporters were barred from the party on December 31, 1902, at which Mrs. Gardner first revealed Fenway Court, but it was inevitable that they would crash this particular New Year's Eve ball. Since the seventies, its hostess had been Boston's most extraordinary and colorful copy. She was so well known that when a letter came to the post office addressed to "Mrs. Gardner, Esq., well-known lady in high life, Boston, Massachusetts," the clerk simply added, "Try Mrs. Jack," and the letter reached her.

For two years the newspapers had been speculating about the curious building rising in this sparsely inhabited, undesirable section of Boston. It was referred to by workmen as "Mrs. Gardner's Eyetalian palace," but it presented a high brick wall and a forbidding, noncommittal four-story façade to the world. Only a favored few intimates had ever been inside. Indeed, the owner had kept its interior so guarded a secret that when she wanted to test the acoustical properties of the Music Room before the New Year's Eve party, she invited for a trial concert a carefully calculated audience: the children from the Perkins Institution for the Blind.

Several reporters did get in that New Year's Eve, some in the guise of waiters and musicians. They watched the cream of Boston society climb a horseshoe staircase at the end of the Music Room to pay homage to their hostess at its summit and then meekly descend the other side.

The woman who received them, now in her sixty-second year, looked remarkably as she had when Sargent painted her portrait fourteen years before. That portrait had created a furor when it was exhibited at the sedate St. Botolph Club in 1888. The subject's alluring hourglass figure had been emphasized by a black shawl tied tightly around the hips over the stark black dress and by a double strand of pearls encircling the waist. The short sleeves revealed the shoulders and the arms, which one ecstatic critic called "perfection—beggaring description," and the low V-neck set off the high, full breasts. The figure looked out provocatively from the background of a painted textile. The pattern made a halo behind her head, causing one gentleman visitor to remark, "Egad, she's had herself painted as a medieval saint," and a Unitarian minister to rejoin, "Leave off the 'medi' and you will describe it."

Mr. Gardner was explicit about forbidding a further public display of the portrait during *his* lifetime. (Mrs. Gardner deferentially kept it hidden from the public even after her husband's death, but insured that it should emerge from obscurity when she herself had disappeared.)

On this New Year's Eve, fourteen years later, the hostess wore a similarly simple black dress. But from her somewhat reddish hair, above wide, enigmatic, blue-gray eyes, two enormous diamonds, which she called "The Rajah" and "The Light of India," rose on quivering wires like antennae.

When the musical program was over, the mirror doors of the Music Room were thrown open. Reporters and guests were con-

fronted with "fairy-land." On this frosty night, under a glass roof
four stories above, bloomed a profusion of carnival-bright, per-
fumed flowers, grouped around a Roman mosaic floor and em-
bracing fragments of ancient sculpture. Hundreds of candles
glowed in the rooms surrounding the court. There, tastefully at
home with Gothic crucifixes, Chinese bronzes, aged and lovely Renaissance velvets and terra-cotta reliefs were old master paintings
of a quality Americans hardly knew. Within these rooms, with
their hand-hewn beams and their brocade-covered walls, the astonishing Mrs. Gardner had created a total, exquisite and wholly personal environment. It was her moment of great triumph. From
now on, through the twenty-two years still remaining of her life,
Boston and the civilized world would, perforce, kneel to her.

Boston had hardly been aware of her until the seventies. She
was a New Yorker, daughter of a well-to-do man who moved
from the importing business to mining. She had married in 1860
John Lowell Gardner, the brother of a friend she met during her
"finishing" process in Paris. Aside from arousing a slight resentment for having captured one of the town's most eligible bach-
elors, the twenty-year-old, reassuringly plain bride scarcely ruffled
Boston society. For nearly a decade she led a quiet, ailing life,
climaxed in 1865 by the death, at the age of two, of her long-
awaited, only son. It was the one cruel blow life dealt her: the only
defeat against which she was powerless. In 1867, the still incon-
solable young woman was carried on a mattress aboard a ship for
the tonic of a trip to Europe. The cure restored her spirit, but the
scars of the tragedy remained and altered the course of her life.

On her return from Europe she began the series of escapades
and unconventionalities that dazzled, fascinated and shocked Boston. As the wife of a member of the impeccably correct Gardner
family and daughter-in-law of that *ne plus ultra,* a Peabody of
Salem, she had a secure niche in Boston society. As a "foreigner"
from New York, she could be considered "on approval" and slightly
suspect, but she could not be snubbed. But it was not her new style

to be the politely accepted and unremarkable stranger. Cleverly, she understood that she could dare attention-getting eccentricity without risking excommunication.

Her friend Bernard Berenson has called her a pre-cinema star, but she was also a pre-publicity agent, with an uncanny flair for attracting the limelight. Against the background of Boston's conservative, concentric society her egocentricity stood out in bold relief. With a sure sense of drama, she capitalized on the contrast between background and behavior.

For decades the newspapers reveled in her escapades. When the Gardners missed meeting a coach to go with friends to a picnic, she persuaded her husband to hire a locomotive and helped drive it at eighty miles an hour in order to overtake the group. Once during Lent she donned sackcloth and ashes and scrubbed the steps of Boston's Church of the Advent. She drank beer at "pop" concerts when other ladies sipped sherry. She sat in the front row at a Jim Corbett boxing exhibition when "nice" women generally did not attend such sporting events. She paraded up and down the Boston zoo leading a lion on a leash. The train of her cerise-and-gold-brocade gown at an artists' ball was borne by a diminutive African in Malayan costume, who carried a tiny dog in his arms. Once she even caused a delicate international incident when, after having been presented at the Italian court, she sent King Umberto yellow roses for his birthday. His Majesty, somewhat nettled by the unconventional gesture, sent an equerry to find out whether the gesture implied the impudent invitation to intimacy which he presumed it did. It required the apologetic explanation of the United States Minister to Italy to persuade him that it did not.

She played her role artfully. Her face might be plain, but her shoulders were beautiful and her figure enticing. Her clothes, ordered from Worth in Paris, were a little more spectacular than those of the other Boston ladies, a little more décolleté, a little more daringly cut, so that young gentlemen in their morning-after-the-ball notes would write of thinking "of the way your dress fits." She and a rival belle had made many spectacular entrances at Boston balls laden with floral offerings from admirers. Aware that the young men were betting about which would have the largest number of tributes at a particular ball, she let her competitor appear first with a funereal array of blossoms and then made a late entrance with a single flower pinned to her dress. When other women were wearing black stockings, she appeared in white ones—and when they followed her lead, she switched back again. Two hostesses at a musicale, seating themselves like bulwarks on each side of their captivating guest of honor, lost him to Mrs. Gardner in spite of their precautions. At a strategic moment, she coughed just loudly enough to call attention to her precipitate dash from the room. Dispatched by his hostesses to see if she were all right, the gentleman never returned. She was aware, of course, that she was vexing the female members of the Boston inner circle. Once when she was asked if she would contribute to the Charitable Eye and Ear she replied tartly that she did not know there was a charitable eye or ear in Boston.

Nor would she concede that her own genealogy was inferior to her husband's. It might be less impeccable by New England standards, but it was a good deal more romantic. By a complicated reckoning she arrived at Robert Bruce and Mary Stuart as ancestors and thus accounted for the "Stewart." She took care of "Isabella" without any complex genealogical justification. She simply equated herself with *all* the Isabellas of history—from Spain to Italy—and so thorough was her identification that she would buy any work of art that was at all connected with any one of these illustrious ladies.

The caprices and escapades and pretentious genealogy focused the spotlight upon her. But even more than attention, she craved admiration—total, universal and submissive. Whether any or how many of her admirers were also her lovers is a question that still titillates Boston dinner conversations. Those who amuse themselves by being accountants of other people's love affairs, basing their reckonings on rumors and the tone of existing letters, come up with a tally that includes as her lovers this prolific novelist, that dandy who committed suicide, and thus-and-so. Old ladies in Boston remember nostalgically how as young girls they were forbidden to meet the "risqué Mrs. Gardner." But Boston was scandalized at the merest unconventionality and she was, indeed, a prodigious and provocative flirt, who wore her conquests proudly, like a coronet. If she had lovers, she acted with the customary discretion of her era. Lest she forget prudence, she had arranged a daily reminder. In her bathroom, there was no swan bathtub in the Potter Palmer manner; there were admonitory mottoes printed on the tiles. Along with the smug proverb, "Good breeding shows," there was, in French, the sage advice, "Think much, speak little, write nothing," and, "Secret of two, secret of God; secret of three, secret of all."

Whether her love affairs were actual or apocryphal, she inspired a special quality of devotion. She could be ruthless and cruel. Her annihilations were less irreparable but almost as effective as those of the Empress of China, whose authority to order actual decapitation she envied. But she could also be soft and *simpática.* She never lapsed into rattling small talk and her presence, like yeast, lifted desultory chatter to brilliant conversation. One of the more broad-minded of the Boston wives remarked, "She made other women's husbands seem more interesting to them." *À deux,* she enabled a man to shine, expand, feel closer to his ideal image of himself.

Her devotees describe her as "a gloom dispeller, corpse-reviver, general chirker-up" (W. Sturgis Bigelow), write of "those evenings at your board and in your box, those tea-times in your pictured halls, [which] flush again in my mind's eye as real life-saving stations" (Henry James), tell her "your letter was a ray of sunshine in this murky, snow-laden sky of the Japanese rainy season" (Okakura-Katuzo), remark, "Dear, dear Lady, it seems me [*sic*] like a dream those days with you" (Anders Zorn), testify that "the effect of an hour with you is that of the Absolute— vertigo, loss of relation, absence in space, time and thought. It is peace, repose, a dream" (Henry Adams), avow that "not a day passes in my life in which there is not a tender thought of you" (F. Marion Crawford)—and more and more such tributes from the hearts of scores of men (and from a few such unintimidated and vital women as Julia Ward Howe and Lady Augusta Gregory), until it seems that she had obtained what Henry Adams said she needed, "not exactly help or flattery or even admiration, but subjects."

Her vanity demanded primacy. She must have the best, and more, and all. If her wishes were thwarted, her appetite was whetted. Those who stayed remote or withdrawn—as perhaps Sargent—or those who declined invitations due to "obstinate insomnia" or previous engagements were pursued, sometimes embarrassingly, with more importunate invitations, thoughtful gifts and impulsive notes. In personal relationships, she brooked no impediment, refusal or defeat. And so it was when she began collecting art.

A hint that anyone else was after an object catapulted her into an immediate purchase. In 1907, her adviser Berenson recommended that she buy two of the paintings which the dealer Joseph Duveen had purchased from the Oskar Hainauer collection. Though it was early in his career, that super-salesman Duveen knew which pictures could be mated with which clients. The "Man" by the Florentine Renaissance painter Castagno was a vigorous condottiere whose bold assurance would certainly flatter J. P. Morgan's historical imagination. The "Lady" by Castagno's contemporary, Piero Pollaiuolo, on the other hand, was a rather homely, sober, middle-class woman, unbedecked with jewels and gilt. Since, notoriously, the one criterion for a Morgan mistress was beauty, Duveen knew the Pollaiuolo woman was not Morgan's type.

Duveen was not interested in wooing Mrs. Gardner, whose income was hardly on the Duveen scale, especially if the act would anger Morgan, who was a man who liked getting *his* way. But the shrewd dealer was glad to do Berenson the little favor of letting the Bostonian buy the unglamorous lady for $58,305. It was small consolation to Mrs. Gardner to be told that she was the "only person *chez nous* . . . who has the culture and depth of taste to appreciate the Pollaiuolo." She had wanted the Castagno, too. She never bought another painting from Duveen.

Sometimes Berenson had to chide his client for her petulant complaints and greediness. "Now, please, be reasonable," he wrote her once, "you cannot possess *all* the great paintings that come on to the market." But no one was quicker than he to try to make up for one that slipped by. One of her greatest pictures, in fact, Titian's "Rape of Europa," was a sort of consolation prize.

Back in 1879, when the Gardners were shepherding Mr. Gardner's three orphaned nephews through Europe, Isabella Stewart Gardner had seen Gainsborough's "Blue Boy" in Grosvenor House in London. The picture worked a spell on her no less potent than it worked four decades later on the Pacific Coast railroad king, Henry E. Huntington. In 1895 she ordered Berenson to get it for her, though he warned her that "bait less than $100,000 would be meaningless." Nearly a year later he felt sure that the Duke of Westminster would part with the little boy, but the bait must be expanded to $150,000. "Be bold," he admonished her. Her boldness extended to a $190,000 offer and the Duke seemed willing. But suddenly he developed a parental affection so strong that it took twenty-five years, a tight financial spot and one of Duveen's most sensational offers to persuade him to part with the boy.

Just when the "Blue Boy" seemed about to find a home with Mrs. Gardner, the Titian came on the market. Thinking that Mrs. Gardner was about to spend $190,000, Berenson doubted that she could afford a $100,000 purchase, too. He recommended the Italian painting to another collector, a Mrs. S. D. Warren of Boston. Then the Duke changed his mind. Berenson had promised never to bring Mrs. Gardner into rivalry—but he could guess her boiling wrath if, deprived of the "Blue Boy," she were to see this prize go to another Bostonian. In a sentence classic for its under-and-over statement, he wrote of the Titian: "It is a far greater picture, great and great though the 'Blue Boy' is." He begged her to cable so that her acceptance would precede Mrs. Warren's written one. Of course she did, and thus came by perhaps the greatest Italian painting in America. Moreover, she had not only snatched it from under the nose of Mrs. Warren, but also of Wilhelm von Bode, who was ransacking Europe to build up the German museums to a glory which would satisfy the cultural ambitions of Kaiser Wilhelm II, a rather richer collector than she. But she was not entirely consoled. Having failed with the "Blue Boy," she never bought another English eighteenth-century painting, and the Romney she already owned is one of the very few pictures with which she ever parted.

Her friend T. Jefferson Coolidge once told her that she was an "Aphrodite with a lining of Athene." As Athene, too, she found Boston her perfect milieu. Of all American cities, it took itself most seriously. It stood for virtue and for intellect. Her dalliances might be in capricious contrast to the former principle; but her interests, her patronage, her income and her deepest friendships were at the service of the latter.

Boston, in those post-Civil War years that Van Wyck Brooks calls its Indian summer, gave a welcoming nod to the French painters of the Barbizon School and a misty day was called "a Corot day." But its deep yearnings were elsewhere. Boston worshiped Italian culture so devotedly, as Brooks points out, that it made "Florence and Venice Bostonian. The fact that Boston girls grew up with Botticelli manners made Botticelli almost a Boston painter . . . Dante, Petrarch, Ruskin and Browning were Boston citizens in their way, although for the good of all, they kept their distance;

and handbooks on Italian art poured from the Boston presses."

High priest of the cult for Italian studies was Charles Eliot Norton, a delicate, fastidious man who had lived in England as a crony of Ruskin, Dickens, Carlyle and Darwin. In 1873, he returned to Boston to become Harvard's first professor of the history of art. There, and in the brown study of his house, Shady Hill, as Brooks says, he preached the gospel of taste "as his forebears preached salvation . . . If the modern world was ugly, it was also base: its baseness and ugliness went together. Taste alone could redeem it."

Norton was precious, exquisite and rather an esthetic prig. It was said that when he entered Heaven he would exclaim, "Oh, no! So overdone!" He was even suspected by some, like William James, of not being "the genuine article." But he evoked a powerful influence in making Boston an oasis in a country both materialist and culturally barbaric.

Isabella Stewart Gardner gravitated to his classes in 1878 and soon her salons became extension courses. In them there gathered such men as the medievalist Henry Adams, Oliver Wendell Holmes in his pre-jurist days, the James brothers, philosopher William and novelist Henry, and Norton's best pupil, curly-headed Bernard Berenson, a precocious, ardent youngster who dazzled his elders.

Dante became practically a Norton protégé. Under the spell of Dante, Isabella Stewart Gardner and the novelist F. Marion Crawford began a romantic attachment in 1880. The books from which they read aloud to each other were interleaved and bound by Tiffany in a volume designed by Crawford. He bought her an Oxford edition bound in soft olive green leather and wrote to her, along with far less literary musings, of "reading our Dante all through again, to the very end." In 1886 she read Dante more analytically with Norton's group, and when under his aegis she began collecting rare books and manuscripts—her first serious collecting venture and one preceding Morgan's by a decade—Dante editions were primary goals.

So, too, began her patronage of music, carried out all her life with a characteristically Gardner combination of indomitable determination and vain caprice. Steadfastly she supported and attended the symphony. She was a fixture at the opera, at which, since she always appeared in her box well before the overture, the audience could debate the relative brilliance of her jewels and her guests. Once she engaged Paderewski to play for her alone, another time to give a concert for which she bought all the tickets and distributed them to Boston musicians. Her salons displayed such musical lions as the De Reszkes and Melba. But she was also generous—sometimes to the point of their engulfment—to promising young composers and performers.

She had, in fact, a restless desire to pursue whatever her friends found exciting, a necessity to be "in the know," whether the subject was Oriental art and philosophy (on whose account the Gardners made a round-the-world trip) or baseball (she once appeared at the symphony with a Red Sox banner on her hat). Norton, who acidly pointed out to his classes that the Greeks did *not* play football, was hardly responsible for her interest in athletics, but he encouraged her in the quest for taste and prepared her for her grandest adventure.

As a girl she had been piloted through the proper museums. After her marriage, she and her husband, like other proper Bostonians, bought such approved evidences of cultivation as tapestries, stained glass and a few French landscapes to go along with the picturesque souvenirs of travel in their Beacon Street house. The young Gardners were not entirely discriminating nor exclusively addicted to Corots and Millets. They also fell hard for a dexterously sentimental Campagna boy by a fashionable Italian painter, Mancini, a lad lower-classed and lower-priced than the Blue Boy.

But soon, magnetized by her circle of writers, musicians and artists, Mrs. Gardner's taste was "advancing." By the late eighties, she was stopping in London to buy pastels from Whistler, commissioning the Sargent portrait and choosing a painting by Sargent's young French friend, Helleu.

There is nothing like a legacy, however, to turn a mere purchaser of art into a collector. In 1891, Mr. Stewart died and his daughter inherited $2,750,000. She ventured into the precincts of the old masters, eager to translate into action Norton's theories of taste. The year that Mrs. Potter Palmer bought her four Renoirs, Mrs. Gardner bought a "Madonna and Child" by Fra Filippo Lippi that later turned out not to be by Fra Filippo Lippi and an "Adam and Eve" by Cranach that turned out not to be by Cranach (changes of attribution which—along with many others—she brusquely disregarded), and, egged on by Helleu, bid successfully at a Paris auction for a handsome Vermeer, which is still a Vermeer.

She bought another painting which is still attributed to the Flemish seventeenth-century artist, Suttermans, to whom it was then accredited. But, ironically, it turned out not to be of the subject on whose account she bought it. It was then said to represent the Duke of Monmouth, illegitimate son of King Charles II. As such, the Empress Frederick of Germany coveted it and made several attempts to get it. Mrs. Gardner was indignant. If ownership depended on the painting being "a family picture" she insisted that she had more right to it than the Teutonic Empress. After all, as she wrote to her husband's cousin, Isabella Stewart and the Duke of Monmouth, however illegimate he might be, were Stuarts before the family "was contaminated by German blood."

With all these new acquisitions, she felt somewhat superior when she arrived in Chicago in 1893 to see her Helleu in the loan exhibition at the Exposition. Hearing that she was going, her friend Henry James inquired charmingly, "Won't there be the Federal buildings, and the State buildings, and then, in a category by itself, Mrs. Jack's building?"

He wrote with the provincial prejudice of the Bostonian. Isabella Stewart Gardner shared his prejudice. When the queen of the "White City," Berthe Honoré Palmer, received her in the battlemented castle, she was rather contemptuous of the Midwest splendor and the contemporary art, symbols of all that made Norton long for the good old days of the Renaissance. She summed up her feelings in the pantry. Mrs. Palmer's eighteen-year-old son, exhibiting the gold and silver plates and the endless towers of porcelain dishes, explained that his mother had fifty of everything. "What does she do," Mrs. Gardner asked acidly, "when she has a really big party?"

The idea behind *her* new purchasing of art had nothing to do with fashionable art or galleries with green festoons and leopard-skin rugs. The idea had been gnawing since 1884, when their trip around the world landed the Gardners in Venice. Mr. Gardner lay in his hotel room fretting with erysipelas. But his "Busy Ella," as he often called her, trudged through two solid weeks of sightseeing. Her carefully dated and annotated albums of photographs of Venetian painting record her indefatigable course. Venice became a must on each of the subsequent biennial European trips, where, in the Palazzo Barbaro (owned by Mr. Gardner's cousins), Isabella Stewart Gardner held her brilliant court-in-exile. Her subjects ranged from Henry James and Anders Zorn to the violinist Tirendelli (in 1892, T. Jefferson Coolidge called him her "new fad") and Don Carlos, the exiled Duke of Madrid. Boston might be her stage: in Venice she felt apotheosized. The hazy dream of masterpieces encased in a permanent Venetian setting began to germinate.

The decisive moment arrived in 1894, when in London she met young Bernard Berenson again. Since Bostonians invested not only in bonds, but also in brains, and since Berenson upon his graduation from Harvard in 1887 seemed to have the kind of brains that made a good investment, a group of his friends raised $750 to enable him to go abroad. He traipsed around Europe training his eye, searching his soul and schooling himself for an ultimate life of exquisite taste and appreciation on the highest level of response. These activities seemed so ephemeral to the syndicate that at year's end it did not renew its investment. But they appealed so much to Mrs. Gardner that she took it up with a new $750.

The syndicate had given up too soon. Even by 1894 it could have claimed dividends. Berenson, approaching works of art as "life-enhancing actualities," had begun writing his remarkable books on Italian art, phrased with grace as well as authority. He had also embarked upon his second, more tangibly productive career. He had become an "expert."

At that period, attributions were made on an optimistic, rather than a scientific, basis. The more affluent the market and the more gullible the buyers, the more optimistic the attributions. In 1852, Melville wrote of "a collection of those wretched imported daubs, which with the incredible effrontery peculiar to some of the foreign picture-dealers in America, were christened by the loftiest names known to Art." The unrestrained use of the loftiest names was, however, not peculiar to these picture dealers. The great painters, it seemed, had painted everything. It mattered not at all that this accomplishment would have made them both extraordinarily prolific and astonishingly inconsistent. Berenson was one of the first to try scientific untangling, and as early as 1891, at the age of twenty-six, he had been summoned to unmuddle the attributions at Hampton Court.

In the process of taking paintings away from certain masters, he was often embarrassed to find that they could not in honesty be given to others, however little known their names. He neatly solved the problem by creating (and sometimes later demolishing) new personalities to whom certain consistent groups could be given. Later he was to codify his findings of paintings by the masters and their pupils and friends in "Lists." They became the Almanach de Gotha of Italian painting. If a painting presumably by Botticelli was not on Berenson's "Lists" it simply could not claim

that peerage. In time, naturally, the "Lists" also became a sort of
Dun & Bradstreet's of art, since the money value of a painting is
directly related to its attribution.

Berenson was later to decry his means of livelihood, saying, "I
soon discovered that I ranked with fortune-tellers, chiromancists,
astrologers, and not even with the self-deluded of these, but rather
with the deliberate charlatans." Nevertheless, his scholarship was
of vast importance and he was to become the most important expert on Italian paintings. Berenson's oracular attributions were to
have such authority that he was eventually wooed and won by
the dealer Joseph Duveen, who found an oracle mighty handy. It
was a mutually lucrative alliance of several years' standing which
ended unpleasantly for both sides.

The attribution of a painting is frequently as unstable as the
position of a French premier. Even the expert himself is apt to be
a fickle bestower. With years of added experience and study to
bolster his findings, Berenson from time to time has changed the
christenings made in his early career, and younger scholars as well
as opportunistic expertisers have played havoc with a good many
more. But the opinion of this exquisite, asp-tongued, utterly charming white-bearded nonagenarian is still the most coveted in the
world, and his revised "Lists," which began to appear in 1958, insure him the respect of even the most cantankerous of scholars for
many centuries to come.

During the summer of 1894, while Mrs. Gardner was floating
genially in gondolas and giving parties that kept the servants up
later than Mr. Gardner thought just, Berenson was beginning the
kind of scouting and arranging which, he wrote, would "in some
sort repay you for your kindness on an occasion when I needed
help." The first repayment was in managing not to insult the reluctant Earl of Ashburnham by offering him $17,000 for his Bot-
ticelli "The Tragedy of Lucretia." It was a capital buy. Five years
later prices had risen so much that Mrs. Gardner would pay
$70,000 for a "Madonna and Child" by the same master. With the

purchase of her first Botticelli, she had entered a new orbit of collecting. Henceforth she would be concerned with masterworks and involved in international intrigue. Berenson's writings and her collection would also generate a taste for early Italian pictures in America. In an article of 1896, Berenson could justly point to the scarcity of Italian pictures, especially early ones, in the United States. The Jarves collection, hanging at Yale University since 1867, was, of course, the unique exception, but it was as little known to Americans as if it had been in Siberia. The somewhat peculiar Charles Eliot Norton never even lectured about the paintings, but, as Francis Steegmuller points out in his book on Jarves, "It is an even more curious fact that in his lectures on art Professor Norton seems seldom to have mentioned any pictures at all."

Berenson continued to repay Mrs. Gardner by becoming her chief adviser. Others helped her: Henry Adams found her magnificent stained glass from St. Denis; Zorn put her in touch with the Swedish consul in Constantinople who got her the rare and wonderful Gentile Bellini drawing; Richard Norton, Joseph Lindon Smith and a score of others scouted for her. She herself found such gems as the tiny, perfect Lippo Memmi "Madonna and Child." But the Gardner collection is essentially of Berenson's making. Most of the paintings came through his recommendation and, with a very few exceptions, he is responsible for the density of unassailable masterpieces that distinguishes it. There are a few disappointments, of course, but only a few, and to more than offset them are many very wonderful paintings he recommended which she did not buy. He was "grieved, grieved" in 1897 when ("that singular lacuna in your taste") she refused a painting by the rare French eighteenth-century master Watteau, which cost but $40,000; he tried urgently over a period of six months to persuade her to buy El Greco's superb, shimmering "The Adoration of the Shepherds," which once belonged to the Duke of Hijar in

Madrid; he entreated her, in 1903, to buy a painting by the great Flemish painter, Rogier van der Weyden, "as one of the two possibly last pictures you can afford . . ." Whether she would accept his recommendations or not, he sought the very best for her, almost as if he were building his own monument. They were both dedicated to taste.

Who else could have advised her so well? The job required wiles along with wisdom. Indeed, he knew his Isabella. "Serpent of the Charles," he called her, and she loved it. He pandered to her genealogical illusions: Titian's "Rape of Europa," aside from the fact that it "is one of the finest Italian paintings ever to be sold," should be hers because "it would be poetic justice that a picture intended for a Stewart should at last rest in the hands of a Stewart"; a not very important or attractive painting by a follower of Titian becomes "in the highest degree valuable" because "it is a portrait of the greatest and most fascinating lady of the Renaissance—your worthy precursor and patron saint—Isabella d'Este, marchioness of Mantua." He catered to her vanity: of the Earl of Arundel portrait by Rubens he wrote, "Who Arundel was, the great ambassador and adviser of Charles I, great patron of arts and letters, I need not tell you"; another time, "I am not going to insult you by talking to *you* about Giotto, nor even of his rarity"; and again, Raphael's "Pietà" could be obtained at a low price because other collectors preferred more "attractive subjects," but, like him, she could "recognize quality regardless of subject." He played on her impatient possessiveness. Sometimes haste was necessary, especially against the omnivorous Bode, but he constantly exhorted her to use "the greatest dispatch," or to "cable immediately," or to "answer at once or on your own head be its loss."

His eulogies of such masterpieces as the Cellini bust and Crivelli's "St. George" were justified. But other, lesser paintings— even those no longer attributed to artists he named—were also "a gem," "an exquisite Bronzino," "Correggio at his finest moment." Indeed, as he admitted not so long ago, "I had to put on the praise of the works of art, as Disraeli said of Queen Victoria, 'not with a trowel, but with a shovel.'"

They tormented each other unmercifully, two vain individualists caught in a curious relationship of affection and annoyance. He denigrated and dallied about decisions on paintings with which he was not directly involved. Once when a friend wanted to buy for her a painting then attributed to Titian he stated categorically that he knew of the picture, that it was not by Titian and was, therefore, not worth more than $7,500. Then he saw the photograph; then the painting. He was enthusiastic. Two years passed: the price rose and Mrs. Gardner cooled. A year later he just happened to be in Forli, saw the picture again and "yearned" for her to have it for $75,000. She did have it. But ironically, by 1930 Berenson had reverted to his original notion. The painting was not only *not* by Titian, but it was at a far remove from Titian. It was by Coello, the Spanish pupil of a Flemish pupil of Titian.

But, in turn, she would taunt him with half-knowledge about purchases she made without him. She teased his curiosity for six months about where she got her Mantegna. He had to beg for information and to entreat her not to be cross with him in six letters before she revealed it came through Richard Norton from Prince del Drago.

One of the Gardner relatives remarked testily that "she helped Berenson more than he helped her." Of course, he received a commission from her—actually five percent instead of the usual ten —and he was put in a favorable position in the art world because of his role as her adviser. But he was indispensable to her. Without him, she could not have had her triumph. And he bought for her not only well but very often at remarkably reasonable prices.

Prices in the years of her most formidable activity—1894 to 1900—had not yet been swollen by the extravaganzas of J. P. Morgan, et al. But the upward trend had begun. Taste was beginning to include some of the lesser-known masters, like Crivelli, and such delightful Sienese painters as Giovanni di Paolo had become, as Berenson told her in 1908, "all the rage, because collectors of *objets d'art* are after him, too." Yet Berenson got her such real bargains as the portraits by Raphael and Velásquez, and he made such coups as finding five panels by Simone Martini— the only complete altarpiece by this Sienese master outside Italy —for only $2,000, which was, as he wrote her, "irrationally priced."

Price mattered to Mrs. Gardner. As compared to rival collectors like Morgan and Henry Walters of Baltimore, her budget was small. Where Morgan's collection was officially worth $60,000,000, hers was estimated at little more than $3,000,000— and the concentration of masterpieces is far greater. She lived regally during her husband's lifetime, but after his death in 1898 she became relatively frugal. She was already obsessed with the idea of Fenway Court, so that every possible penny was allocated to art.

"When she wanted to buy a picture," Mitchell Samuels of French & Company recalls, "she put her servants on rations." This act must have brought them close to a subsistence diet, for even her friends complained of the meagerness of food on her table. Late in life she used to send Morris Carter, director of her collection and a sort of companion-in-chief, to the corner store daily to buy one orange. A meek man, somewhat intimidated by his volatile employer, he acted with intrepid independence one day when he decided to spare himself the morrow's trip and buy two oranges at one time. The saleslady in the grocery store was astonished at the magnitude of his purchase. "The old lady going to have a party?" she asked.

Mrs. Gardner tormented Berenson by delaying checks and then twitting him for "dunning" her for the money. She would upbraid him with reports that someone said she had paid too much for something. Occasionally his annoyance would flare into self-defense. ". . . for the Simones I charged you $2,000 *tutto compreso* and the *compreso* comprehended a good deal. There were taxes, very expensive packing and re-packing, my own commission and the pay for six weeks of . . . skillful restorer . . . not to speak of all of the risk and annoyance."

"Risk and annoyance" plagued a good many collectors, as the American demand for masterpieces and the American willingness to pay staggering prices for them increased in the Morgan era, from 1900 to 1913, and the Italian Government became more and more reluctant about letting its masterpieces go. Collectors and dealers were led to invent ingenious smuggling devices and to indulge in the less original maneuver of bribing willing officials. Italian families also presented a thorny problem. They hated looking at bare spots on their walls. Some of them were touchy about revealing any evidence of straitened circumstances to the world or admitting that greed was stronger than family pride. In particular, they were apprehensive about inquisitive government prosecutors poking around. When these proud aristocrats sold paintings, they usually demanded a copy to serve as a permanent "stand-in."

The manufacture of these *ersatz* pictures—an enterprise still engaged in today—has created a certain amount of additional confusion in the art world. Only in 1954, for instance, did a member of the staff of the Pitti Gallery in Florence admit that the portrait of Tommaso Inghiramī in Fenway Court is the one painted by Raphael and that the version in the Pitti is a replica or copy. That replica is presumably a sixteenth-century one. But there is also a modern copy, made at the time of the portrait's sale, still in the Inghiramī Palace at Volterra.

Some Italians, especially the hungry art dealers, often claim that the originals never emigrated. Sometimes, indeed, they did not. It was to safeguard against this switch-and-double-switch maneuver that Joseph Lindon Smith, when he bought Piero della Francesca's magnificent fresco of "Hercules" for Mrs. Gardner, bound the original in an elaborate web of tracing paper, sealing wax and torn pieces of hotel stationery, of which, spy-like, he kept the matching half.

There was particular "risk and annoyance" about the "Christ Carrying the Cross," attributed to Giorgione, which was owned by Count A. Zileri dal Verme and hung in his Palazzo Loschi at Vicenza. The Count's father had originally bequeathed the painting to the town, but had later revoked that will. The Zileri family was not very loved. Besides being Bourbons and ultra-clerics, they had made the tactless mistake of trying to change the city's annual celebration of Vicenza's victory over Austria from a wine-drenched carnival to a stern clerical affair. The populace's vehement demonstration against the Zileris unnerved them so considerably that they suddenly decided it might be a good idea to give the Giorgione to the city after all—especially since there seemed to be some question about the validity of papa's revocation clause. Berenson finally calmed them and they accepted the copy which still hangs in the Palazzo Loschi. The original made an unobstrusive exit from Italy.

Prince Chigi, Duke of Ariccia, had an even more difficult time than the Zileris with his tenderly beautiful "Madonna and Child of the Eucharist" by Botticelli. Although he was well off, he could not resist the high prices he was being offered for this masterpiece. He sold it. By 1899, the German Emperor and an English syndicate had run the price up to $60,000. "This almost tempts one," Berenson wrote provocatively to Mrs. Gardner, "to join the race for the pure fun of it." It was Mrs. Gardner's kind of fun. The painting, then in the dealer Colnaghi's hands, became hers for $70,000.

Meanwhile, Prince Chigi had been arrested for violating the Italian law against exporting masterpieces. Eventually the upper courts reduced his fine to a mere ten lire, but the case had become a *cause célèbre*.

Since the whereabouts of the painting was not revealed at the trial, the world's press began speculating and each city claimed it was owned by one of *its* collectors. Mrs. Gardner was annoyed, especially when she read that the Chigi Madonna was in America and she knew hers was still at Colnaghi's in London. What was in America was a rather ornamented contemporary copy which had been bought for $10,000 by the traction king, Charles T. Yerkes, whose eye for women was more acute than for Botticellis. Mrs. Gardner finally agreed to have her purchase publicly exhibited at Colnaghi's to show the world that she owned *the* Chigi Madonna and to teach her "over-rich countrymen" not to buy paintings without knowing what they were. Because of Berenson, she knew.

But far easier to be Isabella Stewart Gardner's art adviser than her architect. Willard T. Sears and Edward Nichols had that status—but only officially. The professional gentlemen were treated, at best, as competent draftsmen and, at worst, as irritating obstacles who fussed about such irksome details as city codes and structural safety. Her first idea had been simply to enlarge the Beacon Street house for an art gallery (gossip had it that she was delighted at the idea of thereby blocking her neighbor's light). But by 1896, her husband had agreed to the idea of the Venetian palace on the Boston Fens. After he died, she set to work with Sears on the drawings of the building, which was inspired by the Palazzo Bardini on the Grand Canal.

Fenway Court, down to its last detail, was complete in her head from the start. As a more ordinary woman might light here and there on a bit of fabric for a patchwork quilt she had in mind, Mrs. Gardner went around Europe collecting architectural fragments, from columns to staircases, with absolute certainty of where each would go. With a prodigious memory, an uncanny sense of scale and remarkable taste, she picked up columns from the Ca' d'Oro, bits of stone, ironwork, arches, pilasters, doors, furniture, brocades for walls—a whole kit and caboodle of architectural bits to be fused into the whole. There were no leftovers, no speculative choices.

The building was begun in 1900. Isabella Stewart Gardner's crowning achievement was nearing completion, and nothing must stand in her way. Her imperiousness reached its zenith. Once construction began, she added to her role of architect those of superintendent of work and foreman of each building trade.

With characteristic Boston reticence, Willard T. Sears recorded the exasperating course of the building of Fenway Court. Mrs. Gardner was on the job daily, bringing her lunch like the workmen and contributing her ten cents for oatmeal to purify the drinking water. Perhaps with some unconscious touch of wishful thinking, Sears suggested that an accident policy be taken out for her. She haughtily refused. Whatever righteous satisfaction Sears may have felt when she did one day sprain her ankle was canceled by her appearance as usual the next morning.

She took personal charge of logistics. The hundreds of cases of architectural paraphernalia were unpacked and placed in the warehouse in the exact order in which she wanted them used. Nothing could be removed from the warehouse or carried on the job without her supervision. Once there, nothing could be placed without her direct command. Work was held up for two weeks while she decided on stones for a door; floor timbers could not be laid until she returned from a trip to indicate where each column belonged in the colonnade. She treated foundation walls, retaining walls, metal bracings as ridiculous intrusions, tyrannically ordering them removed as "unnecessary" (and loftily disregarding those which the contractor was later forced to replace). When a city official thwarted part of her scheme for electrical wiring, she canceled it and said she would use candles.

One of the Italian workmen, Teobaldi Travi, called "Bolgi," became her favorite and acted as her personal attendant. Like some medieval herald, he would summon the master workmen she wanted by playing various numbers of toots on a cornet. She dealt with them directly. She showed them how to sponge pink and white paint on the plaster walls of the court and took a broadax in hand to hew a ceiling beam as a model. Her sudden reversals threw work into a turmoil, but it did not matter. The goal was too near. She stopped masons in order to put in extra windows; halted plumbers installing an already approved heating system in order to work out a new one of her own; countermanded a brick facing wall she had looked at complacently for ten days; changed, approved, repudiated all plumbing fixtures; stopped men working in the Gothic Room because they were dropping dust and dirt into the room below, where she was herself oiling and putting up "an old painted ceiling," although the architects insisted the surface was not yet ready for it.

Sears was constantly torn between workmen who wanted to quit because Mrs. Gardner had "pitched into them" and an owner who kept dictatorially ordering him to discharge all the carpenters, fire all the masons, send all the plasterers away. Only once did he take sides: he discharged the floor layers in the Gothic Room for mimicking her when she chided them for not working.

Sears' irritation boiled on December 12, 1901. "When I reached the Fenway house this morning, I found Mrs. Gardner in the court giving peremptory orders for the removal of all the scaffolding at once, saying they must be removed before night . . . I told her that it would be dangerous to attempt to do it with such a rush, that it must be done carefully or someone be killed or badly injured. She said this was all nonsense and that it *must* be removed at once." The outcome of the argument was inevitable. Sears' entry concludes: "All the masons and carpenters were taken from the other work and additional men were sent for and the removal of the scaffold commenced."

Slowly the possessions were moved in, each to its foreordained place. According to plan, everything usable—from cornices to fireplaces—was stripped from the Beacon Street house and her Brookline estate. She was no thrifty housewife. She was simply too vain to let anyone else claim what was hers. Obviously she could not take with her the street number of the Beacon Street house when she moved, but she commanded the new owner to use 150 instead of 152.

Everything was arranged according to its owner's taste, and with extraordinary grace. Things were grouped together for the good and unusual reason that they looked well together. The taste of her time is refined here, but is still revealed in the textiles strewn over tables and chairs and the mating on one shelf of souvenirs and mementoes with such masterworks as a Persian luster plate. Her touch is everywhere, from the little vase of violets under "Christ Carrying the Cross" and the brocade under the Titian (cut from a length of fabric which was also used for a dress) to the scheme of hanging. Berenson had recommended a handsome Manet portrait to take its place in the great tradition of Western painting, but she relegated it to the lesser downstairs rooms along with contemporary works she had bought out of friendship or during her first years of buying.

The peremptoriness, the tyranny, the egocentricity were justified. She triumphed. Fenway Court is, in its totality, a masterpiece of its kind. It is not achitecture, in the sense of J. P. Morgan's Library, which was begun the year Fenway Court was finished, but a delightful ensemble. The eclectic architects of the time were using the vocabulary of the Gothic and Renaissance to make, at its best, a new style: she went them one better, for she used bits of old architecture to create her own style. It is impossible to say where objects leave off and building begins for they are all one and the same. The Morgan Library is stern and resplendent, Fenway Court is charming and feminine, as Venice is the seductive siren compared to splendidly masculine Rome. Where the Library has the beauty of logic, Fenway Court has the captivation of caprice. It is a Bostonian's dream of Italy, but even more it is Isabella Stewart Gardner's dream. The creation of the beautiful environment was also to her an act of virtue. A basically religious woman, she warmed to Norton's belief in the moral nature of art. She believed in salvation through taste. She was saved.

What she did exquisitely, others were to do more crudely. Where she made environment, they made pastiches. Where she bought the bits and created the whole, others were to transplant "the works." Armor, stained glass and Jacobean paneling were to make a baronial bit of Olde England out of dining rooms on Long Island estates. Boiseries and Boucher paintings would transform the boudoirs of *nouveau-riche* millionaires' wives into Rococo stage-sets. Choir stalls would furnish seating for billiard rooms, Gothic arches would lead to w.c.'s, and screens from confessionals would hide phonographs, as many decades later in Hollywood a $10,000 painting by Signac would be rolled back to uncover the movie projector.

Isabella Stewart Gardner's ultimate intention was expressed in stone above the door: "The Isabella Stewart Gardner Museum MDCCCC," and, indeed, Fenway Court had been incorporated as such in 1900. But the inscription was immediately covered with a slab which would remain until her death. The status of Fenway Court as a museum was correspondingly ambiguous. It was open to the public, beginning in 1903 (with $1 tickets available at regular ticket brokers), on certain days according to the owner's whim. It was, however, a seldom whim. She did not mind the public's praise, but she was justifiably put off by its pawing.

Those who could not get in began protesting to the government that Fenway Court was not a real museum and that its art, therefore, should not be allowed duty-free entrance. At the same time that America was encouraging cheap labor to come in, it was determinedly keeping cheap goods out. But the high tariff barrier, extending indiscriminately, also kept out such rather expensive items as Italian Renaissance art.

Mrs. Gardner's friends were sympathetic: Norton castigated the tariff laws as "evidence of our national semi-civilization" and Sargent was upset by the thought of her "being raged about by a U.S. Revenue dragon like the Buddha of your beautiful Kakemona." But the government, newly disposed to placate the have-nots, held firm. In 1904, Mrs. Gardner was out $200,000.

No less resourceful than others in attempting to evade legislation which seemed as ridiculous then as the Volstead Act did later, she inevitably ran afoul of the government once more. "The United States of America vs. Oil Painting et al" was the title of the suit filed in the United States District Court. The objects ranged against this formidable adversary were, in fact, Piero della Francesca's fresco, a marble bust and tapestries from the famous Ffoulke collection. They had been smuggled in as "household effects," valued at $8,000, by a friend of Mrs. Gardner's, but the customs appraiser at Chicago had a sensitive eye for household effects and appraised them at $82,411. Mrs. Gardner had to pay not only the duty of $29,203 and a penalty of $41,205, but, in order to claim them as her property, also the appraised value of $82,411. In 1908, this payment of $150,000 of duty on works of art valued at $82,000 outraged the Boston press. One newspaper pointed out that misguided persons who offended our great and glorious republic by trying to import works of art should, if they wished to be favorably regarded by the law, import duty-free dogs instead.

These substantial dents in her pocketbook and the completion of Fenway Court curtailed purchasing. She bought only what was irresistible and what had a predestined spot. As early as 1906 she began planning to replace the Music Room with a Spanish Cloister below and a huge tapestry hall above. Her fabulous tapestries included one splendid Brussels sixteenth-century set from the Barberini Palace in Rome. They were sold as depicting the lives of Archduke Albert and—magic name—Isabella. Later scholarship has proved that they depict, instead, the life of the Persian Cyrus. Mrs. Gardner might not have minded giving up Isabella, however, to get Queen Tomyris, for Cyrus' adversary was a match even for Isabella Stewart Gardner. Among her lesser pleasures was having her servants waylay and kidnap passers-by in the

Caucasians. When she tired of them as her lovers, she would invite them to look from the windows in her castle, and push them out. Finally conquering Cyrus, Queen Tomyris avenged the death of her son through his trickery, by dipping his head in gore to give him, as she had promised, "his fill of blood."

The Spanish Cloister, finished in 1916, became a setting for Sargent's life-size painting of a Spanish dancer, "El Jaleo." Framed by a proscenium-like Moorish arch and lighted from below, as if by footlights, it is more perfectly displayed than any of her far greater treasures—a final homage to the fashionable painter whom she befriended through a long, ambiguous relationship.

The music, the little suppers, the devotion of old subjects and the spellbinding of new generations of young Bostonians went on. In 1909, she suffered a stroke which left her body paralyzed but her will and energy unimpaired. Her biographer, Morris Carter, tells that in her eighty-second year, sitting helpless in the Venetian gondola chair in which she was carried about, she wrote to a man who had asked about her and naïvely inquired where her house was: "I'm quite an invalid, but cheerful to the last degree. I think my mind is all right and I live on in it . . . I live in one house, everything else having been sold. This house is very nice, very comfortable, and rather jolly. It is on the outskirts of Boston, not in the country. I have filled it with pictures and works of art, really good things I think, and if there *are* any clever people I see them. I really lead an interesting life. I have music, and both young and old friends. The appropriately old are too old—they seem to have given up the world. Not so I, and I even shove some of the young ones rather close. I really have energy."

Boston's rancors and resentments had long been forgotten. Not only Mrs. Gardner's "Eyetalian palace," but Mrs. Gardner herself, swathed in white as Sargent painted her in a poignant watercolor in 1922, had become cherished monuments.

She died on July 17, 1924. Her body lay in the Spanish Chapel of Fenway Court under a purple pall, with a crucifix at her feet and tapers burning at her side. Nuns knelt at two prie-dieus for three days and three nights, and the Cowley Fathers—the oldest order of priests in the Anglican Communion—whom she had befriended, came in their black coats and black shovel hats to pray for her.

She need really not have felt the slightest resentment against her hostess when she visited the Palmer castle in 1893. Though the first Eskimo baby born in the Eskimo colony at the Exposition was made Mrs. Palmer's godchild, had not W. Sturgis Bigelow christened his Chesapeake puppy Mrs. John L. Gardner, called Belle for short? Though Mrs. Palmer was the thinly disguised central character in Fuller's novel, did not Mrs. Gardner figure in three by F. Marion Crawford? And though Mrs. Palmer's name might be immortalized in such transient, small-scale objects as a specially developed pure white petunia and a variety of rose, was not the highest peak in Okanogan County, Washington, named Mount Gardner and the range extending north-northwest called the Isabella Range?

In the end there was, of course, no question. The Palmers' ferociously turreted castle was leveled to make room for a ferociously boresome apartment house; the few dozen splendid paintings were assimilated into the vast collection of the Art Institute; and Mrs. Potter Palmer herself has become only a very likable legend. But Isabella Stewart Gardner's collection, and the writings of the man who helped her form it, set a taste in America for Italian art that the multimillionaires of the Morgan era would follow in grand style.

And Fenway Court remains forever intact, something far more than a museum. It is a memorial—a total, beautiful environment with a concentration of fabulous masterpieces, an environment drenched with the personality of the fascinating woman whose vanity and taste created it. Through it, she still attracts subjects.

The Grandiose Gesture

J. PIERPONT MORGAN

In late March of 1913, at the age of seventy-five, J. Pierpont Morgan lay dying in the corner room of his $500-a-day suite in the Grand Hotel in Rome. On the ground floor, the hotel was besieged by art dealers and antiquaries, impoverished European aristocrats and traders from the Levant. They bore strange burdens of paintings and sculptures, porcelains and jewels, all sorts of artistic odds and ends dredged from cupboards and dragged from attics. Wave after wave they came, only to be repulsed with the regularity of surf on the beach. Upstairs, secretaries disposed of over five hundred beseeching letters a day, while in the art capitals of the world the dealers trembled for fear that prices—which had increased three- to four-fold during the Morgan buying spree of the last twenty years—would tumble from their peaks when the great international banker died.

The clamorous desperation and the apprehension were understandable. The man who lay dying had been the most prodigious private art collector of all time, and now the golden shower was about to end.

Of course, he owned masterpieces of paintings, precious Renaissance bronzes and tapestries stripped from stately English mansions and the Royal Chapel in Granada. But all that was a mere fraction of the splendid abundance.

Even skeptical, reticent museum curators were moved to Hollywood superlatives—"the best," "the greatest," "the most extensive," "the most complete," "colossal"—in describing the vast collection of Byzantine enamels and ivories; the Italian majolica; the German boxwood carvings and silver-gilt work; the rock-crystal goblets (beloved of Renaissance royalty since they allegedly turned cloudy if poison was poured into them); the Oriental porcelains; the watches that had ticked for Napoleon and an Emperor of China; the boxes that had held snuff for such elegant nostrils as those of Catherine the Great; the jewelry that included pieces which seemed precious even to Cosimo de' Medici; the miniatures, those painted "snapshots" of the sixteenth to eighteenth centuries; the incredible collection of illuminated manuscripts; and more and more. All this in numbers that made other collections seem pygmy in size: almost all this of unsurpassed quality.

European competitors in the art market might refer to Morgan as "The Menace," but he was not the only American ransacking Europe for art. The money that came from the metallic ores and the black gold of the earth's crust; the skyrocketing incomes of the victors in the bitter battles over the growing railroad empire; the multiplying dollars of the retail merchants and of the kings of shipping and street railways; the fortunes of the investors in real estate—this wealth of a spectacularly burgeoning economy was being spent lavishly. It was the irrepressible era of Veblen's "conspicuous consumption."

If the new-rich were uncertain or hesitant, there were whole groups of people, from yacht builders to couturiers, ready to instruct them in how to make the best show for their money. Particularly anxious to be helpful were the architects, and they, in turn, had an advantage over the other eager instructors. They could provide not merely a single symbol but, by means of ambient environments, a whole way of life.

Thus they had raised the turrets of the late French Gothic style in New York and such battlemented extravaganzas as the Potter Palmer castle in Chicago. But, as Wayne Andrews remarks in his *Architecture, Ambition and Americans,* patricians and parvenus began to yearn for elegance instead of showy magnificence. And at that point the architects McKim, Mead and White came through with classic, Renaissance-type palaces.

These three became the master designers for the sumptuous pageant. They designed the buildings; they supervised the furnishings; they set the tone for a way of life. No detail was too small for their concern. Helping to relieve the Clarence Mackays of some of the excess wealth yielded by the Comstock Lode, Stanford White (according to Andrews) searched in Munich, Dresden, Berlin and Vienna; Florence, Palermo and Malta; Barcelona, Burgos, Seville, Cordova, Madrid and Lisbon; Brussels, Amsterdam and London; Bordeaux, Marseilles and Paris for the ideal chairs and the perfect tapestries for the $840,000 house at Roslyn, Long Island.

The galvanic redheaded architect would dash into the galleries of the art dealer Duveen and, darting from object to object, indicate "This tapestry for William C. Whitney's house—that statue for the dining-room of Senator Clark." Duveen's was paid $25,000 for making scale models of clients' prospective palaces. They were exquisite little doll houses, complete to hand-woven tapestries in miniature replica and tiny electric-lighted chandeliers. Nor did White find inappropriate the miniatures of the expensive old masters the dealer chose to include.

Many of the magnates were simply acquiring props for their

personal stage-sets. Many of them collected art as a symbol of the prestige to which they believed their power entitled them. Their quest was not for culture, but for the tangible possession of culture. A few had a craving for beauty, especially when combined with excellent craftsmanship. Some were merely indulging the same acquisitive desire that had generated the amassing of their wealth.

These millionaires streamed through Europe by the dozens in those halcyon days between 1880 and 1913 when an income tax was considered unconstitutional. They were buying the superlative and the spurious, the magnificent and the mediocre. There were vulgarians among them, and a few men of taste. But J. Pierpont Morgan, who outstripped them all, was unique.

Morgan was, of course, not only the architect of the biggest trust of all—the billion-dollar U. S. Steel Corporation—but the most aggressive international financier and banker of this epoch of individual might. Twice he stayed America from financial disaster: in 1893, when he shrewdly gauged and supplied the currency needs of the city of New York, and in 1903, when, acting like a one-man Federal Reserve System, he halted a national panic. His influence straddled eleven and a half billion dollars. It earned him the music-hall title of "Morgan, Morgan, the Great Financial Gorgon," and the newspaper nickname of "Pierpontifex Maximus." His power was so pervasive that it could be satirized by peddlers in London selling "a license to stay on earth," signed by J. P. Morgan. He was also a sportsman, a churchman, a philanthropist and a man of the world. But the activity which occupied an increasingly large part of his last two decades and consumed the bulk of his income was art collecting.

Morgan's operations in the art world were on the grand scale of his operations in the field of finance. As he bought a steamship line or a railway system, so he would snap up an immense collection which a connoisseur had spent patient years amassing. In fact, what a dealer calls his "big go-off" in the art world occurred in just this way in 1902.

All museum officials are addicted to greed and necrophilia, and the Metropolitan Museum officials of those days were no exception. The news of the owner's death simply heightened their hopes of getting permanently the huge and then very popular Garland collection of Chinese porcelains which had been on loan. But the owner had inconveniently neglected to make any such bequest. Henry Duveen, Joseph Duveen's uncle, who had a particular fondness for costly, fragile jars, bought them all. Addicted to the habit of early rising which seems common to multimillionaires, Morgan strode in to Duveen's at nine o'clock the next morning. He bought the lot for the Metropolitan and ordered the dealer to procure whatever was missing from the sequences.

Edward Robinson, an early director of the Metropolitan, recalled that Morgan another time went to see a single object in a certain gentleman's collection. But, encountering the whole treasure, he thought, "What's the use of bothering about one little piece when I might get them all?" and did so, then and there. Another time he paused on his way to board a ship for Europe to authorize a dealer to buy a stupendous collection which had just come on the market. One by one, he snapped up almost all the great collections assembled in Europe during the reign of Napoleon III.

No one has ever quite so cheerfully allowed himself to be stalked by art dealers as Morgan. At home in New York, on his annual sojourns in London, Paris, Rome—even when he took the cure at Aix or floated regally in his dahabeah up the Nile—he received them daily.

They would be ushered in to confront the commanding six-foot figure. He would be puffing on a giant black cigar and would temporarily lay aside in a silver box the cards with which he played his incessant games of solitaire. They would look at the massive, square, mustached face with its fierce black eyes, but nervously avert their gaze from the disease-puffed nose, that huge strawberry-purple excrescence which was the bane of his vanity and the easy butt of caricaturists. Like Oriental peddlers, they spread

their costly wares before him, turning his hotel suites into sumptuous bazaars. Daily, too, he would visit their emporia, often spending hours transfixed by the treasures that had been shrewdly
saved for this prince of buyers.

In the hot pursuit, the dealers fought and knifed each other.
They schooled themselves for meetings with Morgan. The gambling operator Dick Canfield, whose solitaire was Morgan's favorite, found it worth his while to offer lessons in Europe to art dealers who wanted to learn Morgan's card games.

Between Morgan's visits the dealers pelted him with letters, offering him in idiomatic translations of their Babel of tongues "the
celebrated pictures," "the multidudinous [*sic*] finest works for the
most modest price of two million marks," "the salt-cellar guaranteed absolutely genuine and old." The United States Consul at
Aleppo suggested three three-hundred-year-old paneled rooms
from a Turkish family; an Italian urged purchasing the Strozzi
Palace.

He listened, he looked. He bought lavishly from dozens of
dealers, antiquaries and impoverished aristocrats in each city.
No Lorelei Lee more hugely enjoyed shopping and never have
there been such grandiose shopping sprees. Only one of a score of
bills in Paris for April and May, 1906, was $770,627. He would buy
a Louis XVI gold box for $21,645 as casually as a commuter picks
up a morning paper, and a few minutes later, with the same
aplomb, spend $200,000 for the Cellini cup which had come to
Adolphe Rothschild via the King of Naples.

When he started buying, his enthusiasm carried him on like a
cataract, until often, as C. Hercules Reed, the distinguished curator of the British Museum, remarked, "he will cumber himself
with things that he would be better without, quite apart from the
fact that they cost him a great deal of money." Yet who would
want to lift the restraining hand?

An audience enhanced his pleasure. The entourage which accompanied him on his triumphal trips abroad frequently in-

cluded, besides a favorite Pekinese and a comfortable battery of
servants, several male companions, a particular—and usually beautiful—lady friend and, as ostensible chaperone, one of his daughters or his widowed sister, Mrs. Burns, who supplied an obbligato
of chirping enthusiasm over works of art and Morgan's comments. Here and there en route a distinguished museum man or
self-styled expert would join the group.

This prodigious collecting of over $60,000,000 worth of art was
accomplished in less than two decades. Obviously Morgan paid
the penalty of extravagant prices. He was too much in a hurry to
allow himself the luxury of a "find" and too imperious to bargain.
As Roger Fry, the English critic, describes it, he would cut short a
dicker by turning his terrific eyes on the dealer and saying, "I've
heard enough. I'll take it for what you paid, plus fifteen percent.
[Fry errs: usually ten percent.] What did you pay?" In a field
scarcely noted for either its scrupulous honesty or its generosity, it
usually turned out that the dealer had paid rather dearly for the
object in question.

Not, they explained, that it was their fault. Their routine
strangely resembled that of the Carpenter in Lewis Carroll's
poem. That gentleman, speaking to the oysters he was about to
devour, said, "I weep for you, I deeply sympathize," and then,
holding his pocket handkerchief before his streaming eyes, sorted
out those of the largest size. Jacques Seligmann, for instance, ran
true to form in the matter of the Swenigorodoski collection of
Byzantine enamels in St. Petersburg. He assured Mr. Morgan that
they were not worth more than $80,000 to $100,000. Then he
sounded the customary note of alarm: someone less scrupulous
than he must be trying to procure them for Mr. Morgan, because
the price was going up. After weeks of petulant defenses of his
heroic efforts against obdurate owners, the dealer quietly bought
the lot for Morgan for $150,000.

The wife of an art dealer was amazed, and somewhat annoyed,
when her husband awakened her at three o'clock one morning

and commanded her to say, "I'll pay you a million dollars for your Gothic tapestries." Sleepily, she protested that she did not have a million dollars and could not see why she should want to buy her husband's tapestries even if she *did* have the money. "Just say it, please," he beseeched her. Realizing she would not be allowed to go back to sleep until she acquiesced to his idiotic demand, she repeated his statement and turned over. At nine o'clock the next morning, the dealer, who took great pride in his integrity, told J. P. Morgan, "I can swear to you on a Bible that at three o'clock this morning I had an offer of a million dollars for these tapestries."

But this man who could acutely gauge the price of a railway system was hardly fooled by the comparatively piddling antics of art dealers. Many offers were abruptly refused: "No—price too high." When he did pay exorbitant prices he knew what he was doing.

As with Gainsborough's "Duchess of Devonshire." The lovely lady had been painted by Gainsborough in 1785. Ninety-one years later, on May 6, 1876, her likeness cost art dealer Sir William Agnew $51,500, the highest price given up to then for an English picture at auction. On May 26, 1876, the painting was put on show in London, in the Agnew galleries, and the banker Junius Spencer Morgan dropped in to order it for his son, Pierpont, who, he explained, had "begun collecting pictures in New York."

It was an act of extreme parental indulgence, because the kind of paintings and bric-a-brac on fringed table covers which Pierpont Morgan had in his Madison Avenue house in those days was far from worthy of the Duchess' company. However, she was to be subjected to even greater indignity than the companionship of some thirsty, morose cows as depicted by Troyon and "Napoleon Planning His Coronation" as detailed by Vibert. That night in the gallery she was cut from her frame by one of a gang of three American thieves, hidden in a mattress in a little house in St. John's Wood and held for ransom. Sir William's fine show of

British imperviousness to both threatening letters and taunting bits of canvas was, in secret fact, due to an unpleasant warning from Scotland Yard that any dealings with the thieves would be compounding a felony.

Sometime later, the Duchess was sealed in the false lid of a Saratoga trunk for the Atlantic voyage and deposited in a Chicago warehouse. Apparently her charms faltered, for by 1901 the last thief tired of her and informed a Pinkerton detective that he would be glad to be rid of her, for a consideration. Morland Agnew, who had succeeded his father in the firm, sped to the designated Chicago hotel, where three rooms with connecting doors had been hired. Money and painting passed unseen from thief to dealer by way of the Pinkerton intermediary in the middle room. The lady's homecoming was garlanded with articles and illustrations. A London soubrette sang a special ballad, "The Stolen Duchess." J. P. Morgan bought the painting.

Prices in the art world can be gently nudged upward by even a bit of publicity. But there is nothing as good as gangsters and a kidnaping. When a clergyman friend was brash enough to ask Morgan what he paid for the kidnaped lady, the banker refused to answer, saying, "If the truth came out, I might be considered a candidate for the lunatic asylum." In point of fact, the $150,000 which Morgan paid seems a piddling enough sum beside the $620,000 which Duveen in 1921 persuaded Henry E. Huntington to give for another English eighteenth-century picture. It was merely of a little boy in a blue suit—the one who had charmed Isabella Stewart Gardner—and he had not even been kidnaped.

Morgan never fooled himself about what he spent. As he confessed to his son-in-law, the three most expensive words in his experience were, justifiably, *unique au monde*. But to make certain that objects were unique in the world, he employed a huge army of experts, whose ranks included curators of the world's great museums as well as obsequious hangers-on and conscientious cadgers.

The curious lot included Langton Douglas, who had given up the priesthood to study Sienese paintings and was produced at the London Burlington House exhibition of 1901 when Morgan asked to be shown around by "somebody who knows something." From that tour came some of Morgan's best paintings, bought at comparatively low prices when gold-background primitives were just beginning a limited vogue. There was C. Hercules Reed, loftily independent, who eschewed personal commissions in favor of significant Morgan gifts to his institution, the British Museum. There were Fitzhenry—"dear Old Fitz"—adviser on miniatures, whom Reed described as wandering "around as usual in a bilingual maze of half-finished sentences," and Dr. G. C. Williamson, a Dickensian fuss-budget. There was William M. Laffan, editor of the *New York Sun* and authority on Chinese porcelains, whom Morgan once ordered to find a cap for a Chinese porcelain ginger jar, "even if it costs me a million dollars" (a challenge met by Thomas B. Clarke, who took over after Laffan died, by the simple expedient of removing a cap from another Morgan vase). There was Wilhelm von Bode, often competing with Morgan in the market in order to fill up the lately founded Kaiser-Frederich Museum in Berlin. There were several trusted dealers. There was the whole staff of the Metropolitan. And there was Belle da Costa Greene.

That young woman, with her slim waist and slanting, heavily lidded green eyes, who looked something like a Chinese firedog, became Morgan's librarian in 1906. Fafnir no more doggedly guarded the gold of the Nibulungs than Belle Greene, sharp-tongued, quick-tempered, hot-blooded, protected her employer against the wily race of art and book dealers and the slurs and denigrations of the malcontented. And it was she who ruled the Library, which more than any of his abodes—the yacht *Corsair,* the house in New York, Cragston on the Hudson, Prince's Gate and Dover House inherited from his father in England—was Morgan's favorite and most apposite environment.

In 1872 the Morgan family had moved from Fortieth Street into a respectably imposing brownstone on Madison Avenue and Thirty-sixth Street. As Morgan's biographer, Frederick Lewis Allen, says, its interior remained dignified, comfortable, undistinguished, although in due course he allowed the drawing room to be done over from more or less Pompeian to more or less French. But by 1900 the autographs, the manuscripts, the first editions, the rare, lovely books which he had been accumulating with increasing enthusiasm from 1880 on were beginning to spill out of bookshelves and to overflow the cellar storage room. The home fires, with three children gathered round, might seem to this sternly religious man to burn more appropriately in a prosaic brownstone in the Murray Hill district than in one of the fashionable Renaissance mansions rising on Fifth Avenue. But culture surely deserved a setting as grand as card playing. That activity was conducted in the handsome clubs that Morgan frequented (and in one of which, the University, the first discussions of the U. S. Steel Corporation took place). So Charles McKim was summoned. The plans for the Library, that would be adjacent to the house, were discussed over breakfasts. On February 28, 1903, they were filed with the city of New York.

The little freely Renaissance palazzo is a triumph of McKim's art. Its steep cost was not lessened by the fact that McKim persuaded Morgan to let him have the pinkish-white marble set without mortar, as the Greeks had done—each block carefully polished to meet exactly, joined only by metallic pins. That operation cost an additional $500,000. But the building is restrained, not opulent; exquisite, not ostentatious. The East Room, lined with books, is regal with lapis-lazuli columns flanking the fireplace and with a Flemish sixteenth-century tapestry above it. What unconscious impulse of guilt or pride determined the choice of this particular weaving? It represents "The Triumph of Avarice," and it includes one vandal stealing leaves of an illuminated manuscript.

Morgan used the West Room, epitome of the Age of Elegance, as his resplendent lair. The red brocade walls bear the coat of arms of the Chigi family of Florence; the ceiling came from a palace in Lucca. The formidable assurance of Renaissance man confronted him in the Castagno portrait (which Mrs. Gardner had wanted) and the loveliness of Renaissance woman faced him in Ghirlandaio's "Giovanna Tornabuoni." Blue-robed Madonnas hung on the walls. Exquisite Renaissance marble busts and bas-reliefs kept company with a ruby-red K'ang Hsi vase, pirouetting Tanagra figures, an elaborate helmet and a Byzantine cist. In the corner, the door opened to the vault which held the precious manuscripts and jeweled bindings.

With monumental aplomb, Morgan settled cozily into the West Room. Louis Sullivan, the ardent, pioneering modern architect of Chicago, had raised a dissenting voice against the eclectic styles and palaces of New York. "Must you wait until you see a gentleman in a silk hat come out of it before you laugh? Have you no sense of humor, no sense of pathos? Must I tell you that while the man may live in the house physically (for a man may live in any kind of house, physically), that he cannot live in it morally, mentally, or spiritually, that he and his home are a paradox, a contradiction, an absurdity?" Perhaps alone of all the millionaires, Morgan gave him the lie. The silk hat struck no incongruous note. There was no contradiction between Morgan and the West Room. He used it as a matter of course for his daily conferences and his committee meetings. During the tense days and nights of the Panic of 1907, the bankers and industrialists whom he summoned shuttled back and forth between the East and West Rooms.

It was Belle Greene who was his frank, often indiscreet, always passionately loyal confidante in the West Room. Smoking her made-to-order Egyptian cigarettes, she chatted with him. In spring, when the tulips bloomed in the Library garden and Morgan was in Europe, letters and, especially, cables sped back and forth. Though Morgan was indifferent to modern art, he was enthusiastic about modern technology. His home was the first in the world to be lit throughout with electric lights, and his message from the Azores to Clarence Mackay in New York in 1906 was allegedly the first cable privately sent. Thereafter he was never without his little cable code book, and messages between "Flitch" (Morgan) and "Morglib" (Belle Greene) were many.

Typical exchanges concerned the Hoe sale of 1911, in which she had planned to spend $110,000 of Morgan's money. She coveted especially a Caxton edition of *Morte d'Arthur* on vellum which she hoped to get for $20,000. Trustfully indulgent, Morgan kept sending cables telling her to go to $75,000 or $100,000 rather than lose, while she kept reassuring him with such messages as, "Hope you will give no attention books being offered Hoe Sale. Prices absurd and evidently made with you in mind. Love. Morglib." The day of the sale she cabled triumphantly, "Bought Caxton irascible intespescas humedos much myrcinite Smith was underbidder," which meant, "Bought Caxton 42,800 dollars much excitement," etc.

Smith, it turned out, was bidding for Henry E. Huntington, nephew of Collis P. Huntington, the biggest of the Big Four of Central Pacific Railroad fortune. In 1913, Huntington was to marry his uncle's widow. He was also, with the expensive encouragement of Duveen, to fall in love with a whole galaxy of English eighteenth-century aristocrats and to install their portraits in ancestral splendor in vast galleries of his San Marino, California, residence. In 1911, however, he was at the less showy stage of book and manuscript collecting, but he was working at it with flamboyant zeal.

Morgan and Belle Greene looked down upon this West Coast upstart. Believing that Smith was paying ten times the value of the books, she wrote patronizingly, "It was rather disgusting to see Mr. Huntington being made ridiculous." She reveals her contempt for Huntington and simultaneously consoles herself about the villainous Smith by concluding, "I doubt if Smith will find any market save Huntington and Hearst."

She rushed like a Valkyrie into the fray when she suspected Morgan was being taken advantage of. Dr. Williamson, an anxious, obsequious, but tenacious old man, found her an unbending foe in their six-year wrangle. The issue this time was a little bronze sculpture of a foolishly grinning, naked urchin riding a shaggy goat. From London, Williamson urgently recommended it to Morgan in 1912 as a piece by the Renaissance sculptor Bertoldo di Giovanni, dating 1460-70. He admitted the owner's price of $10,000 was too high, but was sure that his own dogged efforts could procure it for $8,500—though not a penny less. Morgan, indifferent, replied that he would buy it for $5,000—though not a penny more. The good doctor protested that the subtleties of the art world were beyond him: to his astonishment, the owner had agreed.

When the bronze arrived in New York in January, 1913, it was Belle Greene's not wholly distasteful duty to inform the doctor that there had been a slight mistake in date: the piece was, in fact, about 430 years newer than was alleged. But she was sure that, with his usual tact, the doctor would see that the $5,000 was returned to Morgan immediately. What "a thunderclap, a bolt from the blue" her information was! Modern? He could not believe it!

By the time she convinced him, it turned out that getting the money back was a matter "of extreme complexity." For months his letters sound a tearful threnody. The Prince of Thurn and Taxis, to whom the bronze had belonged, was abroad; the dealer who sold it to Williamson was now "in financial low water" in America; the dealer's father had an inflammation of the lung. But, heroically, he—Dr. Williamson—had extracted $625, which he was returning. Meanwhile, Morgan had died. A new train of sorrowful personal events delayed Williamson's return of the remainder. Belle Greene seized her opportunity. She arranged that when the Morgan estate settled Morgan's bill with Williamson,

$4,375 should be deducted from the amount owing him. The anguished protests carried on until July, 1918, but the ultimate victory was Belle Greene's. She prepared for Morgan's son and his attorney a memorandum—for whose "ladylike restraint" she asked admiration—which finally silenced the doctor.

That Morgan should depend on advisers to assure authenticity was neither surprising nor superfluous. The manufacture of fakes and the perpetration of hoaxes is one of mankind's chronic pleasures. To fool one's fellow man is to feel superior to him. Moreover, his gullibility can be turned to quick profit. There was a brisk trade in false relics along the pilgrimage roads and the Crusaders' routes in the Middle Ages. Enterprising artists of the Renaissance provided convincing fragments of Classical sculpture to suit the prevailing fashion. Indeed, the most accurate index to prevailing taste is to be found in the field of fakes.

For the creator of the fraud, the incentives are rarely mercenary. Usually he craves the sweet, secret satisfaction of seducing by his false self the very persons who have rejected his real self. Hence those like Van Meegeren, who won the unwitting applause of the experts with the religious paintings, which he faked and sold as precious seventeenth-century Vermeers, and their disdain for his own stickily sentimental canvases. Often the forger is moved merely by the challenge of craftsmanship, driven to the most painstaking investigations and most elaborate experiments of alchemy and chemistry to satisfy his perfectionism. But flocks of middlemen are always waiting to harness these talents into commercially profitable channels.

Conditions in the early part of our century were particularly favorable for an epidemic of fakes. The enormous demand for the art of the past was rivaled only by the ignorance of most of the demanders.

Morgan, in a sense, carried his own insurance. He was a man of stern justice and formidable wrath. Only the foolhardy would risk being cut off from the golden patronage. Yet there were conscious and unconscious attempts at fraud. For some of these, he himself was responsible. Bernard Berenson recounts with wicked delight the story about a painting at a London dealer's which had been "faked up" from Rudolpho Ghirlandaio to Raphael. As Berenson tells it, "Said the dealer, 'Mr. Morgan, all the critics say this is not a Raphael, but you and I know it is.' Said Morgan, 'Wrap it up.' " Berenson is apt to take a cold view of the millionaire collectors, but, however apocryphal, the story has a certain symbolic truth. Morgan often went shopping without an adviser at his elbow and made impetuous purchases about which an expert might later timidly suggest an adjustment.

Morgan did not like to be wrong. At his death, there remained in the basement of a dealer's shop in Paris a box of forged champlevé enamels which he had bought from someone else. He knew he had been deceived. He would not return them to the seller— and thus admit his mistake—but neither would he take delivery.

But the percentage of mistakes is very small. As Francis Henry Taylor, the former director of the Metropolitan Museum, pointed out, as a good mathematician Morgan knew enough about the law of averages to risk buying ready-made collections *en bloc*. Moreover, experience is a good teacher, and Morgan, acquiring in vast quantities, had more than a modicum of experience. The art critic Frank Jewett Mather remarked about the specialist: "Where nature has provided fair intelligence, one must die very young in order not to die an expert." The fields in which Morgan specialized were, indeed, those in which he could not be duped.

He even gives the lie to S. N. Behrman's persuasively promulgated myth of the invincibility of Joseph Duveen, who, like the Canadian Mounties, presumably always got his man.

Morgan had been the willing client of Henry Duveen, Joseph's genial, rotund uncle. Young Joseph, an ardent perfectionist, felt his uncle was not realizing the full Morgan potential and begged for a try himself. Accordingly, he arranged a collection of thirty miniatures. He scattered six rare objects among the run-of-the-mill ones that make a wholesale deal profitable. Morgan looked briefly, then asked brusquely, "How much for the lot?" Joseph Duveen, casting a victorious glance at his uncle, answered. Morgan's huge hand unhesitatingly plucked out the six best miniatures from their velvet bed. As he stuffed them into his pockets, he swiftly divided by thirty, multiplied by six, announced what the half-dozen cost and departed.

Uncle Henry smiled benignly at his nephew: "Joe, you're only a boy. It takes a man to deal with Morgan."

Behind the lavish buying, the paid artistic lookouts, the network of dealers and the army of experts, lay a plan. It was a plan so grandiloquent that only a Morgan could conceive of it or fulfill it. He would gather for America an undreamed-of collection of art so great and so complete that a trip to Europe would be superfluous. And he would give this vast and splendid compendium to the Metropolitan Museum.

Morgan had been one of the hundred-odd persons who had contributed to the modest sum of $106,000 with which that museum was founded in 1870. America was getting museum-conscious that year. Boston founded its art museum then and soon such institutions were mushrooming around the country. To the Victorians, capitalism, industrialism and imperialism were not the only progressive forces; there were also those of morality, education and classification.

When Morgan became president of the Metropolitan in 1904, that institution had several times expanded its floor space and now faced Fifth Avenue with a correct McKim, Mead and White façade of Indiana limestone. Its contents were varied. Due primarily to Henry Marquand, there were a few masterpieces by Flemish seventeenth-century painters, whose current vogue in England was spreading to America. There were a vast population of pristine white plaster casts, enough Paris salon paintings to insure the museum's popularity, an extraordinary collection of 650 old-master drawings (sold by Jarves to Cornelius Vanderbilt—also the donor of Rosa Bonheur's "Horse Fair"—who gave them to the museum) and a fascinating collection of Cypriote and Greek antiquities.

The latter had been purchased through the museum's first director, General Palma di Cesnola, a firebrand of a man with drooping white walrus mustaches. An Italian professional soldier, who had trained officers for the Union Army in the Civil War, he had been rewarded by President Lincoln with the consularship of Cyprus in 1865. In those days the controversial island still belonged to the Turks, and the Consul, like so many others in the diplomatic service of the nineteenth century, found archeology more engaging, and often more profitable, than politics.

As its president, Morgan ruled the Metropolitan as autocratically and as bent on its success as if it were one of his industrial corporations. He staffed it with the best experts he could find—and then used them as his personal advisers. He studded the board with millionaire businessmen of his own kind—men like George F. Baker, Henry Clay Frick, John G. Johnson, Henry Walters, Edward Harkness—whose private collecting had some of the feverish enthusiasm of his own. At openings, Morgan would receive like royalty, standing on a near-acre of Oriental rug in the Great Hall. On one occasion he caught sight of a woman in the line who held a baby in her arms and ordered that a $1,000 life membership be taken out for the child (who, ironically, developed cataracts of both eyes by the age of five). But he also devoted much time to museum meetings. No acquisition, no change of architectural detail, no appointment was made without consulting him. He was determined to make the Metropolitan Museum the finest institution of its sort in the world.

Was he then merely the crude checkbook collector, the wholesale buyer of merchandise labeled "Art"? Roger Fry, the English critic he summoned as curator of paintings, wrote venomously of Morgan as a man of perfect insensibility, prodigious vanity and colossal ignorance. Mercilessly Fry described the triumphal passage of *il Morgan* and retinue through Italy: sweeping through "the human flotsam that was drawn into the whirlpool of Morgan's wealth"; kowtowing to a fawning, titled courier; buying heirlooms from pleading owners; blandly accepting such special favors as having the whole wooden floor of the Cathedral of Siena removed so he might see the mosaics, a favor earlier denied to the Queen of Italy.

Fry, the esthete, sensitively on the defensive, jaundicedly anti-American and anti-millionaire, obviously resented dancing to the Morgan tune. It was inevitable that they should clash, as so many millionaires and museum men have since. For many of the latter, intellectual descendants of the medieval scholar and the Talmudic Jew, the world revolves around the nuances and exquisite shading of minutiae; for the former, the issues are big, generalized, demanding sweeping, brusque decisions. Fry dickered to buy a Fra Angelico directly for the Metropolitan. Morgan, ignorant of his maneuver, negotiated for it himself. Across the top of Fry's letter, accusing Morgan of double-dealing, the banker with angry forcefulness wrote to Belle Greene, "The most remarkable letter I ever received." After the break, Morgan remained implacably indifferent to Fry. The moral indignation of the rich has perhaps greater stamina than that of the poor. Before long Fry was urging Morgan to make purchases from which he, Fry, would derive the usual substantial commission.

Morgan was, in fact, no more Fry's checkbook collector, vulgarly using the brute power of the purse, than he was a megalomaniacal, compulsive collector like the later William Randolph Hearst, who not only acquired hundreds of thousands of objects by the carload, but also grabbed up complete Roman temple façades, Gothic monasteries, hundreds of palace ceilings and the like.

Some of Hearst's properties were crowded into that phantasmagoria San Simeon, into which the publisher moved in 1925.

The enormity of its presumption, like the gigantic scale of all Hearst's operations, inspired Aldous Huxley's merciless and wonderful *After Many a Summer Dies the Swan* and the movies *The Ghost Goes West* and *Citizen Kane*. Here in this castle, colossal, even wanton in its castle-ness, were joined the awful and the awesome. With raw insensitivity, exquisite Greek vases, handsome Hispano-Moresque plates, tapestries of unsurpassed quality were joined with fourth-rate paintings of Madonnas, a stuffed owl, a crudely restored façade of a Roman temple and academic sculptures of cast marble as unpleasantly white as a pair of store-bought dentures. On the façade, the teakwood gable of an Oriental pagoda was clutched between pseudo-Spanish-Italian towers. A four-teenth-century confessional served as the elevator, disgorging the castle's owner to a secret door cut into a choir stall—from which he could emerge into rooms of cavernous splendor and gigantic gloom. He could dine, under sixteenth-century Sienese banners, at a refectory table on which, out of sentimental nostalgia for family picnics on this "enchanted hill," paper napkins and ketchup bottles stood with magnificent Georgian silver. Thirty-nine guests could join him, sitting on Italian Renaissance chairs, of which—like much else in this fantastic conglomeration—thirty-eight had been manufactured on the place.

Even this gargantuan castle absorbed but a fraction of Hearst's properties. There was enough to fill two other castles, one of which, in Wales, held his spectacular armor collection, and to cram several enormous warehouses on the East and West coasts. These storage houses contained such items as an entire Spanish monastery. He had snapped this up in 1925 for $40,000. Then he spent $500,000 for the building of twenty-one miles of special-gauge railroad from the monastery site to the main railroad line and for the construction of a sawmill to cut wood for the necessary crates. The dismantling, packing and shipping operation took ten years. When the crates arrived in New York it was discovered that the stones had been packed with straw—a carrier of the dread hoof-and-mouth disease. Each of the 25,000 crates had to be unpacked and repacked. Then they were sent to storage.

Like much else, they were sold in 1941 from Gimbels Department Store, from which vast quantities of Hearst art was dispersed at a year-long sale, the most fantastic art sale of all time (you could get an Egyptian scarab for ninety-eight cents, an Indo-Persian rug for $19,500 or four Renaissance tapestries for $199,894). Yet so gargantuan was Hearst's buying that even today, after generous gifts to museums, and many auctions, the warehouses are still jammed. (If it is true, as his mother allegedly remarked, that "every time Willie feels badly, he goes out and buys something," one can only presume that William Randolph Hearst felt badly most of the time.)

But if Morgan was not the megalomaniacal, Hearstian collector, neither was he a painstaking connoisseur, lovingly seeking out his treasures one by one. What he was, essentially, was the true patrician, to the art-manner born. He did not require art possessions to give him security or to stamp him as a cultivated gentleman. Everything had prepared him to be one: he was born in New England; he was educated in Europe, where he naturally became familiar with art, culture and history from boyhood; he reached young manhood as the son of a respected, wealthy and cultivated Anglo-American banker. He was as much at home in England and on the Continent as in New York. Frederick Lewis Allen observes that it was his nature to pursue "the life of an unostentatious man on a majestic scale."

He collected because he enjoyed shopping. He chose art because he was truly moved by beauty. He chose the art of the past, especially the Renaissance, because he felt at home with it and enjoyed the sense of peership with kings and emperors which owning their objects gave him. Art collecting came as naturally to him as to any prince or patrician of another age. That he was collecting for the public good was merely the accident of his period and of a certain Victorian morality. That he was collecting on

such a scale was due partly to a Victorian admiration for encyclopedic completeness but more particularly to the fact that he
was Morgan, who believed in the biggest as well as the best.

His sensitivity to beauty—especially in quantity—was inborn.
As a boy he collected fragments of medieval stained glass (some
of it incorporated by Cartier's into the West Room windows) : as a
man, waiting for an appointment in the Vatican, he longed for a
bed so he might lie for hours looking at ceiling frescoes by Pin-
turicchio. He knew what he liked. He was as remote from "modern art" as from Theodore Roosevelt's "modern thinking." He
cherished Oriental porcelains, but vetoed other art from the Orient. He had a romantic and historical interest in the way objects
illuminated civilizations. This feeling, plus a love of craftsmanship (an admiration he shared with many tycoon collectors),
made the decorative arts particularly appealing to him.

He purchased by the carload, but he had preferences and predilections. In 1906, when he bought the Gaston Lebreton collection
of faïences and enamels for the Metropolitan, he singled out one
of the 196 pieces to keep for himself because he liked it so much.
His bills are dense with notes that this piece of Limoges enamel or
that ivory was "taken." He was as impatient to get his objects home
as a woman to wear a new hat.

He liked showing off his possessions, especially his huge collection of miniatures, relentlessly trapping a visitor while he went
through them one by one. His attorney, John G. Johnson, recalled
rising with "a nearly broken back" from "the stooping position"
of a long and weary session at Prince's Gate looking "at what
seemed thousands of miniatures, one very much like the other."

There would be no name attached to his gift to the Metropolitan. He gave munificently to his and other churches, to the building of a maternity hospital, to the Wadsworth Atheneum in his
native Hartford, to Cooper Union and museums in Europe, to the
lighting of St. Paul's Cathedral in London and to the reconstruction of the Campanile in Venice, to countless acquaintances and

servitors. But the pattern was rigid anonymity. As his biographer
Allen points out, Morgan believed that a gentleman should not
advertise his benefactions.

Not for him the incentives of certain other magnates, whose
collections for the public would be brazenly and irrevocably
labeled. The Morgan name need depend on no such cheap ticket
to immortality. He might be giving culture to the people, but he
was as aloof from their adulation as he was immune from their
attacks.

His vanity was assuaged in quite other ways. Beginning in
1906, he commissioned almost annually elaborate catalogues of
each part of his collections. Like the mother who told an admiring
spectator, standing above her baby, "Oh, but you should see his
photograph," Morgan delighted in looking at these lavish, hand-
painted, hand-printed, gold- and silver-leafed records of his possessions. Bound in de luxe covers, copies of these catalogues were
cherished by his bed. Others were distributed to the crowned heads
of Europe, who were his chosen contemporary peers and the audience whose approbation he wanted. For even Morgan was not
completely immune from the Henry James sense of American
cultural inferiority. He was pleased when Queen Alexandra
dropped in to see his collection, when Edward VII came to call
and when the Kaiser lunched with him on the *Corsair*. He enjoyed being able to return to the Pope the famous Ascoli Cope
that had been stolen from Italy years before and liked being able
to present Charles V's letter to Luther to the German Emperor.

Nor was anyone more magnanimous than Morgan about helping aristocrats out of temporary trouble. There were the Sackvilles,
for instance. It had cost Lord Sackville a pretty penny defending his
title in the courts against a Spanish dancer who claimed that as the
bastard son of Lord Sackville's father he was legitimate heir to
the title. Morgan kindly replenished the Sackville coffers by buying the famous tapestries from their mansion, Knole, for $325,000.
Apparently he was willing to do more, but, though charmed,

Lady Sackville was proud. She wrote that she wanted "no money, no presents . . . only three things: your photo looking at me full face, my [copy of] Shakespeare, and the two amber vases upstairs you said are not good enough for you."

But it was not to bait royalty or for the sake of European kudos that Morgan let the greatest part of the great abundance pile up in his English houses and European museums. The explanation lay in the American tariff situation.

This barrier, which had plagued Isabella Stewart Gardner in a relatively minor way, was becoming a formidable and expensive annoyance to the big-scale collectors—the "Squillionaires," as Berenson called them—of the Morgan era. Harassed by the necessity of paying heavy levies to get things *in* to America, they were also running into trouble about getting them *out* of Europe.

European dealers might have no qualms about exchanging masterpieces for American dollars, but there were other Europeans, less commercially involved, who felt a patriotic ire at the exodus of their national treasures. France had some restrictive legislation; Italy, already difficult in the eighties, grew stricter in 1909. Britain found the situation worrisome in 1903 and by 1913 reported that the exodus was proceeding at an alarming rate (fifty Rembrandts, twenty-one Rubens, five Velásquez, eleven Holbeins, seven Vermeers were among those listed as having been spirited away to such barbarian areas as American collections and the Berlin Museum). When the British held on to a Holbein that Henry Clay Frick was after, John G. Johnson was moved to remark, "You can count but little on the British love of Art, but upon its *amour propre* you can surely rely." The British had no restrictive legislation at that time, but, whether impelled by love of Art or *amour propre,* no other nation grew so publicly indignant.

Quite a row was raised, for instance, when word got around that Morgan was after Velásquez' "Venus" from Rockeby Hall. The splendid nude, seen from the rear in a pose which some British doctors unromantically recognized as absolutely correct for certain anatomical examinations (and is said to have been used as an illustration at a medical conference), is now in the London National Gallery. But it is there only because Morgan withdrew from the competition and even went so far as to contribute funds toward its purchase. Indeed, there were those unkind enough to hint that some of the munificent gifts by such dealers as Duveen and such collectors as Morgan were sops to quiet the occasional outbursts of patriotic possessiveness.

The combination of American tariff barriers and European restrictions naturally stimulated dealers and collectors to intricate and ingenious smuggling devices.

P. A. B. Widener, the Philadelphia butcher boy who first started making money selling mutton to the Union Army and then made millions out of trolley cars, particularly enjoyed the game of "getting the stuff out." A member of Duveen's recalls that one morning in 1908 an enormous case arrived addressed to Widener. It was so big that it had to be left in the marble court. The millionaire himself arrived to superintend the unpacking. To the undisguised consternation of the Duveen employees, who had been offering Widener their tutelage in art, a huge, four-times-life-size plaster bust of the gentleman in question was revealed. "Come on, open it up," Widener commanded. "It is open," said a horror-struck, stripe-trousered employee. "No, no, open up the bust. Break it open," said the millionaire. Inside was a small terra-cotta figure which had been sold to Widener in Italy as a Michelangelo. His disappointment in discovering that it was a fake was mitigated by his glee in knowing that customs officers both in Italy and New York would never question the over-life-size vanity of an American millionaire.

A year or so before, in Italy, Widener had bought the magnificent Van Dyck portraits of the Grimaldi family, now in the National Gallery in Washington. Motorcars in those days had wide, long exhaust pipes. They seemed irresistible cylinders for rolled canvases. It is said that Widener ordered an extra one made to contain the Van Dycks and then had it neatly attached to the chassis of his car.

One of Duveen's smuggling devices was comparatively simple. A $50,000 tapestry or a $100,000 painting would be folded or rolled into a $200 carved wood chest. The chest was declared at its full value. If the box were opened by some uncooperative Pandora-like customs inspector, Duveen's man would curse the dumb-witted employee in London who had packed the rare object against instructions and would return it immediately. Some of these items made several transatlantic crossings before they came home to roost.

Uncle Henry Duveen had for a long time also been helping Uncle Sam. He had been acting as an appraiser, and although he modestly undervalued his own imports he was reluctant to cast a slur on a competitor's possession by valuing *it* low. But in 1910, through the chattering of a disgruntled employee, Duveen's came a cropper. The government's demands for duty on all Duveen undervalued and undeclared imports prior to 1909 at one point climbed to the astronomical figure of $10,000,000. Lawyers finally whittled it down to a mere $1,400,000. At this point, as S. N. Behrman related it, "the aura of Uncle Henry's benevolent personality shone out to save them. It was an awful lot to ask of an aura, but Uncle Henry's made it." Morgan sent for one of the lawyers, ordered him to "get Uncle Henry off" and obligingly supplied the $1,400,000 that implemented his command.

The irony of the Duveen smuggling case was that it was instigated in 1910, a year after the tariff law had been changed. Morgan had been an influential lobbyist for that piece of legislation.

Theodore Roosevelt was thumping his "big stick" against the millionaire monopolists, but "the interests" were not without friends in House and Senate. Among those who felt rather kindly toward the tycoons was Nelson Willmarth Aldrich of Providence, Rhode Island. He had started life as a grocer, but by taking an astute and vested interest in banking, sugar, rubber, public utilities and tractions, had amassed the fortune of $30,000,000, which made him the richest man to enter the Senate up to that time. He had also developed a discriminating eye, so that the souvenirs he brought home from his Grand Tours in Europe and Egypt were rather remarkable works of art. The duty he paid on them was a good deal less than the $6,000,000 it would have cost Morgan to import *his* souvenirs, but Aldrich could well understand Morgan's moral outrage at being penalized for importing culture and his annoyance at being taxed for enjoying his personal possessions. At the same time, Aldrich was perfectly willing to protect living American artists from foreign competition. This was a field in which he, like Morgan, was conveniently disinterested. The resulting Payne-Aldrich Tariff Bill of 1909 allowed art over a hundred years old free entry into the United States. (It remained for John Quinn, a lawyer whose own collecting was centered in art less than a hundred years old, to force a revision in 1913.)

The tariff barrier had been one obstacle. The housing problem was another. The Metropolitan Museum, whose wings were given the alphabetical nomenclature of orphanages and hospitals, had turned "F" over to the Morgan gift of decorative art from the Hoentschel collection in 1910 (in 1918 it was renamed the Morgan Wing). A new wing—"H"—was then being built, but it was intended for the Metropolitan's accumulating treasures.

The vast Morgan collections would require a new wingful of galleries, but the Board of Estimate of the City of New York balked at making such an appropriation. The year was 1911 and, as Allen remarks, it was politically safer to be against Morgan than for him. Theodore Roosevelt's protests against the uncurbed might of big business had gained momentum. Public indignation was sparked by the novelists' dramatizations of the sins of the tycoons and by their thunderous exposures of conditions in oil fields and meat-packing houses. Honest political reformers and bald opportunists were sweeping into office on the tide of public hostility toward the mighty millionaires.

Morgan himself bore no personal castigation for horrors in the anthracite mines or scandals in the insurance business. But he was called before a Congressional committee (the Pujo Committee) in 1911 to answer for the U. S. Steel Corporation and, in a sense, to defend the whole corporate concept. He was, unquestionably, the symbol of the flagrant influence of wealth. All this had its repercussions on the issue of the new Metropolitan wing. Why, the New York press demanded, should the taxpayers pay to allow Morgan to parade his wealth?

About to give more than $60,000,000 worth of art, Morgan could undoubtedly have underwritten the construction of a wing. But he was obviously too proud to "buy" himself space if the city was indifferent.

But toward the end of 1911, at the age of seventy-three, aware of the implications of his publicly reported "tiredness" and worried about an impending expansion of British death duties, Morgan instigated the Grand Removal of his collections from England to the basement of the Metropolitan. No ordinary shipment, this. In order that everything might be examined and cleared before it was packed and sealed, and thus avoid possible damage from extra unpacking, a special Treasury Department agent and an examiner of the Port of New York were sent to London at Morgan's expense.

The year's packing and shipping job—of a scale and intricacy to make a housewife shudder—began in a special locked room in the Victoria and Albert Museum in London, accompanied by the voluble regrets of the usually reticent British press. With the customs inspector at his side, the dealer Jacques Seligmann was in charge.

Morgan was a man who cut swiftly to the core of a matter and made important decisions with abrupt directness. Yet, like so many of his generation of tycoons, he had indefatigable patience with detail. His son-in-law recalls that when a friend's relative died, Morgan took charge of her trip to the funeral. He even arranged that the cabman waiting on the New York City side of the Jersey City ferry, engaged to take her to Grand Central, would identify himself with a white handkerchief tied to his left arm.

Characteristically, then, he besieged Seligmann with letters and cables from New York, Rome, Bahiana, Assiout. His impatience grew, as if he were spurred by premonitions of death. Finally, the last of the hundreds of cases containing Morgan treasures left England on December 24, 1912.

The cavernous basements of the Metropolitan grew crowded. The Board of Estimate still dallied. In January, 1913, twenty-nine of the paintings were unpacked and put on display. The group included the famous Fragonard Room, a roomful of fourteen paintings by the French eighteenth-century master.

Four of the largest of these paintings had been commissioned by Mme. DuBarry in 1775. According to S. N. Behrman, the lady had refused them because she objected to the canvas called "Storming the Citadel" as too forthright a comment on her relations with the king. "She didn't mind being a citadel," he says, "and she didn't even mind being stormed, but she didn't want it suggested to posterity that the citadel had fallen." But more reliable eighteenth-century gossip had it that DuBarry refused the work because of the canvas which shows the heroine mourning her abandonment by a faithless lover. The permanent display of such a possibility would be apt to make even the most glamorous and secure of mistresses a little edgy. Fragonard had been, it must be admitted, rather tactless and undiplomatic. But he was shrewd enough to remove both the work and himself to his cousin's house in Grasse during the Terror in 1793.

In 1898 the paintings turned up at auction, were bought by Agnew's and sold in 1899 to Morgan for $310,000. Since the financier had no qualms at all about falling citadels or fickle lovers, he had the paintings installed in an eighteenth-century setting at Prince's Gate. The walls, woodwork, mantelpiece, furniture, snuffboxes and carpet were all so perfect and complete as to make

DuBarry, had she but seen them, regret her decision—or perhaps even her choice of patrons. The re-creation of that room was Morgan's one stipulation for the exhibition of his paintings.

At the end of the grueling Pujo hearings, Morgan sailed for what would be his last trip to Europe. He went first to Egypt. Egypt had been a stop on the Victorian Grand Tour, and from about 1875 on, the most worldly of the wealthy Americans were following the standard itinerary. Morgan made the regulation trip up the Nile to Karnak first in 1877, with a whole retinue of family and friends and servants, complete to a fez-hatted dragoman. In those days he traveled in a charter boat and bought odds and ends, rugs and jewelry and scarabs. Later he was to travel in an all-steel vessel made to his order and to buy the lovely alabaster, the dark-hued basalt and the faïence pieces, blue as the desert sky, as they were dug up from four or five thousand years' burial.

Ever since the Renaissance, man has been fairly busy digging up evidence of how earlier members of his species have lived. In the eighteenth century, the writings of Winckelmann about ancient Greece and the excavations at Herculaneum and Pompeii had been spectacular enough to throw Paris into a frenzied Neo-Classic enthusiasm. The savants who accompanied Napoleon to Egypt had turned up some handsome and substantial evidences of a highly developed civilization.

But it was only in the nineteenth century that the archeologists were to make their burrowings systematic. Champollion cracked the secret of hieroglyphics in 1822. By mid-century, digging was in full swing in Egypt and Mesopotamia. By 1875, the civilizations of the Aegean were revealed. Besides adding to the accretion of human knowledge, these forages into the earth were also adding to the possessions of the great European museums.

America had lagged far behind in this digging spree. The fact that certain New England colleges could boast sculptures from Nineveh was due simply to the practicality of certain Congregationalist missionaries who had an eye for a good thing (as others of their kind had a nose for sugar, real estate and such profitable ventures). Museum galleries, however, were relatively barren of ancient art, a situation that was irritating to Morgan.

There was not much he could do about Greece, since that country was acting a little stuffy about foreign digging since Lord Elgin's rather predatory gesture on the Acropolis in 1806. But Morgan appointed as director of the Metropolitan a renowned classical scholar who could purchase wisely from agents. And he imported from Boston two distinguished Egyptologists, negotiated for sites in Egypt, and saw a Metropolitan expedition set out in 1906. The Morgan luck held. By 1908, 185 cases were ready for shipment.

A year later, Morgan began his annual trips to see the Metropolitan's diggings. He hoisted his portly seventy-two-year-old body astride a donkey to ride out to Lisht. He invited intensive briefing on the methods of excavations and the niceties of the reliefs and paintings that were emerging. He trudged over the sands. At Sakara, he sat resolutely on the throne of an ancient priest, his Panama hat squarely on his head, his high collar unwilting.

The mysterious Mason-like ties that bring men of wealth together worked even in the improbable desert setting. Sheik Mustafa Manad, richest man of the oasis village of Karzeh, sat with Morgan in the impassive silence characteristic of the very rich. Three years later, Morgan sat again on the desert with a rather wealthy gentleman from Pittsburgh, Pennsylvania. The press had no report on the laconic conversations between Morgan and Henry Clay Frick, but one wonders what thoughts of Ozymandias' warning to "look on my works, ye Mighty, and despair" passed through the minds of these two whose combined fortunes of over a quarter of a billion dollars rivaled the wealth of pharaohs.

Morgan's personal involvement with the Metropolitan's excavations sparked his concern. He became their generous benefactor. In New York, he busied himself with the arrangement of the galleries and he received at their opening on November 6, 1911. In large measure, this occasion introduced America to great Egyptian art.

But on the Egyptian trip of 1913 his health was failing. He moved on to Rome and managed to put in an appearance at church on Easter Sunday to allay the commercial fears that were revolving around world-wide reports of his illness. But he grew worse, and on March 31, 1913, he died.

The question of permanent space for his art collections was still unsettled. But his will was explicit about his intention "to make some suitable disposition" of these collections "which would render them permanently available for the instruction and pleasure of the American people." He left the treasure to his son with the hope that he would make "a substantial carrying-out of the intentions which I have thus cherished."

The Metropolitan Museum officials were somewhat taken aback. But they gamely—and still hopefully—went ahead and disgorged the boxes in the basement to create a temporary exhibition, which opened in June of 1914. For the only time, the overwhelming collections were seen in their entirety—an abundance of which perhaps not even their owner had been aware.

Ironically, just as the Board of Estimate was jolted out of its righteous parsimony and was ready to appropriate money for a new wing, the Morgan estate's need for cash intervened. John D. Rockefeller, Sr., marveling that Morgan had halted the Panic of 1907, had remarked, "And to think he isn't even a rich man."

The publication of the Morgan will proved the comparative truth of that complacent observation. The art collections were put at $60,000,000 (undervalued, naturally); the rest of the estate —out of which were to come innumerable personal and institutional bequests and trusts—was, at the highest estimate, $68,000,-000. Inheritance taxes on this amount were only $3,000,000 in those days, but the remainder was apparently insufficient to run an international banking business and so, as Belle Greene sardonically wrote in reference to selling a certain book, "it seems we need the money."

The first idea was to get rid as quickly as possible of whatever had not been paid for at Morgan's death. By strange coincidence in this time when dealers feared tumbling prices, the dealers simply could not locate the original owners for whom it seemed they were only go-betweens. The so-called Cellini book cover (which ultimately turned out to be a German pastiche concocted in the nineteenth century), which had come from Maurice de Rothschild, was a case in point. Maurice de Rothschild was in India because, as the dealer confided, "his parents sent him there because he spent a lot of money, speculated on the Stock Exchange and lost a great part of his fortune, which is why he sold the book cover in the first place." Like all the others, he could not be reached.

To try to sell part of the collection quietly was out of the question. Dumping 100,000 shares of U. S. Steel on the market would have been no more conspicuous. And who of the collectors would be altruistic enough not to take advantage of the absence of the big competitor and of his estate's need for cash?

Several dealers, led by Duveen, descended on the premises. The one thing an art dealer likes better than selling a great work of art is buying a great work of art. The more times he can manipulate a change of hands the more productive he finds the object. Obituary pages are required reading for art dealers. Dealers have perfected the art of genteel condolences with insinuated offers of ready cash for the bereaved. In retrospect, it seems almost an act of panic for Morgan's son to have parted so quickly, for instance, with the Chinese porcelains and the Fragonard Room. Joseph Duveen, who had never gotten far with Morgan, now made handsome profits by buying low and selling high to such collectors as Frick, Altman and Rockefeller, whose mouths were watering for Morgan's art. Duveen knew "what's in a name."

There is, indeed, a cachet to an object which comes from a

famous collection. Anything is worth more if it once belonged to a Medici prince or Louis XV, than if its former owners are unknown or it belonged to some worthy but anonymous chap. Thus dealers and museum directors go to painstaking trouble to prepare brochures showing the "provenance," as the previous ownerships and whereabouts of the object are called. Only once did such an elaborate preparation fall flat.

Wartime stringencies in England brought on the market a large marble sculpture of Samson and a Philistine by the Renaissance sculptor Giovanni Bologna. It was a piece that Preston Remington, the curator of Renaissance and modern art, very much wanted for the Metropolitan Museum. Francis Henry Taylor, director of the museum, arranged a gourmet's lunch for George Blumenthal, the sybaritic banker-collector, who was president of the Metropolitan. After lunch, the three gentlemen retired to Taylor's office.

The shy, flustered curator rose to make his presentation while the well-fed Mr. Blumenthal closed his eyes and sat like a sleeping turtle. Remington had never been on such secure ground. Never had there been so impeccable a pedigree. His courage mounted as he made his pitch:

"The statue," he said, "was made about 1565 for Francesco de' Medici, Grand-Duke of Tuscany. In 1601 it was given by the Grand Duke's successor, Ferdinando, to the Duke of Lerma, Prime Minister of King Philip III of Spain, who in turn gave it to his king. In 1623, the succeeding King of Spain, Philip IV, gave it to Charles I of England—who was then Prince of Wales. Soon thereafter, Charles gave it to the Duke of Buckingham. The sculpture eventually found its way to Buckingham House, which was acquired by George III in 1762, and shortly thereafter the statue was for the last time given away, this time by the King to Thomas Worsley, Surveyor General of His Majesty's Works. Worsley, the direct ancestor of Sir William Worsley, the present owner, placed the statue in the courtyard of Hovingham Hall, where it is today."

"Nope," said Blumenthal, hardly stirring, "we don't want it."

"But, Mr. Blumenthal," the flabbergasted curator continued, "this is a great work of art and its provenance is exceptional."

"It can't be any good," said Blumenthal, imperturbably.

"Can't be any good?"

"Nope," insisted Blumenthal, "it can't be any good. Too many people have given it away."

Such skeptics as Blumenthal are rare. In time, the notation "ex-Morgan Coll." could enormously inflate a price. A Morgan object presumably had intrinsic quality and the precious mark of authenticity. More important, like some fetish, it put the new owner into association not only with the remote great of the past, but, even more reassuringly, with the great Pierpont Morgan himself.

The pattern was set. The art collections, whose gathering had been the most regal gesture of the patrician, became, as *Art News* magazine pointed out, the savings department which produced cash whenever it was needed as the world moved from the Morgan to the Morgenthau era. Morgan, though he hardly doubted its value, never bought art for investment. Yet the art for which he paid exorbitant prices turned out again and again to be gilt-edged. Rarely did it yield less than hundred percent profits.

But one wonders whether the need for cash alone accounts for the dispersal of about fifty percent of the collections. Could there have been some purist, puritanical reaction in Morgan's son, "Mr. Jack," some embarrassment at richness and grandeur in a changing world? He was, like his father, so entrenched a symbol of wealth that when anarchists in 1919 chose two rich men at whose doors to leave their bombs, Morgan and Rockefeller were those so honored.

Mr. Jack, too, retired to the West Room, especially on rainy days. But there were no regal levees, no parade of art dealers. He sat in a large chair reading antiseptic detective stories. But whereas in 1914 Belle Greene was "furiously jealous and unhappy" that she could not make a single purchase at an important sale, by 1915 she confided to a friend that "Mr. M. is beginning to show a strong interest in the Library and has promised I may go on collecting books and manuscripts when the war is over." They did go on. Mr. Jack became the Library's earnest, generous benefactor, and in 1924, while still continuing its support, he gave it to the public. (It is now aided and abetted by a committee of Fellows who have enriched as well as administered it.) Yet Mr. Jack felt guilty if he bought without having disciplined himself to study and understand. He had neither flair nor lust for the sumptuous. If the choice from time to time was between selling splendor or securities, was not his decision inevitable?

About forty percent of the total collections did go to the Metropolitan directly, a matter of some six to eight thousand objects which range from the huge, magnificent altarpiece which was commissioned from Raphael by the nuns of Colonna (and cost Morgan $484,000) to gold-diamond-and-enamel eighteenth-century boxes by the dozen. About ninety percent of them are permanently on view and, because of their high quality, are likely to remain there.

Many of Morgan's other vast treasures have passed, via private collections or outright purchase, to public institutions. In the long run, the Morgan collection has become "permanently available for the instruction and pleasure of the American people."

Morgan had appointed himself the responsible organizer, taking advantage of a unique confluence of circumstances: his money, his will to have the best (whether collies or women, yachts or paintings), the still available supply of precious objects and the obvious need for such an assemblage of art in America. The Morgan collections represent the most grandiose gesture of *noblesse oblige* the world has ever known.

Gamesmanship

JOHN G. JOHNSON

John G. Johnson, the son of a Philadelphia blacksmith, was a big, burly man with a massive head, rugged, large features and a shaggy white mustache. He was the greatest corporation lawyer in the English-speaking world. He was asked by Presidents Garfield and Cleveland to sit upon the Supreme Court bench and by President McKinley to serve as the U.S. Attorney General. For seventeen years, he appeared in every great case tried before the Supreme Court and over $400,000,000 was invested in corporate interests on his recommendations. It was said that J. P. Morgan took no important step without consulting him and that lawyers and financiers considered his opinion tantamount to a legal decision. With the largest and most varied practice in the history of the bar, his clients ranged from simple petitioners to the kings of that expanding, trust-dominated era—Frick, Rockefeller, Hill,

Widener, Havemeyer, Morgan. But, as the *New York Times* remarked after his death, "He had the freshness of the amateur," and he pursued intensive practice of the law "not for fame or money, but for the fascination of the game."

It was also the "fascination of the game" that propelled him more and more deeply into the art world and made him a unique and original collector. By the time he died, in 1917, his fantastically overcrowded house on South Broad Street contained over 1,200 objects (now in the Philadelphia Museum of Art), which give a fairly comprehensive view of Western painting. More significantly, they include the finest collection in America of Flemish primitives of the fifteenth and sixteenth centuries, remarkable early Spanish and French paintings and single unrivaled masterpieces of Italian Renaissance and Dutch seventeenth-century art.

At the same time that Johnson was collecting—from about 1880 to 1917—his own clients were stepping all over each other in the expensive scramble for princely immortality. Morgan had set the pace, and, especially in the years after his death, the multimillionaire tycoons were spending their seemingly boundless fortunes in a possessive identification with such of the Olympian great as Rembrandt, Raphael and Titian.

John G. Johnson cast a sardonic eye at this costly chase and set out, in his own way, to beat them at their own game. He would build a collection by depending on acumen rather than money and by seeking pictures rather than Names.

While his tycoon clients were buying three-star items offered by the caterers of immortality, he was acquiring less fashionable merchandise. While they paid obsequious homage to Duveen, Knoedler, Kleinberger, et al., he was hobnobbing with scholars. Intrigued by every aspect of art and the art world, he studied books on painting. He examined sales catalogues as assiduously as he sought out the minutiae of the law. He traced back the histories of paintings and the logic of their attributions with the same diligence that he had applied as a youth to the search of long chains of titles to real estate. Fascinated by the maneuvers of the art world, he learned to evaluate the advice he was given, to see through the schemes of the dealers, to appraise the petulant bickerings of the experts, and in the final analysis, to depend on his own judgment of the intrinsic quality of the work itself.

There was no hint of sour grapes in his decision to play the art-collecting game this way. Even if he had had the wealth to support a journey down the fashionable million-dollar path, he would —out of temperament—have scorned it. He was too much an individualist ever to follow any herd. No matter what the situation, he liked to make his own rules.

Out of deference to his rather social and well-born wife, he would spend part of each summer in her paternal home at Newport. But he paid little attention to Newport conventions. When he felt like it, he would travel by trolley car with his bathing suit rolled up under his trousers. His practice of the law was unorthodox, and in this era of Choate's flowery rhetoric at the bar, his presentations were direct and forthright. He accepted or declined clients with rare independence. While others sought the limelight, he avoided interviews and publicity. At the height of his career, his entire biography in *Who's Who* read, "Johnson, John G., corporate lawyer," and there were those who doubted that he himself had divulged even this illuminating personal information.

In the matter of fees, too, he set his own apparently erratic standards, much to the confusion and annoyance of the rest of the profession. Often he would charge merely ten dollars, which was half the minimum fee for a junior counsel, yet for his defense of the Northern Securities and Standard Oil companies he charged the largest legal fees then known. After trying a case for J. P. Morgan, he refused a check for over $50,000, explaining that he had spent only fifteen minutes on the case and that his services were therefore worth only $5,000. He asked Henry O. Havemeyer for a painting instead of a fee for his defense of the sugar trust—and was profoundly displeased when the Sugar King insisted on giving him $100,000 instead.

But nowhere was Johnson's independent individuality better revealed than in his art collecting. For him, it was intriguing sport. By pitting insight and intellect against mammon and fashion, he was able to surround himself with works of art he very personally enjoyed and to fulfill his aim of making a survey of Western painting.

John Graver Johnson was born on April 4, 1841. He grew up in a plain house, with a brawny, blacksmithing father—from whom he inherited his big, robust frame—and a mother who eked out the family income with a little millinery business—from whom he may well have absorbed a liking for color and form. Elizabeth Graver Johnson had high intellectual hopes for this eldest of three sons. He apparently shared them: he did very well in the public schools of Philadelphia; he trained his memory—later renowned at the bar—by learning Shakespeare and Plato by heart; and as he trudged long miles to school, or delivered his mother's pretty millinery to remote, fashionable addresses, he concentrated on his studies, foreshadowing his capacity in later life to work at law and art almost without respite.

By the age of sixteen he had decided to become a lawyer. He went to work as a "scrivener" in a well-known Philadelphia law office. The painstaking job in those pre-typewriter days of copying out hundreds of legal papers in a round, legible script must have irked him, for as soon as he progressed to more responsible legal tasks, his handwriting degenerated into a scrawl as spectacular as a physician's in its indecipherability. Six years later, in 1863, he was admitted to the bar. His career was interrupted briefly by military service in the Union Army. By 1875 he was chief counsel of the leading trust company in Philadelphia. He was well on his successful way.

Law brought him his bride. Ida Powel Morrell, a widow with

three small children, consulted him in 1875 about salvaging whatever was possible from her late husband's badly depleted estate.
After a four-year courtship, Johnson, at the age of thirty-four, married the handsome, round-eyed lady who was his exact contemporary.

It was an amiably affectionate marriage, which lasted until her
death in 1908. Johnson's affection extended warmly to his three
stepchildren, and Mrs. Johnson's affection was apparently great
enough to keep her from feeling rancor at the fact that her husband considered the social life she enjoyed a waste of time, dodged
her dinner parties by using a back door and, in fact, hardly altered
the work-oriented routine of his bachelor days. Off to the office
at eight in the morning, he would return around six, carrying in a
green bag the books, briefs and correspondence with which, after
a family dinner, he would closet himself in the library until two or
three in the morning.

The acquisition of a family, however, necessitated the acquisition of a house; a house demands furnishings; and in Philadelphia,
where a certain cultural tone had long since been set, furnishings
implied art.

The City of Brotherly Love, with such prominent citizens as
Benjamin Franklin, had been the nucleus of American culture in
colonial times. The strange intertwining of art and science, so
characteristic of the end of the eighteenth century, flourished
there in the versatile and enthusiastic activities of Charles Will-
son Peale and his numerous family. In 1784, having procured a
few mammoth bones, Peale founded America's first museum
of natural history. In 1795 he established its first art school (where
a cast of the Venus de' Medici was "kept shut up in a case and
only shown to persons who particularly wished to see it"), and
that same year he instituted America's first annual art exhibitions.

Boston and Philadelphia were the two cultural oases in mid-
nineteenth century America. Culture in Philadelphia was on a less
esoteric plane than in New England. Bostonians were inclined

even then to take pride in dowdy dress and drab surroundings as hallmarks of good breeding and devotion to the mind and spirit. Philadelphians then, as now, cloaked cultural virtue in rather finer feathers. Handsome clothes, superb cooking and agreeable living were signs of the cultivated man. In the sixties and seventies, as opposed to Boston, Philadelphia was more involved with contemporary civic pride, less busy hankering after dreams of Renaissance beauty. Abstract intellectuality was no enemy to gentility and the amenities. Even the august members of the American Philosophical Society enjoyed a gourmet's table.

When the Philadelphian William P. Willstach made so substantial a fortune from selling saddlery hardware that in 1858, at the age of forty-eight, he found himself in a position to retire, it seemed completely natural to spend the rest of his life collecting fashionable contemporary art to go into his fashionable contemporary house. If art in the home carried intimations of the cultural elevation of the owner, with equal logic art in the city would make Philadelphia "the Athens of America." This was the stated goal of the gentlemen who, in 1871, organized the Fairmount Park Art Association, the first group in America dedicated to adorning public parks and places with statuary. Their up-to-date taste led them to a Dying Lioness, Hudson Bay Wolves and a slightly constipated-looking marble figure called "Il Penseroso." Five years later, when the Centennial Exposition of 1876 was held in Philadelphia, no doubt was left about that city's respect for art: 75,000 square feet of wall space were plastered with paintings, and sculpture jammed more than 20,000 square feet of floor.

By 1881, Johnson, like any other affluent Philadelphian, was paying $450 for a rocky coastal scene by a popular Russian landscapist, and by the late eighties he had become a substantial client of fashionable dealers in Philadelphia, New York, London, Paris and Berlin. His acquisitions represented a conscientious contemporary cross-section, all the way from such traditional items as a discreetly gauze-covered nymph to such advanced ones as paintings by Degas and Pissarro and Manet's spirited painting of the "Alabama and Kersearge." He bought the latter in 1888, almost ten years before even the intrepid Havemeyers bought *their* version of this Civil War engagement, which so engaged Manet. It cost him $1,500. Rosa Bonheur's yellow-spotted hound, which he bought the same year, cost exactly $13,800 more!

By the time a man has acquired 275 items, however, he can hardly be said to be buying just to decorate his house. Johnson found himself in that position in 1892, when he was fifty years old. He had become a collector. He proved it by having a catalogue of his holdings privately printed that year. It was, fortunately, a modest affair—really only a descriptive inventory—for it was barely off the press before he began selling and trading a good many of the objects listed therein. At his death, only 190 of them remained.

When Johnson was just going along buying contemporary art, he had no need of any special strategy. He was doing it so well, in fact, that in 1895 he was appointed to the Fairmount Park Art Association and put in special charge of the Willstach Collection, for Mrs. Willstach had recently died and left their 150 fashionable paintings and $2,000,000 to the city of Philadelphia. He bought for it as he bought for himself. He had one great advantage over other collectors in the contemporary field. He had strong opinions. The collector who has opinions is, ipso facto, one up on those who have only dealers' opinions.

Once, when a group of financiers consulted Johnson about the possibility of their joining in a merger, he cabled them, "Merger possible, jail certain." He was equally blunt and assured in a series of articles called "A Sightseer in Berlin and Holland Among Pictures," which he wrote in 1892 for the *Philadelphia Press* (they were later reprinted in book form). His peppery comments run like this: Of an exhibition of international art in Berlin, "There was nothing by Meyer von Bremer, whose chromos have robbed Americans of hundreds of thousands of dollars. It is possible that he is now dead in the flesh, as he has ever been in the spirit" . . . "Millais exhibited a young girl with chalky face and red cheeks, which is probably the delight of some English owner, who paid a heavy price for what it absolutely without value." Of a whole list of artists' work in the Fodor Museum, founded by a rich Dutch merchant, he says, "Silence is charity." Of a Jules Breton in another Dutch millionaire's collection, he remarks that Breton "treated the Breton peasant as Landseer treated the dog."

But soon the game of buying contemporary art lost its fascination. He was ready to try his hand at the trickier game of buying old masters within his comparatively limited means. He approached this adventure with the same love of strategy that he brought to the law.

He had seen a good many of his contemporaries being duped. He was particularly sympathetic about a Middle Western lumber king. That well-meaning gentleman finally bought a genuine Rembrandt, but, guilt by association being already an accepted phenomenon in America, he could get no one to believe in it since he already owned ten flagrantly spurious Rembrandts. Early in his own collecting career, Johnson had been pushed too far by a rascally pair of dealers who unloaded copies and fakes under illustrious names.

Thereafter, when pictures were offered to him which had Great Names attached, he viewed them with immediate suspicion. His biographer, Barnie F. Winkelman, tells how he once punctured the composure of a self-confident witness with the grim salutation: "Now, Major, let me sharpen my teeth on you." Any painting with a Great Name was immediately subjected to the same relentless cross-examination that he used in the courtroom.

In 1903, a dealer, disposing of a dubious collection of a mysterious marquess on the Riviera, offered him a "Leda and the Swan." The dealer insisted it was by Leonardo da Vinci and was a bargain at 100,000 lire. Johnson began examining the evidence, found several other versions of the painting, and wrote an opinion as exact as a legal brief concluding that the painting was *not* by Leonardo. He also searched back through the records of Leonardo's prices and concluded that if the painting were by Leonardo, the 100,000 lire price was ridiculously low, and if it were not by Leonardo, immorally high. "If I purchased the picture, I would have to rest on its artistic merits," he explained. On that basis, he finally bought it and—anonymous artistic merits being less costly than Leonardo's name—got it for a fraction of the asking price.

Like many other similar decisions to buy on the basis of "artistic merit," this one turned out to have been wise. The "Leda" was later shunted back and forth like an unwanted poor relation by Berenson, who was cataloguing Johnson's Italian pictures, and by the art historian Wilhelm Valentiner, who was cataloguing his northern ones. Berenson insisted the painting was not Italian; Valentiner maintained that "the landscape was Flemish, but the execution was not." After several months of this mutual refusal, Berenson was reminded of "Dante's phrase about those people whom heaven would not have nor hell either." Only in 1912, when Valentiner finally catalogued it as a Flemish copy of a Leonardo, was the "Leda" out of purgatory.

The obvious way to avoid being duped on Names, as Johnson pointed out in his little volume of 1892, was to seek, not Names, but works of art. Accustomed to sizing up the credibility of witnesses and the expertness of experts, Johnson sought out the scholars and experts in the art world who could best assist him in his game of finding works of art. A whole galaxy of these men— Berenson, Herbert Horne, Roger Fry, Valentiner, Langton Douglas—flocked to help him, and he was a great comfort to them. He was after the "off-beat" pictures, the problem pictures, the pictures that intrigued their scholarly minds, the unchristened pictures that held their eyes, the pictures too Unimportant for the Important collectors.

Douglas would tell him of "an amusing picture." Berenson

could suggest a painting which was frankly only a "School of Titian," but he would take it because it was "too good a wine to need a label." Fry, usually more flowery than the others, could write of two panels representing touchingly repentent ladies, Mary Magdalene and Maria Egyptica, by the Flemish fifteenth-century Quentin Maasys: "They are so much your special kind of picture that I can't grudge them to you, though I wish our museum [the Metropolitan] were enlightened enough to want them. They have that peculiar imaginative intensity and intimacy which I find to be the real note of your collection." A trustee of the Metropolitan from 1907 on, Johnson often picked up what the museum trustees discarded as too trivial or "too small."

The scholars could speak to him with a candor that would have lost them their other clients. Langton Douglas could recommend a painting which was "A bit of a wreck, but wonderful, impressive." Berenson suggested a portrait of Lorenzo Lorezano by Botticelli and explained that it had been slightly restored, adding that if it had not been, "it would be bought by one of our Squillionaires." It is one of the masterpieces of his collection. Herbert Horne could say of some Italian panels, "Though they are but 'Trifles,' as you would say, yet they are characteristic of their painter."

They kept their eyes peeled for his kind of picture. They watched forthcoming auctions, recommended buys and estimated fair prices. Johnson was famous in court for sizing up the character of testimony. In one case, where a mass of correspondence had been produced, he realized immediately that there was a gap in the sequence. He prodded the witness again and again until finally the existence of the intervening letter, which contained the material essential to his case, was admitted. In the same way, he could appraise the experts' advice. When he was in doubt, he diligently consulted the priced sales catalogues and art books in his brimming library.

The ploy of indifference to Names saved him heartache when

a painting was robbed of its name. When he was told a picture he liked was *not* by Canaletto, he replied, "Whoever may be the painter, the painting, itself, is one which gives me real pleasure. Be it by Canaletto or a minor Marieschi or old Scott, it will stay with me." He could sit it out patiently while the experts wrangled. Horne and Fry, who had obtained four charming little Florentine predella panels for him, insisted they were by Sandro Botticelli. Berenson claimed them for the close follower of Botticelli whom he had invented and called "Amico di Sandro." When Berenson finally took them away from the friend and credited them to the master, Johnson simply wrote, "I am so awfully glad about the Botticellis. They are so lovely I wanted them to be adjudged as the legitimate offspring."

He could be equally sanguine when the experts raised attributions above his own estimates. When the Swedish authority Oswald Siren declared a handsome early Italian panel of two saints was by the rare and renowned early Florentine, Masolino, Johnson was afraid Siren was "getting a little reckless in his attributions." How ironic Johnson would find the fact that, ever since the National Gallery in London acquired the companion panel in 1950, contemporary scholars have been having an irritable fight, not about whether the paintings are by someone *less* than Masolino, but about whether they are not perhaps by his even greater Florentine successor, Masaccio.

Another Johnson ploy was to disregard a painting's history. "Pedigrees are either manufactured, or if genuine, usually begin a century too late," he remarked in the book of 1892. As dealers like Duveen knew very well, his contemporaries took a different view of the matter. To the industrial princes, there was a certain undeniable reassurance in feeling that you were good enough for a painting that had been good enough for Louis XIV. By 1916 Johnson observed that "a provenance in this country is quite as desirable a subject for exhibition as is the thing it covers." Frequently, because he was willing to forgo such pedigrees, he picked up fine pictures at low prices.

Johnson's most brilliant strategy was his move into the lesser-known, unfashionable markets. Like Napoleon in his early Italian campaign, who, faced with pitting his small army against large forces, won the battle because he studied the terrain and could move with lightning speed, so Johnson surveyed the field of old masters and then moved in ahead of the powerful opposition. As with Flemish primitives.

He bought his first Flemish masterpiece in 1894. It was the tiny "St. Francis Receiving the Stigmata" by the great, rare master Jan van Eyck. He bought it from Lord Heytesbury, whose ancestor, Sir William à Court, had been British Ambassador to Portugal from 1824 to 1828 and had bought the little painting, then called a Dürer, for $40. This gem, the first Van Eyck to reach America, is unrivaled in quality, even by the few later, more expensive arrivals.

By 1902, when a large exhibition of Flemish primitives in Bruges stimulated other collectors to forage in this field, Johnson already had a good head start. He was soon progressing into early French paintings (in 1910 he wrote that if he kept on he would end in the almshouse) and into early Spanish ones. The vogue for these primitives was slower in capturing American than European taste. Even P. A. B. Widener, who trusted Johnson's advice, was not entirely enamored.

Widener and Johnson were good friends. They played poker together and they served together on the Fairmount Park Art Association, where they joined forces in a movement to build a great permanent museum in the park to replace the inadequate Centennial remnant, Memorial Hall. (The agitation, incidentally, continued with endless discussions and shilly-shallying for over thirty years, until, eleven years after Johnson's death in 1917, the present building of the Philadelphia Museum of Art was finally opened to the public.) Widener's eyes were on the expensive Lowland painters, but on his trips to Europe with Johnson he occasionally ventured into another arena. When they were in Paris together one summer, they saw at Kleinberger's two monumental panels by the Flemish fifteenth-century master, Rogier van der Weyden. Kleinberger would sell these altar wings only as a pair. Johnson, already devoted to Flemish primitives, persuaded Widener to buy one and he bought the other. They tossed a coin. Johnson got the panel of the "Virgin and St. John" and Widener, "The Crucifixion." A few months after the masterpieces reached Philadelphia, Widener called upon Johnson. "If you want the other panel, you can have it for what I paid for it," he said. "I can't find a place to hang it where it looks well."

It was not, indeed, until 1912, when Johnson already had a fine holding of "primitives," that American collectors began really to be competitors in this field. That year, the prices for such pictures rose appreciably in the Dolfuss sale. "The 'Wise Men' are turning to the Primitives as a safety valve for their art investments," Johnson wrote to Berenson.

When he wrote in 1892 that by "exercising care, taste and experience, sufficient that is delightful and not too high-priced can be obtained," Johnson had been understating the case. It turned out that his clever strategy brought him even more than was "sufficient."

His already avid collecting accelerated after his wife's death in 1908, and the next year he was puzzling about where to put things. "In the past I have found walls very elastic," he wrote. "I only hope they will stretch a little more." They did not. Two years later he was complaining, "Everything is crammed, even the sides and foots of the beds." A month later, "I now have thirty-five paintings for which I have absolutely no place and even the 'Standing Room' has disappeared." Even when he persuaded himself to part with a large number of things a year later, "the floor is still pretty badly littered up."

But he could not resist any "great temptation. My virtue is Spartan," he said, "only when it is a little one." There were few little ones. "I swear off weekly and seem to swear on semi-weekly," he wrote a friend.

He was determined at one point to swear off Madonnas. In 1910 he wrote Berenson, "I fear that if I have any more Madonnas, I will lay myself open to an accusation of piety which would grant an action for obtaining credit under false pretenses." But he bought some more. "They ought to be interspersed with a few Sabines," he remarked ruefully as he acquired yet an additional two. His colorful and well-known profanity was finally let loose on the subject: "D—— Madonna with Child, whether the Child be within or without." But still he bought more.

By 1915, with pictures littering the floor, covering walls and corridors down through the servants' quarters, hanging not only on chairs and beds, but also inside closet doors, he was literally in danger of being inundated by his pictures. He was seventy-four at the time, defending the Standard Oil Company and meeting the complicated commitments of a crowded legal calendar. Forced to take the time to remove himself from the impending avalanche of art, he found an expedient solution. He simply bought the house next door, built a provisional bridge across, and moved the vast accumulation. The situation was but slightly ameliorated. The still-crowded arrangement hardly constituted a display. It was, as his friend the art critic Frank Jewett Mather remarked, "a convenient form of storage."

This sort of Collyer brothers clutter—in a residence which was virtually a firetrap—not only astonished the students and connoisseurs who came to visit him on Sundays, but was incomprehensible to his clients, the collectors who were out-Morganing Morgan in the splendor of their surroundings. Frick was building his palace on Fifth Avenue; Widener had an impressively large gallery; the banker George Blumenthal and his discerning wife Florence were creating what Johnson called "a unique and very attractive museum home."

Johnson did buy some "English furniture and velvet covers and the like" for his new house. But as Mather observed, he had no sense of the ensemble. He was the sort of man who concentrated thoroughly on one thing at a time, whether the two dozen oysters that he ate regularly at his club for lunch or the single picture at which he chose to look.

Where Morgan had a zest for shopping, Johnson reveled in the ceremony of unpacking. The paintings usually arrived from Europe in batches. Returning late from the office, he would sit down heavily and order his watchman Mulligan to bring up a single one. With the concentrated attention of a burlesque fan at a strip tease, he would watch the painting being disclosed. "He enjoyed it as an apéritif," Berenson recalls, "before sitting down to a heavy, succulent meal of terrapin or canvasback duck."

Johnson was as susceptible to the intimations of immortality as the next man. He always intended to leave his survey of Western painting to the public. By 1909, he decided that it would be wise to justify and explain his unorthodox game to the future. He arranged to have the collection catalogued. He had neither the money nor the inclination for the super-de-luxe variety (remarking wryly that Widener's catalogue needed an athlete to handle it without fatigue), but he wanted a scholarly job. He appraised himself candidly. "Buying on my own sadly uninformed and misinformed knowledge," he wrote in 1909, "I have put my foot in it at times, but I might have fared far worse in the hands of those besides whom base jackals are Innocents—the Dealers in art. Some most lucky purchases at very low prices of works now almost priceless go far to make the final result good. I have been badly used at the hands of a rascal . . . Despite of him, the percentage of fakes is light. In many cases where I took chances, either I could not have gotten advice in time, or advice would have been impossible." The catalogue was necessary. "To have the public hereafter looking at 'geese' designated as 'swans' would turn a gift into a farce," he explained.

Berenson and Valentiner, assisted by other authorities, undertook the formidable task of designating which paintings were geese and which were swans, to say nothing of those which were anonymous webfoots. "You will include or exclude pictures, or attribute them as you deem proper," he told them again and again. It is an activity in which an able curator and subsequent generations of scholars, with a normal amount of disagreement among themselves and with the catalogue (which appeared in 1913 and 1914), have been engaged ever since.

Perfecting his own ploys, Johnson watched the plays of his fashion-following contemporaries. Irony is a quality rarely associated with art collectors. An occasional one will view his activity somewhat sardonically, like Albert Lasker, advertising man and late-comer collector of Matisse, Van Gogh & Co., who remarked that he knew he would have to pay the highest prices to get masterpieces but he did not know he would have to pay even higher prices for the privilege of paying the highest prices. But most art collectors pursue their passion with the deadly seriousness of young lovers.

John G. Johnson, gentle cynic, was a rare exception. He might take himself with some seriousness, but in his illegible scrawl he made regular ironical reports to his friends abroad on the saga of American collectors and collecting in his time.

For a while, the competitive scramble for Dutch seventeenth-century paintings riveted his attention. They were indisputably à la mode. All the collectors—including Johnson himself—had some, and they all proudly lent to the Metropolitan Museum's exhibition in honor of the Hudson-Fulton celebration in 1909. That celebration, honoring the Dutch navigator and the American inventor of the steamboat, was a gala occasion. There was a nine-day regatta; the fleets of the world were anchored in the Hudson River; a reconstituted *Half Moon* cruised up to Albany; and Wright and Curtis, signaling the arrival of the new era of the airplane, flew across the river. The art exhibition held its own among these rival attractions. Containing, with the overoptimistic attributions of the day, thirty-seven paintings by Rembrandt, twenty-one by Hals, twelve by Jacob Ruisdael and six by Vermeer, it was called "a substitute for a trip to Europe" and was valued, not unreasonably, at $10,000,000.

Johnson had long before been amused by the wholesale production of Dutch portraits. After seeing a museum-full of them, he wrote in 1892: "The vanity which enriches the photographers today, if not born in Holland, certainly attained to its full stature in that country in the seventeenth century . . . If, in that country, portraits were not painted cheaply, sitters must have preferred bankruptcy to oblivion." At the time of the Hudson-Fulton celebration, he had been observing the growing vogue in America for Rembrandt portraits. The merchant Benjamin Altman was the special target for his barbs. Altman was a bachelor, a recluse and a rather frugal man, who, as Behrman quotes Duveen as saying, "traveled like a Cook's tourist." The one thing Altman was not frugal about was art, and the one kind of society in which he happily mingled was that of Rembrandt's men and women.

"The 'Wise Men' of America *know,* especially since Mr. Joseph Duveen has confirmed the fact, that Rembrandt is a great artist and they are insatiable in gluttony of his portraits," Johnson reported in the fall of 1909. "Mr. Altman feels, very properly, that he cannot get too much of a good thing. He now has eight. 'Make it a dozen.'" Two months later, Altman was apparently trying to do so. He bought three more Rembrandt portraits for $750,000. "The only consolation he shall find will be in the adage that too much riches is the root of evil," Johnson opined. A few months later Altman bought his twelfth Rembrandt portrait. "How pleased the poor old man would be if he could come back to earth and see how he is adored . . . by the wealthy trader," wrote Johnson.

By 1911, it is Johnson's friend, P. A. B. Widener, who is "cornering the market" in Rembrandt. He is not only after two Rembrandt portraits, but he has also acquired "The Mill." Johnson found it "a noble work, but the price [$500,000] is something *awful*." The trustees of London's National Gallery agreed with him on both counts. They held a consternation meeting over the disappearance of this picture from the collection of the Marquess of Landsdowne to America.

The "awful prices" had a morbid fascination for Johnson. Like a spectator who, horrified, yet remains frozen at the scene of a bloody accident, he was drawn irresistibly to Altman's transactions. Painting by painting, he records the merchant's outlay of $250,000 and more, noting that by 1912, "If the price is sufficiently high, he will probably buy."

It is said that the only thing about which two people can reach total agreement is the amount of money a third should give to charity. There is one other subject of absolute concord: that the amount a third has paid for a painting is too high. Yet Johnson, watching the art market with the absorption and canny knowledge of a tout studying the racing form, had a right to be aghast.

The "awful prices" were making general news even in 1910, when the paintings amassed by Charles T. Yerkes, Jr., were put up at auction. Yerkes, like Elkins and Widener, had made a fortune in street railways. He spent most of it indulging in a chain of love affairs and living in grand style in an Italianate palace in New York. Here he rested his corpulent body in an $80,000 bed that once belonged to the King of Belgium, trod on splendid Oriental rugs, and was surrounded by hundreds of paintings. These voguish art holdings included a few masterpieces, many such overattributed items as his copy of Mrs. Gardner's "Chigi Madonna" and some downright fakes. The sale was a sensation. *Art News* magazine reported that its total "overtopped" all save one of the famous "art sales of history in Europe and America."

John G. Johnson gave Berenson a detailed account: "The Yerkes sale has placed America in the very front rank of art-understanding countries, so far at least as an understanding of art does not extend beyond the ability to pay extraordinary prices. Wonderful discrimination was shown in the purchasing, but not as against fraudulent imitations. No invidious distinctions were drawn in this respect . . .

"A genuine Hobbema went at a reasonable price, and a lot of fake ones followed at figures not very much less . . . a Hals, attributed to Frans, but a work which, owing to the infirmities of his father, his son Herman had obligingly painted for him, went for $33,000 . . . A female lover of the Highest Art succeeded in obtaining a Raphael for $4,000. The only wonder is, as she has plenty of money, she was not obliged to pay $50,000 for it. Prejudiced, as you are, against some of the examples of the High Art which reach this country, I think you would have been compelled to admit it was worth $25 or $50.

"The newspapers, by way of making the people happy who bought some of these very 'important' works, have been giving, since the sale, the prices they realized at the last preceding sale. We can always trust our American Press to do the 'right thing.' Possibly, the 'right time' would have been before, not after, the sale." (Johnson himself bought a painting by Quentin Maasys, appraised at $2,500, for $550.)

He first fixed on Frick at the Yerkes sale, when the coke and steel king paid the top price of the sale—for a robust, fifty-six-year-old lady by Frans Hals—"$137,000 plus ten percent commission to the dealer [Knoedler] who obligingly bought it at auction." Soon Johnson was keeping a tally of Frick's purchases and his taste. In 1911 he remarked that Frick was buying "more Gainsboroughs and Romneys. One of each should suffice, but 'full-lengths' is the slogan."

Frick was worth attention. The dealers who had trembled

early in 1913 when Morgan lay dying had brightened considerably after his death when they realized that, especially in the painting field, his successors and former rivals were trying to outdo him. But they suffered another shock later that year when Benjamin Altman died. Two years later, P. A. B. Widener went. However, that gentleman left not only the largest estate in the history of Philadelphia, but also a son who had inherited his father's taste for expensive masterpieces and an even more discerning and less Duveen-oriented eye.

The dealers could solace themselves with such avid amassers as Frick and Joseph Widener. Johnson noted the shifting positions of these two as the greatest spenders as if he were recording a horse race. Frick was ahead, according to Johnson's book, when in 1915 he paid $1,250,000 for Morgan's Fragonard Room, which had cost Morgan $310,000. But by 1916 Widener was catching up. In addition to paying $500,000 for two of Morgan's great tapestries and over $1,000,000 for second choice of the Morgan porcelains, he had bought two of Morgan's best Renaissance busts, had purchased a collection of prints for $250,000 and was, Johnson thought, "spending his annual income of $1,500,000 in advance on works of art." But then Frick plunged ahead again. He paid Duveen $1,250,000 for the *third* choice of the porcelains and became "the angel of the dealers." Johnson dined at his house, "there being no one present who was not a multi-plutocrat but myself," and was staggered at Frick's frank recital of the prices he had been paying. In March, 1917—a month before his own death —Johnson computed that Frick's "expenditures for each year, for several years, must have been between $2,000,000 and $4,000,000."

Johnson was fascinated and amused, but never disapproving of this expensive activity. Quite the contrary. In 1913, Joseph Duveen found himself stuck with a very great and very costly painting, Raphael's "Small Cowper Madonna." Altman had agreed orally to buy it for $750,000, but by the time the Raphael arrived, Altman was inconveniently dead. His executors felt less than rapturous about the lovely Madonna, even when Duveen reduced the price by $100,000. Joseph Duveen dispatched his genial Uncle Henry posthaste to Philadelphia with the expensive item. Johnson's dislike for art dealers included Duveen, but he strongly urged Widener to buy the Raphael. For $565,000, Widener did. "While I think no museum should spend so much as $565,000," Johnson wrote when the deal was completed, "I feel that Mr. Widener and the seventy-five millionaires ought to do so."

Nor, though Johnson scoffed at Altman's wholesale adoration of Rembrandt portraits, though he put three exclamation points after the prices Widener paid for his greatest Vermeer and his rare masterpiece by Castagno and regularly called the prices Frick paid for his treasures "awful," did he underestimate the splendor of their collections.

They were pursuing what he called High Art. They sought Great Names and paid Great Prices, but undeniably they acquired Great Pictures. The Altman Collection (now in the Metropolitan Museum), the Widener Collection (whose numerous masterpieces of sculpture and painting include the two greatest single pictures in our National Gallery, Rembrandt's "Mill" and Bellini's "Feast of the Gods"), and the Frick Collection with its superb pictures are among the most glorious private collections in the world. Each contains extraordinary numbers of unrivaled and eternal masterpieces by acknowledged great masters.

Johnson died before Andrew Mellon, another Squillionaire who was seeking only the greatest of the Great Pictures, joined the ranks. Mellon's dislike of publicity was so emphatic as to make the reticent Johnson seem an exhibitionist by comparison. Mellon was already worth over $500,000,000 and was director or officer of boards of 160 corporations when, in 1921, his name was suggested to President Harding as Secretary of the Treasury. "I never heard of him," the President replied. Harding's ignorance was shared by the public. But by the time Mellon died in 1937 at the age of eighty-four, having served from 1921 to 1932, he was known as "the greatest Secretary of the Treasury since Alexander Hamilton." He was also rather well known as the man who made the biggest gift to our government that any individual had ever made to any government anywhere.

Mellon was a small-boned, frail man with delicate, tapering hands which usually held a custom-made cigarette-size cigar. He had the alert look of a well-bred terrier, with his sharply defined features set off by well-brushed shiny white hair and mustache and shaggy white eyebrows. Since the late seventies, when both were in their twenties, he and his fellow Pittsburgher, Henry Clay Frick, had been friends, and often partners in financial ventures. They made their first trip to Europe together in 1879, pausing in New York, where Frick looked enviously at the new Vanderbilt mansion. He also calculated that the Commodore must be spending $300,000 a year on its upkeep. On the trip abroad, Frick interested Mellon in art and the young banker returned from Europe with his first picture, a nondescript canvas whose price of $1,000 shocked his Pittsburgh family.

Son of an austere Scots banker, Andrew Mellon maintained a rigid sense of propriety which regulated both his choice and his arrangement of art. According to his friend David Finley, he disliked gaudy colors and was "careful not to hang religious pictures in a room where his friends might be smoking or drinking." The pictures with which he surrounded himself—until the late twenties, when he was fired with a higher purpose than personal enjoyment—were mostly English portraits and Dutch landscapes and, naturally, since the subject was a professional ancestor, a portrait of Alexander Hamilton by John Trumbull.

By 1929, Mellon had determined that America should have a great national gallery of art in Washington, even if he had to build it himself. He began quietly acquiring the kind of work which would set a proper standard of quality. Knoedler's, which was willingly helping him, knew of his scheme, of course, and soon Duveen and the other dealers got wind of it and generously began

helping him, too. In his childhood, Mellon had been given stringent lessons in thrift. They had apparently been well learned: he
managed to reduce the national debt from $24,000,000,000 to $16,-
000,000,000. Thinking in terms of figures with nine zeros during
his office hours, he could hardly have thought it extravagant in
his off hours to be buying many delectable items like Rembrandt's
"Self Portrait," Titian's lady in a green dress, Holbein's endearing
portrait of Edward VI as a little boy—although he paid for each
what Johnson would have called the "awful price" of about half
a million dollars.

In 1930 and 1931, through Knoedler's, he helped the Russians
out of a tight financial spot by buying $6,500,000 worth of master-
pieces from the Hermitage, the museum that had been founded
by the Czars. This was the quietest of all operations, since it
might have seemed somewhat tactless to a disgruntled few that,
in the midst of a devastating depression at home, the Secretary of
the Treasury was spending such sums abroad. The fabulous
transaction included Raphael's "Alba" Madonna, for which he
paid $1,166,400 and which is eagerly inquired for by National
Gallery visitors today, somewhat irreverently, as "The Million
Dollar Madonna"; the same artist's jewel-like little "St. George"
for $745,000; a Botticelli "Adoration" for $838,350; and Jan van
Eyck's "Annunciation" for $503,010, a price that would have fas-
cinated Johnson, who knew Van Eyck when he belonged to lower
price brackets.

Bought through foundation funds and intended for the public,
the Hermitage pictures were secretly stored in a vault in the
Corcoran Gallery in Washington. Neither the public nor the government knew about them or about Mellon's plans until, from
1934 on and off to 1937, his income and his taxes were discussed
in hearings before the Board of Tax Appeals (the testimony filling
10,350 pages). Once the plans were disclosed—and, as S. N. Behrman entertainingly points out, Duveen enjoyed his part in their
disclosure—Mellon proceeded to act.

The architect of the 782-foot-long National Gallery, John Russell Pope, was, fortunately, not so finicky a perfectionist about this building as Charles McKim was about Morgan's Library. He was quite willing to use mortar with the marble. In spite of this, the building, which required eight hundred carloads of Tennessee marble of twenty-three shades ranging from deep rose at the bottom of the façade to pearly pink at the top, cost $15,000,000. Mellon added $5,000,000 for an endowment as well as his spectacular treasures, which were valued at $30,000,000. Congress accepted the incredible gift and approved the plans in 1937 a few months before both Andrew Mellon and his architect died—within a bare twenty-four hours of each other.

With a modesty which is forever remarkable but was in keeping with his shy and taciturn avoidance of the limelight, Mellon had stipulated that the building should not bear his name. Thus there was no name on the portal to steal the show from other donors and no impediment for those who, less disposed toward anonymity than he, wanted their own names immortalized in bronze at least upon the marble gallery walls. Moreover, since he had been dedicated to a small group of only the best pictures (only enough, one of Finley's friends remarked, "to decorate a good-sized duplex apartment"), and since the building was six blocks long, there were acres left to be filled by other donors. By the time the National Gallery opened in 1941, its collection had been expanded by the copious donations of five-and-dime-store magnate Samuel Kress. (The accidental flooding of the basement on opening night caused one wag to refer to the collections as "Watermellon and Waterkress"). Soon thereafter, the gallery was wonderfully enriched with Joseph Widener's great gift.

Had he witnessed Mellon's moves, John G. Johnson would have been both approving of the art and aghast at the prices, as he had been in the cases of Mellon's predecessors. They all belonged to a different league and a different income bracket. It is exactly when Johnson competed with them and went after Rembrandts and

Gainsboroughs and Vermeers and Raphaels—in which the game had to be played the other way—that he most often came a cropper. Playing his own game, with the best scholars and connoisseurs of the period acting as his lookouts and agents, and with his own scholarship far exceeding that of any other collector of his time, he built a quite different kind of collection. It needs no "poor cousin" apology: it is one of which he could well be most personally proud.

Johnson died on April 14, 1917. By his own direction, he was buried without ceremony in the family plot at Germantown. As he had enjoined, there was no monument, but simply "a plain low head and foot stone and coping, with nothing marked thereon except the date of my birth—4 April 1841—that of my death and my name."

His art—with his house at 510 South Broad Street, which would be a museum to contain it—was bequeathed to the city of Philadelphia with the provision that the pictures should remain there "unless some extraordinary situation shall arise making it extremely injudicious." In that case, they were to be kept together at some central site or at an accessible spot in Fairmount Park. Not surprisingly, his executors found it "extremely injudicious" to keep the art in a house which was a firetrap, was hardly practicable as a public gallery and was in a neighborhood where such mundane necessities as parking places were nonexistent. The mansion remained closed and boarded until 1923, when, with no other solution immediately in sight, it was opened to the public. In 1933, the paintings were removed to the Philadelphia Museum of Art—long ago a dream of Johnson's—which had finally been built.

The best 575 of the paintings now hang handsomely in its galleries, arranged chronologically and geographically, with the others in convenient study racks. A mecca for new generations of scholars, students and connoisseurs, the collection now also attracts a wide new public.

Having watched with fascination how the Squillionaires played the art game one way, and having chosen himself to play it another way, John G. Johnson would be amused at the final irony. Reviewing his collection in 1941, *Time* magazine figured out that his postcard-size Van Eyck painting, valued then at $500,000, was the most expensive painting per square inch in America.

Tea and Champagne

CHARLES LANG FREER

The name FREER is disembodied. It is incised in marble over the Neo-Renaissance portal of a national art gallery in Washington, D.C. It is a world-famous name, because it is attached to a collection of Oriental art that is among the greatest of the world and to a representation of James McNeill Whistler that is complete almost to the point of monopoly. But the fascinating gentleman to whom the name belonged insured himself only this monosyllabic, marbleized immortality and carefully concealed from the public the story of his amiable and exquisite life.

Charles Lang Freer dedicated himself to the cultivation of this exquisite, leisurely existence, and his lifetime—from 1856 to 1919 —spanned the twilight years of such a possibility. The clamorous era of the trusts and tycoons boomed around him. Although the thud of Theodore Roosevelt's big stick reverberated loudly, magnificence and opulence were conspicuously the order of the day.

But Charles Lang Freer, a fragile, small-framed man with astonishingly delicate hands and a gracious bearing, isolated himself in a silk cocoon against the showy, boisterous pageantry of his age. He created a private world of refinement and serenity and excellences. Slowly, conscientiously, rather preciously, he nurtured each aspect of his well-tempered existence, until ultimately the man, his surroundings, his associates and his way of life were blended into a single, unified expression of the quintessences and of the exquisite (and expensive) simplicity to which he was dedicated.

Fastidiousness was his persistent and inviolate characteristic. The Vandyke beard which he wore in early life was meticulously trimmed and the closely cropped, almost imperceptible mustache of later years was impeccably groomed. His pince-nez had the most delicate of rims. It pained him when a young niece was sloppy in appearance and penmanship, failing to comb her hair and close her "a's" and "o's." He could not suffer a chef who knew nothing of "pastry-work," and indeed, although over the years he raised their salaries from $60 to $100 a month, many of his chefs were returned to New York from his Middle Western home having survived but a single meal. His finicky scrutiny missed no detail, from the flat silver and the ivory dishes with gold edges on his table to the size of the monograms embroidered on his sheets and pillowcases by the nuns of a nearby convent. The color of the single rose in a vase by the bathtub of a lady house guest was as carefully considered as the frequent order for the best imported caviar from New York. Personal inconveniences irritated him. But although he was impatient with inefficient servants and irascible with stupid acquaintances, he framed his public complaints against such indignities as a washroom on a train being as "cold as a refrigerator car" with punctilious politeness. He was aghast at crude manners, disgusted by rowdiness and offended at anything but the most chivalrous conduct toward women.

When he turned to art, his taste and temperament naturally led him to art of the utmost reticence and refinement: the art of Whistler, the ancient pottery of the Near East and the early sculpture and painting of Japan and China. The cherished work of the trio of American painters—Tryon, Dewing and Thayer—which modern taste dismisses as a revelation of a Victorian squint in the collector's eye, represented for him the same consummate simplicity and refinement.

Especially after 1900, when he retired from business, he pursued perfectionism with single-minded devotion. He countenanced no inharmonious element that might mar the unity of his design. He excluded all trespassers from the cultivated coterie whom he received in his home. A few guests would be welcome at a time. They might be intelligent members of European royalty, or connoisseurs and scholars and amateurs of art from East and West, or a few of the little intimate international group of collectors dedicated to Oriental art. The female guests were usually beautiful as well as cultivated.

The visitors would sit with him on low window seats in a serene, skylit gallery. Nothing cluttered its space: its walls were bare. At a summons, his former coachman Stephen would bring out one or two objects—a Chinese painting and an ancient piece of pottery, a Japanese screen or a Whistler "Nocturne." The guests would give themselves to enjoyment of these for a leisurely stretch before Stephen was bid to replace them with one or two other objects. As the sun set and the light waned on a lovely kakemono, Stephen served the blend of tea the host had perfected—2/3 of the best Ceylon with 1/6 of the best Japanese and 1/6 orange pekoe. Sometimes there might be champagne or Château Yquem, imported monthly with explicit care to vineyard and vintage.

Since the host believed that neither Whistler's paintings nor Oriental art could be seen properly in artificial light, the gallery was not used after dinner. Conversation filled the evening hours; neither cards nor music were supported. Or, to a specially favored lady, Freer might read aloud from his first edition of *The Rubaiyat.*

There was one apparently incongruous thing in the exquisitely refined life of Charles Lang Freer. That was the means by which he made the fortune to sustain it. The fragile gentleman made his money in heavy industry, in the manufacture of railroad cars. But there was no real incongruity. Freer's relation to railroad-car building was a consistent one.

His background was French Huguenot: his first American ancestor in 1670 was one of the original patentees of New Paltz, New York. But the family into which he was born in 1856 in Kingston, New York, was, however proud, extremely poor.

He had to quit school at fourteen. He worked briefly in a cement factory and as clerk in a general store before he caught the attention of Frank J. Hecker, the superintendent of a local railroad. Thus began his association with railroading—but in a manner appropriate and congenial, for Hecker made him paymaster. Freer always liked figures. All his life he thought double-entry bookkeeping one of the most beautiful things in the world. When, at the age of twenty, he accompanied Hecker to Logansport, Indiana, it was to be treasurer of the Eel River Railroad. That sleepy little line, whose sixteen freight cars, six passenger cars and one reliable locomotive trundled daily through the cornfields over thirty miles of track, had little to do then with the rough-and-tumble, cutthroat expansion of railroading in America. In 1879, the Wabash bought the road.

Freer and Hecker then moved on to Detroit and shrewdly started the first railroad-car building shop in the Middle West. Hecker's was the railroading experience; Freer was the organizer and financier. He rarely ventured into the clanging factory, but sat in the office, figuring out such extremely profitable policies as that of employing Detroit's first influx of Polish immigrants at almost starvation wages.

Detroit, at the time, was the pleasantly somnolent city it was to remain until the advent of the gasoline age. In 1892, their business having profited handsomely, Freer and Hecker bought adjoining land on a broad avenue. Hecker, who later became a colonel in the Spanish-American War and clung to his title like a bulldog, inclined to conspicuous consumption: he impressed Detroit with its first turreted and balustraded French château. Freer, leaning characteristically to expensive simplicity, employed a talented Philadelphia architect, Wilson Eyre, to design an informal house for him.

Of shingles and dark, purplish-brown stone, quarried in his native Kingston, Freer's house recalled the shingled villas, with their steeply gabled roofs and round piazzas, which Stanford White, in his pre-Renaissance days, had been designing in the East. Its open-plan spaciousness and built-in seating, its cheerful, sunny exposures and intimate scale were minutely devised to provide the proper environment for Freer's gracious living.

With a perfectionism that rivaled Mrs. Gardner's, but a tact utterly alien to her, Freer fussed with his workmen about the niceties of finish. Courteously disregarding the contractor's disapproval, he instructed them in the way to rust iron with vinegar in order to get a solution which would stain the oak woodwork a warm, brown tone. He made a polite ado about the specially designed lighting fixtures and bothered endlessly over the studded hardware.

Even before he had commissioned the house he had begun to search for the accouterments of the cultivated life. On his frequent trips to New York, he had begun foraging in the properly refined field of etchings.

Many years later, when his well-trained eye was offended by

most of the motley lot he had chosen, the New York dealer from whom he bought them refused to take them back. But in the eighties that dealer was rather more pleasantly disposed toward his lucrative client. In 1887, he introduced him flatteringly as a man with "as good an eye for a print as anyone who comes here" to another customer called Howard Mansfield. A lawyer more interested in Whistler than Blackstone, Mansfield bore Freer off to his bachelor flat on West Thirty-sixth Street. Through the evening hours, he showed his collection of more than three hundred Whistler etchings. Freer was entranced by their subtlety and elegance. "My purchasing," Freer recalled, "began the day thereafter." Having begun, it never stopped. Freer ultimately had the largest holding of Whistler etchings and lithographs anywhere in the world.

Not all of Freer's New York evenings were quite so intellectual. He became a close friend of the pervasive architect Stanford White. The flamboyant redheaded playboy, on whom all eyes turned when he entered the opera, and the quiet, polished gentleman from Detroit would appear together at champagne parties. But they also went together to exhibitions of art. And White, with his intuitive flair for understanding people's tastes and inclinations, recommended to Freer the genteel American painters, Tryon, Dewing and Thayer.

Freer arrived at Dwight D. Tryon's well-groomed studio at an opportune moment. It was the late spring of 1889. The Potter Palmers, pausing briefly in New York on their way to Europe, had come in the day before and admired a painting of a tepee-like haystack misted with moonlight. They told the artist to hold it for a final decision on their return from Europe in the fall. Tryon was so annoyed at their complacency that he decided to sell the picture to his very next visitor. This "Rising Moon" was the first oil painting Freer bought. When the Potter Palmers returned in September, their irritation at finding that "their picture," as they put it, had been sold was scarcely soothed by the discovery that, in a summer loan exhibition at the Art Institute of Chicago, this very canvas had won the $1,000 Potter Palmer prize.

Freer liked Tryon's muted landscapes and Dewing's reticent paintings of women in dimly lit interiors, but he went into raptures over Thayer's unabashed idealization of American virgins. Thayer conceived of them as athletic young women whose innocent countenances suggest the absence not only of any obscene thoughts but of any ideation whatsoever. Of Thayer's "Virgin Enthroned," the Detroit bachelor wrote, "How tender and yet how strong! . . . An emblem of purity: a protest against sin . . . How grateful we should be for such blessings." He solaced himself for the loss of this particular painting to another collector by buying dozens of other Thayers, including his biggest "Virgin." This enormous canvas is an apotheosis of the nineties' idealization of the unsullied young woman which, like "momism" later, was recognized by Europeans as being typically American.

This was an age when any bachelor—and especially an eligible one—automatically enjoyed a deliciously scandalous reputation. Despite the presence of all these robust virgins on his walls, Freer was no exception. A young woman art critic was forbidden by her family to stay in Freer's home. But, according to a contemporary account, the poor girl felt that "her sacrifice on the altar of convention had been rather more than futile, it being, if anything, more respectable to be a guest at a bachelor's house than to have one's expenses paid at a hotel by him."

Certainly Freer's table was continuously graced by one or another decorative lady: beauty in a woman was surely as necessary as in an object. He wrote of the "wicked charms" of his date book, with its "secrets"; his reports of "ripping good times" on travels include discreet references to "charming girls"; and every woman who met him was fascinated by his chivalrous attentions. There were indulgent smiles at rumors of Bacchanalian feasts and Blue Grotto swimming parties which were given at the villa in Capri he shared with a bearded Detroit dandy, and gleeful whispers behind exclusive club doors about certain amazing Japanese paintings which were not shown to female visitors.

These tales and his captivating gallantries supported the Edwardian era's romantic legend of the Casanova bachelor. But legends often innocently deceive. Freer became entangled with no one and no precise or certain relationship can be adduced. His contemporaries of a pre-Kinseyian age never questioned whether this was due to meticulous propriety or disinclination or his delicate health. They insisted upon a bachelor having a "reputation," and where material for legend was lacking, they invented it.

Some of the Detroit industrialists complained that "Charley Freer was no good on a picnic," preferring to talk of the tariff on Italian paintings rather than the price of steel. But he was on intimate footing, especially during the nineties, with the old Detroit aristocracy and he was a popular, founding member of its most exclusive club, the Yontedega, which President Theodore Roosevelt called "the best club in America."

There was little on the artistic level to interest him in Detroit. His business associates owned huge, fashionable canvases as decorative symbols of wealth and culture, and proudly lent them to the Chicago Exposition of 1893. The best-known Detroit collector was Frederic A. Stearns, who made his fortune in the drug business and spent a large part of it on his world travels in the nineties. Like Attila the Hun ravaging Europe, he swept clean the bazaars from Alexandria to Tokyo. By sheerest accident he got a few good things. The bulk of his thousands upon thousands of objects, however, is symbolized by 1,440 pieces of late-nineteenth-century Japanese pottery and a life-size papier-mâché group of Japanese wrestlers. Freer had little sympathy for this lamentable taste. Always anxious to avoid unpleasant situations, he deliberately avoided being introduced to Stearns.

Nor was he much interested in the Detroit Art Museum, which he felt might more justly "run up the ethnological flag" than pretend to contain art. He paid it a dubious compliment. He did not disregard it in his will. He simply bequeathed it prints by a minor Dutch seventeenth-century engraver with $5,000 to complete the collection.

There was one Detroit collector with whom he might have stood on common artistic grounds. James Scripps, publisher of the *Detroit News,* had done rather well acquiring Dutch and Flemish old masters in the auction rooms when he went abroad for his health in the mid-eighties. Often overattributed, the paintings have survived on merit. But Scripps and Freer were kept from artistic intimacy by business enmity. As the voice of the people, Scripps righteously castigated Freer during the Depression of 1893 for continuing to exploit Polish immigrants, rather than hire Michigan unemployed at higher wages. His newspaper regularly criticized Freer as a prince of privilege and made amusing sport of the fact that his political influence had procured a comfortably unnecessary consularship for his Capri companion, Tom Jerome.

Before he settled forever into the cultivation of his own perfect, secluded world, Freer made one big effort for art and Detroit. He was prime mover in the scheme to commemorate the city's bicentenary of 1901 with a $2,000,000 grandiose civic design by Stanford White. The proposed peristyle, linking an esplanade to an island in the Detroit River, was to be climaxed with a 220-foot Doric column, topped by a torch of natural gas, to serve as "Beacon of Commerce to the West." The plans were praised in pulpit and press. The citizens shivered one night before City Hall looking at enlarged stereopticon views of the renderings. But the money was not forthcoming and the Board of Aldermen jeered the artistic dream out of existence.

But, though he was amenable to Detroit society, Freer had begun, as soon as he moved into his house, to create his own handpicked circle. Dewing and Tryon and Thayer were charter members. He advised them on investments and they advised him on wallpaper and the design of his garden. In the mural-conscious decade of the nineties, he commissioned them to decorate the walls of his living and reception rooms. They were his first—and frequent—house guests and surely it was this intimacy that emboldened him in Paris on Monday night, November 12, 1894, to pay an impulsive call on Whistler.

They hit it off at once. Whistler, irascible, hot-tempered, bristling and defensive as a porcupine, responded to Freer's sincere admiration with the generous, amusing and almost tender side of his enigmatic character. There were gay dinners in Paris with Whistler's friends and long hours spent over paintings. Mrs. Whistler, too, adored the fastidious, bespectacled, small-boned gentleman.

Freer so obligingly and efficiently catered to Whistler's whims for such objects as Japanese sashes of special colors that Whistler nicknamed him "General Utility." The most esoteric whim, however, was Mrs. Whistler's. When Freer left Paris in 1894 she asked him on his forthcoming travels around the world to find her a rare singing lark. Deep in the interior of India—where he contracted jungle fever—he found a pair and one survived the trip to Paris. After Beatrice Whistler's tragic death from cancer in 1897, Whistler wrote to Freer:

"She loved the wonderful bird you sent with such happy care from the distant land! And when she went—alone, because I was unfit to go, too—the strange wild dainty creature stood uplifted on the topmost perch and sang and sang—as it had never sung before! A song of the Sun—and of joy—and of my despair! Loud and ringing clear from the skies!—and louder! Peal after peal—until it became a marvel the tiny breast, torn by such glorious voice, should live!

"And suddenly it was made known to me that in this mysterious magpie waif from beyond the temples of India, the spirit of my beautiful Lady had lingered on its way—and the song was *her* song of love .. and courage .. and command that the work in which she had taken her part, should be complete—and so was her farewell!"

Whistler, whom Freer saw on each of his trips abroad, was crucial in his life. Whistler was an esthete, an "exquisite." He was tidy and dapper—with his monocle, his black ringlets setting off his white forelock, his fawn-colored frock coats, black trousers and patent-leather shoes. In an age of clutter, his rooms were sparsely furnished with neat, chaste chairs. A few Japanese objects discreetly decorated the pale lemon yellow and pearly gray walls. He slept in a Chinese bed and the food which pleased his fastidious taste was served on blue-and-white Chinese porcelain. Brilliant, epigrammatic conversation was his relaxation. His love was the Orient. His religion was art. More flamboyantly than could be Freer's style, he nonetheless epitomized all that toward which Freer was yearning. It was Whistler who gave impetus to Freer and he who welded, out of Freer's inclination, Freer's convictions toward the carefully composed, exquisite life.

Freer's opportunity for total dedication toward that end arrived in 1900, when he was forty-four. He helped the American Car and Foundry Company consolidate thirteen car-building manufactories. Then he sold his own interests for several million dollars and retired. According to his good friend Agnes E. Meyer, he was forced to do so because of a severe illness—perhaps congenital—and the fragility it caused. Retirement was a tonic release.

His patronage of Whistler increased: their friendship deepened. Freer cared for the artist when he fell ill in Holland in 1902 and was about to call for him for one of their daily carriage drives in London, on July 17, 1903, when he died. Freer was a pallbearer at the funeral and devoted adviser to Whistler's sister-in-law when she became executrix. His sense of sacred trust also took the form of finicky interference with the smallest details of the many Whistler memorial exhibitions. Once, when the hanging displeased him, he withdrew his loans. He minced no words against the

Pennells when their biography, which he believed was unauthorized, appeared. He could disregard their jealous dismissal of himself, but his delicate nature recoiled at what he called their "spiteful attitude" toward Whistler's sisters-in-law. He found it "not only unpleasant, but caddish to a degree."

What a friend once called Freer's "case of Whistlerism" became more virulent after the artist's death, unaffected by the formidable rise in Whistler prices. By 1906, Freer remarked that people were paying $1,500 for etchings for parlor decoration which had cost but $150 a few years before. A dealer who in 1918 bought Howard Mansfield's collection at auction for $250,000, was able to sell it the next day to a Connecticut collector for $350,000. The rise of the painting prices was even steeper. In 1892 the Luxembourg paid less than $1,000 for "Arrangement in Black and Grey," more popularly known as "Whistler's Mother." In 1903 a painting of equivalent size and quality cost $35,000; six years later, $60,000; and in 1919, the year Freer died, Duveen, who rarely bothered with a near-contemporary and certainly never with an American, paid Whistler the belated compliment of buying "Lady Meux" for $200,000. In 1948, the Louvre insured "Mother" for $1,000,000 and the United States Postal Department commemorated her on a stamp for Mother's Day.

Freer countered the sensational stories of Whistler's eccentricities with dignified silence about their friendship. Yet, inadvertently, it was Whistler who caused Freer's carefully contrived privacy to be punctured.

The publicity came about through Freer's purchase of Whistler's "Peacock Room." It was inevitable. The Peacock Room had been good copy from the beginning.

Whistler's most important early patron had been Frederick Leyland, a Liverpool shipowner. Like many self-made provincial tycoons on this side of the Atlantic, Leyland hoped that art patronage would boost his social aspirations in the metropolis. In 1876 he bought and remodeled a lavish house in London, on the same fashionable street as the Morgan residence. With the able guidance of Murray Marks of Durlacher's, who had helped J. P. Morgan outfit *his* princely surroundings, Leyland filled his house with a showy conglomeration of the world's finest appurtenances.

The dining room was to be the *pièce de résistance*. It was to set off Leyland's two proudest possessions: his blue-and-white porcelains and Whistler's painting of "The Princess of the Land of Porcelain." Henry Jeckyll, the architect's assistant, lovingly undertook the task. He constructed an elaborate thin-shell, vaulted room within the room, with delicate shelving of gilded walnut in the Japanese manner for the porcelain. He was particularly pleased with the Spanish leather he found for the walls. It cost a thousand pounds—but, embossed, gilded and painted with pomegranates and red flowers, it had been brought to England three hundred years before by Catherine of Aragon.

What Jeckyll considered his masterpiece, Whistler damned as pure horror. He persuaded Leyland that the room was inharmonious with his painting, tried toning it down, and just before Leyland left for an extended stay in Liverpool, got permission to make further improvements. It was a classic understatement. Whistler's "improvements" involved a complete, total and irreparable transformation of the room. It became a brilliant peacock preserve. Huge peacocks covered the shutters; peacock breast and tail feathers fanned around the walls; "eyes" of the tail feathers gleamed from the gold-leafed ceiling. The Cordovan leather was completely obscured as the artist worked deliriously on his job through the summer of 1876 and into the next year. His hair spotted with gold leaf, his hands smeared with blue paint, he held daily receptions for his friends and in February, 1877, invited the critics to visit.

Henry Jeckyll, stunned by their reports, came to see what had happened to his handiwork. The poor man was so shocked by the obliterating dazzle of blue and gold that he rushed from the room, with the sound of Whistler's laughter ringing in his ears like a peacock's scream. He was found later babbling of peacocks and pomegranates while he furiously gilded the floor of his bedroom. Hopelessly insane, he died shortly thereafter in a lunatic asylum.

Leyland's reaction was less traumatic, but hardly sanguine. His dining room had been wantonly used for a perpetual open-house; his expensive leather was ruined; and the room was impossible as a setting for his porcelain. When Whistler asked for 2,000 guineas, he gave him instead 1,000 pounds. Whistler was outraged: tradesmen, not professionals, were paid in pounds. He immortalized his revenge at the insult in the final large panel of the room. Here he depicted his "patron" as a rich peacock clawing and clutching at the silver shillings of which he believed himself robbed, and made himself a peacock, poor but proud, disdaining the filthy coins. Leyland risked indigestion nightly in front of this accusation, but sportingly grew to admire the room before his death in 1892.

In 1903, Freer bought the painting of "The Princess of the Land of Porcelain," which had been sold separately from the ensemble. When the dealers Obach & Company procured the room itself, they naturally offered Freer first chance at its purchase. On May 15, 1904, he slipped quietly into Obach's Bond Street gallery and bought the room for an alleged $63,000. Freer found reporters' interest in prices vulgar and thought most art writers insensitive. Only after he extracted a promise of secrecy about his purchase did he agree to let Obach put the Peacock Room on public view in London before shipping it to Detroit.

The exhibition drew a clamorous crowd. News of the sale leaked out and speculations about its purchaser were rife. The *Herald Tribune* scooped the story, but as Freer remained noncommittal, the conjectures continued. Sargent wrote to Isabella Stewart Gardner, who had asked him to buy the room for her, that he thought it had gone to Freer, but he was not certain. By the time the *New York World,* on August 17, 1904, positively reported that J. P. Morgan now owned the Peacock Room, Freer had already sum-

moned Wilson Eyre to design a special building for it at the rear
of his house. It adjoined the new sixty-foot picture gallery which
was created simultaneously out of the upper floor of the stables.

Once it was installed, Freer was besieged with requests to see
the room. Some of the visitors he reluctantly admitted were so artistically uninformed as to inquire whether it was covered with
William Morris wallpaper. None of them was quite as misinformed, however, as the literal-minded Englishman who, having
seen "The Peacock Room" blazoned in London headlines, wrote
to Obach offering "a six-foot long specimen, formerly the property
of Lady Charles Smith of Passingford Bridge, a bird with a pedigree, if you should like to add it to your collection."

Whistler was so famous an enthusiast of blue-and-white porcelain that W. S. Gilbert had satirized him as "a judge of blue-
and-white and other kinds of pottery, from early Oriental down to
modern terra-cotta-ry." He had not really known very much
about "early Oriental," but in the sixties and seventies he had led
the English cult for the porcelains and for Japanese prints, which
had been "discovered" in Paris as packing for china. Much pub-
licized since the time of the Philadelphia Centennial of 1876, the
late ceramics and the Japanese prints as well as costumes and
fabrics were quite in vogue in America by the turn of the century.

Freer began buying Japanese prints in 1892. Later he called
them the mere "skirmish lines of the Oriental advance" and sold
the whole collection. Drawn by their far greater refinement and
stimulated by their relation to Whistler's art, he had also been
buying for as little as ten to fifty dollars such earlier Japanese paintings as were being offered by a few Japanese dealers in Boston and
New York.

Freer had none of the vanity that made Morgan blush about
his errors. In late years, he helped Mrs. H. O. Havemeyer weed out
her collection. One day, when she was disheartened at the large
heap of "discards" and the meager number of the "chosen few,"

Freer tried to console her. "Oh, wait until you see my graveyard," he said, "I have culled thousands to your tens."

Almost as soon as he bought his first Japanese paintings he began to doubt them. The purpose of his trip to Japan in 1895 was to educate himself by looking at great examples in private and temple collections there. It was a considerable education. When he returned he began seeking out the few experts in the little-explored field. So it was that he met some of the New England scholars who had fallen under the spell of the Orient.

Dante had the biggest corner on the minds of the Boston intellectuals, it is true, but it was not a monopoly. Buddha was a strong competitor for those who yearned for an escape from the feverish pressures of the modern world. The voracious Mrs. Gardner had embraced both enthusiasms—Dante through Crawford and Norton, Buddha through Okakura of the Boston Museum.

One of the specialists was Edward S. Morse, the Salem zoologist who taught his science at the Imperial University in Tokyo and collected early pottery. Another was Mrs. Gardner's admirer, W. Sturgis Bigelow. He had worked with Pasteur, but, like Dr. Peter Alden in Santayana's *The Last Puritan,* preferred roaming the Orient to practicing medicine. Van Wyck Brooks tells how, after seven years' study, he was received into the Buddhist communion, and when he lay dying in Boston he tried vainly to persuade a Catholic priest to annihilate his soul. In 1882 these gentlemen went with Ernest Fenollosa to Japan, and Morse wrote in his journal: "We shall see a little of the life of old Japan; I shall add a great many specimens to my collection of pottery; Dr. Bigelow will secure every form of swords, guards and lacquers; and Mr. Fenollosa will increase his remarkable collection of pictures, so that we shall have in the vicinity of Boston by far the largest collection of Japanese art in the world."

Of the three New Englanders, Fenollosa had the greatest influence on Japan, America and Charles Lang Freer. This half-Yankee son of a Spanish musician was born in Salem. He was a sensitive, shrinking young man who went to Harvard in 1866, torn between studies in divinity and drawing. In 1878, when the University of Tokyo opened its doors to foreigners, he went there as professor of political economy and philosophy.

Japan at that moment was indulging in an orgy of foreignism: its old traditions were being scrapped, its art was wholly despised. The lords of the disintegrating feudal system were becoming impoverished and their collections of paintings and bronzes and lacquers were dumped on the market or sold at pawnshops where they could be had for a few yen. Fenollosa found a great ceramic head of Buddha in an ash barrel. Some of the extreme foreignists even burned Japanese art as rubbish. Buddhism itself was in disrepute and the treasures of the temples were also being dispersed and smashed.

Fenollosa, the American, led the esthetic revival. He made inflammatory speeches to the nobles, castigating them for abandoning their birthright. He fought to replace the American and Italian art instructors with Japanese teachers. Finally, as Japanese Commissioner of Fine Arts, he arranged for the registering of all art objects, the restoration of godowns and shrines and the institution of laws governing exports. In 1890 he agreed to go to Boston to take on the new post of curator of Oriental art at the Boston Museum. On his departure, with the court in full regalia, he knelt before the Emperor to receive his fourth and highest decoration. The Emperor told him: "You have taught my people to know their own art: in going back to your own country, teach them also." He took the charge seriously. From 1892 to 1906, he spread the gospel tirelessly to small, esoteric audiences across America.

The Bostonians longed for the East as an escape. As Van Wyck Brooks says, the word "Nirvana" fascinated them (one Bostonian even named his yacht *Nirvana*). They sought, of course, in vain. The artist John La Farge, who made several trips to Japan, wrote to Henry Adams, who accompanied him on one: "If only we had found Nirvana—but he was right who warned us that we were late in this season of the world." But even the quest brought them solace.

It was not exactly Nirvana that Freer was seeking. It was rather more a way of life. Whistler had helped him prepare the design of his life. He found it, ultimately, in the simple perfectionism of Oriental civilization as reflected in its art. And in time this art became an expression and extension of himself.

Fenollosa visited the sensitive collector first in 1900. Diligently Freer applied himself to study. Already wise enough to have recognized the rascality of many of the Japanese dealers, he depended heavily on Fenollosa's knowledge, which was the best of its time. When Fenollosa put on his other hat and offered him objects for sale (he had disposed of his own collection in 1886), Freer bought many of them.

He became more and more possessed by Oriental art. He found himself more and more closely linked with others of his time to whom this art of exquisiteness and refinement also appealed. Neither dilettante nor scholar, he had become something uniquely between the two. He once described a garden he particularly loved as being "not wholly in nor quite beyond the busy world." In exactly such a strange location were the small, exquisite environment and the collection he was perfecting. What had begun as a hobby had become an encompassing way of life.

In 1904, he took the step which would turn it into a respectable career. Encouraged by Fenollosa and Charles E. Morse, a collector of Japanese prints in Evanston, Illinois, on December 27, 1904, he made a formal offer of his collection to the Regents of the Smithsonian Institution in Washington, D.C. The conditions were terse and specific: he would retain ownership during his lifetime; would raise the value (then placed at $600,000) to an even $1,000,- 000; would provide $500,000 and plans for the erection of the gallery. In return, the building would bear his name and be perpetually maintained by the government.

No one before had ever offered the United States Government

a significant gift of art. The offer nonplused the Smithsonian Regents, scientists who had heretofore complacently thought of their museum as a sacrosanct repository of scientific paraphernalia. After stalling as long as possible, they decided to send their executive committee to Detroit to look this suspicious gift horse in the mouth.

The gentlemen charged with the uncongenial task were an educator, Dr. James Angell; a statesman, John B. Henderson; a scientist, J. P. Langley; and the inventor of the telephone, Alexander Graham Bell. They set out on their repugnant journey with Mr. Bell's daughter, Marian, to pilot them through the unchartered land.

Freer gave these "experts" no quarter. Mercilessly he had each of the 2,000-odd paintings and *objets d'art* brought out and displayed separately, Japanese fashion, as was his accustomed style. The performance lasted five days. Marian Bell later told her husband, "The opinion of all regarding this priceless Oriental art was summed up in Senator Henderson's remark, 'The things were all very well of their kind—but damn their kind!'"

The committee duly delivered a skeptical report about his collection of what they called "impressionist art." They tried every device of hedging and delaying in order to bar it from the sacred precincts. Suddenly President Theodore Roosevelt pulled out his big stick. He brought Freer and the reluctant Regents (with whom he had had blistering heart-to-heart talks) together for dinner at the White House on December 14, 1905; he ironed out legal difficulties; he wrote a strong letter to the Chief Justice, who was the Regents' superior. On January 4, 1906—less than a month after the White House dinner—Marian Bell telegraphed Freer that the gift had been accepted.

The news fired him with new high purpose. With Fenollosa, he applied the "fine tooth comb" to the Oriental paintings and got rid of "pesteriferous insects." He laid aside "some of the most beautiful fakes you have ever seen," bought mostly between 1899 and 1901 on the advice of certain Japanese dealers. One of these gentlemen took back without protest dozens and dozens of paintings and potteries, totaling $9,232. Freer's skepticism grew steadily with his education. He even began to doubt—on grounds of their ignorance as well as their guile—the opinions of the currently respected French savants and dealers. He decided again to find out for himself.

Every year between 1905 and 1911 he went on intensive, inquiring trips to Europe, the Near East and the Far East. With letters from President Roosevelt as super-passports, Freer, the ardent, diligent amateur-collector, buying for himself and his nation, had access everywhere. The dapper, fine-grained gentleman, always exquisitely dressed, doffed his derby, his straw boater, his black homburg, his white Panama, and charmed the people of many lands.

"I need all the training and coaching I can get," he wrote home once, "I don't want to buy promiscuously until I know." His knowledge began to outstrip that of his early advisers. Kelekian had introduced both Freer and Havemeyer to the wonders of Persian pottery at the Dana sale of 1898. Freer bought an exquisite piece for $1,750. By 1909, when Kelekian was bidding $12,000 for a Persian plate at auction for J. P. Morgan, Freer was on the spot finding extraordinary examples on his own.

He bought everywhere. His purchases were usually, as he said, "a curious lot, some real treasures, some trash and some mementoes of unusual experiences." Gradually he learned to recognize which were which.

On one trip to Cairo, however, he bought an ancient religious manuscript simply because he thought the pages looked beautiful. He was so skeptical of it that he promised the dealer's son a gold watch if the manuscript turned out to be genuine. Crossing the Red Sea, he unwrapped his purchase, noting again that many of the pages of the two gospels were cemented together at the edges. He grew decidedly embarrassed, and was about to toss this incriminating evidence of his foolishness overboard. But something held him back. In due time, the Egyptian dealer's son got a gold watch. Those fourth-century manuscripts, containing perhaps the most ancient and reliable versions of the death of Christ, rank among the most important ancient manuscripts in existence.

Syria, Turkey, Greece, Japan, Egypt—and finally China. For many years he had wanted to go to China to prove his surmise that the great Japanese paintings were based on even more ancient Chinese ones. For many years he had yearned to find some of the early stone sculptures which were beginning to appear on the market. In 1910, under the auspices of the Smithsonian, he finally penetrated into the interior.

There were hardships and dangers. But there was also the enviably exquisite way of life. Litter bearers, sedan chairs, a guide with a peacock feather in his hat, shelter in Buddhist temples, and gourmet dinners with forty delicately prepared courses served by thirty attendants eased his travels.

His most exciting adventures took place at Lung-men, a narrow gorge of the Yi River, where thousand-foot mountains of solid rock rise steeply from the water. He was lured by the hundreds of sixth-century grottoes, containing Buddhas that range in size from one to sixty feet, which were chiseled out of the mountainside, and by the wondrous sculptured caves that riddled their interiors.

When he set out with his retinue, the two mandarins of nearby Honan Fu supplied him with six armed guards against the dangerous band of about a hundred opium-crazed, bloodthirsty brigands who were terrorizing the region. Freer's suspicion that this precaution was mere Oriental politeness was soon dispelled by news of several murders near the caves.

One afternoon he watched a strange parade wind up the mountain trail: Mandarin Shu, resplendent in dark blue and deep purple silk, beneath a red parasol; his six-foot commander, in a green and scarlet uniform; the infantrymen; and two of the murderers, with ropes tied around their pigtails. They were being led to Honan Fu. The fastidious Mr. Freer listened attentively to the detailed account of the slow, fatal torture that awaited the prisoners there. Later, he noted the scene: "a mingling of shimmering light on the river and the ancient rocky trail, conquest and defeat—the eternal theme, old but ever new."

He felt less poetically inclined about the nocturnal racket that interfered with his sleep. He discovered that his guards were firing blank cartridges throughout the night to keep the bandits at a safe distance. He asked them to desist. Next morning he discovered the price of a good night's sleep: a long row of bandits, whose throats had been slit by his guards, lay outside his temple door.

By 1910, interest in Near Eastern and Oriental art had spread so widely that its chase had become exciting and its prices were advancing sharply. The European dealers were swarming over the Orient, and the Kaiser was using his diplomatic corps to search out art for the German museums. Rising to the occasion, both Japanese and Chinese were turning out devilishly expert forgeries and offering them with convincing tales of thefts from temples.

But despite all the activity, China in 1910 was still the great treasure house. Freer played a smart, tortuous game against the dealers who were always on his scent. He searched tirelessly from province to province and discovered paintings that had been hidden deep in the interor. He trained Chinese boys to scout for him, paid them daily whether they found anything or not, and knowingly bought things he would later discard in order to encourage their efforts for those he would keep. Once he spent weeks on the track of a certain Sung dynasty painting by Ma Yuan, of which he had heard in Japan. The price, when he located it, was a staggering $40,000.

The sensitive, cultivated gentleman had an advantage over the dealers and the German diplomats. As Agnes Meyer observes, Chinese nobles would not sell merely for money. Even when a sale was in the making, they only very delicately conveyed the information that the object might sometime change hands. Freer never grasped. He was equal to the subtleties of this rigid atmosphere of fine perceptions and superb manners. These years of travel enriched his collection and gave it its ultimate distinction, especially in Chinese pictorial art.

Between voyages, Freer gave swift attention to his investments (especially the lucrative Parke-Davis stock he owned so much of) and leisurely hours to the enjoyment of his collection. He was deeply shocked in 1907 when the jealous Harry Thaw murdered Stanford White. In 1908, his "teacher, adviser and inspirer," Fenollosa, died suddenly in London. Freer, who wrote that he felt "quite at sea without a pilot," made a fitting gesture: he paid for the removal of Fenollosa's ashes from Highgate in London to the temple grounds of Miidera, overlooking Lake Biwa in Japan, where Fenollosa had studied Buddhism.

But there were other members of the coterie—old and new—to linger with him in the gallery while Stephen brought out the objects one by one. Having educated him to absolute knowledge of every item in the collection, Freer took pride in Stephen as a personal creation. The bald, heavy-set Cockney, in perpetually unpressed clothes, was the one slovenly note, indulgently accepted, in the exquisite setting. Even Stephen's illusions of grandeur were countenanced by their creator. Freer's secretary once wrote him after a shipment had been received from abroad, "Stephen thinks they are very fine lots and wonders if you've bankrupted yourself. The large Persian sculpture . . . seeming to take his eye, though he feels that both the Larkin and Worch lots are great acquisitions."

Among the new companions were the trio of lovely young women whom Freer called "The Three Graces." One of these was a gray-eyed beauty, Katharine Rhoades, whose modern painting pleased Freer less than her lovely voice, her gentle patience and her devotion as his secretary. Another was Agnes Meyer, a statuesque blonde, ardently enthusiastic about Oriental art, who spent three years learning to read Chinese and dedicated her pioneering book on a great Sung painter to Freer. Another visitor was Charles A. Platt, who came frequently to discuss the plans for the gallery in Washington. Since Freer himself enjoyed art in small, easily assimilated doses, he planned the gallery so that only a part of the collection would be on view at any time. But for the scholars whom he respected and to whom he unconcernedly left the matter of attributions, he provided that the whole collection should be permanently available in storage vaults and stacks. It was a wise move: there were among the Chinese art 1,255 paintings, 678 bronzes, 502 pieces of jade, 487 pottery examples, 567 miscellaneous objects; in the Japanese department 1,863 items—and so on. Loyal to the American trio which he saw as artistic heirs of Oriental art, like Whistler, he provided space for them and dictated that the American group could be neither increased nor diminished.

By 1912, the deterioration of his nervous system was increasing at an alarming rate. The days of adventurous travel were over. By 1915, he had to move to hotel rooms in New York to be near his doctor. His always sandy impatience quickened. He had uncontrollable spells of suspicion and forgetfulness and irritation. But he rallied to a glow of excitement when the huge packing cases sent by his agents in the Orient arrived. As Stephen unpacked the consignments, Freer would go through them, accepting and rejecting.

As he became more and more desperately ill, even painting and pottery and bronzes could not hold him. He turned then to the final quintessence of exquisiteness: jade. He would cling to certain jade pieces, Agnes Meyer recalls, with deep satisfaction and almost religious faith in their restorative power. One of the last objects to reach him was a piece of amber jade shaped like a scepter. It was a musical instrument. At some grand ceremony in the court of the Chou Emperor nearly twenty-eight hundred years ago, it would have been struck to sound its single tone. "It was the best and most refined entertainment the Emperor could offer his guests," Freer explained wistfully. Jade in hand, he lay back, fortified against the severest pain. Frail and wasted, clad in a dark purple dressing gown, his face somewhat yellowish, he had grown himself to look like a Chinese lohan.

Freer died on September 25, 1919. The gallery he had not lived to see completed was opened in 1923; it contained the final 4,811 objects, including the re-erected Peacock Room. The collection was valued at $7,000,000; the building at $1,000,000. Despite the stupefied indignation of Stephen, who believed himself qualified for the job, John E. Lodge of the Boston Museum acceded to the donor's wishes and became its first director. Katharine Rhoades and Agnes Meyer served as trustees. The Freer Gallery today is a pilgrimage spot for scholars in Oriental art and philosophy; a "sight" for those conscientious sightseers in Washington who drop in to it on their way between the Washington Monument and the Smithsonian Institution; and for lovers of art, it is as John La Farge described it, "a place to go and wash your eyes."

Freer has two other monuments. His shingled house still stands in Detroit. It belongs to the Merritt-Palmer School, which has devotedly preserved it. But the once exquisite secluded world is used as a "laboratory of human relations." Freer was always an uneasy man with children, but now the preschool youngsters tumble and play in the erstwhile picture gallery; they stand before easels daubing with finger paints in the wing where the fastidious gentleman once erected the Peacock Room; they climb on jungle gyms in his once tenderly cared for garden. Yet for all the incongruity of its use, the house still evokes the old atmosphere —which can be summoned, too, next door in Colonel Hecker's French château, which is now the home of Baldwin pianos.

A more fitting monument to Freer is the one the Japanese erected to his memory in the Koetsu temple in the suburb of Kyoto. It is a natural rock, suave and beautiful in form, about three feet high and six feet long, curving gently upwards. It bears a carved inscription and stands before a green screen of trees. At the dedication ceremonies, with exquisite appropriateness, the Japanese placed tea and champagne upon the rock.

The Last Word

THE HENRY O. HAVEMEYERS

He was the plunger, she was the thrifty one. He brought to collecting the nerve that marked his shrewdly brilliant operations as founder and virtual controller of the sugar trust, one of the largest and most notorious monopolistic combines of that fabulous era. She brought to it so eager a desire to be an "original" that she encouraged their venturing into the vanguard. Accustomed to volume, he liked buying by the carload. Entranced by associations and adventures, she enjoyed tracking down the single object. The difference in their temperaments, the similarity of their taste and their mutual dependence on the perceptive advice of Mary Cassatt made Mr. and Mrs. Henry O. Havemeyer a remarkable collecting team.

Although he died in 1907, and the collections which enriched the Metropolitan Museum (and account for such of its most popular paintings as Greco's "View of Toledo" and Goya's "Women on a Balcony") were given only after her death in 1929, the name "The H. O. Havemeyer Collection" stands for both Havemeyers and carries intimations of marital solidarity.

Henry Osborne Havemeyer and Louisine Waldron Elder were married in 1883, when he was thirty-six and she was twenty-nine. (He had previously been married to her aunt.) He was already moon-faced, with steely, pale blue eyes, a firm, mustached mouth, and a bulky, imposing figure that seemed built to fit in a dignified frock coat. She had a strong-featured face, brightened by amused, intelligent gray eyes and an ingratiating smile. Each of their very definite personalities was fully formed. Each had already approached art characteristically.

Henry Havemeyer's grandfather was a German immigrant who founded a bakery in Greenwich Village in 1802 and five years later gave it up to begin refining sugar in the same locale. Henry Havemeyer's father did so well with the business that when he died in 1891, he left his sons several million dollars and a factory that loomed imposingly on the Brooklyn shore of the East River. Young Henry—or Harry, as his friends called him—inherited not only money and a flair for the sugar business, but also a taste for good living. He had been brought up in a comfortable overstuffed house among numerous decorative and anecdotal paintings.

Among his friends was an amiable, methodical, much-traveled gentleman artist, Samuel Colman, who painted picturesque watercolors of Italy in hot, pure tones. Together they visited the Philadelphia Centennial of 1876.

Henry Havemeyer, introduced like thousands of other Americans to the exotic art objects of China and Japan, took his first step in collecting. It was no timid step. It was a splurge, predicting a pattern of art buying that would persist all his life. He had been trained to think in wholesale terms. The sugar business was a volume business, dealing with such vast quantities that the fractional differences of an eighth or thirty-second of a cent per pound could mean a fortune. Many years later, the five-and-dime magnate, Samuel Kress, conditioned by huge inventories of small items, could not bear to buy even Duveen's and Wildenstein's most expensive paintings except in "lots." Henry Havemeyer confined his wholesale buying to rather less expensive objects, but within this area his enthusiasm knew no bounds. In Philadelphia, he bought Japanese lacquer boxes, gold and silver brocades, lustrous silks, sword guards and carved ivory inros by the dozens and dozens.

Although he seemed to believe that if one is good a dozen are better, Henry Havemeyer did not buy objects just for the sake of shopping. He deeply enjoyed those for which a place could be found in his house. He bought things because they appealed to him and would have bought some of his most renowned Chinese porcelains even if, as his wife said, they were Hindustani or from the Sandwich Islands. The fact that scholarship concerning Oriental objects was in its infancy in America in the eighties and nineties did not faze him at all. He knew what he liked and finicky scholarship annoyed him.

Professor Edward Morse came down from Salem frequently to examine the Havemeyers' Oriental pottery. Mrs. Havemeyer later recalled his "ferreting out the enigmas of province, clay, kiln and maker . . . leaving cigar ashes in his trail, which he carefully deposited in the jars and vases." Mr. Havemeyer lost his patience with the constant examination of seals and kiln marks and suggested that the professor quit scrutinizing the bottoms of the jars in order to admire their beauty from above. When Morse protested that he was working on a history of Japanese pottery, Mr. Havemeyer warned him not to get his history as upside-down as he did the jars.

Not only did Mr. Havemeyer know what he liked, but he also liked getting what he liked. Time and again he made rapid decisions to buy, even when prices seemed high. He was convinced not only that each work of art would increase in price in the future, but also that in the art market, as in any other, it was legitimate to ask "what the traffic would bear." He would point to the watch Jurgensen made for him in Norway. "I could have bought a dollar watch—there *are* dollar watches," he explained, "but I wanted one of Jurgensen's because they are the best in the world. He took into consideration my desire, the excellence of his work and the limitations of his production and charged me $800. He was fully justified."

He was a born competitor. A spirited rally in the auction room or maneuverings against another collector for a dealer's prize appealed to his sporting blood. In collecting, as in business, the more formidable the opponent, the greater the zest. In 1894, he found the triumphal clash with the famous European collector, Count Commando, for Manet's "Le Bal de l'Opéra" heady tonic. At the Gillot sale of 1904, when he found that his competitor for a certain Japanese screen (of dubious attribution) was the mighty Berlin Museum, he ran the price up over eight times its appraised value.

He was intensely stimulated by the spirited bidding at the Dana sale of 1898, where Kelekian introduced him to the beauties of Persian pottery. Charles Lang Freer was there, too. That fastidious gentleman from Detroit found competitive bidding against his social peers distasteful. Since the merest unpleasant association connected with the acquisition of a work of art sullied his enjoyment of it, he habitually refrained from auction battles with his acquaintances. But he was bitterly disappointed that Mr. Havemeyer had procured a particular piece which he deeply desired. At the end of the sale, Kelekian confided this information to Mr. Havemeyer. "We don't need it, let him have it," the Sugar King replied magnanimously.

Again and again in the auction galleries, the most splendid booty fell to "Henry Henry," the name under which he bought. Equally often, the extravagant determination behind his order to "buy" shot the prices skyward. His orders occasionally unnerved the employees of the auction galleries. At one sale, a Mr.

Kirby, who had been given a Havemeyer imperative about a small, lustrous pink vase, quailed at the prices which he found himself bidding against his aide, "Miss Rosie," who was acting for Sir William van Horne of Canada. Nervously about to falter, he consulted Mr. Havemeyer's brother. "Follow instructions," he was told. "You know Mr. Havemeyer." This unswerving resolve to get what he wanted, regardless of price and obstacles, won the Havemeyers many masterpieces that his more financially conservative wife would have lost.

Henry Havemeyer had a quick, hard mind and extraordinary powers of concentration. He would plunge into a subject, give himself to it, master it and then turn his terrific energy elsewhere. He explained to Freer, when the Havemeyers paid a visit to Detroit in 1906, that there were times when he could not "disengage himself from the most active material things," times when music claimed his entire attention, times when fine arts were his only desire. "I am glad to say," the sensitive and somewhat specialized Mr. Freer wrote to a friend, "that he was in the latter mood while he was here."

With this power of concentration, Havemeyer quickly developed a discriminating eye, especially for three-dimensional objects. Like J. P. Morgan, Henry Walters and so many other male collectors, he responded particularly to craftsmanship and form. He kept two handsome Greek fourth-century helmets and several Chinese bronze jars in his library. He caressed them frequently, like a blind man experiencing their shape.

The slow conversion of this enthusiasm for objects to an enthusiasm for paintings was accomplished by two of paintings' most ardent disciples, his wife and Mary Cassatt. A man accustomed to having his way, Henry Havemeyer was abrupt, bluff, cold to the outside world. He was genial to his friends and warm-hearted and generous to his family in general. But he was an adoring slave to his young wife, Louisine.

Louisine Waldron Elder was born in Philadelphia in 1855, daughter of George W. Elder, a sugar refiner who had been in business with Henry Havemeyer's father. Louisine Elder spent much of her girlhood being piloted through European museums and galleries, but her headquarters was Madame de Sartre's socially correct, cultivated *pension* in Paris.

The Elder and Cassatt families had belonged to the same intimate Philadelphia circle. When Mary Cassatt settled in Paris in 1874, she looked up Louisine Elder and found the young woman eager to learn about modern art.

A year later she led twenty-year-old Louisine to a color shop and advised her to buy a pastel of a ballet rehearsal by Degas. Louisine, who had been saving out of her fifty-dollar-a-month allowance to buy a Pissarro and a Monet, was proud of her advanced taste, but the strange pastel, with its asymmetric composition and boldly sheared-off figures, confused her. She recalled later: "I scarce knew how to appreciate it, or whether I liked it or not, for I believe it takes special brain cells to understand Degas. There was nothing the matter with Miss Cassatt's brain cells, however, and she left me in no doubt as to the desirability of the purchase and I bought it upon her advice." Louisine Elder gathered the necessary $100 by borrowing from her sister. Later she learned that these 500 francs rescued the poverty-stricken Degas from a decision to abandon art.

Her allowance was small, but once having acquired the taste for owning modern art, she learned to save and budget. It was a habit she never lost. Even when she became enormously wealthy, she remained a rather frugal woman. She ran her household simply and without waste. The children were not permitted to bring home guests for meals without a few days' advance notice. On a wintry afternoon in 1913, she invited her sister to accompany her to the exhibition of pictures to be sold at the Borden sale, in order to look at Daumier's poignant "Third Class Carriage." She authorized Durand-Ruel to bid the record-breaking Daumier price of $40,000, but she insisted that she and her sister use public transportation to and from the auction room.

In the early Paris days, her careful budgeting allowed her to purchase many prints, pastels and watercolors. Her gumption helped. She even presented herself to that eccentric and unpredictable artist, Whistler. She announced that she admired his work, told him she had thirty pounds to spend and inquired what she might have. The triumph of her resourcefulness was five lovely pastels, color notes on brown paper for his etchings of Venetian scenes.

Not only careful about money, she thoroughly enjoyed bargaining. After her marriage, she once found in Spain a ring she wanted to buy for Miss Cassatt. She offered the shopkeeper half the price he had asked. The man refused it. When they left the shop Mr. Havemeyer chided her for going too far. "You know you overdo things. You can't expect a man to sacrifice his goods just to please you," he said. At that moment the merchant ran down the street after them, willing to accept her offer. Mrs. Havemeyer smiled archly at her husband. But often her bargain hunting, especially after her husband's death, led her to dubious paintings.

She was a secure and totally ingenuous woman who never bothered with analyzing or philosophizing. She believed that good was rewarded and bad was punished and these concepts not only governed her life, but figured in the bedtime stories that she later told her children. She could meet every situation with a buoyant, almost Pollyanna sunniness.

She was a bride of only one year, living in a fairly small brownstone on East Thirty-sixth Street, when she was first confronted with a taxing problem that was thereafter to be hers: the disposition of her husband's wholesale purchases. He announced casually one morning as he left for the office that a case of Japanese tea jars would arrive later in the day. Uninformed about what a tea jar was anyway, she was astonished to discover that the case contained several dozen small boxes. Each of these enclosed a some-what smaller box, which contained a little silk bag which, in turn, yielded a small, soft clay jar, usually not more than three and a half inches high. The jars were dark brown with splashes of var-ious color glazes. "My brownies," she called them, as she gazed at the rows upon rows, "as varied as the smile of as many lips, as varied as the twinkle of as many eyes." Bewildered but pleased, she selected those she liked best and packed the rest away in the storeroom—as she would later pack away scores of other "brownies," since Mr. Havemeyer ultimately acquired 475 tea jars.

She was fortunate later in having a vast storeroom. It had, even-tually, to accommodate hundreds upon hundreds of other hetero-geneous objects from the Near and Far East which caught her husband's fancy. Indeed, the diminution and even disappearance of the attic has had as much to do with the changing pattern of collecting as any other factor. Without the yawning recesses, the omnivorous collector today finds he has reached the point of in-undation far earlier than his predecessors did. He is apt to buy less and, with the added inducement of a tax-deduction, apt to give far more quickly to museums and other educational institu-tions.

The orderly and good-humored way in which Mrs. Havemeyer packed, labeled, stored and kept track of the vast accumulation raised housekeeping to a science as methodical as public account-ing. Before her death, she marked with a "Z" myriad objects which she deemed worthy of the Metropolitan and then wrote voluminous notes to her children telling them in which cupboard or which case or which box they would find a particular peachblow jar or Greek Tanagra figurine. The lessons of this I.B.M.-like domesticity were fortunately taught to the Havemeyers' younger daughter, Electra, who inherited, in virulent form, her father's magpie proclivities.

Mrs. Havemeyer's reward for her efficiency at inventorying was a chance to indulge her cherished talent for decorative effects.

However much she despaired of finding a place for yet five more Chinese rugs, she delighted in expressing her individuality through tasteful arrangements of Chinese porcelains, Rakka pottery and Italian glass. Her passion for new and original ways of decorating extended even to the design of the cocoa-colored uniforms in which she clad her maids and to the gold and black checkerboard patterns on her coachman's buttons. At one point she had a spell of what amounted to a stenciling mania. She took the design from a Chinese rug and stenciled it on the floor; she stenciled it on some velvet draperies; she stenciled it on some closet doors; and she might have gone on stenciling it elsewhere if her husband had not warned her, "Look out, Louie, you'll be stenciling yourself."

The twin characteristics of self-assurance and naïveté marked every aspect of her life. They enabled her to speak fluent, incomprehensible Italian without a blush, to take singing lessons without a shade of embarrassment and to feel totally unconcerned about being married in a pink gingham dress. They equipped her to charm her husband into acceding to her whims. And these qualities of confidence and artlessness emboldened her toward "originality." She could never resist what she called "the last word," whether a hunting picture by Courbet or an attitude toward women's rights.

In 1884, a little more than a year after the Havemeyers' marriage, their first daughter, Adaline, was born. Their son followed in 1886. Perhaps with some unconscious identification with the powerful Romans, his father named him Horace. When their third child appeared in 1888, Mrs. Havemeyer decided to counter Roman with Greek and named the little girl Electra. One wonders what prompted her to commemorate the name of a woman famous above all else for having committed avenging matricide. But Mrs. Havemeyer doubtless looked at the sunny side and admired the classical Electra's qualities of loyalty and family pride.

At the same time that the Havemeyers' family was expanding, so was their fortune. In 1887 Mr. Havemeyer founded the sugar trust. Its success was phenomenal. Within fifteen years its profits were $150,000,000, and a share of American Sugar Refining Company stock bought at par had already paid 136 percent dividends. There was a saying on Wall Street that the stock market gave the sugar trust as much profit as the sale of sugar. But even within two years, the trust showed profits of $25,000,000. By 1889 it was obviously time for the Havemeyers to build themselves a proper house uptown.

Their architect, Charles Haight, who was later to flower into the Neo-Gothic style and build Vanderbilt Hall at Yale, understood that the Havemeyers had the position, courage and taste to be "different." The massiveness and simplicity of their house at 1 East Sixty-sixth Street made it conspicuously unlike its fancier neighbors. It was rather Romanesque in feeling, with rough, cliff-like walls. It had a bulging bay on the Fifth Avenue corner and an arched entrance placed discreetly on the side street.

But the interiors were really "the last word." Once after a strenuous afternoon of calling, Mrs. Havemeyer told her husband she felt dizzy from being ushered into one room after another all decorated in Louis XVI of "unqualified similarity." By employing the Tiffany Studios to do *their* interiors, the Havemeyers ran no danger of having their house look similar to any other in the world.

The Tiffany Studios had been founded in 1878 by Louis Comfort Tiffany, the thirty-year-old son of the famous jeweler. He first studied painting with Mr. Havemeyer's friend Samuel Colman, and he traveled abroad as far as Algiers. En route, he became greedily enamored of every rich decorative style he encountered: the Moorish style, Japanese art and artifacts, and above all, the sinuous, flowing forms of the new esthetic movement known as "art nouveau." Thereafter, his own rich confections mixed together strange and exotic elements from Near and Far

East and from nature itself, made stranger, more exotic, sometimes grotesque and outlandish, sometimes marvelous and beautiful.

Tiffany Studios, true to the tenets of William Morris, was dedicated to the harmony and apotheosis of all the crafts. It could take care of its clients' needs lock, stock and barrel—but never have lock, stock and barrel been so exotically and sumptuously custom-made. Aside from its work in glass mosaic and stained glass and the creation of the iridescent Favrile glass for which Tiffany is best known today, the firm also built furniture, made special lighting fixtures, cast ornamental bronze, hammered wrought iron, hand-blocked wallpapers, and wove and dyed rugs and textiles to order. Having provided a style of living to which its clients soon became accustomed, the Studios was also considerate enough to insure the continuation of this style after death by offering specially designed Tiffany monuments and memorials.

At least a little bit of Tiffany was as *comme il faut* as a gown from Worth or a Corot landscape. When McKim, Mead and White decorated the interior of James Gordon Bennett's 226-foot steam yacht, the largest privately owned pleasure craft then in existence, the fireplace of the 16-by-24-foot salon was of glass work by Tiffany. Mrs. Potter Palmer commissioned Tiffany embroidered tapestries for her Lake Shore Castle, and the beautiful actress Lily Langtry ordered Tiffany bed hangings and coverlets for her London hotel room.

By allowing the Tiffany Studios to do their complete interiors, the Havemeyers got the full *tutti-frutti*. Samuel Colman, who had by then become famous for making Tiffany clients "color conscious" and transforming a taste for drab, neutral interiors to an enthusiasm for glowing harmonies, worked with Tiffany on the Havemeyer house. They designed every detail, down to the hammered table silver in designs adapted from the Japanese. If the interiors were a trifle less rich than Tiffany's own, which had a bit of the rajah's palace about them, the designers left no square inch untouched and no source of inspiration untapped.

Mrs. Havemeyer was thrilled that the Byzantine chapels of Ravenna inspired "our white mosaic hall and ten pillars at the entrance of our gallery," and that the staircase derived from the one in the Doges' Palace. The Venetian rulers may have had the Adriatic outside: the Havemeyers had a fountain *in* their entrance hall, a fountain, Mrs. Havemeyer explained, that "was allowed to splash but a few drops at a time."

The walls of their music room were covered with Chinese embroideries. On the blue and gold Chinese rugs stood special, richly carved furniture rubbed with gold leaf and varnish to look like the ivory inro that inspired it. The furniture and woodwork in the library were based on Viking designs and Celtic motifs. In order to stain the oak woodwork the exact color of a Japanese lacquer panel he admired, Mr. Colman invented a system of acid staining that intrigued Mrs. Havemeyer so much she busily diverted herself for many years experimenting with it elsewhere.

The library ceiling was a sensation. Mr. Colman remembered the rainbow stacks of Japanese textiles that his friend had purchased thirteen years before at the Philadelphia Centennial, and Mrs. Havemeyer, of course, was able to lay her hands upon them. In his Newport studio Mr. Colman fashioned a mosaic design of these multicolored silks, outlined them with heavy braid and framed the panels with carved gold moldings.

When visitors exclaimed at the resplendent lustrous ceiling, Mrs. Havemeyer would call their attention as well to the library walls, since, as she said, backgrounds were one of her hobbies. Instead of the "murky red velvet" of the dealers' sanctums and the "red satin brocade" to which most of her fellow collectors were prone, the walls of the library were pale olive in tone. She found the whole rich mélange "modestly submissive" to the eight Rembrandts—including the superb "Gilder" and Van Bere-

steijn portraits—the austere Bronzino and several other masterpieces (and some not-so-masterpieces) that graced the library
walls.

These original and extraordinary interiors were compensating
attractions for the unmusically inclined among the guests who attended the Sunday afternoon concerts. Mrs. Havemeyer took great
pride in these musicales, which were inaugurated shortly after
the house was completed in 1890. At exactly three thirty-five on
these Sunday afternoons, Mr. and Mrs. Havemeyer parted the
heavy curtains leading to the music room and the portly gentleman led his wife to their seats. For these occasions Mrs. Havemeyer wore one of her grand Worth dresses. The versatile couturier appropriately designed, for this somewhat stolidly built figure, gowns a little more matronly, a little less daring and svelte
than those he concocted for such other customers as Mrs. Jack
Gardner and Mrs. Potter Palmer. The hostess' alert eyes were
alight with excitement as the "A" was sounded on the grand piano,
the Queen Anne's lace-inspired chandelier was dimmed and the
room hushed to silence.

The program usually consisted of a vocal solo and two quar-
tets by a well-known chamber-music group. Mr. Havemeyer not
only owned a couple of Stradivarius and the "King Joseph"
Guarnerius violins, but he also played a violin—with more vigor
than virtuosity—every morning before he went to his office. Even
his wife, whom he most affectionately indulged, dared not interrupt these private matinal performances. On certain Sunday afternoons, the host sat in with the professional group.

Precisely at five the concert was over and tea was served in
the dining room. "Fat Kate" and Mary Sheridan, the two upstairs
girls, were given alternate Sunday afternoons off despite the expected company. Directly after Sunday lunch, which the family
ate in the breakfast room, the cook sent up a platter of soda biscuits, some pâté and cream. Under the diligent direction of their
mother, dressed in pre-festival gingham, the three children mixed

the pâté and cream and spread it on the biscuits for the afternoon's repast.

Mr. Havemeyer, like most of the magnates, was not a very loquacious man. Even when discussion turned to so heated a topic as the trusts, he was apt to contribute only some such laconic remark as the fact that the price of sugar to the masses had decreased since the sugar combine was formed. His wife, on the other hand, had, as a friend put it, "the gift of gab." Although her husband teased her about it, she hugely enjoyed chattering with her guests. Long after he had retreated to her upstairs sitting room, she would be energetically answering her friends' questions, pointing out the special lighting Tiffany devised for the pictures and telling her "little stories" about various acquisitions in the two-story upstairs gallery.

Aside from the obvious attractions of the pictures and the cases crammed with Cypriote glass and Chinese porcelains, the gallery became a topic of animated conversation by virtue of its "golden" or "flying" staircase. A narrow balcony with an alcove ran around the second story of the picture gallery. The spectacular staircase was suspended, like a necklace, from one side of the balcony to the other. A curved piece of cast iron formed the spine to which, without intermediate supports, the stair treads were attached. The sides of this astonishing construction, as well as the balcony railing, were a spider web of gold filigree dotted with small crystal balls. The concept of a construction in space was revolutionary indeed for 1890, and its daring was dramatized by a crystal fringe on the center landing which tinkled from the slight motion when the staircase was used.

In the early days, the gallery was filled with the usual anecdotal paintings and with landscapes by Tryon and Dewing. After the turn of the century, the Havemeyers' painting collection not only improved in quality, but it so vastly increased in quantity that they had to build a second skylighted gallery on the first floor, covering the whole back yard.

Louisine Havemeyer, herself well schooled by Mary Cassatt, began to educate her husband to the appreciation of paintings as soon as they were married. He was an apt pupil. Within six years he had progressed from the anecdotal realism of the salon painters to the higher realism of Rembrandt and the Dutch. Then she enlisted Miss Cassatt as her co-instructor.

At the exhibition of paintings to be sold a few days later at the Secretan sale in Paris in 1889, Mrs. Havemeyer called her husband's attention to a large "Landscape and Deer" by the vigorous nineteenth-century painter Courbet. He led her instead to a pristine, neatly put together Dutch seventeenth-century interior by Pieter de Hooch. "That's the sort of thing to buy," he said. As she phrased it, "He had not yet reached Courbet."

Miss Cassatt averred frequently that "he learned by leaps and bounds . . . more quickly than any collector she ever knew." His conversion to the Courbet in the Secretan sale was certainly rapid. By the morning of the sale he decided he wanted it. The fact that it had been previously "knocked down" to the Louvre only whetted his appetite for Courbet. Before the Havemeyers left Paris, they had purchased a landscape, the first of their thirty-five superb examples of Courbet's work.

Soon the ladies were educating him to other modern painters. Once, early in 1894 he told his wife he was going to stop in at an exhibition at Durand-Ruel's. "If you find any Manets there, be sure to buy me one," she said casually. He did. He bought her a still-life. He confessed that the other Manet, "Boy with a Sword," was "too much for me." He referred, of course, to the bold, simplified style of painting rather than to the price of $3,500. Not completely sure of his affection for Manet, he limited their subsequent Manets to small, amiable canvases.

Then one day, when Miss Cassatt was making one of her rare visits to America, she and Mrs. Havemeyer decided to help poor Mr. Havemeyer "through the ordeal of deciding on a large Manet." The two women dropped into Durand-Ruel's New York gallery and purchased Manet's spirited painting, "The Alabama," and his huge, forceful "Bull Fighter." When Mrs. Havemeyer demurred that her husband might think the latter too big, Miss Cassatt told her dryly, "It is just the size Manet wanted it, and that ought to suffice for Mr. Havemeyer." It did. It also inspired him to assuage his belated annoyance at having let the "Boy with a Sword" slip past him by making a series of brilliant buys—including the two other great life-size bullfight pictures, "Majo" and "Mlle. V. in the Costume of a Toreador" (rather broad-minded purchases, since he abhorred bullfights), the portrait of George Moore (one of the most popular paintings in their home) and the daring "Le Bal de l'Opéra," so daring, in fact, with its sea of black top hats, that it inspired ridicule from many of the Havemeyer guests. Mrs. Havemeyer found this so irritating she removed the painting to her private sitting room.

Such was the pattern. Miss Cassatt was the introducer, the explainer, the interpreter who infected Mrs. Havemeyer with zeal about an artist. Then Mrs. Havemeyer would gently call his work to her husband's attention. Quite quickly he would respond and the big guns would come into action.

Occasionally thereafter each of them might find something on his own, but most often they were led to their remarkable paintings by Miss Cassatt. She accompanied them everywhere: when a dealer led them to see a Courbet in a blacksmith's shop (though the blacksmith refused to sell); to find a magnificent portrait of Louise Colet by Courbet at an impoverished family's home; to a dentist's to buy two Degas; to Vollard's to buy Cézannes. They went with her often to Degas' studio and to Durand-Ruel's gallery in Paris, where their patronage made that of Mrs. Potter Palmer seem picayune indeed.

Neither of the Havemeyers bought without the other's approval, but Mr. Havemeyer often gave in to his wife's whims and enthusiasms. There was, for instance, the question of nudes. Mr. Havemeyer felt strongly that it would be improper to include nudes in their collection because of their growing daughters. His wife had agreed.

But one day in 1890 she went into Durand-Ruel's New York branch. There she saw a painting of a half-length nude, a fleshy young girl with her arms raised above her head, holding a branch of blossoming cherry. It was the very painting that Miss Cassatt had particularly praised in 1881 when she introduced Louisine to Courbet's work in an exhibition in the foyer of the Théâtre Gaité in Paris. Mrs. Havemeyer sent it home, braced for her husband's full disapproval, even though it was only half a nude.

"Surely you are not going to buy that," he said. She admitted she would like to. "I shouldn't do it, if I were you," he replied ominously. Feeling firmly defiant, she kept the picture a few days before returning it to Durand-Ruel. Mr. Havemeyer said nothing until he noted its disappearance. "I knew you wouldn't want it," he then remarked complacently, his "enough rope" theory having apparently worked. His smugness unloosed a flood of protest. She wanted it very much; it was one of the loveliest pictures she had ever seen. "If I had it," she told him, "I would keep it right there in my closet and not hang it in the gallery at all, but just go there and look at it all by myself."

The next day the Courbet arrived at the Havemeyer house with word from Durand-Ruel that "Mr. Havemeyer had ordered it sent home to Mrs. Havemeyer." Never underestimate the power of a woman. The painting was hung in the gallery. Not only did Mr. Havemeyer frequently lead his friends to that picture and say, "Next to the Rembrandts, my favorite," but several other of Courbet's marvelously sensuous nudes, full length as well as half, entered the Havemeyer collection. He even acquiesced when she begged him to buy the great "Woman with a Parrot," although they both agreed that this painting, in which the seductive nude sprawls on her back, with her head and cascade of red hair thrust toward the spectator, had best be sent immediately to the Metropolitan Museum.

Many collectors hold the consoling belief that if a nude is intended for public rather than private viewing, her acquisition is a respectable rather than an indiscreet act. The root of their ethical decision may be that there is safety in numbers, or perhaps the cognizance that museums are "educational institutions." The Havemeyers made distinctions about *which* nudes might best be publicly rather than privately viewed. Andrew Mellon was apparently less flexible in this regard. Besides having a delicate sense of the inappropriateness of hanging religious pictures in smoke-filled rooms, the banker shied away from the idea of having pictures of any unclothed ladies on the walls of his home. His haul of masterpieces from the Hermitage included—for $544,320—Titian's "Toilet of Venus." Since she was destined for the eyes of the potentially largest public art audience in America, he accepted the likeness of this luscious lady without even a trace of his customary compunction. He even went so far as to visit the Venus in the impersonal setting of the Corcoran Gallery vaults, where she was stored pending the building of the National Gallery.

Besides acquiescing to his wife's whims, Mr. Havemeyer liked to indulge her with surprises. He enjoyed dropping into a dealer's on his way to or from Wall Street and buying some little treasure that he knew she would want. Thus one afternoon he paid a few hundred dollars for the original set of Whistler's Venetian etchings—those famous etchings for which she had purchased the color notes so many years before. Such gifts pleased her. As she once told an inquisitive guest, "I prefer to have something made by a man than to have something made by an oyster," and indeed, she rarely wore the fabulous string of sixty-one Oriental pearls that he had bought at the Philadelphia Centennial.

The Havemeyer collection would be remarkable if it contained only its wonderful French paintings and Degas bronzes or its fine Oriental and Near Eastern art (Mrs. Havemeyer was a devotee of Fenollosa and never missed one of his lectures unless it unhappily conflicted with her Tuesdays at home, which were as sacrosanct as her Sunday musicales). At the time of its purchase, all this art—like the employment of the Tiffany Studios—represented "the last word" of the best, advanced taste. But the Havemeyer collection is yet more remarkable because, under Mary Cassatt's guidance, the collectors also sought those old masters who made a link with the moderns. Thus they ventured into the little-known field of Spanish art.

That great adventure started in 1901, and they went foraging first in Italy. They were a party of four: Mr. and Mrs. Havemeyer, Mrs. Havemeyer's sister and Miss Cassatt. Mr. Havemeyer usually sat in stony silence in the carriage while the jabbering of the three ladies eddied around him. Occasionally he would have talks on politics and world affairs with Miss Cassatt, whose sharp, masculine mind he respected even beyond the boundaries of art.

Italy was hardly virgin territory for American collectors. Most of Mrs. Gardner's masterpieces were already installed in Fenway Court and J. P. Morgan was the proud possessor of a good many great Italian pictures. But the Havemeyers could hardly have done worse.

They fell into the hands of an impoverished German whom Miss Cassatt had known years before in Italy when he was sculpting *putti* and small objects. He had subsequently married an admiring little Italian, who claimed to be *persona grata* with the Italian nobility, and now worked for a dealer. With rare poor judgment, Mr. Havemeyer and Miss Cassatt rose to his bait and employed him as the Havemeyers' private and exclusive agent.

He provided them with adventures whose cloak-and-dagger aspects appealed to Mrs. Havemeyer. There were secret visits to the darkened, shabby palazzi of the poverty-stricken Italians (whose walls seemed to fill miraculously again with family treasures after each sale to gullible Americans). There was an uncomfortable excursion up into the hills, where they had to masquerade as wine merchants and indulge in wine tasting so that they could be led casually to the villa in the vineyard and then sneaked into a chapel that contained a painting attributed at the time to Filippo Lippi. He also unfortunately provided them with more than two dozen works of art bearing such celebrated names as Raphael, Andrea del Sarto, Titian, Veronese, Donatello and so on. Of all these ambitious attributions, only two have survived the tests of time and scholarship: the superb Bronzino portrait and the handsome Veronese "Boy with a Greyhound," both in the Metropolitan.

In Spain it was a different story. Charles Deering of Chicago, who lived in Spain part of each year, had developed an adventurous passion for Spanish primitives, and some of the European collectors were interested in later Spanish paintings, especially in Velásquez' canvases. But there was so little vogue for Spanish art that many wonderful paintings were to be had for low prices. It was as profitable for dealers, agents and owners to be honest as dishonest. The errors were usually due to ignorance, not wiles.

Madrid's great museum, the Prado, was a revelation. Mr. Havemeyer maintained that, after the Spanish-American War, the United States should have demanded the Prado as an indemnity instead of the Philippines. The Havemeyers fell under the spell of El Greco's intense, flickering paintings. They grew possessive.

Miss Cassatt rose to the challenge in no mean way. Ingeniously she managed to meet the Infanta's godson and to locate Greco's marvelous full-length portrait of Cardinal don Fernando Niño de Guevara; his only known landscape, "View of Toledo"; his huge "Assumption of the Virgin"—and for good measure, Goya's splendid painting of some women on a balcony, which she remembered having seen in Spain many years before.

Mr. Havemeyer had rather strict notions about the propriety of portraits, which were always being shaken by the respected Miss Cassatt. There had been trouble in Italy about a painting, then attributed to Veronese, presumably of the artist's wife. Like Morgan and Frick, Mr. Havemeyer believed that if an artist was going to paint a portrait of a woman, she should be a beautiful woman (or, if the artist was Rembrandt or some northerner, at least a good, homespun woman). He found the beefy, middle-aged, determined-looking woman in the so-called Veronese distinctly disagreeable. He had fallen in love with Botticelli's lithe, lovely "Venus" and felt frustrated that he could not lure her from the Uffizi. Mary Cassatt pleaded the case of the Veronese, saying that sixteenth-century women *"were* full breasted and *did* wear tight bodices." Mrs. Havemeyer wanted the Veronese, too. Unlike Mrs. Gardner in almost every way, she shared the Bostonian's sanguine feelings about portraits of ugly women. Mr. Havemeyer still yearned for the Botticelli, but the odds were against him. He bought the alleged Veronese.

But in Spain, when Miss Cassatt enthusiastically described the Greco Cardinal wearing big tortoise-shell spectacles, he was adamant. "What!" he exclaimed. "Spectacles in a portrait! I would not consider it. They must be terrible." Of course, by the end of the visit he deferred to Miss Cassatt's judgment and started negotiations for this superb portrait as he had for the Greco landscape (which cost only $14,000) and the Goya women.

He was put off again, however, when the critic Theodore Druet in Paris offered them a portrait by Goya of Queen María Luisa of Spain. It would be difficult to find a subject more unattractive than Charles IV's wife. Madame de la Tour de Pin, who had served as her lady-in-waiting when the monarchs were held captive by Napoleon at Bordeaux, described Her Majesty's neck as "the blackest, dirtiest, skinniest" she had ever seen. Poor María Luisa also had dry, frizzled hair, nasty birdlike eyes and a hideous nose. The artist pitilessly presented her distasteful face as she stood arrogantly clad in a sumptuous yellow satin gown. "Well, Goya never did a finer bit of painting than that dress," Miss Cassatt observed. "All right," said Mr. Havemeyer, "we'll buy the dress and take the Queen with it." (The painting is now considered a copy after Goya.)

The Havemeyers virtually opened the market for Grecos and

Goyas in the United States. Besides their Grecos, they were ultimately to have twelve Goyas (including the fine pair of the
Sureda family, for which they paid less than $8,500, and the
portrait of the Duke of Wellington, for which they paid $3,400).

They had refused Greco's "Assumption of the Virgin." Every
time his wife wanted a big picture (such as Manet's "Christ with
Angels"), Mr. Havemeyer would warn her that he didn't know
what she would do with it, and every time she managed to rehang the galleries to find a place for it. But this thirteen-foot-high
"Assumption" nonplused even her. In 1906, Durand-Ruel came
across it again in Spain. Its price was only $17,000. In order to pro-
tect it, Mr. Havemeyer bought it and offered it to the Metropolitan at cost. The trustees turned it down because, they said, "they
had acquired a finer one." The "finer one" was "The Adoration
of the Shepherds." Recommended by Fry, it was the one Berenson had unsuccessfully urged on Mrs. Gardner. It was not the
quality of the Greco that concerned the public in 1906. Greco
was so little appreciated as a painter that one reader of *Art News*
magazine characteristically called the painting "a jumble of
carelessly thrown together, badly drawn human figures not worth
$50." The Havemeyers relinquished the "Assumption" to Durand-
Ruel and Miss Cassatt recommended it to the Art Institute of
Chicago. Martin Ryerson enabled that museum to buy it, but such
are the ways of the art world that it cost the Institute $53,000.

The Havemeyers' Spanish paintings remain unsurpassed. But
Mrs. Havemeyer liked telling the story about Granada. "It took
some time 'to do' Granada, but it took very little time for Granada 'to do' us," she recalled good-humoredly. After many persuasive and highly secret conversations with the owner of an antique
store, they bought several thousand dollars' worth of Moorish
tiles "from the villa of Charles V at Guadix." When the 250
cases arrived two years later, their contents were declared modern. Mrs. Havemeyer, looking on the bright side, decided they
were handsome anyway. She stored most of them in the stable,

but, unable to resist a personally devised decorative effect, she used a few on an addition to her Stamford home.

On December 4, 1907, Henry O. Havemeyer died of a ruptured pancreas in his home at Commack, Long Island. Just before his death, Mr. Havemeyer told his eighteen-year-old daughter, Electra, "Boss, take care of your mother." Mrs. Havemeyer needed taking care of. Her mother had died within a few months of her husband. Electra sensibly bore her off to Europe, where, in Spain, she rallied sufficiently to buy three more Goyas.

Mrs. Havemeyer continued her art collecting, her Sunday musicales and her Tuesdays at home after her husband's death. She was a hospitable woman. One of the few visitors against whom she ever demurred was Isabella Stewart Gardner, who requested to see the collection on a Saturday morning in 1901. "Doesn't she know that Saturday morning is reserved for cleaning?" Mrs. Havemeyer grumbled to her husband.

After Mr. Havemeyer's death, as the fame of the collection grew, so did the number of callers. Mrs. Havemeyer graciously received such "lions" as Baron Kamura, the Japanese envoy to the United States during the Russian-Japanese War; Lord Kitchener, who tenderly fondled a peachblow vase; and Helen Keller. She passed many afternoons chatting with Mr. Freer.

More and more, however, she engaged her passionate enthusiasm in the cause of woman's suffrage. Back in Madame de Sartre's *pension* in Paris she had known the granddaughter of Lucretia Mott, the Quaker who in 1848, with Elizabeth Stanton, prepared the first woman's rights convention, in Seneca Falls. She always liked the story of Mrs. Mott's reply when Mrs. Stanton proposed including woman's suffrage in the platform: "Why, Elizabeth, they will think thee crazy."

Mrs. Havemeyer was a logical feminist. Of all the new ideas, "votes for women" was the most compelling one. She was a woman of determination and purpose. Cherishing the notion that women, if properly educated, would become more intelligent than men, she had even gone so far as to make her eldest daughter a guinea pig to prove her point. Adaline was pushed through lessons so that she could enter Bryn Mawr at the age of fifteen. If Mrs. Havemeyer was disappointed that Adaline rebelled against this intellectual determinism by choosing early domesticity, she took it with her usual sunniness. She specifically left to Adaline a Corot painting of "Mother, Child and Nurse," with the comment, "To Adaline, because she loves children."

She stoutly maintained that her husband believed in the enfranchisement of women and had stood beside her when, as a bride, she signed a petition to Albany. But many of her relatives and friends decried her radical activity. When she lent her art collection for a suffragette benefit exhibition, several collectors refused to attend and even threatened to withdraw their patronage from Knoedler's, the gallery which had lent its premises for the show. The disapproval daunted her not at all. She proceeded to give a speech, which the eminent art critic Royal Cortissoz described as "sluicy."

She was, obviously, an asset to the National Woman's Party. The presence of this wealthy, respectable, elderly woman, with her white hair still worn in a dignified pompadour, was in itself "good copy." She was a proven organizer. Who else could so successfully have conducted a campaign to send seventy thousand pounds of homemade jam to wounded soldiers during two years of the war? In addition, her "gift of gab," her inner confidence, her ingenuousness and her agile mind made her an ingratiating speaker.

She lapped up her audiences' applause and enjoyed playing to her gallery. Once she set her small grandson on a chair and said, "Friends, if the *men* of your generation will not grant us justice now, you may be sure this generation will." She toured New York state in a little laundelet car which she called her "Jewel Box." Balancing a big, fancy hat on her head, she held aloft the "Torch of Liberty" and delivered dozens of speeches. She devised a little model of the *Mayflower* which she called the "Ship of State," whose electric wiring was attached to a battery in her automobile. She wove endless speeches around the theme of the "Ship of State" ("Women were good ballast on the *Mayflower,* why not on the Ship of State?"). She was especially proud of her dramatic finale. As she said, "When you give us freedom, my Ship will look like *this,*" she pushed the button so that thirty-three tiny lights, including red and green port and starboard ones, outlined the "Ship of State."

She was the heroine of two special schemes concocted by the energetic ladies of the National Woman's Party. The "Torch of Liberty" was to be transferred from the New York suffragettes to their Jersey sisters in the shadow of the Statue of Liberty. Mrs. Havemeyer gaily set sail wearing a black dress, a white flowered hat, elbow-length gloves and a banner saying "Votes for Women" across her now copious bosom. When they reached the halfway mark, it appeared that unfortunately the New Jersey ladies had forgotten to get a license. Even the seasickness induced by waiting in a choppy sea did not quell the indomitable Mrs. Havemeyer: she rallied as the Jersey sisters hove to.

She was such a success, in fact, that the Party decided her participation in their most dramatic demonstration was a necessity. Convinced that the suffragette amendment would be defeated in Congress in 1919 because of President Wilson's "faithless words from Paris," they decided to burn the President in effigy. If all went well, the perpetrators would be arrested and jailed. Then they could gain glaring national publicity by touring the country in a "Prison Special" railroad car. The ladies were nothing if not honest. In order to qualify for the railroad trip you had actually to be imprisoned.

Mrs. Havemeyer was summoned to Washington and obediently packed her "grip" with a warm wrapper and a bottle of disinfectant. A flag was thrust in her hand. She was directed to lead the demonstration and to make the first speech. She felt as calm as if she were going to play croquet.

With one exception, everything proceeded according to plan. The police began hauling away the suffragettes—all except Mrs. Havemeyer. Captain Flathers, the round, red-faced police captain, just hadn't the heart to arrest this nice sixty-four-year-old lady. The more flagrantly she tried to defy the law, the more concerned the kindly gentleman became. Her efforts were not helped by the fact that she could not get a match to strike in order to ignite the bundle she was to throw on the effigy. But the resourceful ladies kept supplying her with other bundles which had already begun to burn. They were too much for Captain Flathers. He reluctantly led Mrs. Havemeyer into the Black Maria.

Sportingly, she spent the night with the thirty-nine others in the police dormitory (the younger ladies graciously gave her "first call on the lavatory") and stood in the crowded waiting room of the jail along with several ladies of the evening. Their case histories titillated some of the suffragettes and roused them righteously to promise future reforms to help their fallen sisters. She stoutly chose five days' imprisonment instead of a five-dollar fine and went with twenty-eight other suffragettes to be incarcerated in a disgraceful jail, discarded ten years before as unfit even for hardened criminals.

The ordeal of the night in the jail faded before the wrath of her family and friends when they read the next morning's paper and discovered she was a jailbird. She was bombarded with telegrams accusing her of disgracing the family's name, warning her she had lost her citizenship and the legal right to sign checks and declaring that she would be, as she said, displayed "as on an oyster shell in society."

Since she had "done the trick" and was qualified for the "Prison Special," she acceded to the demands, paid the fine for the rest of her sentence and departed. After the "main part of the family" welcomed her back, she consoled herself against the disdain of the disapproving by recalling others who had gone to jail for their beliefs: John Bunyan, Galileo, Martin Luther and Joan of Arc. She was the hit of the strenuous tour and of the big closing rally in Carnegie Hall.

Mrs. Havemeyer made a will in 1917 leaving everything to her children. Before her death from heart disease on January 6, 1929, she had added three codicils that changed it completely. The first of these gave the Metropolitan Museum 113 works of art; the second added 29 pictures; the third authorized her son Horace, as executor of her estate, to give to the museum such works of art not mentioned in her will as he chose and directed that the three children might select from the remainder.

The way in which Horace Havemeyer, Adaline Frelinghuysen and Electra Webb carried out this authorization was a tribute to their upbringing. Mrs. Havemeyer had been a virtuous and conscientious mother, "ever," as she said, "seeking ways to interest my children." They had been given works of art from time to time; they were encouraged to pursue music; and, fortified by afternoon naps, had been taken to see Terry and Irving perform Shakespeare. Despite the muckrakers' virulent attacks on the sugar trust, the children were taught to feel at ease with wealth and to respect the public responsibilities it entailed. Like the Southerner for whom "damyankee" is one word, Mrs. Havemeyer invariably addressed her offspring as "Dearchildren." The Victorian phraseology of her admonitions make these sound sanctimonious, but she was earnest in her teaching that they should remember how "blessed" they were and that they should "try to equalize the sum of human happiness and share the sunshine that you have inherited."

What is essentially *their* gift to the Metropolitan is an example of astounding generosity. The bequest was increased from the 142 objects she had specified to 1972 items. Far more significant than the quantity was the quality. Edward Robinson, director of the Metropolitan, wrote in the catalogue that accompanied the temporary exhibition of the collection from March to November, 1930: "They seem to have assumed that their Mother wished the Museum to have the best of everything she left and to have done their utmost to carry out this wish." Perhaps even more remarkable was the next statement: ". . . at the same time avoiding embarrassment on our part by including things which we might not really desire."

In addition to heeding the "Z" which had indicated her own evaluations of the objects fit for the museum, the children consulted the various curators and whatever errors crept in are on the museum's own head. The heirs further enhanced the bequest with gifts from their own collections. It was not politesse but truth that made Mr. Robinson characterize the bequest as "one of the most magnificent donations ever made to a museum of art." So it was and so it has remained—although its extent and complication are not apparent to the museum's casual visitor. Unlike the banker Jules Bache and the merchant Benjamin Altman, both of whom specified that their collections must be kept intact and fenced in by the donor's name, Mrs. Havemeyer attached no restrictions save those that the objects be known as "The H. O. Havemeyer Collection" and that acceptance should be "for permanent exhibition." Scattered in their appropriate places, they add immeasurably to the glory of many of the museum's departments.

Today the fashion for private art collecting has veered almost exclusively to paintings (and sometimes sculpture). Those like Robert Lehman and Samuel Untermyer who continued the older tradition into the present are rare. There are many reasons for the shift. Modern interiors and modern taste eschew the crowded room in favor of the uncluttered one and the busy look for the stark one; the size of living space has shrunk; there are no longer servants to dust and care for objects. Likewise, it is paintings, rather than objects, that attract the public in museums. Thus the paintings in the Havemeyer bequest overwhelm the rich multiplicity of the collection, especially since these superb pictures are by artists who, "the last word" then, are popular favorites today. Few people attach the name Havemeyer to the Persian lusterware, the Chinese rugs, the Oriental potteries and porcelains and objects, the Cypriote glass and the extraordinary prints which are not only beautiful in themselves but also evidences of the eclectic, catholic taste which was characteristic of almost all the great collectors of the Havemeyer period.

Even after the supremely generous gift to the Metropolitan was subtracted, the Havemeyer collection contained fabulous treasures for the heirs. With more amiability and less friction than usually marks such sessions of allocation, the three children—as if they were choosing "sides" in a children's game—bespoke in turn for this Goya, that Rembrandt, this Degas, that Manet.

The well was still not dry. There was enough left quantitatively to fill a ten-day session at the American Art Association Galleries auction rooms in April, 1930, and qualitatively to attract the best collectors. John Ringling, who was simultaneously finding gargantuan acts for the circus and the biggest possible Baroque pictures for his Venetian palace at Sarasota, Florida, bought a "Lady with a Guitar" attributed to Goya. The heaviest buyer was the pert, aggressive collector Chester Dale. In addition to purchasing several paintings by Mary Cassatt and a haystack by Monet, he paid the two highest prices of the sale. "Portrait of a Young Girl," attributed to J. L. David, cost him $26,000. The auction audience stirred with consternation and surprise when he bid up to $24,000 for a Cézanne called "L'Enlèvement."

Some of the family's holdings were subsequently sold. A few—such as Goya's portraits of the Suredas and Manet's "Gare St. Lazare"—have been given to the National Gallery. Others have been handed down to interested grandchildren and great-grandchildren of Louisine and Henry O. Havemeyer. Many of the remaining Havemeyer treasures are slated for permanent public exhibition in a small town in Vermont. But that event belongs in the story of the Havemeyers' youngest daughter, Electra, who inherited a passion for collecting that rivals her father's and a taste which embarrassed her mother.

Americans in Paris

GERTRUDE, LEO, MICHAEL AND SARAH STEIN

It has been said that as many people claim to have discovered modern art as there are cities claiming to be the birthplace of Homer. The most convincing of the contenders are the four members of the Stein family—Gertrude, Leo, Michael and Michael's wife, Sarah. They were not only discoverers but effective publicists and patrons. Within the family circle, however, there was a petulant dispute about priority.

Who, for instance, was actually responsible for buying Matisse's "Woman with a Hat" from the Paris Autumn Salon of 1905? Credit for the purchase was worth the wrangle. It took more than a little courage to buy a picture so jeered at that the artist dared visit the show only once and his wife not at all.

The exhibition was notorious. Here were paintings such as the world had never seen, violent in distortion and riotous in color. Water was pink; flesh was green; brush strokes appeared slapdash. The paintings looked barbaric, pulsing with a fierce energy. Canvases by such young, little-known men as Matisse, Derain and Vlaminck filled the central gallery. As the story goes, when the critic Louis Vauxalles saw a small Renaissance-type bronze sculpture of a baby standing in the middle of these savage works, he remarked, "Ah, Donatello, *au milieu des fauves.*" And of all the paintings by these fauves, or "Wild Beasts"—as they have been known ever since, even now that they bring prices approaching $100,000—Matisse's "Woman with a Hat" was the most ferocious.

Said Sister Gertrude, who had determined almost from babyhood that she wanted "gloire," the painting seemed perfectly natural; she could not understand why it infuriated everybody; *she* wanted it—though her brother, she claimed disparagingly, preferred a conventional painting of a white-clad lady on a green lawn. Sister-in-law Sarah said that *she* suggested the family make the purchase because of the "unprecedented magnificence of its color" and because it reminded her of her mother. Brother Leo saw no family resemblance at all. In fact, he found the picture "a thing brilliant and powerful, but the nastiest smear of paint I had ever seen." But, "since it was what I was unknowingly waiting for," he managed to get over the unpleasantness in a few days. Stressing the personal pronoun, he remarked, "*I* had bought my first Matisse." He had "discovered" him at the dealer, Vollard's, a year before.

There was no controversy about who first "discovered" Picasso, but plenty of bitterness about who really appreciated and understood him. Leo came upon his work in 1905. He used to while away the time with Sagot, a dealer on the rue Lafitte, an ex-clown with a pointed beard who chewed on a piece of licorice and gossiped about art. Sagot directed Leo to an exhibition of Picasso's drawings. He is "the real thing," Sagot told him. Leo bought one. When he returned to Sagot's with Gertrude, the dealer showed them Picasso's tender "Young Girl with a Basket." On one point brother and sister agreed. Gertrude was "repelled and shocked by the drawing of the legs and feet." But Leo bought it. He had "discovered" Picasso.

During the next two years, Leo and Gertrude bought many other paintings by Picasso, who was then in his romantic, rather sentimental "blue" and "rose" periods. By 1906, Gertrude had posed ninety times for the Picasso portrait now in the Metropolitan Museum. Picasso was on the verge of his cubist phase and Leo's enthusiasm was growing tepid. When Picasso turned the corner and began to reconstruct the world into cubes and planes, Leo called the paintings "fantastic contraptions" and "scrap-bag assemblages." Gertrude glowed. She insisted that what Picasso was doing in paint, she was doing in words. As she wrote later of her alter ego, every time she met a genius, a bell rang. The bell rang three times: once for herself, once for Picasso and once for Alfred North Whitehead, the mathematician. She did not do very much about Whitehead, but she kept the bell pealing loudly for the other two. Long before public relations became a profession, Gertrude Stein became her own best press agent and Picasso's best publicist.

Sarah, on the other hand, did her enthusiastic bit for Matisse, who, in turn, called *her* the "really intelligent, sensitive member of the family." His appraisal was hardly disinterested. She was a devoted pupil; during the years 1905 to 1907, she and her husband Michael were Matisse's most important patrons; and when in 1906 they returned briefly to San Francisco to see what damage the earthquake had done to their home, they brought Matisse canvases along and sought converts in America.

It was an undertaking not without hazards. The "startling news that there was such stuff in town has been communicated," she wrote to Gertrude. "Oh, Albert Bender has been our most faithful and devoted, as always . . . but his devotion hardly stood the test of the *'femme au nez vert.'* . . . Upon his demand, I assured him that perhaps he'd better spare himself this test, as I knew his belief in my infallibility was something very dear to him. 'No,' he said, '*I* shall never, never, never say, as others have, that you are crazy.' Well, he saw it—for two minutes he was speechless—then he meekly inquired, 'But don't *you* think you're crazy?'" Crazy or not, the Michael Steins were responsible for the framer George Of buying a Matisse—the artist's first sale in America. They also so intrigued another San Francisco lady, Harriet Lane Levy, that she and her friend Alice B. Toklas soon came to Paris to look for themselves. Miss Levy, under Sarah's direction, was to become another Matisse collector.

But Leo Stein licked his wounds. "I was the only person anywhere, so far as I know," he wrote testily years later "who in those early days recognized Picasso *and* Matisse. Picasso had some admirers and Matisse had some, but I was alone in recognizing the two as important men."

The "two important men," like almost all the other pioneering artists and writers, musicians, collectors, bohemians and intellectuals, doers and re-doers, prodigies and parasites, met each other at the Saturday night salons at 27 rue de Fleurus, where from 1903 to 1914 Leo and Gertrude Stein lived in as harmonious a relationship as was possible between a brother and sister caught in a dramatic psychological conflict.

There were five Stein children: Michael, the eldest, born in 1865 —then Simon and Bertha, whose humdrum lives need not concern us—then Leo, born in 1872, and Gertrude, in 1874. They were all born in Allegheny, Pennsylvania, where their father, Daniel Stein, of German-Jewish descent, was in the retail clothing business. The year Gertrude was born, Daniel quarreled with his partner brother and bore the family off to Vienna. Six years were spent in Europe, while a tutor, a governess, a nursemaid and instructors of riding, music and skating took charge of the children. Just before they left Vienna for a final year in Paris, the well-to-do little Steins posed for their picture: Michael, aged thirteen, stands with crossed arms and legs, independent, grave; Gertrude's pudgy little four-year-old body strains at its velvet dress and big eyes stare from her chubby face; Leo, aged six, languishes on a pillow, pale, curly-headed, his morose expression in sharp contrast to the jaunty Tyrolean hat in his hand.

In 1880 the family settled in San Francisco, where Daniel Stein became involved—for better and worse—with street railways, cable cars, mines and the stock market. The mother was a patient, conscientious, singularly dull woman, whose health gradually deteriorated until she died in 1888, when Gertrude was fourteen.

The father, always unstable, erratic and addicted to one dietary or educational fad after another, became increasingly eccentric. The already peculiar household lost any semblance of order or routine. When Daniel died in 1891, Michael, who had returned from Harvard and was now first assistant superintendent of the Omnibus Cable Company, took charge of the family's financial affairs. He became legal guardian of Leo and Gertrude, who moved to Baltimore to make their home with their mother's sister.

What Leo later referred to as "the family romance" between himself and Gertrude began when they were toddlers. In California, their closeness grew through their directionless childhood. By the time they reached Baltimore—Gertrude, a plump, hearty extrovert; Leo a thin, moody introvert—the unconventional, egotistic pair were deeply devoted.

Their college years—with Leo at Harvard and Gertrude at Radcliffe—overlapped. He was a meticulous, concentrated student. She rode rapaciously through her courses, drawn especially to philosophy and psychology, where she became the prize, and most original, pupil of Hugo Münsterberg and William James. At one examination session, her note, "Dear Professor James, I am so sorry but I do not feel a bit like an examination in philosophy today," elicited the answer, "Dear Miss Stein, I understand perfectly how you feel. I often feel like that myself."

In 1895, Michael Stein married Sarah Samuels, a San Franciscan who had been studying conventional painting. She passed the ordeal of meeting her strange, intellectual brother-in-law and her robust and critical sister-in-law, who would suddenly thrust a volume of Browning at her and command her to read out loud. Privately, maternally, she worried about their unconventional dress and ideas, as her husband would later worry about their extravagance.

Separated in the summer of 1895, when Leo went around the world, Leo and Gertrude spent most of their other vacations together, traveling in Europe. For a few years their graduate work at Johns Hopkins was simultaneous. Then Leo left for Europe, where he began to look at art even more seriously than ever before, to paint earnest, mediocre pictures and to contemplate writing a book on Mantegna, which, like so many of his projects, was never even begun.

Gertrude continued at Johns Hopkins Medical School, now fascinated and involved, now bored and impatient, her originality and inquiring defiances the delight of her brilliant professors, the bane of the standard ones. Flunking a perfectly ordinary course in obstetrics, she failed to get her degree, refused to take the summer course which would give it to her and abandoned medicine and pathological psychology as a career. After a few restless years, in the fall of 1903 she came to Paris and settled with Leo in his two-story studio apartment at 27 rue de Fleurus.

They were a conspicuous pair. Leo had a tight, intelligent face with small, squinty eyes and a large, mournful nose. In later years, he looked like Jimmy Durante turned intellectual, but in these early days his face was smothered in a rabbinical beard. Gertrude already had a massive, monolithic body. She wore her hair in a topknot above her strong-featured, Buddha face. They both sported sandals which were notorious even in Paris. Gertrude's, worn with thick woolen stockings, had toes which were described as looking like the "prow of a gondola." The poet Guillaume Apollinaire called them "bacchic sandals," but the manager of the Café de la Paix, less romantically inclined, denied the Steins entrance because of their footgear.

They also both wore brown corduroy. Bernard Berenson, on whom the Steins descended in Florence, carried an indelible image of Gertrude: "Her apparently seamless garment made her look like the proto-Semite, a statue from Ur of the Chaldees. I was always in trepidation that it would someday fall down." One summer in Florence, Leo and Gertrude came regularly to Berenson's library in his villa, "I Tatti." Stretched out on their stomachs on the floor, they smoked cigars and drank lemonade as they looked at old manuscripts and books. "The books showed evidence of their visit," their host recalls dryly.

Leo Stein took himself seriously—almost rudimentarily. He never tired of tracing his own ideas, emotions and hiccups back to first principles. In 1902, he was already taking himself seriously as an esthete. Although, like Gertrude, he had been enthralled as a child by the waxwork realism of the "Panorama of the Battle of Waterloo" and moved by Millet's "Man with a Hoe," he was, by his own admission, esthetically precocious. By the time he was fourteen, he had grappled with and conquered such problems as "composition" and "significant form."

He was a man who, as Berenson put it, "was always inventing the umbrella." Incessantly he evolved new versions of pragmatic philosophy and such neat esthetic formulae as "art is where construction and composition coincide."

Having scrutinized, studied and dissected the old masters, he began searching for valid contemporary expression. He bought a tepid British impressionist painting in 1902, significant because it made him feel "like a desperado" and because it proved that "one could own paintings even if one were not a millionaire." He bought another in Paris (the innocuous lady on the lawn which Gertrude falsely credited to a later date), important as paying "his fee to the Paris art world." But he was depressed about his search. The contemporary art he encountered in the salons and the galleries seemed to him hackneyed, spiritless, dull, reiterated.

The Steins were not Berenson's type. Gertrude offended the esthetic sensibilities which Berenson had been refining for so many years, and he found Leo a tiresome bore. But he could not resist a man who lived in his mind (even when he considered the mind mediocre), and so he was willing to rescue Leo from his intellectual funk. He told Leo to go to the dealer Ambrose Vollard and look at Cézanne's paintings.

Thus it was Berenson, who had thrown his own lot so wholeheartedly with the Renaissance, who pointed the way to modern art. Berenson also became Matisse's first spirited public defender. Outraged at the puerile criticism of a Matisse exhibition in the *Nation,* he wrote a lively letter to that magazine in 1908. He called Matisse "a magnificent draftsman and a great designer" who had found "the great highway traveled by all the best masters . . . for the last sixty centuries at least." As soon as his letter appeared in the *Nation,* Gertrude Stein began badgering him to devote all his energies to propagandizing Matisse. He politely declined. He had been moved to his peroration more by his annoyance at the foolish, hackneyed criticism in the *Nation* than by dedication to the artist.

Those who were angered that he would not take up the cudgels for modern art took malicious delight in slanting the story of Berenson's subsequent encounter with another contemporary artist. The story concerned the murals for the lunettes in his library at "I Tatti." He decided that they should be covered with pale, unobtrusive floral arabesques. For this job he commissioned an artist friend, Piot, whom Mrs. Berenson found personally charming. Piot duly and agreeably produced sketches for pale, unobtrusive floral arabesques. The Berensons approved them and set off for America.

Like Whistler, Piot apparently could not restrain himself when confronted with wide, empty spaces. To the Berensons' justified consternation, he covered the lunettes with hot-toned landscape scenes, à la Puvis de Chavannes, populated with figures whose muscular development, à la Signorelli, looked like an advertisement for Bernarr McFadden's health courses. Berenson, who had been one of the advocates of legislation in Italy forbidding the destruction of any work of art, was in a somewhat embarrassing position. His way out of the dilemma was simply to have the offensive paintings covered. Hidden, they are still unharmed on the library walls.

The incident, however, furnished combustible fuel for his antagonists in London and Paris. Led by André Gide, they spread the story that Berenson had debated between Matisse and Piot, had decided Piot was the better artist and had gotten his just desserts. Obviously Berenson would hardly have considered Matisse, famous for his exuberant, insistently bright paintings, to do reticent arabesques.

But back in 1903, when Berenson was still the Steins' hero, Leo followed his advice and went to Vollard's. His conversion to Cézanne was immediate. He bought a work by that great precursor of twentieth-century painting, and his sagging faith in modern art rallied. That summer in Florence he compounded his enthusiasm for Cézanne at the villa of Charles Loeser, the wealthy son of a Brooklyn merchant, whither Berenson had also directed him.

There is a certain protocol in the way collectors assign their pictures to various parts of their dwellings, a protocol as rigid and indicative as the seating of guests at an ambassadorial dinner. P. A. B. Widener was quite frank about this etiquette. When he commissioned Berenson to examine his collection, he asked for three lists: paintings good enough for the gallery; paintings which should be relegated to the bedrooms; paintings which should be thrown out. The public rooms of Loeser's villa were crammed with Italian Renaissance paintings, bronzes, faïences and drawings. Leo Stein found Loeser's many Cézannes in the dressing rooms and bedrooms.

By the time he returned to Paris in the fall of 1903, Leo was ready for the new art. Gertrude was energetically embarked on her career as a writer, but she found time to join him in his quest.

Michael had been doing well in San Francisco. He worked for Collis P. Huntington at a large salary and shrewdly invested the Steins' money in schemes like San Francisco's first apartment building. But in 1902, when the workers on the cable cars struck, he found himself embarrassingly on the side of the unions. "Sally," he announced, "there is no place for me in management." He resigned his job and moved to Paris with his wife and seven-year-old son, Allan. (Shortly after Allan's birth Sarah had written, improbably, to Gertrude, "Go and get married, for there is nothing in this whole wide world like babies—Leo to the contrary notwithstanding.") In the reunited family, Michael took the back seat. But he was always the stabilizer for his complicated siblings and his excitable, determined wife. Leo and Gertrude "sat on his doorstep for meal-tickets," as a friend put it, and everyone else came to him to solve their problems.

Together, the four Steins made looking at and buying art a family adventure. Their means were small, but the new art was cheap. They went to Berthe Weill's tiny gallery, to the big conventional salons, to the "independent" exhibitions and, perhaps most often, to Ambrose Vollard's. This astute dealer, who was to handle the work of most of the important artists of his time, remembered them in his strange, junk-shop-like gallery. Leo would sprawl in an armchair with his feet high up on a bookcase (it was one of his many temporary remedies for digestive troubles). Gertrude would squat on a chair, roaring her much renowned, richly resounding belly laugh—a laugh like a beefsteak, one friend described it; a laugh that had glory, another put it. Sarah touted hard for Matisse. But Leo in those days was the leader. The brave new collection was growing.

The Steins' acquaintance with Matisse deepened into friendship when they bought "Woman with a Hat" and agreed to pay
his asking price of $100. They became friendly with Picasso
through Henri-Pierre Roché, whom they called "the great introducer." Roché, journalist and artist, was a tall, redheaded man
with a romantically sorrowful face, whom Leo described as being "all ear" and Gertrude as one "who was always listening." He
was the sort of man who knew "everybody," and in those early
days before, as Gertrude says, "everybody brought somebody" to
their salons, he was just what the rather ambitious Steins needed.

The "come-on" to the Leo-Gertrude Saturday nights was, at
first, Leo's Japanese prints and, as one habitué cynically remarked,
the long loaves of French bread and platters of ham and cheese
that stood in the center of the studio on the Renaissance refectory
table behind a large, overstuffed couch. But soon the spectacular
attraction was the Steins' collection of contemporary and near-
contemporary masters. From 1905 to the beginning of World War
I, 27 rue de Fleurus was the most vital and exciting center of
modern art in the world.

There were Picassos, large and small, of harlequins and tenderly awkward young girls, and there was his commanding portrait of Gertrude with its grave, mask-like face, of which she said
later, "And I was and still am satisfied with my portrait of me, it
is I, and it is the only reproduction of me which is always I, for
me." There were rows of carnival-bright paintings by Matisse, including a robust sketch expressing exuberantly his own "Joy of
Life" and his powerful, violently distorted, literally "Blue Nude."
This bold painting disturbed most of the visitors. One of them,
seeking desperately for something agreeable to say to Matisse
about it, ended up remarking, "I don't think I could take that
pose," to which Matisse replied charmingly, *"Et moi non plus,
madame."* But Gertrude would soothe aggressive spectators by telling them that her janitor's four-year-old son, when he first saw the

Blue Nude, "cried out in rapture, 'oh la la, what a beautiful body of a woman!' "

There were luscious little Renoirs and hot-toned, patterned Gauguins. There were paintings by Vallaton and Manguin, now almost forgotten; there was a little Daumier, a little Greco, a Toulouse-Lautrec. And there were small Cézanne watercolors and larger Cézanne landscapes in oil and a big portrait of Madame Cézanne. The paintings were hung close together, two to three deep, and odd bibelots stood on top of Renaissance chests, so that the room had a cluttered, Victorian look which made the modernity of the art all the more astonishing.

Soon "everybody" came to the salons. Apollinaire brought his friend Marie Laurencin, who peered near-sightedly at the paintings through her lorgnette. She sold her first painting to the Steins —an ingenious quadruple portrait of herself and Apollinaire, Picasso and *his* current friend, doe-eyed Fernande Olivier. The painters Derain, Vlaminck, Braque (who asked diffidently, "What do they want of us?" when Roché first invited him to attend), Pascin and Delaunay came. The American painters Maurice Sterne, Marsden Hartley and Alfred Maurer came—and Maurer would reassure dubious visitors that, of course, the Cézannes were finished—why else would they be framed? The far-sighted and courageous dealer, Daniel Kahnweiler, who promoted the cubists, came. So did Edward Steichen, a young man who was to find in photography a great twentieth-century art form and who was to be a courier of modern art to America. The splendid Russian collector, Sergei Shchukin, came. The German, Hans Purrmann, who, with Sarah Stein and Patrick Henry Bunce, was to start Matisse's school, came. The hot-tempered collector from Philadelphia, Dr. Albert Barnes, the inventor of Argyrol, came, waving his checkbook. Even the Berensons occasionally came.

There, in 1906, for the first time, Henri Matisse and Pablo Picasso met each other. Picasso, then twenty-five, looked like a small-boned gangster, or as a friend of Gertrude Stein's said, "like a good-looking bootblack," with a thatch of black hair curving down over one of his enormous dark eyes. Matisse was then thirty-seven. Leo described him as "bearded, but with propriety; spectacled neatly; intelligent; freely spoken, but a little shy." Fernande Olivier recalled that when they met, Matisse was very much master of himself and shone imposingly against Picasso "who was always a bit sullen and restrained at such encounters." "They were," she concludes, "the two artists one paid the most attention to."

The Saturday night salons were an international pre-café society—Russians, Poles, Scandinavians and Germans along with English, Americans, Spaniards and French were there. The Steins' salon was the artists' showcase and press conference. It was the crossroads and the vortex. Perhaps no other collection was ever so effective a stimulant and catalyst.

Leo, pontifically divulging the contents of his encyclopedic mind, would hold forth on the enchantment of calculus and the Cavalier poets, on William James and Gesta Romanorum, and revert intermittently, crusadingly, to dissertations on the validity of modern art. Unlike the brash and brutal Dr. Barnes in every other respect, Leo Stein shared the Philadelphian's abhorrence of "twaddle about art instead of hard-headed common sense." He never "enjoyed" a painting. He struggled to discover why he felt it had power. Once acquired, a picture became like a microscopic slide to a scientist.

Gertrude, who knew what she liked and what she wanted to like and didn't care why, spoke little. She usually reclined on a chaise longue. Occasionally she would join Leo in patronizing the new Americans who were not yet initiated into the mysteries of Cézanne and Picasso or, egged on by confederates, would proceed from bantering to bullying. Her resplendent laughter made a throbbing obbligato to the evening's talk.

The Michael Steins had rival Saturday nights at their home on the rue Madame. Their walls were covered exclusively by Matisses—all the important Matisses of the years 1905 to 1907, in fact, that were not at the rue de Fleurus. Although, as an asp-tongued friend of Gertrude's remarked, Sarah saw herself as a provincial Madame de Staël, the Michael Steins were less ambitious and less exhibitionistic. *Chez* Michael Stein, life was bourgeois and cozy. There was less bohemian atmosphere, and there were fewer intellectual pyrotechnics at their house than at the Leo-Gertrude salons. The Michael-Sarah evenings ended early, so that people went first to the rue Madame and then to the rue de Fleurus, where the gatherings lasted until two or three in the morning.

When the artists left, they would hail a yellow fiacre to take them back to their world of Montmartre or would storm through the streets of Montparnasse. They all had a sense that these were their heroic days. Picasso would shoot a pistol in the air out of sheer exuberance. Roché, drunk, would go to Braque's to look at new paintings, fall asleep and awaken staring at an African mask, new enthusiasm of the pre-cubist painters.

Among the habitués of 27 rue de Fleurus and the rue Madame were Doctor Claribel and Miss Etta, the Cone sisters of Baltimore (reputedly but not actually distant relatives of the Steins), on whom the catalytic properties of the collections had a potent effect.

The spinsters' devotion to each other lasted a lifetime, perhaps because their temperaments were diametric complements. Picasso called them "The Miss Etta Cones," but once a little girl bringing them flowers differentiated between them more perceptively by giving Dr. Claribel flame-colored sweetpeas and Miss Etta a reticent bouquet of violets.

Dr. Claribel was a pathologist. In the days before Johns Hopkins would accept female medical students, she went to Women's Medical College in Baltimore, did graduate work at the University of Pennsylvania, was a resident at Bloakley Hospital for the Insane and assistant to a Hopkins pathologist. She studied abroad and did research in Germany, making some pioneer discoveries about relationships of cells and fat in the skin. She was, however, congenitally dilatory and tardy. Other people usually managed to publish similar research conclusions ahead of her. It bothered her not at all. The energetic intention was always as good for her as the act. She always intended to read newspapers. At her death, there were trunks full of newspapers she had never gotten around to reading.

Monumental, Dr. Claribel had a noble head, with an arched, strongly jutting nose and a firm mouth. She dressed the part of a grande dame. Her clothes, invariably black, were made for her by Madame George in Paris, who charged her twenty-five dollars more than any other customer because so many hooks and eyes were required on her high-necked dresses. She strode down the aisle of the Lyric Theatre in Baltimore with Hindu silver skewers spiking her coiffure, pendants of Renaissance jewels shelved on her bosom, and shawls from the Orient, Africa, Italy and Spain massed over her shoulders. Once the Kaiser instinctively offered her his arm when he saw her waiting in the lobby of the Munich Opera House, so duchess-like was her appearance. She usually took two seats for concerts and lectures, using the second to hold her mountains of shawls, packages, and a bulging hand-tooled French leather briefcase-bag which was a habitual accouterment.

She was an imperious woman, who insisted upon having her own way and her comfort. Gertrude Stein told about the evening that Dr. Claribel and Miss Etta found themselves in a European town with only one not very well appointed hotel. Miss Etta urged her sister to put up with it as they would have to stay there only one night. "Etta," answered Dr. Claribel, "one night is as important in my life as any other night and I must have my comfort." When World War I broke out, Dr. Claribel was in Germany. It is said that the reason she remained there throughout the hostilities is that she refused to share accommodations. (Another friend counters this explanation by saying that Dr. Claribel remained in Germany because she heard people were having to undress before the officials in order to be searched at the border.)

Miss Etta was the quiet one—shy, indulgent, patient—the one who remembered to order ice cream in fancy molds when they entertained in their Baltimore apartment, and the one who ordered the workmen to wear immaculate white gloves when they handled the paintings. Still a large woman, she was smaller scaled than Dr. Claribel. Her hair and face were softer. She wore precious laces from their textile collection draped around the collars of all her dresses. Whereas Gertrude Stein wrote to Dr. Claribel about art and literature, her letters to Etta dealt with such enlightening subjects as the purchase of corset covers or the decision to wait for Etta's "over-seeing eye" before having some blouses of "tan cawdrey" made up.

One winter in Paris, while Dr. Claribel was away in Germany, Gertrude Stein gave Miss Etta the manuscript of *Three Lives* to type. So well bred and unassuming was Miss Etta that, having failed to ask permission to read it, she typed the manuscript letter by letter and read not a word of it. Besides being able to type, Miss Etta played the piano and studied French, Biblical and Talmudic literature. But her real career was being Dr. Claribel's companion.

In 1905 they came to Europe on the first of thirty-two trips based on Dr. Claribel's medical studies. They were house guests of the Michael Steins. Through Sarah they met Matisse, who became a warm friend, and they bought the first of the forty-three Matisses that were to make the Cone collection, after Dr. Barnes', the greatest collection of Matisse paintings and sculptures in America.

Through Gertrude they met Picasso. He had been working on the large painting of the family of saltimbanques. Hundreds of related drawings dotted his studio in a tenement in Montmartre. During the summers of 1905 and 1906, the Cone sisters bought for pittances thirty-six of these drawings, literally off the floor. And, like the Steins (and later John Quinn), the Cone sisters kept Picasso supplied with coveted colored comic supplements from American Sunday newspapers.

The curious apartment on Eutaw Street in Baltimore which the sisters shared with their somewhat "weak sister" brother, Frederic, was railroad in plan, really three apartments of small rooms joined together. Frederic and Dr. Claribel would formally ring the front doorbell of Miss Etta's apartment when they appeared for their daily lunch. The apartment was jammed unpretentiously with Oriental rugs of high quality, Renaissance and Queen Anne tables and chairs, red damask and embroidered burgundy velvet. Bronze sculptures jostled Dutch brass jars filled with haphazard, flamboyant flower arrangements. The pictures crowded the available wall space.

There was something of the squirrel-collector in all three of them, although Claribel, who had picked up dozens and dozens of sea shells as a child, was the most avid buyer. She could never bear to buy one of anything. She even bought two of the same book, in case she wanted to give one away—but she never did want to. When the husband of a friend looked unhappily at the tie she gave him for Christmas and admitted that her choice the year before was more to his liking, she grabbed his arm and led him back to a chest in which she had stashed away over six dozen neckties. At Miss Etta's death, the executors found two and a half dozen pencil sharpeners, one hundred leather book covers, dozens of Liberty scarves, fifty-two candlesticks, and enough paper clips, rubber bands and pads of paper to stock a five-and-ten-cent-store counter.

This same wholesale approach marked their purchase of textiles (the collection ranks as the finest of its kind in America, including Persian cloths-of-gold and gossamer scarves embroidered by the ladies of Turkish harems); of laces (Miss Etta began with lace in 1905 with the most delicate of bobbin work); and of Renaissance and Baroque jewelry, dazzling, chunky, intricate, fabulous; of African and Asian jewelry and coral pieces by the several score.

But Dr. Claribel's penchant—counterpart, in these days of pre-Freudian unself-consciousness, to Gertrude Stein's predilection for buttons—was for boxes and chests. The Cone sisters had hundreds of boxes, from pocket-size snuff boxes to gigantic armoires, from Japanese lacquer chests to heavy Dutch wardrobes, endless boxes-within-boxes and chests with drawers-within-drawers. In a particularly beautiful Spanish box, Dr. Claribel kept her mail, unopened and unanswered.

And there was, of course, the painting collection. Besides the Matisses and the Picassos, there was work by Renoir, Van Gogh, Cézanne and Manet, a collection of 180 items (outside of prints and drawings) which, when it went to the Baltimore Museum on Miss Etta's death in 1949, was valued at $3,000,000.

Gertrude Stein liked to say that it was she who made the Cone sisters go to Picasso and "buy something." Sarah Stein used to insist that unless she herself were present to make Etta buy a particular Matisse, "she would slip through my fingers."

But, in fact, the Cone sisters bought what *they* liked. With two exceptions, what they liked were paintings which, within their own frame of reference, were gentle rather than violent, sumptuous and splendid in color as their beloved Near Eastern textiles. One of their few "violent" pictures—and it was, of course, Dr. Claribel who leaned toward it—was Matisse's "Blue Nude," which went from Gertrude and Leo's collection to John Quinn and, after his sale, to them.

Dr. Claribel died in 1929, worried that Baltimore was not yet ready for such modern art; and indeed, the community thought the two ladies a little bit touched. But Miss Etta determined that, through education, even sleepy, conservative Baltimore might be prepared. During the remaining twenty years of her life (she was seventy-eight when she died), she worked on the collection. She added precursors like Delacroix and Courbet. She forwent insurance so that she might use the money to round out the Matisse collection. She not only sent Matisse an annual birthday cable, but she also bought one of his pictures almost every year. The result is a remarkable record of Matisse—Matisse in the mild, rather than in the raw.

Once they had gotten started, Dr. Claribel and Miss Etta knew what they wanted. But many of their best paintings once belonged to the Steins, and without the Steins and the Stein collection, they might never have begun.

By 1910, the tenor of the Leo-Gertrude salons had changed. Alice B. Toklas, a thin, dark and intellectually quick little gnome, who was to become famous as the "subject" of Gertrude Stein's autobiography and later as the author of a cookbook, had joined the household. Leo had already met Nina Azais, the luscious, sympathetically loving former artist's model whom he would finally marry in 1921. Leo was becoming increasingly irritated by Picasso's cubist explorations and considered his work—like Gertrude's—"the most God-almighty rubbish that is to be found." He was growing bored with Matisse's painting. He was even beginning to judge Cézanne a "squeezed lemon," an opinion which later caused Picasso to remark, "You can bet that Leo never tasted a drop of that juice." Leo grew increasingly remote. On the Saturday nights he retreated to an adjoining room. "He had tired of the mob," says the critic-painter Walter Pach. "He wanted to talk stomach-ache and politics and esthetics—but mostly stomach-ache."

The inevitable divorce between Leo and Gertrude came in 1914. Dr. Barnes received the most succinct account. Leo, whom he met on the street, told him he was moving to Italy. "I can't stand Gertrude. She's crazy," he explained. When Barnes told Gertrude he heard Leo was moving, she said, "That's fine. You know, he's crazy."

It was an oversimplified explanation, but like most oversimplifications, it had truth in it. Two more neurotic personalities would be hard to find. The fact that Leo was so bogged down by his neuroses that his talents and capacities were rendered almost impotent and that Gertrude so accepted and reveled in hers that they determined a whole extrovert way of life did not make the situation any easier. She demanded constant, extravagant praise of herself and the extension of herself in her writing. But Leo found her prose gawkish gibberish, the result, he claimed, of her inability to compose a lucid sentence. He, in turn, accustomed to being the master of the relationship, resented her growing independence, and though his demands were less flamboyant than hers, his need for ego-building admiration was no less insatiable.

He had another oversimplified explanation for their break: "Gertrude and I are just the contrary. She's basically stupid and I'm basically intelligent . . . She was practically inaccessible to ideas and I was accessible to nothing else." And here, too, there was truth.

Dispassionate thoroughness was Leo's hallmark. Cerebrally, relentlessly, he pursued whatever subject hooked his questing mind, whether a faddish theory of starvation to cure "appetitelessness," the ways to cook zucchini (he achieved twenty-seven, including one recipe with walnuts) or the precise definition of poetry as distinguished from prose. Gertrude, on the other hand, greedily embraced everything and anything. She gave herself expansively and jovially to all relationships—whether the subject was Bertrand Russell or a naïve doughboy. Though her enthusiasms might wear themselves out and her friendships end in quarrels, she trusted first sight and first instinct. Paintings, for Leo, were essentially only instruments for philosophizing and analysis; for Gertrude, who enjoyed artists even more than art, they were the revealing expressions of creative personalities.

Like all other divorcees, Leo and Gertrude divided their personal property. Leo took most of the Renaissance furniture. Thereafter, Gertrude filled 27 rue de Fleurus with chintz and more amply commodious chairs. Leo was to get most of the Renoirs and

Matisses; Gertrude was to keep most of the Picassos and almost everything else. The Cézannes were to be divided. After reviewing their agreement, Leo wrote her, "I hope that we will all live happily ever after and maintain our respective and due proportions while sucking gleefully our respective oranges."

Leo's orange was not particularly juicy. Soon after the separation he wrote a few articles for the *New Republic* and a dense, dreary book called *The A.B.C. of Aesthetics*. But it was to his neuroses that he applied himself most strenuously.

He decided that he was subject to three major complexes: an inferiority complex, a castration complex and a pariah complex. He was equally devoted to all three. Like Edwardian ladies who carried their pug dogs with them everywhere, so Leo bore his complexes with him and petted them publicly. Freud was not yet fashionable when Leo first heard of him, before World War I, but he felt the Viennese's theories were what he was waiting for. He tried his own analysis. Then he underwent treatment with two Freudians in America in 1915, but he did not think much of it, remarking later that he wondered where psychoanalysts kept their successful cases. "They must keep them in safe deposit vaults," he concluded. He became intrigued with Trigant Burrow's revolutionary idea of group analysis. But he finally worked out his own system, acting himself as interlocutor and witness.

It became an overpowering absorption, prosecuted with such thoroughness that he finally claimed he could hear his own screams as he emerged from his mother's womb. It was a pitiful, painful odyssey. In 1920 he wrote, "I have exorcised the great fear." In 1930, "I have finally resolved the problems of my neurosis." In 1935, "I finally decided at six o'clock this morning that I was completely cured of my neurosis." In 1947, at the age of seventy-four, he felt he finally had his "feet on bottom," and he did, indeed, face the fact of having intestinal cancer with gallant equanimity.

Gertrude, meanwhile, pursued "gloire" ever more fervently. In

Alice B. Toklas she found companion, disciple, amanuensis, protector, housekeeper, general manager and a talented needleworker, who covered footstools and chairs with cubist paintings translated into petit point. Miss Toklas and Miss Stein made an even more astonishing-looking pair than had Leo and Gertrude. Alice B. Toklas' intent little face, sharp as a raccoon's, and her black-clad figure contrasted with Gertrude Stein's imposing bulk and her large face which, under its short, mannish haircut, began to look at once imperial and peasant-wise. Once in Spain, so her recent biographer, Elizabeth Sprigge, relates, she was mistaken for a bishop who was expected in a certain little town, and the villagers queued to kiss her ring. When she made her triumphal lecture tour in America in 1935, crowds gaped at the voluminous lady who wore a peaked hat and elaborately brocaded and embroidered cerise vests under squarish brown tweed suits and walked with a rollicking gait.

Seriously and earnestly she poured out torrents of prose and sportingly faced the struggles of getting it published. She had absolute faith in its worth and bitterly resented the fact that the little magazines *transition* and *Transatlantic Review* paid as much attention to James Joyce as to Gertrude Stein. She had her disciples as well as her detractors. One critic would call her "The Mother Goose of Montparnasse" and another described her prose as "Chinese water torture: it never stops and is always the same." But still another would insist that she was "a sort of Typhoid Mary of prose style, infecting to some degree a lively percentage of those who came within range of her wondrously commonsensical mind," and E. M. Forster maintained, "There is nothing to ridicule in such an experiment as hers."

But whether she was taken seriously or ridiculed, the important fact is that she became, within her lifetime, as "historical" as even she had wished. In the late twenties, among the eggheads, the sentence from her "An Elucidation," "Suppose, to suppose, suppose a rose is a rose is a rose is a rose," became a cliché. In the mid-thirties, after the American production of *Four Saints in Three Acts* (with Virgil Thomson's scintillating score and Florine Strettheimer's delectable décor), "Pigeons on the grass, alas!" became a part of common campus lingo.

After Leo's departure and the end of World War I, many of the old friends were gone and the sense of pioneering diminished, but in their own ways, Gertrude and Michael and Sarah carried on.

The Michael Steins, with their divorcée friend Gabrielle Osorio, moved into the rue de la Tour. Their Matisse collection was depleted. They had yielded to the artist's persuasion and allowed nineteen of their great Matisses to go to Germany in 1917 for a one-man show. When the United States entered the war, the paintings were expropriated and the German dealer greedily bought them up at low prices. After the war, the Steins' friend Purrmann tried to get them back, but through further chicanery on the dealer's part, the paintings ended up in the hands of the two Scandinavian collectors who had been angling for them for years. The missing nineteen hardly made a dent in the Matisse treasure that the Michael Steins still owned—including the 1916 portrait of Sarah with her warm, wide-eyed, heart-shaped face, and Michael with his detached, reliable look—but the Michael Steins began partially to make good their loss by buying still more Matisses.

Michael, who had enjoyed the South of France during the war, began to get restive in Paris. Sarah, a doting and overprotective mother, wanted to stay in Paris to be near their son, Allan. They compromised on a Paris suburb, Garches. At an exhibition in 1925, Michael Stein and Mme. Osorio were intrigued by the photograph of a house by the young Swiss architect Le Corbusier. They approached him about building their house at Garches. Thorny, vain and independent even as a young man, the talented Le Corbusier viewed his first big private job with skepticism. "I have to be very careful when I take clients," he announced, "so that they won't spoil my house with their furniture."

Although Le Corbusier was making chairs of metal pipe, the Renaissance furniture that the Steins had bought in Florence in 1904 somehow passed muster. Le Corbusier built them a flat-roofed house, with floors that cantilevered out from interior exposed posts. It had an "open" plan, ribbon windows and so many terraces that it was named "Les Terraces." It was one of the first of what he called "machines for living" (a phrase with which his detractors have hounded him ever since, although he wrote at that same time that " 'a machine for living' was a step on the way to architecture," a "credo" that would lead to poetical expression). The neighbors jeered at what, in their most polite moments, they called "a box with windows." But Les Terraces attracted a large enough number of international intellectuals to satisfy the local Madame de Staël (who served them homemade ice cream on Sunday afternoons). Le Corbusier and Matisse met at Garches. The architect had not thought too highly of the painter until he heard Matisse remark to his host, "This young man has talent." Thereafter Le Corbusier referred to Matisse as "a great master."

Meanwhile, Gertrude's salons were flourishing. Everybody who was somebody continued to come to 27 rue de Fleurus—and so did everybody who thought he was somebody and everybody who was "nobody"—young artists, young writers, young musicians, sightseers, curiosity seekers, and the doughboys of World War I —as G.I.'s would come after World War II.

Where Leo had abandoned modern art, Gertrude took it up. In pinning down Leo's position as an art collector, the scholar Alfred H. Barr, Jr., never an extravagant man, reached the apogee of guarded exactitude: "For two brief years, between 1905 and 1907, he was possibly the most discerning connoisseur and collector of twentieth century painting in the world." Gertrude's contribution could be less precisely pinpointed and her impact was more forceful.

Indeed, the first of her writings which had been published in America were "Portraits" of Matisse and Picasso. They had appeared in 1912 in a special edition of *Camera Work,* published by Alfred Stieglitz. By the end of his life, Stieglitz, still evangelistic and ardent, wrapped himself not only in a flowing black cape but also in an enveloping cloak of mystic poetics and enjoyed being the cult figure for solemnly adoring disciples. In the early years before World War I, he was an energetic, gifted and imaginative photographer, who had opened a little gallery at 291 Fifth Avenue in order, courageously, to exhibit photography as a fine art. (So advanced was the notion of photography as an art that Edward Steichen had to support himself by painting in order to have time and money for photography.) By 1908, spurred by Steichen, Stieglitz was expanding his gallery to include work by the advanced painters and sculptors. Matisse had been given his first American show at "291"—his first one-man show outside Paris. Picasso, Braque, and the Americans John Marin, Charles Demuth and Georgia O'Keeffe (whom Stieglitz married) had all made American debuts under Stieglitz' aegis. "291," with its white walls and revolutionary paintings and photographs, was one of the rare and lively meeting places for the early defenders of modern art in America.

It was reported later that Stieglitz accepted Gertrude Stein's "Portraits" of Matisse and Picasso principally because he did not immediately understand them. Nor, indeed, did a great many other people. The insistently repeated statements that Matisse was "one that is clearly expressing something" and that Picasso was "one having something coming out of him something having meaning" did little to make these artists more intelligible to those who were finding their art somewhat obscure. Yet these "Portraits"—like the dozens of others that Gertrude Stein was to write about the dozens of other artists who, at least temporarily, captured her interest—were like publicity releases. In their curious, monotonous way, they had some instinctive sense of each artist's art. Their subjects gained stature for the limited, but taste-setting, audience which read them.

Gertrude Stein tried, after Leo's departure, to keep pace with the new art. Excited about Picasso's cubism, she became a devoted admirer, purchaser and friend of the lyric Spanish cubist, Juan Gris. She liked Picabia, who did a portrait that made her look as if she had been shaved for the last mile, and Jacques Lipchitz, who made a handsome sculpture that gave her majesty.

Although she far outdistanced Leo in her appreciation of the cubist and post-cubist painters, as the critic, James Thrall Soby, points out, "like nearly all collectors, she was capable of appreciating to the full only one generation of living artists." She kept trying to hitch on to the younger generation and she knew and encouraged a number of young men. One was Pavel Tchelitchew, the one she preferred of the group she called "the russians." She pointed pridefully to the fact that "Picasso had been drawing three heads in one. Soon the russian was painting three figures in one." But she quickly had enough of each of these younger men, and the only one whose work she bought in quantity was Sir Francis Rose—a distinctly minor artist—of whom she confessed she liked the man as well as his art.

That you were dropped by Gertrude Stein was unimportant; that she had taken you up was what counted. She had no doubts about her capacity to be the arbiter of modern art. Her opinions were expressed with the finality of papal encyclicals. She was so much the energizer, so much the catalyst, so much the overbearing spokesman, so much the taste-maker for the hordes of pilgrims that flocked to see her and her collection, that, as one critic remarked, "It must be very hard to paint unless you know Gertrude Stein." After her death, Yale University arranged an exhibition called "Pictures for a Picture of Gertrude Stein," which included paintings by all the artists about whom she had written. Almost every important painter of her time was represented.

In 1935, Gertrude Stein's autobiography of her alter ego, Alice

B. Toklas, was published. An easy, entertaining, gossipy book, it was a vast popular success. "That farrago of rather clever anecdote, stupid brag and general bosh," Leo called it. "There is almost nothing in the period before the war with which I am not acquainted, and there is nothing that she has written that is true." It was an opinion which, in somewhat milder form, was also held by, among others, Matisse, Braque and Tristan Tzara, who formalized their protest in *transition,* and by Ernest Hemingway, who never forgave her for what he considered gross falsifications.

Perhaps it was the combined success of Gertrude's *Autobiography* and her American lecture tour that spurred Leo to settle down to write *Appreciation: Painting, Poetry and Prose.* He was hampered by the fact that she had "first innings" and "told or mistold most of the amusing anecdotes," but he did set forth, in his final chapters, *his* version of the pre-World War I days at 27 rue de Fleurus. More significantly, the book is his esthetic testament. "Appreciation," for him, "names all the ways in which we regard those things that we do not define, measure or directly use" and art is that which "renews appreciation." With a directness and clarity rare in the cant-ridden, cliché-sodden field of esthetics, he develops his thesis and lucidly explains his own appreciations and nonappreciations.

While his book was in the publisher's hands, on July 27, 1946, Gertrude Stein died of cancer. Leo read of her death in *Newsweek.* He wrote to Dr. Barnes, "It surprised me, for she seemed of late to be exceedingly alive. I can't say it touches me. I had lost not only all regard, but all respect for her."

His own book appeared, nearly a year later, on June 24, 1947. Gertrude's massive shadow reached from the grave to obscure his limelight. Almost without exception, the book reviewers chose this occasion to discuss the relationship of Gertrude and Leo, to contrast their personalities and to compare their accounts of the heroic days of early-twentieth-century art. By the time the disappointing reviews reached him in his villa at Florence, he knew he, too,

Mrs. Potter Palmer, 1905

MRS. POTTER PALMER

1850 - 1918

Mrs. Palmer, 1892   Mr. Palmer, 1892

The Palmers' Castle, Chicago, 1882–85

The Picture Gallery, 1892

Renoir:
"Two Little Circus Girls"

Zorn: "Mrs. Potter Palmer," 1893

Zorn: "Isabella Stewart Gardner," 1894

MRS. POTTER PALMER

1850 - 1918

Mrs. Gardner,
1888

Mancini:
"Mr. Gardner," 1895

Sargent:
"Mrs. Gardner," 1922

ISABELLA STEWART GARDNER

1840 - 1924

Fenway Court, Boston:
The Titian Room

Fenway Court, Boston:
The Court

Sargent: "Isabella Stewart Gardner," 1888

In Egypt, 1909

In Rome, 1907

J. PIERPONT MORGAN

1837 - 1913

At Göttingen, 1857

Morgan Library, New York, 1902–06   The West Room

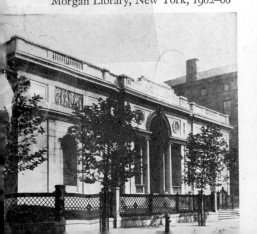

J. Pierpont Morgan, 1903

Rand: "Benjamin Altman" (1840–1913)

Henry Clay Frick (1849–1919)

Sargent: "P.A.B. Widener" (1834–1915)

John: "Jos. E. Widener" (1872–1943)

JOHN G. JOHNSON

1841 - 1917

Van Eyck: "St. Francis"

Haeseler: "John G. Johnson"

The Drawing Room, Philadelphia, 1880

In Japan

In Egypt

In Capri

CHARLES LANG FREER

1856 - 1919

Freer's House, Detroit, 1892–1904

Whistler: The Peacock Room

Charles Lang Freer, 1916

Memorial to Freer, Kyoto

Courbet:
"Woman with Parrot"

El Greco:
"Cardinal de Guevara"

The Picture Gallery, 1890

MR. AND MRS.
H. O. HAVEMEYER
1847 - 1907
1855 - 1925

The Music Room, 1890

Mr. and Mrs. Henry O. Havemeyer, around 1898

Picasso:
"Leo Stein," 1906

Picasso:
"Gertrude Stein," 1906

Matisse:
"Michael Stein," 1916

Matisse:
"Sarah Stein," 1916

Leo and Gertrude's Apartment:
27 rue de Fleurus, 1907

Alice B. Toklas and Gertrude:
5 rue Christine

Leo, Allan, Gertrude, Sarah, Michael Stein

THE FOUR STEINS

Michael and Sarah's Apartment:
3 rue Madame, 1907

Le Corbusier:
Michael Stein House, Garches, 1927

Quinn, Fernande, Picasso, Roché   Satie, Quinn, Brancusi, Roché

John: "John Quinn," 1923

Quinn Memorial Show, 1926

The Armory Show, New York, 1913

John Quinn

JOHN QUINN

1870 - 1924

Quinn Family, Fostoria, Ohio

Miss Dreier with
Coco and Brancusi's "Bird"

Miss Dreier with
Marcel Duchamp

KATHERINE SOPHIE DREIER
1877 - 1952

Library, West Redding, Conn., with paintings by Duchamp

Katherine S. Dreier

Dreier Family, Brooklyn, 1885

Grace and Edward Root, 1918

In Texas, 1906

EDWARD WALES ROOT

1884 - 1956

The Homestead, Clinton, N.Y., 1849

Edward Wales Root

Burchfield:
"Childhood's Garden," 1917

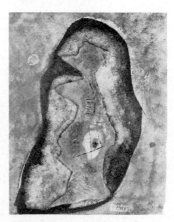

Stamos:
"Monolith," 1947

JOSEPH H. HIRSHHORN
1899-

Hirshhorn at School, 1913

The Gallery, New York

Hirshhorn in New York Office

View from Hirshhorn's Desk

Mrs. Webb with Hunting Trophies

1958, TIME, Inc., Richard Meed
SPORTS ILLUSTRATED

Mr. J. Watson Webb
at Westbury, Long Island

Cassatt:
"Mrs. Havemeyer and Electra," 1896

Shelburne Museum, Shelburne, Vt.

Schumatoff: "Electra Webb"

ELECTRA HAVEMEYER WEBB

1888 -

"Mary O'Connor"   The "Ti" and Lighthouse, Shelburne Museum

Parsons: "Cunne Shote"

Remington:
"Coming Through the Rye"

Hopewell Culture: Raven Pipe

The Private Gallery, Tulsa, Okla.

Thomas Gilcrease

Gilcrease, 1910

THOMAS GILCREASE

1890 -

Lenbach: "Peggy," 1902   Tanguy: "Peggy," 1939

"Art of This Century," N.Y., 1942

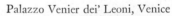

Palazzo Venier dei' Leoni, Venice

Peggy Guggenheim, 1955

PEGGY GUGGENHEIM

1898 -

THE ROCKEFELLERS

The Cloisters,
Fort Tryon Park, N.Y.

M. Zorach:
The Rockefeller Family

David Rockefeller's Living Room
with Cézanne and Seurat

Abby Aldrich Rockefeller

John D. Rockefeller, Jr.

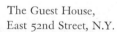

The Guest House,
East 52nd Street, N.Y.

Blanchette and
John D. Rockefeller III

Nelson A. Rockefeller

Picasso:
"Girl with Mandolin"

NELSON A. ROCKEFELLER

1908 -

Calder: "Mobile"
in Pocantico Grounds

Museum of Primitive Art,
West 54th Street, N.Y.

had cancer. One letter cheered him: Dr. Barnes found *Apprecia-tion* "a knock-out" and made it compulsory reading for the students in his unfriendly fastness in Merion, Pennsylvania.

Still trying to fathom and analyze the differences between Gertrude and himself, Leo Stein died on July 29, 1947.

In 1935, the same year that Gertrude's *Autobiography of Alice B. Toklas* appeared and she made her triumphal tour, the Michael Steins moved back to the United States. Michael had been yearning for a long time to say "Good morning" instead of *"Bonjour."* After Hitler seized power, he insisted upon their departure. It took a long time to sell the Le Corbusier house—as Gabrielle Osorio says, "Those who had the money did not have the taste"—but finally they did. Then, accompanied by the Cone sisters, who they felt "knew the ropes of travel," the expatriate couple, with Gabrielle Osorio, Allan's ten-year-old son, Danny, some of the Renaissance furniture, and all the Matisses, came home. Soon they settled in a large, rambling, nondescript house in Palo Alto, California.

No one jeered at *this* house. This time, no one ridiculed the Matisses. When they were exhibited at the San Francisco Museum in 1935, no one paid them much heed. Michael Stein, always the least assuming and most stable of the lot, died of cancer in 1938. As far as the community was concerned, Sarah Stein was a nice, elderly widow, taking care, not only of her grandson, Danny, but also of two other very young grandchildren, Allan's children by a second marriage, who came to America for the duration. Madame de Staël had become Grandma. But soon, as it always does, the word got around. Stanford University professors, Stanford students, pilgrims from the East, museum directors and collectors began to call.

By this time, Sarah, too, had assumed a somewhat pyramidal, monolithic figure. Her hair made a frowsy halo around her head. Her face was still alert and intelligent; her manner friendly.

Eagerly she led her visitors through reminiscent, anecdotal tours. Unpinning the safety pin and unwrapping the bath towel in which she kept them wrapped, she would pick out Matisse letters and read them aloud. Proust-like, she was transported back to the days when she was not only student and perceptive patron, but also Matisse's very dear friend and confidante.

Pointing to the "Woman with a Hat," which Gertrude had sold her in 1918 for $500, she would exclaim at its vibrant colors and muse about it. "And to think that when she posed for those frenzies of colors, Madame Matisse was wearing a black dress, with only a small piece of orange ribbon at the neck, and a silly black hat loaded with black feathers!" In the dining room, she poured tea, appropriately, under Matisse's wall-filling canvas of a tea party of 1918. Her eyes glinted with pleasure. "Guillaume Apollinaire was trying to buy it for another client. But he wanted Matisse to change the eye of the woman on the right because he said it looked unfinished. I grabbed it as it was. Whenever people told Matisse something looked unfinished, he'd say, 'I'll finish it in the next picture.'" She showed the drawing Matisse had swapped her for the samovar in the painting; a Picasso drawing traded for one of her incredible shapeless kimonos; and the vast, unexpected treasure purchased in those brave, remote days. Her allegiance to Stanford grew steadily. In the mid-forties, she changed her will so that the collection would go, intact, to that university.

But by 1947, things had changed. Michael, Gertrude and Leo were dead. Sarah Stein lived on in two things: the Matisses and her twenty-year-old grandson, Danny. They turned out to be incompatible loves. Danny, with a talent for writing, was spoiled and undisciplined. He had developed a taste for race horses. It was an expensive and unproductive taste, but his grandmother indulged it and even bought him a ranch. By 1948, the Matisses were going to foot the bills.

Sarah Stein's mind began to wander and cloud. Devoted friends like Mrs. Walter Haas had begged her, were she ever forced to sell, to let them have first choice of the paintings. They would, of course, pay her fair prices, and they knew that, in an increasingly confused state, she was no match for certain dealers who had begun to descend like vultures upon her. In 1949, she did sell "Woman with a Hat" and the sketch for "Joy of Life" to Mrs. Haas, in whose apartment they now hang handsomely with works by Braque, Henry Moore, Rouault and exquisite Oriental and Gothic objects. A few other paintings were also sold to friends.

But behind everyone's back, she fell prey to certain calculating dealers. It is said that she sold over two dozen Matisse bronzes for the shockingly low sum of $750; that, after finally winning an argument for a reasonable price for an oil painting, she would "throw in" some Picasso and Matisse drawings. She allegedly parted with a fine Cézanne for $4,500, because, as she explained, "The dealer told me he'd give me every cent he had for it and that was all he had." It was visibly breaking her heart to sell the beloved Matisses. But however much she loved Matisse, she loved Danny more. "Art isn't really so important," she would bravely tell her friends.

As the sad debacle swept on, Sarah Stein's mind deteriorated. During the last three years of her life she was rarely lucid. Matisse had been keeping up a loyal correspondence. In 1951, he sent her an illustrated book via Elise Haas. Its inscription read: *Á Madame Michel Stein, mon amie qui m'a si souvent soutenu dans mon faiblesse. H. Matisse.* She was beyond comprehension. On September 15, 1953, Sarah Stein, the last of the fascinating quartet, quietly died.

After Sarah Stein's death, Elise Haas bought the monumental Matisse portrait of Sarah, and a Chicago friend, Nathan Cummings, bought the portrait of Michael. They were presented to the San Francisco Museum as the nucleus of "The Sarah and Michael

Stein Memorial Collection," magnets, it was hoped, to attract as many as possible of the objects of the collection which had had very real and personal meaning to its owners.

Leo's collection had also been dispersed. Since self-analysis is not a lucrative employment, Leo had gradually parted with almost all his possessions. In 1947 he sold one of his last remaining objects, a Picasso drawing, to pay for radium treatments.

Gertrude had always hated to part with anything. Her drawers and closets were such nests of profusion that back in the thirties her friend Thornton Wilder persuaded her to start packing stuff off to Yale University and to will that university her manuscripts, letters and memorabilia. According to her friend Janet Flanner, Gertrude felt she had no right to sell art except to buy a necessity and then would sell to suit the necessity. She sold some paintings to cover living expenses during the first war, others to pay for the installation of electric heating, for the printing of an edition of her books, and, in 1937, for the move with Alice B. Toklas to a new apartment. But she managed to hold on to most of her art. She made specific disposition of a single picture in her will. Picasso's portrait of her was given and bequeathed to the Metropolitan Museum of Art, whose venerability must presumably have seemed to impart the proper "historical" tone to subject and artist. Most of the rest of her collection remains still on the walls of the rue Christine apartment, with Alice B. Toklas as consecrated custodian. At her death, the art will go to Allan's three children.

Gertrude, Leo and Michael and Sarah Stein were not collectors of modern masterpieces. Dozens of their successors can more justly claim that title. They acquired many fascinating and illuminating paintings, but only a very few were of the first order of magnitude. Yet the impact of the Steins was formidable. They altered the whole atmosphere of modern art. After the Steins, no self-respecting intellectual could ignore it. By becoming patrons of the great modern masters at crucial moments in their careers, the Steins gave these artists—especially Picasso and Matisse—influential boosts. The catalytic action of their salons and of Gertrude's writings brought these artists prominence and clients. The Steins were hardly everyone's dish of tea: they often offended sensibilities far less refined than Berenson's. Roché, their great introducer, had the tact, for instance, not to introduce the collector John Quinn to Gertrude, but even Quinn's way had been prepared by the Steins. When, in 1913, modern art burst upon the American public in the notorious Armory Show in New York, some of those who had helped select it and many of those who supported it had received initiation or indoctrination at 27 rue de Fleurus and 23 rue Madame.

Patron

JOHN QUINN

By the time he died, in 1924, at the age of fifty-five, John Quinn had become the twentieth century's most important patron of living literature and art.

He had gathered a stupendous library of over 12,000 items. There were first editions of the work of almost every significant modern writer and fine editions of the classics. The manuscripts ranged from all of Joseph Conrad to James Joyce's *Ulysses*. He had been one of the organizers of the Armory Show, the exhibition of modern art which jolted the American public as no other artistic event has before or since. His private collection of painting and sculpture had become braver and better than any other. Letters, which were to fill thirteen volumes of typescript, were testimony to the friendship, the patronage, the assistance he had given to dozens of great literary and artistic—and many political—figures of our time. He counted among his close, true friends Lady Gregory, the Yeats family and Joseph Conrad; Ezra Pound, T. S. Eliot and James Joyce; the musician Erik Satie and the statesman Poincaré; the artists Walt Kuhn, Jacob Epstein and Augustus John; Derain, Segonzac, Matisse, Picasso, Brancusi.

But the library was sold at auction in 1921. After his death, his family drew a silken curtain of silence around his life. The paintings and sculptures were dispersed here and abroad. Kept behind locked doors in the New York Public Library, the fabulous correspondence is available only to qualified students. And today the name of John Quinn is all but unknown.

John Quinn, tall and commanding, had a clean, clerical look and a profile as fine as that on a Roman coin. He was an extraordinary man—exhilarating, fascinating and often exasperating, a man of magnetic charm, Rabelaisian wit and flashing tempers that lowered his level brows and turned his marine blue eyes dark. Nothing about him was tepid or moderate. Capable of benevolence and tenderness and of nourishing friendships, he could also storm into black rages and Napoleonic insistence (it was said he discharged a law clerk every month). He was a Don Quixote, passionately magnifying his fervid enthusiasms and his unremitting prejudices.

Whenever Quinn irritated him, his artist friend Walt Kuhn, with the snobbism of a born New Yorker, would remark acidly, "The trouble with you is you never got away from Tiffin, Ohio." Kuhn's taunt was not entirely fair. Quinn had been born, in 1870, in that small town on the Sandusky River, but by the time Kuhn first met him—around 1910—he had already become a cosmopolite. Yet Kuhn's barb always stung. Quinn's loyalty to his simple middle-class Irish parents back in Ohio put him doubly on the defensive.

John Quinn's first escape from the small-town small talk which suited the other members of his family as they rocked on the porch of their white frame house, was into the blood-and-thunder tales of pirates and the adventures of Deadwood Dick and Calamity Jane. His next idols were Helen of Troy and Buffalo Bill. He was born a little late to gaze upon her famous face, but, at the age of thirteen, he did see his other idol, traveling a hundred miles by himself from Fostoria, to which the Quinns had moved, to the town where the Buffalo Bill show was playing.

Soon he outgrew swashbuckling heroes and dime novels, but he had developed a lifelong zest for reading and a lightning-swift memory. One morning in 1922 he received from T. S. Eliot a first copy of *The Waste Land*. He summoned a lovely lady with a melodious voice to read the lengthy poem to him while he shaved. Thereafter, he could recite it without an error. He maddened his dinner guests by completing the Shakespearian and Latin quotations over which they hesitated and he regularly confounded his opponents in court with his infallible memory.

At seventeen, he was on his way. After a year at the University of Michigan, he became secretary to ex-Governor Charles Foster of Ohio. He promptly fell in love with the boss's daughter, but he did not ask Annie Foster to marry him. The Fosters, whose home town of Fostoria was named after Annie's grandfather, were rather high-toned, and even though theirs was an ex-gubernatorial mansion, they were somewhat choosy about who was received in it. John Quinn refused to subject his mother to a possible snub.

It all turned out for the best, for he soon outgrew Annie Foster, whose persistent small-town chronicles of sickness and death irritated him for years. He was, moreover, temperamentally unsuited for marriage. The more worldly and attractive and sought after he became, the more cynical he grew about it. Although he adored women, he adroitly avoided the altar. His many conquests included the aristocratic and the "violet-crowned," as well as a troublesome harpy who wrote to him once from Naples, "I am sitting here looking at Vesuvius. Vesuvius is looking at me. We are both burning."

When President Harrison appointed Annie's father Secretary of the Treasury in 1891, Quinn accompanied the ex-governor to Washington. Studying at night, he took his law degree and then used his savings for a year at Harvard under Thayer, Santayana and William James. He entered the New York bar during its heroic days, got involved with the sensational insurance company investigations that were rocking New York, and in 1906, when he was thirty-six years old, founded his own firm.

Nothing pleased him more about the law than the chance to use it, like a knight-errant, in tilt against oppressors. At Harvard, when a policeman unjustifiably laid a hand on him, he speedily knocked the officer down so that he would be arrested and have a chance to vindicate in court the delightful right of any citizen to do likewise. He enjoyed playing Lancelot in the courts for the Irish Players in 1911, when the self-righteous sent police to close Synge's *Playboy of the Western World,* and jousting against the Society for the Suppression of Vice in 1921 by defending Joyce's *Ulysses.*

He was particularly effective about an oppression that hit him personally. The tariff law of 1909 had finally exempted from duty art over one hundred years old. But as Quinn heatedly pointed out to several congressional committees, this leniency benefited only such wealthy gentlemen as Messrs. Morgan, Widener and Altman, who bought expensive old masters and, as he once said, "kept their optics on the Coptics." The restriction discriminated not only against those artists who were still alive and kicking, but also against those—like himself—who were helping to keep them alive and not kicking.

Almost single-handedly he got the tariff law changed and was largely responsible for its definition of art. Several years later he was hoist by his own petard. He bought some ceramic plaques and jars by Rouault. The customs officers looked at the definition of art and, finding no mention of ceramic sculpture, declared that these jars were not works of art. They were, therefore, although totally useless, objects of utility and, as such, dutiable. Quinn's fury flared. When he discovered that he was being penalized by his own definition of art, he grew even angrier. He said he felt like the Irishman who hurled a rock into a group of Irishmen, ran up the hill like the devil to watch the brawl and said to a passer-by, "See that fight down there? I started it!" He fought the case in the customs court before Justice Waite. When he lost, he carried the fight to a higher court and won. The fact that he witheringly referred to the Justice throughout as "The Appraiser" may have left an indelible mark on that honorable gentleman.

In 1938, it was Justice Waite who gave a new, liberal interpretation to the definition of sculpture in the tariff law. The issue this time was not ceramic sculpture, but Brancusi's bronze, "Bird in Flight," which had been imported by the Steins' friend Edward Steichen. The tariff law defined a sculpture as an object that truly represented human or animal form. Uncle Sam's agents diligently examined this sleek bronze object, but finding that it looked more like the shaft of a propeller than a bird, they ruled that it was not art but a dutiable manufacture in metal. Steichen produced an illustrious parade of witnesses in the customs court. They insisted that it *was* sculpture and that it *did* represent a bird, although Steichen himself confessed that if he "would see it in a forest," he "would not take a shot at it." Justice Waite said some difficulty might indeed be encountered in associating the object with a bird, but he recognized that a "so-called new school of art" had been developing and as this was the original production of a professional sculptor he let it pass as art. Quinn's "Appraiser" became a limited hero.

Though Quinn was a fiery fighter in the courts against oppression, he was cool-headed, astute and respected by the respectable in corporation and financial law. He was sole counsel for the National Bank of Commerce and principal legal adviser to men of such substantial means as Thomas Fortune Ryan, who paid him not only a handsome annual retainer, but also the social compliment of sharing with him the crimson Renaissance brocade he had brought from Italy for the upholstery of his own palatial furniture. It was from the virtually one-man practice of corporation and financial law that John Quinn derived the income he spent on the art and artists of his time.

Law was his livelihood, but in his Irishness John Quinn first found his identity and Ireland was his path to splendor. A supporter of the Home Rule movement and a starry-eyed advocate of the Irish Literary Revival even before his first trip to Dublin in 1902, he swept into Ireland's most stirring and romantic period.

Chivalrously he placed his charm, his intelligence, his influence, his enthusiasm and his money at the disposal of the cause. All were welcome. Accepted like manna from a well-endowed heaven, he was catapulted into the center of the charmed circle. The young man who once feared his mother might be snubbed at Fostoria, became the tenderly cherished favorite of Lady Augusta Gregory, the forceful leader of the Irish Players, who warmed to his beguiling smile and called him "The Wonder of the Western World." He breakfasted and lunched with William Butler Yeats, tramped through Dublin with the poet-painter George Russell (AE), argued with George Moore and admired his Manet and Degas paintings, busied himself with Gaelic leaders, met James Stephens, Arthur Symons, John Synge, and heard James Joyce read an unpublished poem after warning his listeners that he cared not a straw what they would think of it.

Later, in America, Quinn railed against his Irish dinner guests who, he said, having been starved so much of their lives, paid more attention to the food than the conversation. But apparently on home ground the culinary attractions were not so distracting. He found the talk at the dinner parties at Dublin's Hotel Shelburne sparkling. And all the while, he was buying books and manuscripts as well as paintings by English and, especially, Irish artists.

He had found his world, though its horizons would widen, and discovered his way of life. As a patron, he could enlarge and intensify his existence. He could blend with the magic of genius.

John Quinn collected the artists along with their art. One of his early acquisitions was the English painter Augustus John, a Francophile who in 1911 led Quinn out of Anglo-Celtic insularity into the artists' cafés of Montparnasse, traveled with him through Romanesque churches in the South of France and introduced him to champagne. He also introduced him to the dealers Durand-Ruel and Vollard. Quinn was regularly absorbing most of John's output (by 1915 he had the dubious distinction of owning the largest collection of John in the world), and the artist did not mind sharing his patron with such of the safely dead and noncompetitive as Cézanne, Gauguin and Van Gogh, whose work Quinn bought.

Augustus John's American counterpart in Quinn's life was Walt Kuhn. Quinn met Kuhn through Frederick James Gregg, the art critic of the *New York Sun,* an Irishman as redoubtable and impassioned as Quinn himself, who was making American art *his* crusade.

Kuhn painted circus folk and apples in a tough, objective way. Quinn bought so many of these paintings that some of the less favored artists called him "Kuhn's milk-cow." Quinn liked the man as well as the art. Kuhn's hard-boiled lust for life appealed to him.

The two tall figures—the one dressed in artist's tweeds, big-featured, with high, broad cheekbones, the other with his fine, ascetic head rising like a statue from the pedestal of his high stiff collar—were a familiar, almost conspiratorial pair. Quinn usually lunched at the Bankers' Club, but he would sit late into the night at the Round Table at the artists' hangout, Mouquin's. He and Kuhn drank beer under the pearly nudes by Bouguereau and Correggio in the old Hoffman House bar and smoked ten-cent perfectos from the Hoffman House box with its world famous nymph-and-satyr trademark (a favorite comic lithograph of the time showed a hobo gazing at the nymph and saying, "I've been all

over the world looking for that creek, but darned if I can find it").
They appeared as pirates at the Kit Kat Klub balls.

Quinn's spirit warmed to the free and easy camaraderie of artists and writers and his vanity was soothed by their respectful—
and often grateful—friendships. He was difficult in many relationships. He was impatient with stupidity, sensitive to criticism
and enraged by inefficiency. He would reduce a secretary to tears
if pencils were not properly sharpened, and deliver orations, like
some wrathful Demosthenes, to moving men who neglected to
wear gloves while handling Brancusi's brass sculptures.

He was more humble, more careful in his friendships with artists. But even these were subjected to more than ordinary strain if
he felt "driven" or taken advantage of. At one point he turned on
Augustus John, who, it was said, was making derisive remarks
about Quinn's disloyalty in switching to living French masters.
Quinn called John "yellow, a double-dealer, an ingrate," and contemplated dumping all his John holdings on the market. Then he
relented and the deep friendship was recemented.

For years Quinn supported with both filial and financial devotion John Butler Yeats, W. B. Yeats' venerable expatriate father,
who had been holding a concentric court in New York from 1908
on. Then, at the end, when the ailing John Butler Yeats kept craftily postponing his promised return to Ireland, Quinn flew into
periodic rages, afraid the old man would die on his hands (which,
indeed, he did). But each tantrum was offset by acts of tender
kindness, and finally it was Quinn who attended to J. B. Yeats'
funeral, arranged for the old man to be buried in the Adirondack
property of a friend and paid for an appropriate tombstone.

Quinn's furies were sudden and short-lived, his repentance persuasive and his kind heart usually overflowing, so that he was most
often indulgently forgiven and the friendships survived their
scars. The final judgments of his friends agreed with William Butler Yeats': "I have known no other so full of over-flowing en-

ergy and benevolence, and this always arising out of his nature like a fountain and having the quality of his nature. I mean his benevolence expressed him as a work of art expresses the artist." He got along best, of course, with those like Kuhn, whom he respected.

It was Kuhn who got him involved as lawyer and supporter of the Armory Show, which began with the rather tame idea of showing American art. Arthur B. Davies was responsible for the change. Kuhn and the other realist painters of the founding group had little in common either artistically or socially with Davies, a reticent man who painted unicorns and languishing maidens, but, to a group in need of money, Davies had one irresistible attraction.

He was confidant and adviser to some of the wealthiest, most art-minded women in New York, who liked his schoolteacher looks and trusted his refined manners and taste. These good ladies —three of whom rumor later identified as Gertrude Vanderbilt Whitney, Miss Lillie P. Bliss and Mrs. Cornelius J. Sullivan— opened their checkbooks once again.

Davies, now in charge, changed from recluse to commander. The original idea, as Kuhn said, had been to enliven the American show with "a few of the radical things from abroad," but Davies saw a chance to confront America head-on with European modern art. Davies, Kuhn and Walter Pach, the painter and critic who was then living in Paris, were so bowled over by what they saw in Europe when they went around looking for "the radical things" that they earmarked hundreds of them to be shipped to America. When the Armory Show opened on February 17, 1913, the American paintings were a pale rim around the blazing, dominant core of art from abroad.

Under the cavernous vault of the Sixty-ninth Regiment Armory in New York, burlap-covered and evergreen-festooned partitions made a honeycomb of galleries. Within these were statues of attenuated ladies by the sculptor Lehmbruck and ovoid heads and birds by Brancusi; paintings with searing color by Matisse and the other "Wild Beasts"; paintings with cascades of black-gray-brown rectangles by Picasso and the other cubists; carnival-bright abstract designs by Léger and Picabia; dozens and dozens of astounding and astonishing things. The initiated had had a glimpse of Picasso and Matisse in the Stein salons at 27 rue de Fleurus and at the rue Madame and in Stieglitz' white-walled gallery in New York, but with the Armory Show modern art exploded like a bombshell on the American consciousness.

The press laughed, jeered and ridiculed. Brancusi's compact cube of a sculpture called "The Kiss" inspired a poem which began, "He clasped her slender cubiform / In his rectangular embrace . . ." and ended, "He kissed her squarely on the lips." Marcel Duchamp's "Nude Descending a Staircase" was the most incendiary item in the altogether combustible show. This picture, which today looks like a mild prophecy of the stroboscopic camera, was castigated as "an explosion in a shingle factory" and parodied in a cartoon of a subway rush hour called "The Rude Descending a Staircase." It particularly irked those who came to see the nude and could not find it. Eventually, *Art News* magazine offered a ten-dollar prize for anyone solving the puzzle. No one did. In the *New York Times,* Kenyon Cox called the whole show "pathological."

But news of modern art had been spread across America. It made copy for headlines and subject for conversation. Soon John Wanamaker's department store ran an advertisement announcing "Color Combinations of the Futurist Cubist Influence in Fashions," and a Tin Pan Alley hit tune was called "That Futuristic Rag."

A record-breaking 129,000 people crowded into the Armory. They, too, laughed and derided, cheered and defended. The operatic idol, Enrico Caruso, made parodies of the paintings which he tossed to the crowd. J. P. Morgan's son stormed around the galleries protesting to everyone that it was a damned outrage to have to pay a quarter to see this stuff. President Theodore Roosevelt had strong personal antipathies, but he hailed the freedom that allowed this art to be produced and exhibited. Everywhere there was fervor, excitement and heated argument.

Quinn relished the fight. The cause of modern art had become a crusade for which he could be impassioned crusader. He was not only the sponsoring committee's lawyer, but, as its most distinguished "front man," he had delivered the opening address and had written stirring articles in its defense. When he piloted such V.I.P.s as President Roosevelt through the excited crowd, he tried to charm them into acceptance of the new art.

He was the hero of the party that was held late on the night of St. Patrick's Day, when the doors closed for the last time on the clamorous public. The Armory echoed with the noisy strains of an Irish band and the staccato poppings of champagne corks (it was said that Quinn supplied the champagne). A parade of the artists and their girls, the students who had sold catalogues and served as guides, and the organizers snake-danced jubilantly through the galleries. Marching, cheering, waltzing and drinking they celebrated the victory of the revolutionary new art. In the midst of the carousing, there were speeches and toasts.

"To the Academy," one artist shouted mockingly.

John Quinn rose. "No, no! Don't you remember Captain John Philip of the *Texas?* When his guns sank a Spanish ship at Santiago, he said, 'Don't cheer, boys, the poor devils are dying.' "

The Armory Show made Quinn a real collector. Visiting it, he began to consider paintings aside from personalities. He spent $5,868.75—and since the unit prices were low, he became the possessor of a great many of the "radical things from abroad." He had bought beautiful Redons, which he particularly liked, and Segonzacs. Stimulated by the controversy, he had purchased work by those who had been special targets of attack: Brancusi, Derain, Duchamp and Duchamp-Villon. And later that year he relieved Gertrude and Leo Stein of Matisse's controversial "Blue Nude," which had been lent to the Armory Show and burned in effigy when the exhibition moved to Chicago.

Others, too, had bought. A new group of collectors began to emerge. The prices were lower, but the rivalry for pictures and prestige within the modern field would soon be as keen among the new collectors as it was among the old-master amassers who, later this same year, after J. P. Morgan's death, would descend competitively on his collection.

According to Kuhn, it was Quinn's prodigal buying that had spurred the Chicago lawyer, Arthur Jerome Eddy, to buy. Eddy was already predisposed. He was an urbane, courageous man who enjoyed shocking his stolid colleagues with his enthusiasm for the new. He had been one of Whistler's first patrons (he wrote a book about him in 1903) and had bought Manet's "Philosopher" when Manet was hardly known in America even to the Havemeyers.

It was said that Eddy was the first man in Chicago to ride a bicycle and the first man there to own an automobile. There was no question that after his trip to New York in February of 1913 he was the first person in Chicago to own paintings by the "Wild Beasts" and some of the most bewildering cubist pictures in the Armory Show. In 1914, he wrote the first book in America to deal with cubism. As the critic Milton Brown says, it reads like the impassioned plea of a defense attorney for his client, but it is still valid and informative today.

Quinn's hours at the Armory Show were crowded in after the working day and in the evenings and Sundays. He had innumerable irons in the fire, which an almost superhuman energy kept at white heat. As if he had some premonition of early death and an insatiable zest to live life fully, he drove himself hard. As Elizabeth Yeats said, "He could not be half-hearted."

His law practice was pressing. He played a role in national politics although he scorned the small-mindedness of politicians and described one Democratic bigwig as "a digestive tract, a voice, a bush of hair above each ear, glazed eyes, no will." He became influential in international affairs: he advised the British

and French ambassadors during World War I; defended the con-
stitutionality of the Trading with the Enemy Act successfully
before the Supreme Court. He was an ardent Francophile, and his
hatred of Germany and Germans was massive, second only to his
dislike for Jews. He disgorged both his prejudices once in writing
to a friend that, "Disraeli was an actor, a charlatan and a Jew;
but Disraeli fooled only a few, beginning with the old tub of guts
who was then the German Queen of England."

He found time for golf, which he played badly; horseback riding, which he did well; and walking, which was really a sort of
rapid striding that exhausted his companions. On Sundays he
would keep three secretaries simultaneously occupied around his
dining-room table. He dictated to one on legal matters, to another
about transactions for art and literature, and to the third he gave
twelve- and fourteen-page letters to artist and writer friends abroad.
He read voluminously, disposing of most books in an hour, and
diligently followed auction catalogues. He was besieged by persons
making legitimate requests and by Irish gougers. Frequently he
would blow up in profanity, vow he would never give another cent
to anyone, then make another fabulously generous—and often sentimental—gesture.

He had been too bitten by the excitement of the Armory Show
and too smitten with the artistic camaraderie it provided to give up
that sort of situation completely when the show closed. The fight
was being carried on in a number of new little galleries and societies, causing *Art News* magazine to complain in February of
1914 that there were current at that time "six exhibitions devoted
to the 'Faddists.' " For one of these John Quinn was responsible.
He had yielded easily to the persuasions of Davies, Kuhn and
Pach that he interest himself in a commercial gallery. With no
one's persuasion, except perhaps the lady's own, he chose the Carroll, at 9 East Forty-eighth Street, which was being run by a lean,
long-legged, handsome girl named Harriet C. Bryant. He sent
Pach abroad to arrange for exhibitions of the advanced Europeans

and corralled Kuhn and Davies to advise on the Americans.

Then he became the big buyer that kept the gallery going (he had to go to the dealer Montross only for his brave Matisse purchases). His taste for high-keyed paintings and for paintings with bounce and punch was developing and so was his perception. "Cubism," he wrote to a friend in 1915 apropos of a show at the Carroll, "is, of course, only a stage. It may be a window opening on a blind alley or a window broken through to eternity." Either way, he was willing to buy it.

It was in the Carroll Gallery that Quinn and Dr. Albert C. Barnes first clashed. Barnes looked like an aggressive dentist. He had a squarish, heavy-set, ruddy face, with stern eyes behind metal-rimmed glasses, and neatly trimmed thick hair. He was already known for his egoism and his "terrible temper." That two such forceful individualists as Quinn and Barnes would clash was inevitable.

Two years Quinn's junior, Barnes was born in 1872 in the toughest section of South Philadelphia, a circumstance about which he remained belligerently defensive the rest of his life. His father was a butcher, companion in the slaughterhouse to old P. A. B. Widener, who shifted from carcasses to trolley lines and made the fortune he spent on old masters. Albert Barnes' father stayed in the abattoir, so he had to make his own fortune. He worked his way through medical schools and universities here and in Germany. In 1907, the year after Quinn started his own law practice, Barnes, at the age of thirty-five, discovered the antiseptic Argyrol (which he allegedly never patented in order to keep its formula a secret) and promptly became a millionaire.

An old schoolmate, the painter William Glackens, rescued the *nouveau-riche* Barnes in the nick of time from spending his money on a "correct collection" of Barbizon School paintings. Barnes trusted Glackens because they had once played sand-lot baseball together, and allowed himself to be led to paintings by the French impressionists and post-impressionists, especially Cé-

zanne and Renoir. Leo Stein had obviously never been near a baseball diamond, but Barnes trusted him, too, because—also a James-
ian pragmatist—Leo shied away from any emotional twiddle-
twaddle about art. Stein steered him to early Picassos and Matisses.

Like Leo Stein, Barnes choked over Picasso's cubism, but, unlike Stein, he kept on and on with Matisse. His enormous holdings
included eventually the greatest collection of Matisse in America,
along with a fabulous number of Renoirs—a circumstance which
prompted Bernard Berenson to ask him, with wicked innocence,
"Why do you have fifty of the same paintings by Renoir and fifty
Matisses all the same?"

Where Quinn often bought as an expression of faith in a man or
a movement, Barnes from the start set out to get the best and was
always convinced he had it. Possessor of a few Renoirs and
Cézannes at the time of the Armory Show, he stormed into the
exhibition, looked around and proclaimed loudly that he had better stuff than anything there.

If the superiority of his possessions was questioned, he spewed
abuse upon the detractor. In 1937 the Philadelphia Museum declared that the version of Cézanne's "Bathers," which P. A. B.
Widener's son, Joseph, had given it, was larger, earlier and better
than Barnes' version. Barnes retaliated by calling Widener a
"boob" about pictures (he graciously granted him some connois-
seurship in the matter of race horses) and the Philadelphia Museum "a house of artistic prostitution." Shortly thereafter, Barnes
and Joseph Widener found themselves in adjacent deck chairs on
the *Normandie*. "We just sat there, side by side," Barnes said, "a
couple of millionaires on the luxury liner *Normandie,* just as his
old man and my old man once worked side by side in a slaughterhouse." Not a single word passed between them.

In the course of his voracious collecting, Barnes did come across
a great many bargains, such as his Soutines, which he bought early
and cheap. But not quite as many bargains as those of which he
boasted. For most of his long life—he died in an automobile acci-

dent in 1951 at the age of seventy-eight and was collecting up to the very end—he paid the increasingly high prices which, to Quinn's jealous annoyance, he could comfortably afford. In 1942, he paid what was then a record-breaking price of $185,000 for Renoir's "Mussel Fishers at Berneval." One rare defeat concerned Mrs. Havemeyer's single Renoir. In 1922, Barnes offered her $10,000 for it, a price then 'way above the market. "Thank you, Dr. Barnes," that spirited lady replied, "when I need $10,000, I'll let you know." But only occasionally was he thwarted. By the time he died, his collection—though neither as bold in individual choice nor as adventuresome in spirit as Quinn's—had become the best of its kind in America. However, comparatively few people have ever seen it.

The chip on Dr. Barnes' shoulder made Atlas' burden seem light. Even Quinn's fiery rages were mild compared to Barnes' tempers. Quinn was basically a loving man whose essential mood to the world was one of graciousness. Barnes was a hostile person with very few real friends (Katharine Cornell, Charles Laughton and ex-Ambassador William C. Bullitt were among them), who faced most of the world as an aggressive, angry opponent. Ambivalent, contradictory, unpredictable, he expressed his enmity, as his biographer McCardle says, "like a combination of Peck's Bad Boy and Donald Duck." He once sent word to Walter P. Chrysler (especially despised since he was rich) that he couldn't be disturbed from his "strenuous efforts to break the world's record for goldfish swallowing" and sent a message to a dowager who came to call that "Dr. Barnes has just died." The obscenities with which he seasoned his letters to individuals and institutions were as adolescently exhibitionistic as chalk scrawls on a barn door.

In the early twenties, he lent some of his pictures to the Pennsylvania Academy for an exhibition. Several alienists wrote that the paintings were proof of the insanity of artists. Barnes reacted to the criticism as if it were aimed at him personally and grew increasingly vindictive against the public.

In 1922 he founded the Barnes Foundation and endowed it with ten million dollars. Shortly thereafter, he barricaded himself at Merion, Pennsylvania, behind a belligerently spiked iron fence and lived in almost pathological isolation in his half-million-dollar limestone palace. There he found security in a group of erratically chosen students, almost all of whom docilely accepted his pragmatic esthetic theories for the privilege of living with his art. Many of them, however, including a secretary who had to take dictation in a steam bath, remain his devoted disciples. Almost everyone from the outside world who asked to see his collection was refused, a situation that has been only slightly mitigated since his death.

The clash with Quinn occurred over some paintings by the American impressionist, Maurice Prendergast. Barnes wanted them, but, still early in his collecting career, balked at the price. He wrote acrimonious, insulting and finally obscene letters to Harriet Bryant which Quinn, in the role of Cyrano, answered with a sassy and profane volley of his own. The peppery correspondence made titillating reading at the Round Table at Mouquin's. But it so shocked the painter's brother, Charles Prendergast, who had a strong New England sense of propriety, that Quinn finally allowed Miss Bryant to capitulate. Quinn considered Barnes a brute who, with enormous means, had acquired little better than a good dealer's stock. He was gleeful as a small boy when Barnes met a come-uppance, such as Davies' refusing Barnes access to his studio or Picasso's refusing to sign some early drawings that Barnes bought, unsigned, in New York.

Barnes' defensiveness was morbid. Quinn's was not. But Quinn was more than ordinarily touchy. He met Ezra Pound in 1915, when the poet was visiting America from England. He admired Pound's talent, his sharp mind and wit. He entertained Pound frequently at home and gave a spirited party for him at Coney Island, at which J. B. Yeats rode on an elephant and Quinn was exuberant in the shooting gallery.

Pound's bread-and-butter letter to his American hosts was a snide article in the *New Age,* which said, "One looks out across America to men who collect autograph manuscripts of William Morris and faked Rembrandts and faked Van Dycks." He sneered at the "dead ones" in America.

Quinn was convinced that he was Pound's sole target. He wrote an infuriated defense. He *had* had autograph manuscripts by William Morris and also by Meredith, Swinburne and the like, but he had sold them two years before for what they cost in order to buy art. He listed an inventory of his advanced modern paintings to prove he was not a "dead one." Neither Quinn's inclinations nor his income had ever brought him near the purchase of a real Rembrandt, much less a faked one, but he even rose to that accusation. He insisted that by inserting the word "original" in the tariff law's definition of a work of art, he had done more than anyone else to stop the importation of reproductions (i.e., fakes). His conclusion was succinct: "I can think of no one to whom modern art owes a greater debt."

Certainly, thereafter, there was no one to whom Ezra Pound owed a greater debt. He skillfully smoothed Quinn's ruffled ego. Then, to prove his good will, he generously offered his services in advising Quinn how to spend his money. The beneficiaries of this advice were, of course, Pound and his friends in the Vorticist movement—that short-lived offshoot of cubism, with which Pound had just gotten involved—and his friends in the literary magazine world.

Quinn bought many sculptures by Pound's Vorticist protégé, Gaudier-Brzesca, before the talented young Frenchman was killed in World War I. He bought even more paintings by the Vorticist Wyndham Lewis, since he was not killed but went right on painting prolifically. Quinn yielded to Pound's pressures for a Vorticist show in New York, paid all the expenses, and when war prevented the return of the objects, bought most of them himself.

Pound's investment counseling led Quinn to pay publishing

bills for the *Little Review,* one of the most venturesome of the "little magazines" that mushroomed after World War I, and to add Pound's friends to the roster of those for whom Quinn was acting as provider, legal adviser and—as Quinn said in a particularly exasperated moment—"petty literary agent."

Quinn enjoyed Pound's literary circle for the rest of his life. But by 1920 he had tired of "the Wyndham Lewis art junk" with which "Pound saddled me." A strategic event in 1918 had changed his attitude toward buying art and a new acquaintance had materialized to help him fulfill his new intention.

On February 5, 1918, John Quinn was operated upon for the removal of a cancer of the intestine. He recovered from the dread operation and the prognosis was presumably favorable. Many men triumphing over a skirmish with death spend the rest of their lives shopping around for passports to immortality. Quinn, victor in this bout, determined instead to affirm even more forcefully his mortal life. His satisfactions had come from patronage of the living. But now he would jettison the extraneous and disregard the mediocre. He would keep the stardust pure.

Much of his patronage had been based on a compulsion to do —a favorite phrase—"the sporting thing." The sporting thing covered a wide territory. It involved buying from friends and friends' friends, advancing money on works of art to be produced and buying because of an artist's "hard work" or because he "did not care for recognition" or because he was "sincere."

In 1920, Quinn wrote to a friend, "I am going to do it no more . . . I have long since passed through and beyond the time when I want to purchase the art of men . . . because of anything except that it is art." But not just any art. "A man does not go out fishing merely to catch fish irrespective of their quality or breed," he wrote. "He goes out for bass or trout or other game fish: so it is with pictures." He knew the fish he was after, for he already had some fine specimens in his collection: Brancusi, Picasso, Braque, Matisse, Derain, Rousseau, and perhaps even a recently dead fish or two, like Seurat. And he knew the quality he wanted: the most intense, unqualified expression; in short, the best. But, being "only a hard working lawyer and not a capitalist," the number of works he could acquire at any time would be limited. He was more reasonable, less greedy than Mrs. Gardner. "One can no more buy all of the beautiful works of art that one sees than one can marry all the beautiful women that one meets," he remarked.

Art collecting became his most fervent activity. But he was too busy to do it alone. The new acquaintance who helped him with his selective fishing and landed most of the masterpieces of the collection was the Steins' old friend Henri-Pierre Roché, whom Leo had called "the great introducer."

The epithet was to become apotheosized in the Roché-Quinn relationship. At first Roché in Paris acted like a Seeing Eye dog for Quinn in New York, finding the things Quinn said he wanted and those Roché decided he should want. Roché's gossiping nearly killed the goose that was laying golden eggs of ten percent commissions, because the French dealers began talking of Quinn as a "wholesale buyer from photographs." Easily ignited, Quinn was enraged at the implication, for he bought from photographs only things by men whose work he knew well.

In 1921, Quinn came to Europe and Roché's big introducing act began. These weeks in Europe—and three more in 1923—were perhaps the best of Quinn's life. Quinn was exuberant, charming, carefree; Roché was lively, knowledgeable, willing to smoke black cigars and talk art far into the night; and the third member of the trio was Jeanne Robert Foster. She was an American, with burnished golden hair, black eyes and a lilting voice, who had written several volumes of verse, had been on the staffs of *Review of Reviews* and the *Transatlantic Review,* and was an intimate of the Yeats circle in New York and the "little magazine" group in Paris. The days were sun-filled with laughter and excitements. Roché and the lady, indulgent, adoring and entranced, catered to Quinn's whims and lightning desires. They clambered with him over the battlefields of Brittany; tagged behind him, as if with blinders on, through the Uffizi to the three things he wanted to see; smiled at his delightful irreverence in churches.

In Paris, there were hours in Braque's outlandish studio above the roofs of Montmartre, visits with Matisse in his garden at Clamart, talks at the Gustave Moreau Museum with Rouault, pale and pinched, to whom Quinn had been regularly sending $600 a year above his purchases. There were dinners and lunches with Picasso and Fernande, who were spending the summers at Fontainebleau. Brancusi cooked pullets on his forge and served them, with wines and Rumanian liqueurs, on a round white plaster table freshly scraped for the occasions. After dinner, Derain would mount one of Brancusi's white pedestals and freeze into poses of classical statuary; Brancusi would reminisce about his Rumanian boyhood; Erik Satie would speak of modern music or tell how he asked the stern-faced Marine, on guard in an elaborate uniform outside the Palais de Justice, "At your age do they still dress you like that?"

There were hilarious, ridiculous golf games at Saint-Germain and Chantilly. Satie, dressed in a black bowler and tight black jacket and carrying an umbrella, followed the play like a demoralizing spy. Brancusi, dressed equally incongruously in a gray hat shaped like an inverted chamber pot and the clothes of a ragpicker, lunged at the ball as if he were striking a hammer on his forge and invariably missed it. Until his death in 1956, Brancusi kept above his bed the little white canvas golf bag that John Quinn gave him as a memento of these occasions. When Satie was not present to be witness, he claimed it as a championship prize.

There were long lunches with Joyce and Pound, at which Roché found the conversation "too Irish" for comprehension. There were affectionately tender visits to Augustus John's cherished sister, Gwen. Quinn rushed around Paris to find a singing canary for Marie Laurencin. He gave wonderful dinners—fried sole and magnums of champagne—at Laperouse for all the artists. Pascin delighted him with the story of a dinner Barnes once gave in Paris to which he told Pascin to bring his friends. Pascin, who was apparently a friendly soul, arrived with fifty guests. When the bill was presented to Barnes, the chemist looked coldly at the waiter. "A gag?" he asked. Pascin passed a hat around, paid the bill and rushed out in the street to give the surplus to a prostitute.

Quinn bought heavily from all these artists—their boldest, most concentrated work. He outlined a program of acquisitions for Roché to follow in his absence. A voluminous correspondence of letters and cables documented the active transactions: "Brancusi, the more one has, the more one wants"; Picasso's large and small versions of "Maternity" and a dozen or so more; Derain; Braque; but no Modigliani; no Chirico; no Delaunay ("I liked him in 1914 and got six or seven, but, basically, Picasso and Braque *are* Cubism"); no English paintings, they are "too solid, too much like furniture"; and certainly no German art ("You say there is a very intense and marked movement . . . I would like to have a 'very intense and marked movement' of Germans to hell or the Argentine or the headwaters of the Amazon in Brazil or the Sahara desert").

The public saw evidence of Quinn's brave taste in 1921. Quinn, Miss Bliss, Mrs. Havemeyer, and a few other intrepid souls persuaded the Metropolitan to hold a post-impressionist show. It was not a very daring step in 1921, but it seemed so to the venerable trustees who belonged in the Morgan camp and had been skittish about modern art all along. Out of a sense of obligation to buy something from the sensational Armory Show in 1913, the Metropolitan had purchased a Cézanne, but its director tried to suppress that fact from the press.

Quinn's paintings, with their strong, essential statements—especially his early Matisses—were the salt of the show. They seemed "difficult" even to the financier Sam Lewisohn, who had propelled his father's collecting expertly into the post-impressionist field and considered himself rather advanced. One of Quinn's distinguished legal friends consoled Lewisohn. "Whenever I stumbled on anything particularly outrageous, it was from the John Quinn collection," he said. One day at the Bankers' Club, the president of a large insurance company said, "I hear you own some of these crazy modern things, John. Why?" Quinn answered sweetly, "Don't you know that little poem by Dean Swift, 'The little money that he had / He gave a home to house the mad / Convinced that Spanish, French or Dutch / No people needed it so much.' "

The press, too, singled out Quinn for personal attack. Joseph Pennell, Freer's old anathema, charged that Gauguin and Van Gogh represented the same form of degeneracy that brought on the war. An anonymous circular signed "A Committee of Citizens and Supporters of the Museum" also called the pictures "degenerate" and the result of Bolshevist propaganda which was trying to destroy the existing social order. Quinn wrote the vehement answer to what he labeled this "Ku Klux art criticism." Although there were some ardent collectors, the American public was obviously not yet ready for even this mild dose of modern art.

Its reluctance was confirmed the next year when the dealer Kelekian, who had begun his American career selling rugs in Chicago in Mrs. Potter Palmer's day, put some of his modern paintings up at auction. "The Kelekian sale (total $254,879)," Quinn reported to Roché, "would have been a slaughter, an Armenian slaughter, Kelekian being an Armenian, but for the fact that many pictures were protected or bid in on behalf of Kelekian—only $91,000 worth being actually sold," and, he added confidentially, "had not Kelekian bid up two pictures he knew Barnes and Lillie Bliss wanted."

Miss Bliss need not have felt too badly had she known of this manipulation. The picture she was bid up on was Cézanne's "Still Life with Apples" and it cost her $21,000. A few years later she turned down $150,000 for it (and it is now one of the Museum of Modern Art's masterpieces). Other Kelekian prices were low indeed. The Detroit Museum bought a Van Gogh "Self-Portrait" for $4,200. Quinn got Seurat's "La Poudreuse" for only $5,200 (by 1939, Kelekian valued it at $100,000).

Quinn's pace accelerated. There were still injuries to be avenged, chivalrous acts to be performed. Don Quixote's windmills were being more clearly seen, but they were whirling faster. He helped form the Sculptor's Gallery; staged a Brancusi show in it; argued successfully before congressional committees to keep art on the free list against strong sentiment for rising tariffs; fought against the sales tax on art.

Defending and buying modern art were still the sporting things to do, but in his new mood Quinn occasionally lapsed into the un-sporting. He bought some excellent Oriental art, including white jade (which he removed when his Tammany friends came lest they snuff out their cigars on it), a bronze head from Siam, "not because it was old, but because it was . . . as beautiful as though it had been made by Brancusi today," and, for $18,000, his one old master, El Greco's "Christ Driving the Money Changers from the Temple."

There comes a time in every collector's life when he covets above all else a painting which is "unobtainable." So compulsive is this whim, in fact, that dealers often obligingly make pictures temporarily unobtainable in order to increase their desirability.

In John Quinn's case, the object of frustrated desire was "The Circus," the last great canvas which Seurat painted before his death. It belonged to Seurat's disciple, Signac, who guarded it possessively and deemed any suitor other than the Louvre unworthy. In later years Roché spun a romantic story of Quinn's courtship, wherein Signac succumbed to charm and sincerity. In cold fact, Quinn and Signac never met during the year-long wooing in which Roché acted as go-between. Finally, like most other "unobtainable" pictures, "The Circus" became obtainable at a price.

The price, in this case, was 150,000 francs, the highest price Quinn paid for any picture except the Greco. A year later, the year of Quinn's death, the painter-amateur Frederick Clay Bartlett of Chicago bought Seurat's large "Grand Jatte" for $24,000, for which, a few years afterwards, a French syndicate offered him $450,000. At the time of the Museum of Modern Art fire in 1958, this painting (lent by the Art Institute) was insured for $1,000,000. What might have been offered for Quinn's picture will never be known. It was the only painting for which he made disposition in his will: he left it to the Louvre.

Quinn lived in a large apartment on Central Park West. Only his bedroom, an incongruous re-creation of Tiffin, Ohio, with over-large furniture, childish paintings of the family by his sister Jessica, and family photographs, had a semblance of order. The rest was crammed and jammed with books, paintings and sculptures. Possessions even crowded the furniture, covered with Mr. Ryan's Renaissance brocade, and the two tall bishop's chairs (one habitually Quinn's) in the living room. A large so-called art room in the back held the highest concentration of things, so many, in fact, that circumnavigation was perilous.

Both Quinn and his well-trained manservant had an uncanny knack of locating what he wanted. Without hesitation, he could pluck a particular manuscript or painting from the precious litter or choose strategic works to show Picasso's various phases. He could also, when he felt like it, spitefully suppress a picture from an annoying guest. He always kept a few things out for his own contemplation, changing them from time to time and involving himself emotionally with them. He had no inclination for hoarding. He never considered putting anything in storage. He liked his possessions where he could get his fingers on them.

But in 1921 he decided to auction his library. His ostensible reason was that he was going to have to move to a smaller apartment. But that was not true. He wanted to have as much money as possible to spend on art. As he once said, "When one is really

'hit' over a work—like 'The Circus'—one will do almost anything
to get it. It is interesting and sometimes depressing to be so 'hit.'
But it spoils one for milder joys." As his passion for painting increased, he was being "hit" more and more often. It was becoming
a costly addiction.

He always had a nervous abhorrence of talk of sickness and
death, but, an avid reader of medical literature, he surely understood the seriousness of his own condition. It must have seemed
time to him, in 1921, to arrange his affairs so that he could keep
on indulging his passion for art without jeopardizing his family
responsibility.

His mother, two sisters and a brother had died, one after another, in 1903. He was profoundly shaken by these deaths. Another sister, Clara, had entered the Ursuline convent at Tiffin,
where she became Sister St. Paul. He had an uncle, Dean Quinlan,
pastor emeritus of the Catholic Church near Peoria, Illinois, of
whom he was very fond—"a wonderful man with a heart as big
as a tree." But the full force of his affection and strong family feeling was turned on his sister Julia Anderson, who had married a
pharmacist in Fostoria, and on her daughter, Mary, who was born
in 1907.

He doted on his little niece. She and her mother spent many
months of each year with him in New York before the Anderson
family acquiesced to his wishes and moved permanently to an
apartment there in 1918. Like a benevolent tyrant, he insisted
that Mary must have the best of everything as he saw it, from education to blouses from Paris. He made her write letters home
and edited them himself, chiding her if she wasted paragraphs
describing the weather, which, he pointed out, was always either
fair or foul, hot or cold, wet or dry, and could be quickly disposed of. Seurat's "The Circus" arrived the day of Mary's sixteenth birthday (brought up perilously on top of the elevator cage)
and he hung it in the foyer so that she would see it immediately
when she arrived for the dinner party he was giving her. It al-

ways pained him that he could do so little for Sister St. Paul. But for Julia and for Mary, he wanted to do everything while he lived and after he died.

On the back of each of the volumes of the auction catalogue of his library, he ordered printed Edmond de Goncourt's famous instructions about the dispersal of *his* works of art. That great nineteenth-century amateur had ordered that his treasures should "not be consigned to the cold tomb of a museum and subjected to the stupid glance of the careless passer-by," but that they should be dispersed at auction "so that the pleasure which the acquiring of each one of them has given me shall be given again, in each case, to some inheritor of my own taste."

But despite the brave quotation, the parting with the library was a wrench for John Quinn. These books and manuscripts "which contain a world of beauty and romance and enshrine records of friendships and interests and enthusiasms," he wrote in the catalogue foreword, "seem to be a part of myself, even though I may smile a little at my feeling."

The sale took place in five sessions between November 12, 1923, and March 17, 1924. The press signaled its success, but Quinn wrote to a friend that it had been "a fearful slaughter." Less the fifteen percent commission for the auction house, he realized only about $180,000 for the 12,000 items, of which the Conrad manuscripts accounted for $109,000. "The dealers have been having a Roman holiday out of it," he wrote, "buying valuable books at practically their own prices."

While the sale of the books was going on, Quinn was still buying pictures. Besides Roché, he had such other benevolent informers as Picasso. It was Picasso who earmarked for him the haunting painting, in a moonlit desert, of a sleeping gypsy and a silent, inquisitve lion by Henri Rousseau. It was his last purchase. By April of 1924, the cancer, presumably excised six years before, had metastasized. His lungs and liver were affected.

For several years he had been privately debating the disposition of his collection. He rejected the idea of "leaving these things to the Metropolitan. They would not be appreciated in New York." And although he indignantly defended American culture when an Irish friend scoffed at it, he had his reservations. "American art politics bore me," he wrote once. "I hate the puritanism of this country, its banality, its crudeness, the insanity of its idea of speed, its lack of taste and the mechanization of life that is almost universal here. The damned country is too big."

His enthusiasm for Ireland had also cooled considerably, because of its rigid moral censorship and its neutrality during World War I. Ireland had been his vaulting point: America his means: but France was his glory. His best paintings were French, French in spirit and in style, painted in France: "They belong to France, which I love." He contemplated providing for a committee, which would include Arthur B. Davies, to select those works which were "of museum rank and importance" as a gift to the French Government for the Louvre or the Luxembourg, as it saw fit. "When I come to make the decision," he wrote, "it will be carefully thought out."

He kept putting off the decision. Quite possibly his disappointment at what the library sale had realized (he had anticipated $250,000) influenced the decision he finally did make. Desperately ill, on July 22, 1924, he wrote a final will. "The Circus" was left to the Louvre (neither the Louvre nor the Luxembourg at that time had a single example of Seurat's work). He specified that the rest of the collection should be sold, according to written directions to his executors. The receipts of the sale, along with the bulk of his estate (about $500,000), was designated for his sister Julia Anderson (but not to her husband or his relatives) and her issue, Mary, with a provision for the medical care of Sister St. Paul.

Six days later, having made his peace with the Church, John Quinn died. He was buried in the family plot at Fostoria, Ohio, under a Celtic cross.

John Quinn would have enjoyed reading the letters that came

from the artists to his sister and to his lovely companion of the last eight years. They enshrined him as patron and friend. Picasso wrote, "It is rare to find an amateur of painting who really loves pictures. He, he loved them. And what agreeable and natural friendship one could have with him." Braque said, "What a real man, who knew what he wanted. What an honest man—an intense personality—a challenging spirit always ready to fight for his ideas." Satie called him *"un bon type, quel chic type."* Brancusi wrote of his generous soul and said, "He was a friend."

There were letters from many of his writer friends. Lady Gregory wrote, ". . . so much kindness, and sympathy, gone from my life—and from the life of many—for those whose weakness was helped by his strength, their poverty by his open hand, are very many." Even James Joyce, who had been angered at the sale of the library, including his *Ulysses* manuscript, forgave him and wrote dryly to a friend, "He had many good qualities."

Quinn had provided in his will that Jeanne Robert Foster prepare the correspondence for the New York Public Library. She fulfilled her task intelligently, devotedly and discreetly. Quinn had also indicated that, if permissions from living writers were obtained, a selection of the correspondence could be published. Mrs. Foster offered her services, but was refused. Mrs. Anderson consulted a few of the writers, but when they denied permission she abandoned the task. Someday, if this correspondence is published, much of Irish history and twentieth-century literature and art will be illuminated.

And the art collection? Quinn had directed that Arthur B. Davies and Henri Pierre Roché be called to advise, respectively, on the American and French art, indicating whether the best prices for various objects could be obtained here or abroad and at public or private sale. Lawyers are famous for writing impossible wills for themselves. Quinn was no exception. His written instructions to his executors were doggedly specific and hamstrung his advisers. It was as if, characteristically, he still wanted to be in control, but also as if, uncharacteristically, he viewed the situation with short-sighted panic. He went so far as to admonish his executors that it would be "better to take a loss than to carry them [the objects] over for more than two years."

All the advisers—Davies, Roché, Pach, the dealer Joseph Brummer, Frederick James Gregg, Jeanne Foster—urged the executors to hold the art and sell it gradually. They all foresaw the consequences of dumping this incredible, advanced treasure on a market still lukewarm toward modern art. Here were more than fifty Picassos, among them major and strategic works; twenty-seven Brancusi sculptures; nineteen Matisses, including his most forceful expressions; eleven Seurats, which was almost a corner on the artist's oil paintings; Redons; Picabias; and so on. Memory of the Kelekian sale was vivid. The advisers urged not only delay, but also publicity schemes, a complete memorial show before dispersal, a full-dress catalogue.

They met obdurate resistance. The National Bank of Commerce, which was one of the executors, was in a panic to be rid of the embarrassing stuff as quickly as possible. "Say, Pach," one of its officers said, "we don't want Wall Street to be laughing at us as the Cubist bank."

Quinn's sister, Julia Anderson, like the executors, clung to the letter of Quinn's written instructions. Never completely at home in the world of modern art, she was perhaps also hurt by the clause in her brother's will about her husband (Quinn had nothing against his brother-in-law, but was the kind of man who believed no one was ever quite good enough for a member of his family), and she was being publicly harassed by the harpy, who, always troublesome, had now become unbalanced and embarrassingly difficult. Bewildered, Mrs. Anderson, like the executors, was anxious to have it all over and done with. She wanted to remove her family from the spotlight of John Quinn. Ever since, attorneys have protected his heirs from inquiry and interview.

The sale of the art was hurried. Against these odds, the advisers did their best. Brummer sold a few things privately. Roché and Marcel Duchamp bought the twenty-seven Brancusis. Two thousand, eight hundred items were chosen for the presumably more advantageous Paris market, to be sold in October, 1926. They included the Rousseau "Sleeping Gypsy" of which the poet Jean Cocteau wrote extravagantly in the catalogue ". . . a phenomenon, a unique piece, the hub of the wheel, the dead center, the heart of the hurricane, the sleep of sleeps, the silence of silences . . . painted poetry," and about which a Paris newspaper headline asked, "Which Idiot Will Pay the Big Price for 'The Sleeping Gypsy'?" (the dealer Bing did, $15,600, and many years later the painting became one of the Museum of Modern Art's most prized pictures).

The rest of the collection—about 500 pictures and 300 sculptures —was sold in New York in February, 1927. Some of the works were sold earlier from a Memorial Show at the Art Center, which, of course, contained only a fraction of Quinn's collection. The critic Henry McBride reported that it "drew a steady audience of 'the best people' who made valiant efforts to 'understand.' No doubt some of them succeeded."

The highest prices of all American sales were $8,000, which the dealer Durand-Ruel paid for Puvis de Chavannes' "Beheading of John the Baptist," sold by him to Quinn for an eighth that price in 1911, and $1,225 for Matisse's brilliant "Bowl of Apples." Quinn had spent about half a million dollars on art. The total sales realized over $750,000. Crazy modern art, it seemed, was a good investment. But the advisers had been right. In terms of what these things would have brought a few years later, the Quinn sales were—as the gentleman himself said of his book sale—"murderous, a complete murder." Even in 1927, the public was not yet ready. It was twenty years too soon for the "Wild Beasts" to be popular; it would take thirty years before a cubist picture would bring $100,000.

But some of the collectors were eager even then. Quinn pictures began to enrich the holdings of others. Miss Lillie Bliss, the Walter Arensbergs, even Dr. Barnes were among those who bought directly from the sale. Dr. Claribel Cone finally fell for Matisse's "Blue Nude," the strongest and still most controversial work in the sisters' collection. The dealers who bought—and held —reaped the big benefit.

For the public, John Quinn passed into obscurity. But to students of Irish history and literature, he is a remembered titan. And to those "in the know"—to the institutions and individuals who own the works he bought (from the Museum of Modern Art in New York to the Courtauld Institute in London, from Sam Marx in Chicago to Chester Dale in New York and R. Sturgis Ingersoll in Philadelphia)—the label "ex-Quinn Collection" still carries an alchemy.

In his instructions to his executors, John Quinn had dared one wistful hope, "the possible contingency" that Arthur B. Davies might get up a fund of $250,000 to buy the best of the French and some of the other paintings.

Davies was eloquent in his despair at the dispersal of the collection. But the man who had come through so magnificently for the Armory Show failed to persuade any of the ladies to open their checkbooks in this emergency. Yet over their teacups, Miss Lillie Bliss and Mrs. Cornelius Sullivan deplored with him the loss of the Quinn collection and pondered whether, if New York had had a permanent museum for modern art, Quinn's art might not have been saved. They began talking about doing something to correct the situation.

And John Quinn himself? Engaged in some excited act of phantasmal patronage behind the Pearly Gates, in 1957 he surely paused to look down at crowds pushing into the Picasso exhibition at the Museum of Modern Art. Undoubtedly he cornered a fellow spirit to tell him, "See that fight down there? I started it."

Propagandist

KATHERINE SOPHIE DREIER

Katherine Sophie Dreier's opinions were convictions; her suggestions, edicts. She was accustomed to being obeyed. But when she brandished her cane autocratically at the American artist Joseph Stella and commanded him to paint the Brooklyn Bridge "this way, not that way," he went right on making it look the way he wanted. A common friend explains his unique independence: "He was a very exuberant male and wouldn't listen to any old maid."

The description would not have pleased Katherine Dreier. She thought of herself in somewhat more grandiose terms. "I am the reincarnation of Frederick Barbarossa," she remarked casually one day.

There were many who agreed with the self-appraisal of this militant woman. John Quinn was one. Those of the artists whom she sponsored, supported and held in what one of them called "a feudal formation with herself as seigneur" were especially aware of the German Emperor complex.

But there were others who, less romantically, saw the robust lady as the prototype clubwoman, who proselytized modern art in the same way that her sisters crusaded for the heroic female causes of the day: woman's suffrage, labor legislation for women and women's trade unionism.

In 1911, as a matter of fact, she pinch-hit for one of her sisters and appeared as a fraternal delegate at Carrie Chapman Catt's international suffragette meeting in Stockholm. With her Wagnerian proportions, her reddish blond hair piled on her head like an elaborately heavy hat, her determined jaw and strong nose, she was indistinguishable from the other dedicated and combative ladies.

As ardent and forceful as they, she fought for a cause even less popular than theirs. It had fewer adherents and no established programs. But the time was crucial for her enterprise. In the strategic period between the Armory Show of 1913 and the founding of the Museum of Modern Art in 1929, she performed almost single-handedly a courageous service for modern art. She propagandized it, she supported it and she formed a collection (now at Yale University) which is "a living historical expression" of a dynamic period in art.

That Katherine Dreier would have a cause was inevitable. Born in 1877, she was the youngest daughter of Theodore Dreier, a black-bearded German who fled Bremerhaven after the Revolution of 1848 to find freedom of thought and action in America. In the new land, the rebel worked conscientiously and profitably to the top of an iron import-export business and, having arrived, held high posts in upright community organizations.

Respectability had won over rebellion, but he squared himself with his conscience. His four daughters and one son were reared on Responsibility. Neither gossip nor small talk was tolerated in the dining room of the house in fashionable Brooklyn Heights. The daily diet was good works and improvement of the intellect.

With this diet, his wife, who was a pastor's daughter, was in full agreement. She supplemented it by rigorous emphasis on religion. Once when Katherine injured her knee sliding down a banister on a Sunday morning, she felt far more remorse than pain, because she had not wanted to go to church that day. Mrs. Dreier also believed in keeping the children busy. Their leisure was filled making flowers out of feathers, modeling roses out of clay, taking lessons in painting, piano and horseback riding, reciting Schiller, singing hymns and helping the cook shell green peas. The disciplines paid off: all the children distinguished themselves.

The good works were allotted as full-time careers to Mary and Margaret and Henry; the intellectual enterprises to Katherine and the eldest daughter, Dorothea. Katherine had been earmarked by her parents for a musical career, but, like Dorothea, she chose painting, in which she had dabbled from the age of twelve. So strong was the sense of social service, however, that she made that an additional part-time activity. She helped found the Little Italy Settlement House, one of the first in Brooklyn, and later in life worked tirelessly for the vacation home for tired working women which her mother had founded.

She studied painting for many years in Brooklyn and traveled extensively abroad. Determinedly improving her mind, she sought out artists and intellectuals wherever she went. She settled in England in 1911, where she met Henry James and Sargent and various of the esthetic expatriates and the British esthetes. But theirs was not to be her world. All that remains of that period are rumors of a painfully unhappy love affair and, incongruous with all else in her library, a complete set of Oscar Wilde.

She quit England and toured the Continent with gentle Dorothea. In Holland, Dorothea ventured with a social worker's concern into the coal miners' huts to sketch their wretched living conditions. There she contracted the tuberculosis of which she would die ten years later. Katherine, meanwhile, met Van Gogh's sister, embarked on a translation of her book on the artist and bought "a beautiful little Van Gogh, the first as far as I know owned by an American."

The Armory Show opened soon after she returned to America. Katherine Dreier began to warm up for her crusade. The fact that one of her own paintings had been accepted for the exhibition was as unimportant as the still-life itself was unexceptional. But her indignation at the attacks on modern art as charlatanism and chicanery was momentous. Later she would employ the letters column of the *New York Times* as outlet for her righteous anger. At this moment she decided the way to refute the charges was by "getting to know the artists" and helping them.

Once Katherine Dreier set her mind on something, nothing deterred her. Her persistence was always remarkable. Once when the Dreier children were small they were deposited with their grandparents while their parents traveled abroad. Each of them was given one egg at breakfast. Every morning two-year-old Katherine repeated doggedly, "Katie two eggs," until after two weeks of her insistence, the grandmother capitulated. Katie alone of the brood received a double portion thereafter.

Her determination to get to "know the artists" led her finally to a curious and strategic friendship with Marcel Duchamp, whose "Nude Descending a Staircase" had been the *cause célèbre* of the Armory Show. Duchamp had the precise, aristocratic features of a Clouet portrait, a sprightly, somewhat surrealist wit that impelled him later to submit a urinal as a work of art in a Society of Independents exhibition, and the kind of esoteric intellectualism that made him a champion at blindfolded chess. Ten years her junior, this suave Gallic artist became the guide, adviser and loyally filial friend of the earnest Teuton. He was the one person to whose influence she was susceptible, but even with him she kept her independence intact. She saw much of him on a five-month trip to the Argentine, but her published travelogue bears the explicit subtitle, "From a Woman's Point of View."

Duchamp brought her to the home of Walter Arensberg, where the idea of a new society of artists was being hatched in 1916. The idea was a Society of Independents—a sort of free-for-all organization which would give any artist a chance to exhibit in a huge, nonjuried annual exhibition.

Walter Arensberg's mind was as intricate as the inside of a calculating machine. It led him to two dedications: one was the deciphering of symbols and supposedly cabalistic signs in Shakespeare's plays in order to prove the authorship of Francis Bacon, and the other was the sensitive purchase of cubist and surrealist modern art—by such men as Duchamp, Klee, Brancusi, Picasso —in which intellectuality was the touchstone. He had discriminating and cerebral taste. Arensberg entertained himself with such pastimes as writing free verse; joining Duchamp in what the critic Milton Brown calls "verbal jugglings, pranks and mental 'hot foots' "; and supporting the avant-garde "little magazines" and even littler art galleries of the fomenting period.

Katherine Dreier seemed a rather heavy-footed guest in the nimble gatherings at the Arensbergs' Fifty-seventh Street studio. Walter Arensberg showed his coolness to her bluntly, but through Duchamp she had become part of the Arensberg circle. Once installed, she was far too valuable and durable a figure to be dislodged.

Moreover, she had proved her eligibility. She had painted some rather talented abstract portraits of her new artist friends, and Duchamp's dadaist masterpiece, "TuM," which incorporates an actual cleaning brush and a sign-painted finger-pointing hand, was already in her library. Though Duchamp might feel that she "accepted it on faith," she had, nonetheless, accepted it and paid cold cash for it. She might trudge along after the fleet, esoteric humor of Duchamp, et al., like an admiring, gawky girl trying clumsily to follow the lead of an exquisite tango partner, but she had earned the privilege of being there. A simple, open person, she might miss the recondite nuances, but she loved being part of the group. Later, she wrote often of the "gaiety and humor we created."

Even Arensberg had to acknowledge her committee-woman talents. She was given an important sponsoring role in the Independents' organization, whose first exhibition opened on March 6, 1917, at the Grand Central Palace. Duchamp, who had been leading the dada movement in America—that protesting movement that by nihilism mocked at all entrenched tenets and conventions—sent his "ready-made" object, the urinal, entitled " 'Fountain' by R. Mutt." It splintered the society. The "hanging committee" hid it behind a partition. The majority of the artists condemned Duchamp's impudence, but a small group championed his independence. (Stieglitz photographed the object and the American painter Charles Demuth wrote an ode to R. Mutt.) Walter Arensberg bought the "Fountain."

The show had been interesting and exciting, but the importance of the Independents began petering out almost as soon as it was over. The cognoscenti faithfully visited the galleries showing modern art, and men like Quinn and Eddy and Arensberg were buying it. But the relationship between modern art and the public, which had been boiling at white heat at the time of the Armory Show, had cooled considerably. It was, in fact, hardly a relationship at all. The Society of Independents exhibitions had not accomplished a liaison. Katherine Dreier, for whom the Independents had furnished a firmer toe hold on a cause, now decided to turn her prodigious energy to remedying the situation.

She formed a group to exhibit, publish and propagandize modern art. Marcel Duchamp and the surrealist photographer Man Ray attended its accouchement. Since Miss Dreier's idea was to promote "Art, not personalities," Man Ray obligingly baptized the group "The Société Anonyme, Inc.: Museum of Modern Art,

1920." Miss Dreier liked explaining his joke. "Since 'Société Anonyme' is also the French for 'incorporated' and as we incorporated, we became Incorporated Incorporated," she would say, laughing heartily.

The capricious gentlemen were also responsible for the self-mocking symbol of the laughing ass, but no one but the lady could have written the massive, upper-case prose that proclaimed its Educational Aim for the "study in America of the Progressive in Art, based on the Fundamental Principles."

The two rented rooms on the third-floor front of a house on East Forty-seventh Street, which was the headquarters of the Société Anonyme, had that derelict look which seems the common aspect of offices devoted to good works. The extraordinary and advanced art which hung on its walls and filled its closets came first from Miss Dreier's own collection. But immediately she began buying for the Société.

Like the social reformers of the day, she was motivated both by dedication to the Cause and by sentimental commiseration. What maximum hours and minimum wages were to her sisters, the movements—cubism, expressionism, dadaism, surrealism, futurism, constructivism—were to her. Her sisters' concern about the working girls killed in the notorious Triangle fire was mild compared to her agitation about the plight of the artists. Where the amelioration of poverty was at stake, considerations of taste or quality or enjoyment were not permitted to interfere. If these incidentals collided with the rescue of an artist from obscurity, they had to give way. She was particularly ardent in promulgating the cause of the postwar German artists, with whom, unlike John Quinn, she felt a personal affinity.

She plugged hard for the emotionally expressive art of such men as Franz Marc and Heinrich Campendonk, who only recently, more than thirty years later, have begun to be fashionable (and high priced) in America. At the Bauhaus, that famous German laboratory school of modern art and architecture, she found Kandinsky and bought enthusiastically his improvisations and nonobjective paintings and became his ardent champion in America. She brought to America the poetic fantasies of Paul Klee and the jewel-like *collages* of Schwitters, both of whose work has become delectable to American collectors since the late thirties. (It became particularly enticing to G. David Thompson of Pittsburgh. He almost cornered the Klee market in America and bought enough Schwitters to cover a long corridor like wallpaper. His Klees and Schwitters, along with scores of Giacometti sculptures, are the central attractions of his marvelous, little-known collection.)

She went about indefatigably ferreting out artists. In the process, she came across such star performers as the brothers Gabo and Pevsner, who were making space a positive element in abstract, geometric constructions of celluloid and metal. She bought her first piece of Gabo sculpture in 1922 out of the exhibition of constructivist art in Berlin—a piece which provoked the press to call the artist "mad." It was a kind of art she liked and understood. She found the Dutch painter Mondrian, who was reducing nature to a mystical rationale by means of primary colors and rectangles. Interested in theosophy and religion, she responded to his Fundamental Principles. She bought paintings by Léger, whose rhythmic transformations of machines had not attracted John Quinn. She sought out the advanced American painters, whose lack of recognition was massive, from abstractionists like Mac-Donald Wright to expressionists like Burliuk.

Unquestionably Marcel Duchamp's fine French hand guided the choices of work by such witty painters as Miró and by so suave a sculptor as Brancusi, to say nothing of the art of his brothers, Villon and Duchamp-Villon, and his own. She trusted Duchamp, admired him, accepted most of his recommendations. Yet she was never bulldozed by anyone. Nor did she ever bargain.

The collection became a vast compendium of the movements of modern art by men great, good and mediocre in great, good and mediocre examples. No preciously selected group of masterpieces, it represents Katherine Dreier's exuberant espousal of modern art.

It was not the personal accumulation of a "collector," but the instrument for the activities of the Société Anonyme. The institution was not only America's first museum of modern art; it was also the first place to organize traveling or road shows. Exhibitions, usually with the tie-in feature of a lecture by Miss Dreier, or, occasionally one of the artists, and often Miss Dreier without any accompanying exhibition, went, as she put it, "from the Colony Club on Park Avenue to the Workers Club on Union Square, from the Jewish Community Center in the wilds of Brooklyn to the finishing schools of Washington, D.C." The exhibitions were important landmarks. So were the publications on what, to John Quinn's annoyance, Miss Dreier possessively referred to as "her" subject.

Especially in the years 1920 to 1923, the Société spread the gospel of modern art vehemently and effectively. It was Katherine Dreier's show. She financed it, for the other financial aid was nominal. She made its policies and program and ran them. Names like Kandinsky and Campendonk as first vice-presidents were only symbolic. Duchamp was the stimulus, but she was the dynamo.

In 1929 two events, of somewhat unequal significance to the world at large, left her shaken. The first was the depression, which hit her hard. The second was the birth of the Museum of Modern Art, for Miss Bliss and Mrs. Sullivan had attracted an energetic ally, Mrs. John D. Rockefeller, Jr., and the teacup talk had resulted finally in the founding in New York of a long-needed, permanent, well-endowed organization. The Société Anonyme hardly filled that bill. The Société was really an intrepid beachhead landing. Moreover, as frequently happens, the explorer who has the courage, energy and autocratic hold necessary to seize new territory is, by those very qualities, ill equipped for the next stage of colonizing with permanent installations. Katherine Dreier was upset by the depression. She was merely patronizing about the Museum of Modern Art. "Well, they're copying us," she said. And truly, she had cleared the way.

Once she yanked back eight items that she had lent to the Museum of Modern Art because she accused the director, Alfred H. Barr, Jr., of being "derisive" when he included the art of children and the insane as comparative material in a surrealist exhibition, an action which, in turn, provoked the *New York Times* to query editorially, "Why does Miss Dreier merely like the work of painters who pretend to be insane and become indignant when she sees the real thing?" But on the whole, her relations with the Modern Museum were friendly and she lent generously when requested. In 1946, she sent a group selected as "Collectors' Favorites," which included paintings by Kandinsky, Léger, Campendonk, Schwitters, Villon and Katherine Sophie Dreier.

As it turned out, the birth of the Museum of Modern Art had virtually no effect on the Société. By 1929, the Société's propaganda job had been successfully accomplished and its impresario had more or less retired to her enormous house in West Redding, Connecticut.

The Brancusi and Lembruch sculptures stood graciously in the green garden. Inside the house, abstract paintings lined the walls of rooms crowded with baronial furniture from Brooklyn Heights, a hodgepodge of antimacassars and tassels. In 1942, these furnishings were moved to a much smaller house in Milford. Here the paintings were displayed against a blue wallpaper with an aggressive pattern of pink and silver leaves, which one visitor still claims was hung upside-down. The surplus art was stored in a rather airless barn.

Occasionally she emerged to buy a painting. Most of the time she stayed at home. Artists came to see her. To the young ones she was a heroic, already historic figure who, at the time that American collectors like the banker Henry Goldman were boasting, "My taste stopped in 1669—that's the year Rembrandt died," had brought to America the work of rather more recent Dutchmen like Van Gogh and Mondrian. She wrote dense books on subjects ranging from *The Invisible Line* to *Shawn, the Dancer* and occupied herself with music and theosophy.

But her real mission was readying the Société's collection for Yale University. She had chosen Yale because she wanted the collection to continue "working." She saw it as a kind of moral yeast, which would lift the young, by its challenge, from "falling into a set pattern of standards" and would "revitalize them and create an inner moral courage and discipline to be true to the best in themselves."

On October 11, 1941, Charles Seymour, president of the university, did his bit in revitalizing the undergraduates by accepting the 616 items by 169 artists from 23 countries for the Yale University Art Gallery. Katherine Dreier began using her rather limited income to fill in gaps in the collection which, in the early days, had been filled with loans from such collectors as Arthur B. Davies and John Quinn. George Heard Hamilton, professor of art history at Yale, whose bland, round-eyed baby face belies his learned and vigorous mind, was assigned to Miss Dreier for the duration of the cataloguing.

Once, many years before, Miss Dreier had considered asking another art writer to catalogue the collection. Neurotically afraid of drunks, she never served liquor. But when she saw how exhausted that gentleman looked after his day-long survey in the barn, she broke her rule and magnanimously offered him a single glass of sherry. No such social relaxation was offered George Hamilton. Her hair was white and she looked like a benign grandmother. Her health was failing and she walked with ever increasing difficulty. But neither authority nor energy was enfeebled. Week after week, day after day, Hamilton shuffled through the objects under her martinet's eye until the catalogue was finished in 1950.

She lent her influential name to every event that was concerned with the furthering of modern art, sponsoring such exhibitions as the one the surrealists put on in 1942, but she emerged to lecture only once in this later period. That was in 1948, in her seventieth year, when under the ponderous title, "Intrinsic Significance of Modern Art," she delivered, spiritedly, the Trowbridge Lectures at Yale.

In 1951, the collection of the Société Anonyme was declared closed and the Société itself dissolved. Duchamp, other old friends, and new friends from Yale had been constant callers. In the evenings, they would watch Katherine Dreier heave her heavy body into the open elevator that Duchamp had charmingly decorated with *trompe l'oeil* wallpaper. She made a lordly ascent. Perched on her shoulder was the sulphur-crested cockatoo, Coco, which she had bought many years before in the Argentine and to which she was sentimentally attached. He was an indignantly unfriendly bird, who terrified such gentle visitors as her sister Mary by making crash landings, with clutching claws, upon their shoulders, but who tenderly ate bread from its owner's mouth. Coco and she fell ill at about the same time, but, obviously of less stamina, Coco succumbed first. It is said that no one dared tell her; they simply put the bird in the deep freeze. On March 29, 1952, Katherine Sophie Dreier also passed away.

She had served her Cause well, without misgiving or respite. She believed in reincarnation, but it would seem that her soul has not yet found its new lodging. Modern art has known no other so fervent a propagandist, although in Peggy Guggenheim, a woman of quite other temperament, the Cause was to find an impresario.

The Quiet World

EDWARD WALES ROOT

Edward Wales Root lived in a quiet world. It was a world whose
scenery was composed of nature and art; a world of lily-shaped
elms, bluejays seen startlingly bright against a brown landscape,
iris hybridized to perfection of color and shape, and of paintings
—American paintings—which were lyrical in feeling and whose
emotion had been recollected in tranquillity.

As a son of Elihu Root, Edward Wales Root had been born into
a quite different world of tense political and economic drama and
of international excitement. Already a successful corporation lawyer when Edward was born in 1884, Elihu Root served subsequently as Secretary of War under McKinley and Theodore
Roosevelt and as Roosevelt's Secretary of State. An urbane man,
with an inquiring mind and an epigrammatic humor, he was
the most admired member of the Cabinet and an influential in-

ternationalist. Edward Root recalled that when he was a child
the house in Washington, D.C., was frequently "cleared like the
decks of a battle-ship" for grand social functions. There were elaborate social occasions, too, during summer vacations in South-
ampton and in Clinton, New York, and meetings with powerful
political figures on trips to Europe, Cuba and Labrador.

But out of necessity, Edward Root chose another way of life.
He was left a prisoner of almost total deafness from an un-
diagnosed mastoiditis at the age of three. Perhaps because she was
ridden by some unconscious feeling of guilt, his mother schooled
him never to allude to or explain his affliction. He was not permitted to betray it by using the rudimentary hearing aids of the
time. He was instructed to force himself to lead an outwardly
normal life. None of the childhood playmates, whose voices he
never heard, knew he was deaf. Even in college, only the most ob-
servant could read a betrayal of his condition in the wistfulness
of his smile and the alertness of his eyes. At social gatherings
he would lurk quietly in the background until he saw someone
about to pose a question. Then he plunged desperately into an
uninterruptable monologue to avoid being thought rude for not
answering a query he knew he would not hear. When a pretty
young girl performed on a guitar, he kept his eyes on one of her
feet, following the rhythm as she tapped it out with her pink
satin slipper.

The deafness and the discipline accustomed him to self-reliance,
intense concentration and the habit of reflection. He read greedily
and thoroughly. As a substitute for oral communication, he took
to jotting down every musing and idea. Most of all, he trained
his eyes. They became his salvation and his bridge to the world.
At once imaginative and methodical, he used them both to see
and to observe.

When he looked at art, he really looked. His well-trained eyes
could discriminate and recognize quality in the very new and still
strange. He came upon American art at the beginning of this cen-

tury at a fascinating and transitional moment in its history. Offering a release from deafness, the pursuit of art became the core of
his life. He watched American painting move through changes
as rapid and strategic in their way as were the developments in
the international and social arena in which his father was engaged. When Elihu Root died in 1937 he was a respected, conservative elder statesman. But Edward Root moved forward with
each chapter of his time, his enthusiasms as fresh and revolutionary in 1956 as they had been in 1907. He trusted his eyes so
completely that neither preconceived notions nor prejudice nor
fashion could obstruct their direct vision. His taste was formed
by his concern with quintessences rather than extravaganzas and
by his profound affinity to nature. His background and his experiences directed him, unlike most other collectors of modern art,
to American paintings. He looked in American art for that which
would satisfy his particular taste and sensitivities—and he found it.

By 1920—at its exact mid-point—his life came into focus. In his
quiet world, philosophy and way of life, nature and art were in-
separably intertwined.

Even before his death on December 5, 1956, at the age of seventy-
two, Edward Root still had a boyish aspect. He was a tall, long-
limbed man who walked softly from the long habit of not disturbing birds and butterflies whose private busyness he liked to
observe. He usually wore a bow tie and casually comfortable blue-
gray tweeds whose sleeves, like those on a fast-growing child,
were, rather endearingly, an inch too short. The schoolboy impression was reinforced by his pink cheeks and by the way his short
hair seemed to fit snugly on his head like a skullcap, but most of
all by the look of absolute candor in his large blue eyes and the
motility of his face, which transparently betrayed every mood. Except for the whiteness of his hair, he looked, in fact, remarkably
as he had in 1905 when, at twenty-one, he graduated from Ham-

ilton College in Clinton, New York, a well-educated, well-bred, attractive young Phi Beta Kappa.

Upon graduation, he had to choose a career. His handicap forced the choice. The strain of putting on a hollow act of laughing and smiling at strangers' inaudible conversations was becoming heavy. He chafed under the burden he felt he was imposing on friends, to whom "one passes as a sort of telephone conversee to be rung up with a shout every now and then when the conversation lags." He decided to become a ranch hand in South Texas, where talk would be less a part of life than action and where the few laconic comments of the cowboys, bellowed in the open air, would be audible even to his dull ears.

In Texas he clung to the quaint habit of brushing his teeth, but he managed the hard life well, rejoiced in the loud words of the riders and contemplated staying on after the year's trial. On a visit East, he changed his mind. The snatches of conversations he could hear there were more rewarding than all the audible shouting on the range. Charles Dana, the publisher of the *New York Sun,* told him, "You can live more in a day in New York than a lifetime in Texas." Edward Root agreed. He accepted a proffered job on the *Sun.* But he kept his silver spurs, lasso and chaps. The battered cowboy hat he habitually wore around Clinton made him a hero for generations of small boys, whom he never disenchanted from the conviction that the two moth holes in the crown had been caused by Indian arrows.

In the little cubicle which was the editorial office of the *New York Sun* in 1907, Edward Root had a jolting surprise. It had never occurred to him that when fiery Irishmen argued they would raise their voices to a pitch higher than that of the cowhands in the wide-open spaces. But when the art critic Frederick James Gregg and the editorial writer Charles Fitzgerald got going on the subject of modern art, Edward Root could hear every word.

Fitzgerald had seen the "Wild Beasts" in Paris, but the modern art that inflamed their discussions was by a number of former

American newspaper illustrators who, under the influence of an artist called Robert Henri, were learning that realism had a grand tradition in Hals, Goya, Daumier and Manet. These painters were vigorously depicting the back streets and slum life of New York and so antagonizing the polite art audience and the gentlemen-artists of the National Academy that they earned themselves the name of "The Ash Can School." Henri, George Luks, William Glackens, John Sloan, Everett Shinn, along with Maurice Prendergast and Ernest Lawson, and later George Bellows, made up the group which was also known, less colorfully, as "The Eight."

After hours, the impassioned polemics would continue in Mouquin's, that proto-café society restaurant where, a few years later, John Quinn would join the group. Mustached gentlemen and elegant ladies, whose elaborate hats were skewered into their high coiffures, sat on a banquette that ran around the room under a continuous band of mirrors. At a round table in the center, the artists, newspapermen, critics and writers had established squatters' rights. Besides the two charming, redoubtable Irishmen, Gregg and Fitzgerald, there might be the critic James Hueneker; the novelist Booth Tarkington; the sculptor Jo Davidson and other artists who were finding exhibition space in the West Eighth Street Studio of that far-sighted patron, Gertrude Vanderbilt Whitney. Among the regulars were Lawson, taciturn, with a face like Shakespeare's; and, exuberantly drunk, George Luks, whom Richard Harding Davis called "the best two-fisted bar-scrapper in the world."

All this vehemence astonished Edward Root. Matters of culture and literature had been discussed in his home with traditional Anglo-Saxon restraint. Now he had entered a world where grown men were "arguing, going like hammer and tongs," as he recalled it, "about contemporary art as if it were a vital part of life—as if it were something you got mad about like politics and finance and law."

If the excited verbal engagements shocked him into an awareness of the vitality of art, the experience of seeing how the artists lived shocked him into action. When Gregg told him Lawson was "hard-up," Root withdrew his $250 savings and went to see Lawson's work. He envisaged artists' studios as high-ceilinged rooms in which beautiful nude models lounged on Algerian carpets and white bear rugs. He found Lawson's paintings, unmounted and unframed, leaning against a kitchen table in a sordid little tenement trap. Walt Kuhn, before the days of the John Quinn bonanza, was sitting there with his legs up, drawing for the old *Life* magazine pre-Disney insects wearing large shoes and carrying umbrellas. "One of Lawson's paintings moved me a little," Edward Root said, "and I bought it."

It was the first step toward becoming a collector of contemporary American art, a rare field in which to specialize. What little market American art has ever had has been local rather than international. Even in 1899 it was noted that, lacking a fashionable world market, "big names" and social prestige, American art had no appeal for the majority of collectors who wished to be in vogue or were buying for investment or immortality. In the past, there had been the lone pioneer collector, Luman Reed, who died in 1836. Among Edward Root's few closer predecessors, there were two eccentric and entertaining nineteenth-century gentlemen, Thomas B. Clarke and John Gellatly.

Thomas B. Clarke was an elegant man, with precise features and hair as white-gold as the head of the cane he carried in later years. Aline Bernstein, the actor's daughter who was to become famous for her theatrical designs, lived next door to Clarke's lace-curtained house on East Thirty-seventh Street when she was a young girl, and knew him well. His life "was caught in two passions," she recalled, "first and foremost a love of art, second the pursuit of pleasure. He rode that passion like a handsome yacht riding a blue and wavy sea; that passion was not only for the ladies, but for food and wine, flowers and rides to the country, and wonderful parties at Claremont or Delmonico's."

The son of a schoolteacher, Clarke began collecting in 1865, when he was fourteen. Wandering around Chinatown, he found his attention snagged by a black jar with white hawthorn blossom decoration which he saw gleaming among a window-full of junk. "Too dear for boy, seven dollar, cheaper ones, here, twenty-five cent, thirty cent, seventy cent," the Chinese storekeeper told him. He pulled back a soiled curtain and revealed shelf upon shelf of porcelains in lovely shapes and unfamiliar, glowing colors. The fourteen-year-old boy bore home a peachblow vase for eighty-five cents, left a gold cuff button as deposit on the black hawthorn jar and bought it ultimately out of payments from his fifty-cents-a-week allowance. Clarke's porcelain collection eventually became fabulous and famous. As fortunes piled up in the expanding economy of the eighties and nineties, and the millionaires began desiring elegant trappings for their plush new surroundings, Thomas B. Clarke sold to them. He became Morgan's adviser on porcelains and catalogued the banker's collection.

Soon after he fell under the spell of porcelains, Clarke spent a hundred dollars for a meticulously rendered "Brook Trout." But his first serious love affair with an important American painting occurred in 1869, when he bought a landscape called "Grey Lowering Day" by George Inness. Clarke kept on buying in the seventies the work of the painters then known as "The Younger Men," men like Inness and Winslow Homer. He became their friend as well as their patron. A gregarious man who cut a fine figure, he used his social position to influence his friends to buy paintings, too, and he promoted American art in the Century and Union League Clubs. When his American paintings were exhibited at the end of 1883, it was the first show of its kind ever to be held anywhere.

As Aline Bernstein remarks, "Once he started to collect, it was like a disease that had to run its course." One by one he built up collections, tired of them and auctioned them off, his passion fixing not only on paintings and porcelains but also on English furniture, Greek vases, brass jars, Syrian glass and Italian faïence.

He tired of the American paintings in 1899. The Clarke sale made headlines, and its total of $235,000 astounded the press. Many records were broken: Inness' "Grey Lowering Day," for which Clarke had paid less than $3,000, went for $10,150; Winslow Homer's "Eight Bells" brought an unprecedented $4,500. One by one, Clarke built up and sold his other collections. He spent the last years before his death, which occurred in 1931 when he was eighty-eight, building a brand-new one of American portraits from the seventeenth to nineteenth centuries.

John Gellatly, ten years Clarke's junior, also died in 1931, a month before Clarke. Thin, hollow-cheeked, with dark, liquid eyes and a tidily trimmed mustache, he was a dapper man with a supercilious sneer. Born in New York in 1853, he was orphaned early and brought up by an uncle in the drug business. Gellatly worked for a while in the London branch of the firm, but shortly after his first marriage in 1883 he left the concern and went vaguely into real estate and insurance. It is said that his fortune began with the sale of the old Holland House, which was willed to him by his first wife on her early death.

He began spending that fortune on art and *objets d'art,* of which he ultimately acquired over 1,600 items. Strange, brooding, somewhat mystical, he was particularly attracted to the inscrutable beauty of glass and jewels (he owned the 475-carat emerald cup of a seventeenth-century Mogul emperor of Delhi) and to the poetically mysterious paintings of Albert Ryder. He owned seventeen of these, along with work by a variety of other artists including Dewing and Thayer. (It was he, in fact, who bought Thayer's "Virgin Enthroned," which had moved Mr. Freer to such pious thoughts.)

His vast collection—of which the paintings number 142—was valued in 1929 at $5,000,000. He decided to leave it to the United States Government. No Smithsonian Regents came to look this gift horse in the mouth, as they had when Mr. Freer made his offer of art twenty-five years before. The Senate and the House simply passed resolutions and on May 19, 1929, accepted, to come to the Smithsonian after his death, the entire Gellatly collection.

Barely four months later, Gellatly, aged seventy-six, married a woman forty-three years younger than he, a granddaughter of a senator from Georgia, whose stage name was Charlyne Courtland. The lady was somewhat bitter when she discovered *after* the ceremony that the United States Government rather than her pretty self had dower rights to the $5,000,000 collection and that her spouse had left for himself only an annuity that paid scarcely more than $3,000 a year. She was so bitter that she soon moved to a separate apartment, hounded her husband in the courts for $450 monthly support payments and, after his death from pneumonia in 1931, appealed unsuccessfully to Congress to reject the collection. Her scorn was mighty. She told the press that Gellatly had given the collection to the government, and thereby impoverished himself, in order "to pose as a philanthropist."

Ironically, Gellatly's philanthropy is little known. His *objets d'art* and his paintings are barely noticed in the vast accumulation of the Smithsonian Institution.

Both Clarke and Gellatly stopped short of the new generation of American painters that Edward Root saw confounding the art world at the turn of the century—the realists who seemed very brash and outrageously impudent, and such of the American impressionists as Maurice Prendergast. These were the young men who instigated the Armory Show of 1913, but it boomeranged for them because the much-publicized French copped most of the sales. Edward Root was one of the few who "bought American" there. He was tempted by the French "Wild Beasts" and the cubists, but he settled on a landscape with figures by Maurice Prendergast.

He was motivated both intuitively and consciously. Like his father, he had strong pride in his American heritage: his ancestors were among the first to venture from England in the seventeenth century and to push westward with America's frontier, until, their restless urge over in the mid-nineteenth century, they settled in upstate New York. But he also felt protective and grateful to the struggling American artists who had released him into the visual world and to men like Luks who had introduced him to a boisterous Bohemia so unlike the polished world in which he grew up.

Yet these were uneasy, floundering years for Root. He quit the *Sun*. By day, he studied painting with Luks. He continued painting later both as a hobby and as an exercise in analyzing form and color. At the end of his life, he delighted his doctor with a series of *collages,* which he called "pill-ages" because they were composed of bright, multihued barbiturate and miracle-drug capsules. By night, in these early restless years, he wrote sophomoric editorials for *Harper's Weekly* and struggled futilely at a novel. He regularly bought paintings from the artists in their studios, American Chippendale furniture ("my wooden chattels") from auction rooms and methodically built and read a thorough library of literature and history. So assiduous and diverse was his application that when Elihu Root was sent secretly by President Wilson in 1917 to see Kerensky in a last peace hope, it was Edward Root who briefed his father on Russia. Despite Luks' ebullient friendship, Edward Root's life grew increasingly inward and solitary. Directionless, lonely, and taut with the strain of deafness, he had a physical breakdown in 1916 that landed him in a rest home on the Hudson.

In this improbable setting, he met his future bride. Grace Cogswell of Albany, New York, had come to the haven to escape a difficult stepmother situation. She had the kind of square, strong-featured, thoughtful face that you come across above a white ruff in Dutch seventeenth-century portraits. He admired her prowess at baseball; teased her about her deep Puritanism; sympathized with her love of nature; responded to her forthright intelligence; and was attracted at the way she turned a perceptive phrase as a more flighty young woman would flash a pretty ankle. He wooed her gallantly and timidly. They were married late in 1917 and spent the war and postwar years in Washington, where Root worked for the Red Cross.

She was a most excellent consort. She accepted his deafness tacitly. She managed adroitly to counteract his childhood shame about using a hearing instrument. Unobtrusively she maneuvered conveniences: a chair strategically placed; a dinner party arranged according to the decibels of voices; brilliant overhead lights to facilitate lip reading. As deftly and subtly, she managed the last five years when angina pectoris was a threatening reality. They both pretended to believe whatever flimsy pretexts she invented when she transplanted close to the house the sweet wild daphne and white trillium from a part of the forest he could no longer explore. Once when their friend Alexander Woollcott told Edward Root that Grace should be given an honorary degree of Master of Arts, Edward Root countered by saying, "Yes, Master of the Wily Arts." Their constant intimacy was protected by an almost Victorian respect for each other's privacy.

Entranced by her gentle, unassuming husband until the day he died, Grace Root became his secret Boswell. Late at night she surreptitiously filled notebooks with such of his trenchant or amusing comments as, "You fight with only a wooden sword on matters of taste," or, "Dimming your lights when you drive at night is like throwing kisses: sometimes the gesture is returned, sometimes not." She noted such of his pastimes as "spouting Swinburne in the shower" and keeping a tally on whether he passed more blue-haired women or more men wearing hearing instruments on a given stretch of Madison Avenue.

Edward Root found himself in 1920. Distressed for a long time by the spectacle of people "diseased by dutifulness," he had been searching for the courage to live simply in order to enjoy and understand living. By accepting a job as teacher of art appreciation at Hamilton College he could do so.

He could also move into the family homestead and bask in family tradition. His grandfather Oren Root had begun teaching mathematics at Hamilton College in 1849. He had built a serene Greek Revival house and planted rolling acres of the Mohawk Valley with elms, spruces and a rich tangle of myrtle and exotic seedlings gathered from his botanist friends. Edward Root had loved the Mohawk Valley from the summer days in his childhood when he diligently collected caterpillars and watched them turn into butterflies. It was a landscape, he wrote later, "to arouse indeterminate desires and bestow sensuous delights—a proper nursery for the poet, the artist and the man of thought." In this nursery, he could be all three. He could also devote himself to the rare kind of collecting that became his way of life.

Collecting was part of the Root heritage. Grandfather Oren, as his son Elihu had written, "collected" not only trees, but also "black sumatra game chickens, peacocks, plants and geological specimens. I have seen him fondle a beautiful geological specimen, patting and gazing at it as a mother would a baby."

Elihu Root liked collecting trees, too, and both he and his son Edward put themselves to sleep at night recounting the Latin names of the more than fifty varieties they planted on the Hamilton campus. Elihu also inherited his father's attachment to geological specimens. Fortunately, his law practice was more lucrative than his father's academic career had been, for the geological specimens *he* liked were emeralds and rubies. He would carry a few around in the pockets of his well-cut suits and fondle them in a similarly maternal way.

Edward Root's collecting had less to do with fondling and caressing. He had very little pride in possession. He was always, even in his personal relationships, the observer. He collected things in order to observe them intimately, study them, analyze them, understand them and by this profound appreciation and love come closer to the excellence of life. They were instruments of faith.

Paintings were only one of the things he collected. They were infinitely more precious, but not really different from many other creations that, by the beauty of their form, "called your attention," as he once said, "to the world in which you live." Thus, iridescent butterflies; ladybugs and less gay, more martial-looking beetles; sea shells; trees; vintage wines; daffodils and lordly iris seemed to him also witnesses to the possible perfection of life.

His Odyssey was personal. So was his choice of paintings. Time and again his unclouded eyes led him to painters whose work would later be fashionably approved. The list of his discoveries and early recognitions is long. He "discovered" in 1929 the early (1916-1917) watercolors that Charles Burchfield had discouragedly put aside. He saw the originality and power of these anthropomorphic landscapes, where houses have leering faces, the wind is a ghostly phantom and trees reach up with menacing claws. Not only did he buy many of them, but he persuaded the dealer Frank Rehn to promote them. As a result, Burchfield was able to quit his frustrating job designing wallpaper and devote himself to painting. In 1944, Root was among the first to respond to the new American abstract art. He was the first in the East to buy the canvases over which Mark Tobey spread the magic of his "white-writing"; the first to purchase Theodore Stamos' imaginative visual metaphors of nature; one of the first to approve Bradley Walker Tomlin's poetic tick-tack-toe-like patterns.

Although he championed diverse styles, his taste was consistent. He was a meticulous man. His study was filled with dozens of little file drawers, neatly labeled from "Tobacco" and "Matches" and "Hybridizing Tools" to "Fishing Flies" and "Photographs of Italian Renaissance Paintings." Astonishingly, each one contained exactly what it was supposed to. He liked a similar orderliness in paintings. The abstract paintings he bought were never the "messy" or "smudged" ones.

Always he responded to work that had a closeness to nature, whether in the concentrated close-up of a poppy by Charles Demuth or in a canvas in which Rueben Tam set waves and winds battling in a color fugue. He did not care for expressionist painting; and the "social consciousness" canvases of the thirties, which ignited a collector like Joseph Hirshhorn, interested him not at all. The only inconsistent pictures in his collection are those he bought for teaching purposes, such as a tightly embroidered landscape by Lucioni. He hung this, with wry humor, in the guest room for such conservative visitors as his banker brother, who would consistently and innocently fall into his trap by telling him at breakfast how much they loved it.

Once he believed in a painter, he bought his work consistently over the years. The fascination of cultivating daffodils and hybridizing iris found its parallel in being involved with an artist's growth. With the flowers, he had control. Like the mother of a first baby, he kept painstakingly accurate records of each blossom's growth, measuring and recording height, width, foliage, date of opening. (At one point he named his various varieties after the faculty and recipients of honorary degrees at Hamilton, but the crossbreeding led to such embarrassing nomenclature that he reverted to the practice of baptizing them after favorite heroes and heroines of fiction.) He had no desire to control the artist's growth, but he had a deep need of paternal involvement with it. His own son's interests lay more in Elihu Root's directions: the navy and public affairs. Young artists like Theodore Stamos and Jimmy Ernst became other sons, who, in some subtle way, made him feel fulfilled. He stood by them even in lean creative years: trees in his orchards did not bear abundantly every season. But if he discovered he no longer "really saw" a painting, he would get rid of it. He always pruned deadwood.

"Teaching," he explained once, "is getting someone off balance emotionally. You have to shock them." He jolted stolid football captains out of visual stupor by making them look at snow through a prism. He would show them a Sung painting and then lead them out to look at the mists in the glen. He unfolded the magic possibilities of color by twirling cards attached to the treadle of an old sewing machine. The calloused hands of farm boys were made to hold cubes, spheres and cones until they had a feeling for form. Beginning in the twenties—thirty years before the notion of visual education had even occurred to most institutions—Root was finding ways to open unseeing eyes.

He tried to be an evangelist who "could bring emotion to a point where intuition began to work." Then he would leave his students and move to New York for a few months to haunt the galleries and to buy. (His mother's death in 1929 and his father's death in 1937 gave him a tidy income.) Grace Root never asked if he had bought a painting, but she could discern that he had by the restless way he kept looking at the door. When a painting arrived, he would prolong his anticipation as long as possible. Unlike Johnson, he would delay unpacking it until after his dinner. Then, fastening on it, he carried it around for several days, trying it in different lights. In New York, he spent most of his time with artists and citizens of the art world (he had removed his name from the Social Register, remarking that more of his friends were listed in the Manhattan telephone directory). Then he would return, with his new acquisitions, to Hamilton for the third semester. In "The Studio," a large, uncluttered room he built in 1922 and in the fireproof "pocket-gallery" in which he housed his collection from 1931 on, he tried to teach the young men "appreciation as a part of life."

When he first started teaching, Edward Root lugged with him everywhere a hearing instrument weighing seven and one-half pounds, "the weight," as he put it, "of an average baby." So extraordinary have been the technical advances in hearing instruments that by the time he died, he was wearing simply a light metal band that held a small white button behind one of his ears and carrying a small vacuum tube in his shirt pocket. "My hearing has gotten steadily worse," he remarked shortly before his death, "but I hear increasingly better." In 1932, the bone-conduction receiver was a revolutionary step; in 1940, Sonotone's first wearable vacuum-tube model was made available. Edward Root waited until his wife had gone to market and then he put on the new instrument. He met her at the door with an expression of transfixed wonder. "I've heard my first symphony," he said. He rushed over to a musical neighbor and begged him to explain the scales. He sat up most of the night working them out, with variations, on score paper. The neighbor was awakened early next morning by the sound of Edward Root quietly tapping out scales on the piano.

From that point on he tried to balance the visual world with the aural one. He added musical recordings to his list of collections. He went avidly to concerts. Grace Root's secret notebooks began to be spotted with such of her husband's offhand comments as, "Mozart is angelic and athletic," or, "I like Mendelssohn's overtures; he makes grand whoopee," or, "Brahms is autumnal, regretful and noisy." He found Heifetz had "like Ozymandias, a sneer of cold command," thought Mitropoulos in the lively passages "shook his shoulders like a dog coming out of the water" and decided that the conductor Cantelli "must have lived with his tailor at least a month to be able to present such a perfect back." As with painting and architecture, his interest in music embraced the present along with the past. Bartók was a special enthusiasm. He even took his wife to 301 West Fifty-seventh Street to see where Bartók was writing his third piano concerto just before he died.

In 1953, the Metropolitan Museum of Art broke a precedent. Edward Root was invited to show his collection there. It was the first time that the Metropolitan had exhibited a private collection of contemporary art. It was also a rare gesture on the part of an institution that for most of its life had been somewhat reluctant about American art. In 1906, the department-store king, George A. Hearn, had presented the Metropolitan with a $100,000 fund (later doubled) whose income was to be used for the purchase of

American art. It was as if a rabid Puritan had been left a bequest to be used exclusively for the benefit of fallen women. In the twenties, Edward Root made one attempt to influence a Metropolitan purchase. He was presumably permitted to make this attempt because his grandfather, Salem Wales (editor of *Scientific American*), had been one of the Metropolitan's founders and his father and brother had served successively on its board. Root was very fond of Edward Hopper's detached, lonely, very American landscapes. He persuaded the Metropolitan purchasing committee to look at Hopper's "Blackwell's Island." "The average age of the purchasing committee was seventy-two," Root calculated, "and none of them liked anything more modern than the Barbizon School and certainly nothing American." The painting was rejected. The Metropolitan bought an American painting every now and then, but the income from the Hearn fund was accumulating in an embarrassing way and the ire of American artists was building up, too. Finally, in the late forties, the Metropolitan began a series of placating and finally encouraging gestures and purchases.

The Root collection had been invited not because of its size (at its largest, it numbered only about 220 paintings and 150 drawings) or its cost (Edward Root spent probably less than $110,000 on art) or its comprehensiveness (many gifted, acknowledged Americans were absent), but because of its quality and its revelation of a sensitive, personal taste. It was also unique in its adventuresomeness. The only other collection of American art which could rival it in the early periods had ended with its owner's death in 1934. It had belonged to Ferdinand Howald, an Ohioan who graduated in the first class of the engineering department of Ohio State University. Howald made his money out of the coal mines of West Virginia, but he was somewhat more squeamish than the tycoons of an earlier day. His sensitive nature was so shocked by two mine explosions about 1914 in which seventy-one of his employees were killed that he sold his interests and devoted himself, primarily under the influence of the Daniel Gallery, to buying American art. His collection, a conscientious cross-section of conservative and advanced art, was divided between his niece and the Columbus Gallery of Art in 1931, three years before his death. Root's more personal collection uniquely spanned the whole period up to the avant-garde present of the fifties.

Root never intended to leave his collection to the Metropolitan. He had deep regional feelings. For a long time the art department at Phillips Andover Academy had shown sympathy with his aims and he had served on the board of its Addison Gallery of American Art. Some of his paintings were willed to it. But once the Munson-Williams-Proctor Institute in nearby Utica, New York, hired an active director, Root transferred his allegiance there. He guided the museum's purchasing, made gifts and urged the choice of a distinguished modern architect for its new gallery. He left his few contemporary English paintings, by such men as Tunnard and Sutherland, whose feeling for nature he enjoyed, to his wife. The bulk of his collection went to Utica. "The Homestead," which Oren Root had built and in which Edward Root found his quiet world, will, under Grace Root's guidance, become an art center.

On May 26, 1957, a memorial concert for Edward Root was held at Hamilton College, in the chapel, which had been designed by Philip Hooker, an eighteenth-century American architect on whom Root had written a monograph. The Budapest Quartet appropriately played Beethoven's Quartet in A Minor, Opus 132, and the first movement of Bartók's Quartet No. 2, Opus 17. Shafts of sunlight played over a vase of flowering white dogwood, daffodils and a spray of orange azalea which stood on the altar. The cross was not in evidence. It had been removed by the artist friend who had arranged the flowers. He felt compelled to remove it, because that morning he had found a poem which Edward Root wrote shortly before his death:

When the loons were calling
From the dark reflections of the hills
In the quiet water,
And the east turned to ashes,
And the zenith to roses,
And the stars came out one by one,
I used to think:
Was it so great a disaster
That so many people no longer believed
That the Universe was made by a little old man with a beard?
(Not even Michelangelo could do the impossible.)
And we who have an affinity
For the beetles, the trees and the flowers,
Who have no father to cry out to,
No cozy little world with man at its centre;
Let us contemplate the stars;
And if we feel lonely
Let us also feel proud:
For the dignity of man is relative
And to be even so small a part of so great a thing
is greatness.

Little Man in a Big Hurry

JOSEPH H. HIRSHHORN

Joseph Herman Hirshhorn followed none of the standard professions of the Brooklyn tenement district, thickly populated with
Jews from Eastern Europe, in which he came of age. He became
neither Dead End Kid, nor gangster, nor murderer; neither play-
wright, nor actor, nor artist. But the slum environment provided
him with an incentive and his Eastern European Jewish ancestry
shaped his dreams.

The incentive was primary. It was to rid himself forever of
"the bitter taste of poverty." He knew that taste literally. His
widowed mother, Amelia, emigrated with her thirteen children
from a small village in Latvia in 1905, when he was six years old.
Her six-day-a-week, twelve-hour-a-day job in a sweatshop pocketbook factory yielded twelve dollars a week. There was never very
much to eat. Once, memorably, there was nothing. A three-alarm

fire in 1908 burned some of the tenants to death, routed others out of windows to become impaled on a fence below and sent Amelia Hirshhorn to the hospital. The children fended for themselves. "I stayed alive on garbage," Joseph Hirshhorn recalls. He became so devoted to the notion of wiping out that unpleasant flavor that he amassed a fortune said to be more than $130,000,000.

In this tenement district, the Jewish immigrants, with bearded faces and shawl-covered heads, sat for tedious hours in the waiting room but rose respectfully to their feet when the doctor entered. They jammed the Yiddish theatres and made heroes of the actors. They eyed the artist with awe, revered the writer. Having suffered centuries of persecution, enforced rootlessness and the terrors of insecurity, these Jews worshiped intellect and art as evidences of stability and eternity and as a means of grasping hold of life. In this environment, Joseph Hirshhorn was brought up to respect "the professional, the talented man." Fifty cents a week out of Amelia Hirshhorn's sweatshop earnings went for piano lessons for the children and another fifty cents for payments on a piano. Joseph Hirshhorn was subsequently to translate his admiration for "talented men" into such widespread patronage of living American artists that he has become the single largest collector of their works.

This man who bears the title of "Uranium King" is now fifty-nine years old. He is a tough, wise-cracking dynamo with a mind like an accelerated precision tool, the seasoned gambler's sense of the calculated risk and a big heart as sentimental as the calendar art he first admired. Five feet, four inches short, becoming a touch portly but still walking with a fast, bouncing gait, he has the mobile, tragicomic face of the classic Jewish comedian. His rapid-fire speech is a personal vernacular which hits hard with any direct, colorful word or phrase that is used to mean what he wants it to mean. All his life he has been a little man in a big hurry and everything he has done has been a one-man show.

It has been said that John D. Rockefeller's fortune was a historical accident. Joseph Hirshhorn nudged history in the pursuit of his. Many of the tycoons of the nineteenth century made their millions out of America's natural resources, but by the time Hirshhorn came on the scene there were no more golden eggs. The goose had been domesticated and regulated. Hirshhorn found a new goose. He discovered Canada, a country riddled not only with such old-fashioned metals as gold, iron and copper, but such Buck Rogers ones as uranium and taconite.

He foresaw the potentials of the northern land as early as 1933. Never recondite or reticent about his ideas, he took a full-page advertisement in a Canadian newspaper announcing in very bold-face type, "My Name Is Opportunity and I Am Paging Canada." The ad was an invitation to do business with Hirshhorn, one of the few brokers' brokers in Toronto, but its text, as *Fortune* magazine explained, was "pure Hirshhorn—a kind of rousing mating call from a man who had found the financial market of his dreams."

Those dreams started when Hirshhorn, at fourteen, became a twelve-dollar-a-week office boy. Six months later he was charting stocks and analyzing their zigzag course with the shrewd attention of a Damon Runyon character studying a racing form. At the age of seventeen, with a capital of $255, he set himself up as a broker on the New York Curb Market. Wiggling his fingers in the frenetic deaf-and-dumb language of that trading post, he made $168,000 in the first year. In 1924 he left the Curb and soon emerged as a brokers' broker. By 1928 he was making profits of over $2,000,000. Queasy about the boom, in the spring of 1929 he pulled out of the stock market with $4,000,000 just before the bust. Then he played his money wisely in its subsequent gyrations.

Tales of Canadian gold lured him north. In mining he was to make his big killings and his costly mistakes. In mining he could try his iron nerve, test his instinct for a long shot and exercise his hard business sense for moving fortuitously in and out of stocks.

He found his affinity in uranium. He owned 470 square miles of uranium-bearing land and had a mine producing the coveted element by 1950. But in 1952 he made his most spectacular gamble. Others had paid no attention to geologist Franc Joubin's theory that uranium lay richly beneath the surface of Ontario's bush-covered Algoma Basin. They maintained that if uranium were present it would show up in the surface—which it had not—and dismissed the tantalizing buzz of the Geiger counters as the result of commercially worthless thorium. Hirshhorn, however, listened to Joubin's theory that uranium had been "leached" out of the surface. Early in 1953, he put up $30,000 for deep diamond-drilling tests. In May, fifty out of the fifty-six samples at the assay office proved Joubin right.

Hirshhorn immediately instigated a fantastic maneuver to stake the biggest secret claim in history. Scores of mining licenses were taken out in deceptively scattered points; fishing and hunting licenses were obtained to allay the suspicions of vacationers along a main highway and the Canadian Pacific route; dozens of stakers in pontoon planes were dispatched to unidentifiable parts of the jack-pine-covered land to follow the siren tick of Geiger counters; lawyers were alerted. By July, Hirshhorn had acquired 1,400 claims covering 56,000 acres in the shape of a backwards-S, with thirty miles between the southern and northern points. In record time, two enormous mines were operating in this so-called Blind River area.

The frenzied operations that produce Hirshhorn's fortune are carried out in two unpretentious offices: behind JOSEPH H. HIRSHHORN on frosted glass in a venerable downtown Broadway building in New York and behind JOSEPH H. HIRSHHORN on fluted glass in a sleek marble building in Toronto. The walls of each are plastered with paintings and on every table and available foot of floor space there is a forest of sculpture. The same crowded arrangement occurs in his Fort Lee, New Jersey, home and in his suite in a Toronto hotel. Still more paintings and sculptures are installed in a two-room apartment in an East Sixty-seventh Street house in New York.

But Joseph Hirshhorn's art collection is like an iceberg. What is totally visible is only about an eighth of what exists buried in closets, storerooms and warehouses. Neither he nor anyone else knows exactly how much or what this thirty-five years' accumulation represents, not even the young man Abram Lerner, whom he hired recently to begin finding out. So far, Lerner's estimate is about 1,800 paintings and 450 pieces of sculpture. But no tally will ever be final as long as Hirshhorn lives. Every few days, Hirshhorn will call Lerner and say, "I did some damage." Translated from Hirshhorn-ese, this means that at least six sculptures and about eight to a dozen paintings, by anyone from Stuart Davis to Arshile Gorky, will be coming up.

The only safe assumption, in fact, is that there will be more objects in the future rather than less. Hirshhorn not only is addicted to collecting, but he likes buying in quantity. He could no more think of buying a single object out of an exhibition than he could dream of purchasing a single unit of a stock issue. "I'm gaited that way," he explains. "I'll go all the way on something or not at all. One time in the forties, I had four houses. I had nine pianos and four Capeharts, which is factual. The Capehart people sold a library of records—classical and everything—in a concentrated form. I had a set for each house." Similarly, he cannot function with just one telephone. In the early days in Toronto, he had by his desk an elaborate switchboard, which was nicknamed "the pianola," on which he played to keep in direct touch with a dozen cities. Today he operates with merely two telephones in each office (in New York, one is black, the other gold), which have a total of fourteen possible connections. He habitually keeps two phone conversations going simultaneously, and carries on an obbligato with a third person in the office.

Hirshhorn's tempo in the art market matches the *vivace* rhythm of his life in the business world. He is always in a hurry. Where other men will ask a hovering head waiter, "What's good?," he will demand, "What's ready?" Since even that inquiry takes time, his favorite restaurant at lunch time is the Automat. Operating at a frenzied pace and under needling pressures that would debilitate most men, Hirshhorn literally has "to steal time to buy art." He will leave a board meeting half an hour earlier than an appointment with the dentist requires and spend those thirty minutes in a gallery, or he will simply get up and say, "Mind if I step out a minute?," and then will "grab a cab and go to see some pictures."

His practice of buying art in quantity and his lightning decisions are somewhat unnerving to dealers in American art. Unlike dealers in old-master and impressionist art who own and can manipulate their holdings, and even unlike most dealers in contemporary European art who buy an artist's output and thus control its price, dealers in American art generally work on a consignment basis. At best, they take thirty-three and a third percent of the comparatively small sale prices which American art, with its primarily national market, can command. Most dealers in American art have small businesses, make slim profits and spend a great deal of time nervously persuading uncertain clients to consider a single purchase. Even an Edward Root is a phenomenon for them.

A friend describes Hirshhorn swooping into the gallery of a rather fragile dealer who holds only a few timid exhibitions each year. "Joe rushed in and bought five Walt Kuhns," he says. "In half an hour that dealer's life had changed: he was developing a tic." A more seasoned merchant says it takes him an hour to recover from one of Hirshhorn's visits. Lerner recalls that during his first week as a green hand at the A.C.A. Gallery in the nineteen forties he was alone in the exhibition rooms when the unknown, dynamic little man bounced in. " 'You be a good boy, and I'll take that one, that one, that one and that one,' he said. I just stood there waiting for the keeper to come and get him," Lerner recalls. That Hirshhorn should buy art—like everything else—in quantity and in haste seems so usual to his business aides, however, that they find one vocabulary suits the two activities. "He paid out $3,500 in a couple minutes the other day," one of them remarked, "one 'unit' cost $850."

Because he expects a wholesale rate for his quantity purchases from a dealer and will never submissively pay what is asked, Hirshhorn is known along Fifty-seventh Street as a "tough cookie." Most collectors bargain, but many disguise such tactics by conducting financial negotiations in delicate, *sotto voce* queries and answers. Accustomed to these techniques, one rather idealistic dealer forwent an important sale rather than subject herself to what she called Hirshhorn's buffeting tactics. It is not that Hirshhorn hangs on to his money in a miserly way. "Money comes easy to me," he says. Having made and lost millions of dollars several times, he has a rare sense of security. He is an obdurate and successful bargainer because he enjoys the hassle. Like other victors of such negotiations, he relishes the sense of power and the sense of assurance against having been taken advantage of.

What appeals to him in both business and art is the opportunity to test his judgment. "It gives me a kick," he says. In business, he will listen, at least for a split second, to engineers, geologists, lawyers, politicians before he makes a decision. In buying art, he acts entirely on his own. "I don't ask the advice of anybody," he says truthfully. "I don't care if my grandfather or my friends or anybody likes it."

That statement includes his successive wives. His first wife, Jennie Berman, whom he married in 1922, was tolerantly acquiescent about his purchases. His second wife (1945), Lily Harmon, was a painter and sympathetically interested. But she was not permitted to participate in his collecting. He was indignant at any implication of her influence on his taste. When an exhibition catalogue credited some loans to "Collection of Mr. and Mrs.

Joseph H. Hirshhorn," his temper flared. There is no possible chance for such an error in his present marriage (1956), for Brenda Hawley Heide Hirshhorn is indifferent to his collecting, prefers dancing with her husband to gallery trotting with him and would rather discuss television programs than art. Her attitude suits Hirshhorn, who has always enjoyed any lone-wolf operation. Once in the early days of his business, when a man asked him for a job in his organization, Hirshhorn snapped back at him. "What organization?" he demanded. "There is no organization, there's only me."

He likes to test his judgment in the art field by spotting what he calls "comers." Many of the well-known artists in his collection— Burliuk (Katherine Dreier reported that he bought dozens from that artist's first one-man show in the early thirties), Kuniyoshi, Evergood, Levine, for instance—were little known when he first bought them. When he finds a "comer," such as Carroll Cloar, whose knowingly naïve paintings he likes, he buys especially heavily. Similarly, he enjoys collecting an older artist who he thinks is insufficiently appreciated. "Eilshemius," he says, "I'm a madman for Eilshemius. He was in the basement in the 1870's and he came up for a while with the Independents, but in my book, he excites me, even today."

In business, he savors the dollar profit that substantiates his hunches. "I'm not an investor, I'm a speculator," he told Emmett Hughes of *Fortune* magazine. "I'm not interested in the blue chips and their dividends—they're O.K. for grandma and the kiddies. I've always wanted the proposition that costs a dime and pays $10."

Since he has been buying American art of all kinds in large quantities since the thirties, he owns work by many artists whose sale today would net him the kind of thousand percent increase that interests him, though the dollars-and-cents profit would be infinitesimal in the Hirshhorn scale. But he does not look for "comers" in order to make financial profits. He has never sold any of his American paintings. The only pictures he has ever sold are his two first purchases and a small group of French impressionists and post-impressionists that he bought without conviction and unloaded at one point in the forties when he desperately needed cash. He has never bought American art for either investment or speculation. He finds his satisfaction by seeing his judgment vindicated, not in the rise of market values, but in the subsequent approval of his "comers" by museum men and art critics.

So little is he interested in selling, in fact, that he resents requests to do so. One English dealer put him to the supreme test, offering two fine bronzes by Henry Moore and Reg Butler (both sculptors whom Hirshhorn admires intensely) in exchange for Hirshhorn's small, rather unimportant, early painting by the American abstractionist Jackson Pollock. "This is *my* picture," Hirshhorn told him haughtily. "I'm not a dealer. I don't trade in pictures."

If Hirshhorn does not buy art for investment or speculation, neither does he buy it for prestige. He has never been interested in the trappings of the rich. He likes "nice things," as he puts it, and remembers that when he had only two shirts, his sister kept them laundered so that "I was always the neatest, cleanest kid in the class." But "nice" does not mean flamboyant. His clothes are impeccable but conservative. The jewelry he finds by darting into Sixth Avenue antique shops is interesting rather than expensive. The furniture in his various offices and dwellings is unpretentious Early American, acquired over the years at auction sales.

Nor has he used his collection for social climbing. In 1952 he helped form the Rio Tinto Mining Company of Canada, Ltd., offspring of a hallowed British firm. In the process of trading his vast mining empire to the new company in exchange for a controlling share (55 percent) of its stock and chairmanship of its board, he came in intimate contact with such aristocratic Britishers as the late Earl of Bessborough. Hirshhorn made no effort to change his style. As Emmett Hughes reports, he would "chew his unlit cigar unremittingly and jar leisurely British discourse to an end with a phrase like 'Let's cut out the baloney and make a decision, eh?' " or toss aside the elderly lord's solicitous advice to slow down by saying, "Look here, Earl, I got plenty of health." When the Rio Tinto meetings were held in London, Hirshhorn invited the British sculptor, Henry Moore, to join him for lunch at the executives' large round table. He spent the whole hour discussing Moore's new work and telling his mining colleagues, "This is a great man here, a very talented man."

Obviously, if he had had any intimations of social prestige through art he would not have "bought American." Recently a few rich collectors have begun to add such now securely respected American artists as Ben Shahn, John Marin, Stuart Davis, Alexander Calder, Edward Hopper and Jack Levine to their Correct Collections of French impressionist and post-impressionist art. But, as it was in Thomas B. Clarke's day, American art is still socially inferior. If Hirshhorn had wanted art as a social entrée, he was in a financial position to hire the best advice and buy the best canvases and to pay for their reproduction in color in influential art books.

The only fashionable pictures he ever bought, however, were not even remotely fashionable when he bought them and chic had nothing to do with their purchase. They represented the fulfillment of a tenement-house kid's dream: they were the biggest, grandest apotheosis of calendar art he could find—a tremendous soulful-eyed dog by Landseer, and a Madonna, with lilies as well as soulful eyes, by Bouguereau. He paid for both out of his first fortune in the twenties.

Joseph Hirshhorn became an art collector for two simple, fundamental reasons. He grew out of his early environment with a huge, often indiscriminate but passionately real love for art and an almost compulsive concern for the artist's welfare.

He began to exercise both the love and the concern strenuously in the late thirties. "The money had begun to accumulate and I started going to the galleries." He was excited by what he saw. These were the days of "social consciousness" and the "American scene." Realism, which has always been a significant strain in American painting, had gained a new momentum and, in the canvases of many, had acquired a new point of view. There were still reportorial realism and poetic realism: to these was added critical realism. There was indictment as well as comment.

A detractor of Hirshhorn remarked that this socially conscious art—with its bloated capitalists and gaunt sharecroppers—was good for Hirshhorn's conscience. More accurately, it was in agreement with his conscience. There is nothing specious in Hirshhorn's identification of himself with "the little man." The fact that he is worth millions simply makes him a "little man" who has happened to make good in the financial world.

The social art of the late thirties and early forties may have been the easiest for him to respond to, but it had no exclusive claim. Along with Prestopino's high-keyed scenes of construction workmen and trolley-car riders, Gropper's windbag senators, Shahn's terse statements and Evergood's underfed tenement children, he liked Raphael Soyer's melancholy middle-class interiors, Eilshemius' poetry, Weber's emotionalism and Marin's dynamics and—far in advance of his time—Gorky's poetic abstractions. He was intoxicated, too, by the freshness in the work of many young men who had just emerged from their first opportunity under the heroic patronage of the Works Progress Administration.

He has continued buying the work of his early affections, but has progressed, along with American art, to some of the abstractionists and the new realists of recent years. Predilection for the strong statement is the only discernible line of taste in this vast catholic enthusiasm. Even when he turns to so reticent a master as Mark Tobey or as lyric a one as Rueben Tam—where Root chose the example with poetic sensibility, Hirshhorn will pick the one with maximum emotional impact. His method of buying, like panning for gold, results in a large amount of dross for every few nuggets. His best things are splendid and unsurpassed; some of the rest is mediocre. His "taste," in the objective terms of critics and museum directors, seems to have grown strikingly over the years, and now good far outnumbers bad. These days, except for purchases which, despite his pious denials, are eleemosynary in motive, the mediocrities are few. The consensus is that in sculpture his eye is almost infallible: he seems to have an intuitive flair for three-dimensional objects.

As exciting to him as the paintings he saw in the thirties were the "talented men" he met. He was introduced to dozens and dozens of American painters, old and young, who were hanging around the galleries where the dealers keep a perpetual open house. He felt a burning sense of obligation toward them. Other rich men might be buying Rembrandts and Renoirs, but those artists were long since past having to worry about paying for their sons' doctor bills. "These guys did have to worry," Hirshhorn says, "they had to worry about plenty. I'd take 'em out and buy 'em proper nourishing food and lend them money. And I'd buy their pictures. But I wouldn't buy what I didn't like. I'd give a guy two hundred bucks, but not buy his things."

The unpublished subsidies have been consistent and plentiful. Hirshhorn melts at an artist's plea for help. Anonymously and quietly, he has handed out thousands of dollars. Many artists have also asked him for financial tips on investments. Joseph Hirshhorn wrestles with his conscience on such occasions. After warning sternly that "you guys oughtn't to get into gambling," he obliges. He is less hesitant about giving tips to others than the "talented men." In fact, he has a propensity for giving them rather urgently. Peoples' friendly feelings toward him have a direct ratio to the success or failure of the gamble. One erstwhile friend, who was badly burned along with Hirshhorn in a Philippine gold-mining project that produced no gold, admits he must have had larceny in his own heart to fall for the investment. Others are less apt to blame themselves for yielding to temptation. From Hirshhorn's point of view, he is simply offering little men like himself the chance to share in what seems like a promising venture. If they are not "gaited" to gambling, it is hardly his responsibility.

His direct concern for the artist's welfare in terms of appreciation and sales is so strong that it has of necessity to be communicated to others. "Joe waxes very emotional about art," says one of his *Guys and Dolls*-type aides. Every few months, Hirshhorn will buy three dozen copies of Sheldon Cheyney's *Modern Art* and two dozen copies of Alfred H. Barr's *What Is Modern Art?* and press them on acquaintances like a zealous Bible distributor. It seems incomprehensible to him that others should not feel a similar solicitude about artists and a similar satisfaction in helping them. As if he had found an irresistible formula, he told his secretary, whom he had ordered to call some Canadian friends about a contribution toward an Ottawa museum purchase, "Just tell 'em they'll be benefactors of art."

His sense of obligation toward art has neatly meshed with his obligation toward Canada. The suspicion and chilliness with which conservative, rather anti-Semitic Canadian society first greeted Hirshhorn have made him sensitively proud of having earned a reputation of developing rather than exploiting the country. "I came not with a carpet-bag, but with money and faith," he says. He found Canada a country whose cultural resources were even less developed than its natural ones; he has consistently promoted this less profitable exploration.

A few years ago he was interviewed on Canada's most important personal-appearance television show. The Rio Tinto deal had just been completed and Hirshhorn stood at a dazzling summit of success. The nation waited for the boastful pretensions appropriate to a Uranium King. They saw, instead, a little clown who puffed his cigar toward the camera and said casually, "Hope the smoke doesn't get in your eyes." They heard him brush quickly over his regal position and force the cameras to follow him to the paintings by young Canadians which covered the walls of his hotel rooms. He mentioned each artist by name, talked about the paintings and, as if he were giving his audience confidential tips on the market, told them, "I want you to keep your eyes on this guy," or, "Dwell on this fellow."

His dream of founding the town of "Hirshhorn" in the Blind River area was a grandiose scheme for helping in one consummate act Canada, art and the little man. For years the bleak horror of mining towns had seemed but an alternate nightmare to metropolitan slums. He set engineers and surveyors laying out a city along Lake Huron's blue bay with its mountainous backdrop. As designer, he hired Philip Johnson, whose architectural hallmarks are elegance and dignity. The fleet, sophisticated architect and the garrulous, hurrying magnate, his eyes popping with excitement, trudged through pine and birch woods envisioning Hirshhorn, Ontario.

"This is going to be an esthetic town—laid out for growth," Hirshhorn announced. "It'll have a big square—like in Italy—with sculpture. I've got a big Henry Moore and I'm getting an Epstein, a big one. I'll have a museum there, too. Paintings belong to the public. Maybe the miners won't be different because of the beauty, but their kids will." A few months later, Johnson brought to the hotel suite a pristine model in black and transparent lucite of a tall slab building and several lower ones grouped around what would have been a city square to rival those of the past. "He danced a jig," says Johnson, "and said, 'We gotta do it,' and wanted to rush out to buy a big Picasso sculpture."

They had completed the first housing for workers when Hirshhorn's vaulting hopes were smashed. Citizens of the old lumbering town of Blind River, nine miles away, had been reveling in the Klondike tempo and boom dollars from the uranium strike. In no uncertain terms they made it clear that they would resent the competition of a neighboring town. "I had wanted to help Canada," Hirshhorn explained, "but if they didn't want it, I couldn't do it. I didn't want to impose the town on them." Nothing has ever hurt him as deeply.

Though the residents of Blind River were not receptive to his ideas, a few cultivated Canadians began to see what his dynamic interest and bulging pocketbook might mean to Canadian culture. Hirshhorn had been giving and lending rather generously for some time to the Toronto Art Gallery. One day the customs officer called to say he would have to pay duty on Henry Moore's handsome sculpture, "King and Queen," which he was importing to show at the Gallery. With characteristic impatience, Hirshhorn turned brusquely from the phone to an aide, said, "Hey—they want me to pay duty on the Moore. Do something. Get that law changed," and went on with his conversation on the other telephone. In nine months, Canada had repealed its tariff on contemporary art, a step whose accomplishment had taken the United States Congress several years.

In the process, certain Members of Parliament became aware of Hirshhorn as a collector. Governor General Vincent Massey invited him to an interview, lined a red carpet with cabinet ministers and told Hirshhorn, "You can awaken Canada culturally with your energy. Lend your art." The direct results of this request were big loan exhibitions of Hirshhorn's collection at the art galleries in Ottawa and Toronto, both of which were opened with official fanfare and brass.

Soon Hirshhorn was being wooed more systematically. At the time that he was focusing on modern sculpture for his projected city square (and extending beyond American art), he became interested in ancient sculpture, especially that of the Etruscan, archaic Greek and pre-Columbian periods. "I liked it for the 'tie-in,'" he explained. "When I was at the sculptor Marini's studio in Italy—nineteen hundred and fifty-four, about—I saw an Italian book about the Etruscans. Marini took a lot from that old art— and so did Henry Moore—and lots of others. The tie-in is clear." He bought a few dozen small pieces.

At the strategic moment when the plans for the town of Hirsh-horn collapsed and the new interest was growing, the personnel of the Royal Ontario Museum, which has an extraordinary and little-known collection of Oriental and ancient art, moved in. They offered guidance, supplied digested literature and, it is said, even subtly steered to Hirshhorn a dealer who handled ancient objects on which they cast covetous pauper's eyes. Soon the museum was proudly displaying as "Lent by Joseph H. Hirshhorn" one of the most important eighth-century Etruscan bronze figures in exist-ence and several other notable objects, including a horse's bit made in Greece in the eighth century B.C. This compact, intense little sculpture, with two horses joined by a twisted rope of bronze, is one of Hirshhorn's favorite objects, possessing emphatically the three qualities which express his esthetic: it is "clean," has "guts" and is "realized." (He also likes paintings to "sing" and to make him "feel weak.")

Soon he was guest of honor at a dinner at an exclusive club given by tycoon trustees, the president of a university and sundry other important persons. There was banter and good will. At one point Hirshhorn said, "Hell, I shouldn't even be here, I'm not a member of the museum." He was told, "It will cost you one dol-lar." He promptly said, "Here's your one" and put a hundred-dollar bill on the table.

He was equally quick when the climax of the dinner was reached. A dealer, self-styled as "The Einstein of Archeology," held forth on some unique pieces of carved ivory which he al-legedly said had decorated the bed of a king whose name ap-peared eighteen times in the Bible. The museum could have these carvings and become a Mecca for the mere sum of a half-million dollars. "Wonderful," countered Hirshhorn, "we should certainly get them. Now *you* are fortunate in being able to do something for Canada. Sell them for a *quarter* of a million dollars." It ap-peared that the dealer's passionate love for Canada had already worked its spell to drive the price down to the $500,000 mark,

which sum, it also appeared, must be paid at once lest the option
lapse. The company turned expectantly to Hirshhorn.

But they misjudged him on several scores. Hirshhorn's entire
collection of American art probably cost less than $2,000,000. Al-
though the prices of the ancient art were fairly steep, for more
than two decades he has been accustomed to thinking of the prices
of works of art in terms of hundreds of dollars and, occasionally,
in a four-figure category. The purchase of a $500,000 object was
simply not his style, especially when there were no artist's grocery
and dentist bills involved. Nor was it his style to be Canada's big
Mr. Moneybags donor. His mission, as he saw it, was to encourage Canadians to support their own artists and museums. He offered to underwrite the half-million dollars for a year. Consider-
ing what Hirshhorn could have realized on that sum in a twelve-
month period, it was a very generous gesture. But after a few
desultory pledges, the Canadians let the affair drop.

Joseph Hirshhorn does want to be a donor, but only in terms
that are natural for him. In 1956, he set up the Joseph H. Hirshhorn Foundation. He speaks of creating "an active museum,
which will also be a salon for the younger painters, giving them a
chance to show."

The first step was hiring Lerner to investigate the art holdings
which might go into the museum. The two rooms on Sixty-seventh
Street were rented to serve as an organized storeroom, but when
Hirshhorn saw them, he said, "Oh, Al, let's make it nice." He
turned them into a minor private gallery into which he can pop
to look at his purchases in the course of rounds to the galleries to
make additional ones. It is a typically Hirshhorn retreat: it has two
telephone lines. It has also become typically Hirshhorn in its clutter. This man who does not sell his art, nor give it away (even if
his children ask for a painting, he will go out and buy another
by the same artist, rather than part with one he owns), keeps
"doing more damage," as he puts it, every week.

Since thought and action are almost simultaneous for Hirshhorn, it seems astonishingly uncharacteristic that he should talk about a museum and do nothing about starting one. Some of his intimates believe the delay is deliberate. They think he is avoiding precipitate commitments because he still secretly cherishes the idea of founding somewhere the town of Hirshhorn. It would have the city square with magnificent large-scale modern sculpture; the masterpieces would be in an adjacent gallery; and the rest of Hirshhorn's art would go into public buildings and public housing. Art would be a living thing in the community. Such an act would seem logical for this collector: he would be creating a beautiful environment for the "little" men and honoring and being patron of the "talented" ones.

When the final idea does jell, he will clutch a telephone and start the project toward its mercurial fulfillment.

Americana

ELECTRA HAVEMEYER WEBB

Usually ebullient, Mrs. Havemeyer was downcast. Electra! Electra, of all people! She had pinned her artistic hopes on this youngest daughter as she had groomed her eldest one to fulfill her aspirations of the Educated Female.

Electra had conscientiously been taken on innumerable sight-seeing-buying trips abroad ("Look at that dumb-bell," sister Adaline taunted, "never going to school!"). Miss Cassatt was her "dear Auntie" and had even painted her, when she was a little girl of eight, with Dutch bob and frank eyes, whose stalwart little body was pressed against her mother's bosom. All the artistic exposure and advantages had seemed, to Mrs. Havemeyer's delight, to be paying off when she and Electra went to Spain after Mr. Havemeyer's death in 1907. Electra used her own money to buy Goya's charming portrait of a grave little girl in a white dress.

But now, a few months later, here was eighteen-year-old Electra toting home in the back of her car a huge piece of carved and painted wood. It represented, life-size, an Indian squaw with feathered headdress, holding a box of cigars, one of the vanishing tribe of "Cigar Store Indians" which so prominently identified tobacconists' shops from 1850 to the turn of the century. She had paid twenty-five dollars for it, she announced proudly, and it was intended for the covered porch of the Havemeyer house at Commack, Long Island.

Mrs. Havemeyer flinched, but she held her tongue and continued to expose Electra to Art. When, in 1910, her daughter became engaged to J. Watson Webb, she joined forces with his mother, Mrs. W. Seward Webb, in determining where and how the young couple should live. They settled on a rather grand house in Syosset, Long Island. Mrs. Webb thought it would be nice to have big chairs in the living room and Mrs. Havemeyer thought Moorish furniture would be lovely in the den and she sent an agent abroad to buy a handsome set of Chippendale for the dining room.

The good ladies underestimated Electra. Defying parental guidance, she persuaded her husband to auction off the somewhat stuffy Syosset house. He was ardently occupied with polo (ultimately he became a ten-goal man playing on three winning U.S. International teams) and was delighted to move into a small house in the gay polo world of Westbury. His young bride's delight was intensified by a formal parting with the Moorish chairs.

When Mrs. Havemeyer came to see the new house she was as much appalled by "the smell of those awful polo ponies" as by the waves in the painted maritime wallpaper in the dining room, which, she declared, made her quite seasick. She surveyed the American furniture, the patchwork quilts, the hooked rugs, the pewter, the bowls of glass witch balls, the carved eagles and tradesmen's signs. "How can *you,* Electra," she asked in exasperation, *"you,* who have been brought up with Rembrandts and Manets, live with such American trash?"

Electra Havemeyer Webb not only lived with it very happily, but she continued to collect American arts and crafts with the avid and insatiable enthusiasm that had propelled her father toward the pursuit of Japanese tea jars and ivory inros.

She had inherited his urge for magpie collecting undiluted. In both cases, moreover, the small unit price of the coveted objects and the large income at hand for their purchase worked conveniently to encourage wholesale accumulation.

When she was a little girl she had not one but seventeen turtles (all of whom traveled with her). Her Grandmother Elder interested her in dolls, making exquisite pearl-studded satin dresses for the tiny creatures. From the beginning, she preferred possessing them to playing with them. Her doll collection was eventually to include dolls made of Bisque, china, papier mâché, wax, wood, shells, rubber, rawhide, gutta-percha, rag, celluloid and all manner of other materials; dolls small as a fingernail and dolls nearly life-size; dolls made to display fashions and dolls representing English peddlers; dolls for play and dolls which performed to the tinkle of music boxes. She could resist none, nor their accouterments. She even persuaded the man who made her riding habits to sell her, for a doll, the prancing horse and tiny sidesaddle that he used as a tradesman's sign.

With the same keen eagerness for encyclopedic quantity, she progressed to other categories. Ultimately she was to acquire in the neighborhood of 125,000 objects, a number which, if similarly inventoried, would fill a volume thicker than a Sears, Roebuck catalogue. These possessions included whole collections of quilts, rugs, furniture, pewter, glass, ceramics, toys, carriages, sleighs, tools, folk art, bonnets, hatboxes and decoys. Her passion finally flared toward the full-scale and she went on to collect a real covered bridge, a lighthouse, a stone jail, a wood meeting house, a completely equipped country store, a schoolhouse, several dwellings, a locomotive and the S.S. *Ticonderoga,* the last sidewheeler in the world.

Out of all this fabulous accumulation, eleven years ago she began creating and is still adding to a unique and fascinating outdoor museum at Shelburne, Vermont.

Electra Havemeyer Webb is now a woman of seventy with fluffy white hair, blue eyes and a small, sturdy figure. Always active, but never frantic, she so efficiently organizes her extraordinary flow of energy that she accomplishes an enormous work load which includes running and fussing with her museum, being a devoted grandmother to twelve grandchildren, dashing off to Scotland for a spot of grouse shooting and up to the Adirondacks after deer, badgering the Metropolitan Museum to provide a proper catalogue for her parents' collection, typing most of her own letters, feeding her Shelburne terriers, running elaborate households in New York and Vermont and chasing off after a cache of snuffboxes or a rare patchwork quilt.

Open, ingenuous, unanalytic, as generous of herself as of her goods, she walks the world with a merry heart and an affectionate curiosity. She lives by a set of proverbs and platitudes as basic and homespun as the *Farmer's Almanac,* such as, "Laugh and the world laughs with you, Cry and you wet your shirt," "No matter how you get knocked down and no matter how often, it matters only how you get up again."

Unabashedly, she counts the blessings that enormous wealth, family life and an unfettered mania for collecting have brought her. As outspoken and friendly with a gardener as a grandduke, as willing to pitch into any menial task (except cooking) as to receive at a granddaughter's debut, she combines inviolate dignity with folksiness. She is, as a colleague put it, "the damndest grande dame."

That Electra Havemeyer should have expended her compulsive

passion for collecting on Americana is not at all surprising. She was neither hostile to nor unappreciative of the Rembrandts and Manets or the Chinese bronzes or the Tanagra figurines of her parents' choosing. Indeed, since her mother's death in 1929, she and her husband have lived graciously with a good many of each —plus Degas, Corots and such manner of things—in their New York apartment.

But surely deep down the little girl reacted against the Tiffany extravaganza and the presence of Great Art in the Havemeyer house. Perhaps when she came in after school and had to tiptoe past the somberly splashing fountain up the back stairs to avoid illustrious visitors in the music room or the gallery she determined secretly that when she grew up *her* home would never be a "museum." In even the most devoted and admiring child, the ego has a way of asserting itself. By declaring her own taste, Electra Havemeyer, in the most polite and respectful fashion, made certain her independence. And what more logical choice for her than objects created by anonymous craftsmen rather than by Great Names, objects simple, forthright and unpretentious which seem indeed to exist for a world created according to human, rather than godly or abstract or esthetic, specifications?

The J. Watson Webbs' little house in Westbury kept being expanded to accommodate the temporary needs of dinner parties of twenty given in honor of the Prince of Wales and the polo teams from France and the Argentine and to fulfill the more permanent requirements of five successive children. But the collections grew faster. They spilled out over the confines of rooms and closets. They would have inundated the inhabitants had not Mr. Webb arranged for some extra rooms in the building he had constructed to house an indoor tennis court and swimming pool. The first Cigar Store Indian, a figure as commanding and capable as Mary O'Connor, the nursemaid of two generations after whom she was affectionately named, held place of honor. She was joined by other polychromed squaws and braves. Nearby there were duck decoys, ships' proud figureheads, weathervanes carved by spirited anonymous artisans and magnificently powerful eagles made by a then-little-known Pennsylvanian called William Schimmel. Furniture, pewter, glass, rugs, quilts, hatboxes covered with early views of Yale University and the Lake Erie canal, the dolls and toys took over the new rooms.

It was easy to find these things in the 1910's and 1920's, and they were cheap. Mrs. Havemeyer was not the only one who was candidly skeptical of her daughter's taste. It was not until the mid-twenties that Early American crafts began widely to be sought after as "antiques." Only toward the end of that decade were the sculptures and paintings appreciated as art (and that phenomenon largely due to the enthusiasms of such artists as Elie Nadelman and Hamilton Easter Field, who collected them, Holger Cahill, who exhibited them at the Newark Museum in 1930, and dealer Edith Halpert, who promoted them as "ancestors" of contemporary American art). In the twenties, not many disagreed very strongly with the greeting of sundry Webb children: "Mother? Oh, she's out in the tennis court with her junk."

Electra Webb's enthusiasm for things American was reinforced by her husband. For J. Watson Webb, a tall, lean man with a Yankee dryness of humor and sparseness of speech, Vermont had always been home. His father, Dr. W. Seward Webb, was a handsome, bearded man with big ideas and energy to match. A practicing surgeon, Dr. Webb obligingly gave up medicine when he married William H. Vanderbilt's daughter, Lila Osgood Vanderbilt, because it was said not to be chic for a Vanderbilt to marry a surgeon. Thereafter he devoted himself grandly to the apparently more acceptable pursuits of railroading, horses, dogs and the land. By 1886, he had acquired what is still the Webb estate—a handy parcel of 4,000 rolling acres sweeping up the east shore of Lake Champlain. He planted trees, improved farmland, became president of the Wagner Palace Car Company and the Rutland Railroad, and builder of the Adirondack Division of the New York Central.

Electra Havemeyer first grew to know Vermont when she came up for glittering house parties in Shelburne House. Nonchalant about private railroad cars and great wealth, she took in her stride the butler from Blenheim Castle and the hundred and ten rooms which curved in an arc on the crown of a hill above formal terraced Italian gardens. She was rather more impressed by the Webb's general-studded genealogy and their deep involvement with American history. Having accompanied her own father duck shooting and on trips to the West, while Mrs. Havemeyer stayed securely home with art and musicales, she had learned to love animals, sports and the great outdoors.

The Webbs, too, loved these simple things of life, albeit in a somewhat insouciantly unsimple way. She was taken sailing on Dr. Webb's private yacht against the inky blue backdrop of the Adirondacks, played on the private golf course (the second course to be built in America) and rode to the hounds with young J. Watson Webb. Her young beau took her to see Dr. Webb's hackney breeding barn. Dr. Webb begrudged his horses no comfort. The indoor riding and exercise ring of this magnificent wood and stone structure was an ample 375 by 85 feet.

Then J. Watson Webb led her to a small brick, typically Vermont house at the southern end of the property. He admired it so much that he had saved it from ruin by patching its roof and boarding its openings. For the first time, Electra Havemeyer, who had been avidly collecting objects, became aware of the beauty and historic interest of a building. Innocently unaware that everything is grist to the mill of the born collector, J. Watson Webb had as little idea of what this introduction to American architecture portended as he had later of what would happen when his young bride announced casually one day that she would like to try her hand at a rifle so that she might accompany him on deer hunting trips. With her first white-tailed-deer-head trophy, her zest for collecting and her enthusiasm for hunting game animals flared into fervent concord.

Americana is available in New England; big game is not. Soon the Webbs were off to Eastern Canada for moose and then to Alaska in search of the larger species. Between 1931 and 1941, they made seven trips to Alaska and the Canadian Northwest, penetrating into more and more remote regions. In the days when charter flying was still hazardous, they flew over wasteland and tundra to the west side of the Alaska range.

Electra Webb was enraptured. Usually the only woman in the party, she was as at home in this man's world as her mother had been with a trainload of suffragettes. Resourceful, once when her jackknife blade was missing, she used the can opener instead, to slit a deer and remove its intestinal organs with surgeon-like precision. The afternoon she shot her first bighorn sheep, darkness fell before she could reach camp. The guide skinned out the head and the cape. Draped in it, she sat out the frosty night by a fire on the timber line. Not even this dampened her spirit, and if it had, there would have been a set of silver-lining proverbs to dry it out. On one trip her nine-year-old son, Harry, tented with her. Her enthusiasm for hunting and her sympathy for a fellow collector stiffened her constitution so that she could even stomach his current hobby of boiling the skulls of squirrels and other rodents in a basin on her small stove in order to extract the teeth for his collection.

Zealously she set about collecting fine representative specimens of each animal. Superlative moose, Dall sheep, bighorns, mountain goat, elk, caribou, grizzly bear, black bear and brown bear were added to her bag. One of her brown bear weighed 1,400 pounds. Mounted, his eight feet, one inch tower over the small huntress. The quality of her North American big game collection is unsurpassed by that of any woman's and many of her trophies stand high in official records.

Even courage is relative. Cheerfully, Electra Webb will tell you it takes more fortitude to start a museum than to face a charging grizzly bear. "Ideas just come to me," she says. The idea of having a museum came to her after her mother's death in 1929. Long since, the little brick house on the Webb estate that Watson Webb had rescued had become the nucleus of their summer home in Vermont. Like the Westbury one, it had been expanded with innumerable wings. Under the new roof there stretched an attic as large and lofty as a grand ballroom. The house was furnished with Mrs. Webb's Americana, but fifty times as many things as were in the house were in the huge trunks that stood in neat, imposing rows down the spine of the attic.

"Once you're a collector," Electra Webb declares, "you buy something and you can hide it in a bureau drawer or pack it in a trunk and it doesn't matter. You know you have it. Some collectors have the place and look for the piece," she says, "not I. I buy the piece and then I find the place." But places were running out.

In 1947 she seized her opportunity. Dr. and Mrs. W. Seward Webb had died. The family gathered to discuss what should be done with the splendid collection of carriages in which Vanderbilts and Webbs once rode in style.

Here were the George IV phaeton, the dark green brougham, the Victoria, all specially made by Brewster; the graceful, open Calèche, made in 1890 for Dr. Webb by the famous French carriage makers, Million et Guiet, an enviable sight when it was driven in Central Park with the two matched Webb horses, 17.1 and 17.2 hands respectively; the handsome Berlin with its exquisitely tufted satin interior; the tub cart in which J. Watson Webb, aged two, had shared the reins with his sister Fredericka, aged four, having been given riding and driving lessons before he could walk. What should be done with these and dozens of other vehicles that were polished and glittering testimony to the vanished age of the carriage trade?

Electra Webb took what she calls "my first little step." If the other members of the family would also contribute their portions of the carriages, the J. Watson Webbs would buy a small piece of property and construct an appropriate building for their public display. She had been collecting long enough to know that one thing leads to another and she was not averse to nudging each one along.

The Webbs secured some eight acres of land on Route 7, south of the village of Shelburne. Soon eleven abandoned Vermont barns and two grist mills were being demolished to supply hand-hewn beams for the cathedral-like framework of a large horseshoe barn. By the time it was complete, Electra Webb, with squirrel-like diligence, had collected by gift and purchase a vast number of additional carriages, as well as fire equipment, wagons, sleighs, coaches (including the Liberty coach which broke the world's record for speed in 1901 when its owner and his friend—James Hazen Hyde and Alfred Vanderbilt—ran it, using seventy-eight horses in all, from New York to Philadelphia in nineteen hours and thirty-five minutes).

Indulged by a husband with a weakness for early Vermont buildings, she could begin collecting architecture. A beautifully proportioned, pinkish-red-brick schoolhouse of 1830 was moved from Vergennes. A small barn followed. The one existing building on the grounds was enlarged. The handsome Stagecoach Inn, built in 1783, eight years before Vermont joined the Union as the fourteenth state, was re-erected.

Word that a significant piece of New England architecture was about to be destroyed made Mrs. Webb react as predictably as a Pavlov dog. She responded with alacrity to news that the Vermont Highway Department was about to replace the last double-lane covered bridge in Vermont with a wider, steel crossing. This picturesque 168-foot structure of 1845 spanned the Lamoille River at Cambridge, Vermont, thirty-six miles away. There was neither river nor stream nor gully to justify its re-erection on museum grounds. Mrs. Webb created a necessity. She had a large lily pond dug to make an impassable gap between Route 7 and the museum property.

One day she was sitting at the edge of the road in her car, watching the huge hand-hewn beams of the bridge being put together one by one. A gaunt Vermont farmer, who had paused to watch the complicated process, spoke to her.

"You know this Mrs. Webb?" he asked.

"Yes," she replied. "Very well."

"Crazy, ain't she?" the Vermonter remarked. "Durn sight cheaper to fill in that pond than build this here bridge."

Not one to brood, even over such discouraging reminders of Vermont thrift and logic, Electra Webb went on her sunny, busy way. She began dipping into the apparently bottomless reservoir of her personal possessions. She found appropriate furnishings for the schoolhouse, from stove and desks to fractur drawings and copy books, from little jackets to hang on the clothes pegs to small boots to be tossed carelessly beneath them. She skimmed off the top of her endless supply of pewter, glass, china, dolls, doll houses and toys to fill a house she called "The Variety Unit" and arranged in the small barn the cream of her collections of hatboxes, rugs and quilts (the latter the best in the world). Into the Stagecoach Inn went her superb folk-art sculpture (of this, her favorite of her multiple holdings, she says, "I try to find the art in folkart"). The pattern of the Shelburne Museum was emerging.

It was by no means the first "outdoor museum" in America. Beginning in the mid-twenties, certain Americans began to interest themselves in their own back yards. American crafts and folk art were only one discovery. Historians began reinterpreting our past and biographers breathed life into our heroes. The expatriate writers, straggling home from Europe, their *valuta* spent and their ideals frayed, began to explore the vast *terra incognita* which was their homeland. Painters were beginning to open their eyes to the American scene, of which they were to make a dreary and chauvinistic cult in the thirties.

Here and there across the land, other Americans were beginning to realize that it was not only the Indian and the buffalo which were vanishing. Usually energized by the sap still trickling down from proudly nurtured family trees, small, earnest groups were repairing and restoring individual buildings. Such a pioneer connoisseur as Henry Dupont, slowly searching out objects of only the highest quality, was beginning to make his great mansion, Winterthur, the most exquisite reincarnation of its kind.

Other Americans, looking beyond the single structure, were deploring the disappearance of the frontier town and the ruthless engulfment of the American village. In 1925, a group of log cabins was moved into Decorah, Iowa, and opened to the public. The first of the "reconstruction villages" or "outdoor museums" had been born in America. Today, more than thirty restored villages dot America east of the Mississippi alone.

In Dearborn, Michigan, there are the Henry Ford Museum and Greenfield Village, where the oldest windmill in the United States vies with Thomas Edison's workshop and the courthouse where Lincoln practiced law. In Sturbridge, Massachusetts, inhabitants masquerading in period costumes dip candles before eighteenth-century hearths and shoe horses in a nineteenth-century blacksmith shop. In Williamsburg, Virginia, the once proud capital has been restored and reconstructed on the grandest and most scrupulously accurate scale of all. Along with exhibitions of James Fenimore Cooper memorabilia and America's most famous hoax, the Cardiff Giant, a whole village has been reconstructed at Cooperstown, New York.

The Shelburne Museum, which opened to the public in 1952, was a late-comer. But from the start it was unique. It is neither a reconstruction nor a restoration, although it contains something of both. Some of its oddly assorted twenty-nine buildings (now on twenty acres) are furnished according to period, others give shelter to various portions of Mrs. Webb's Americana. These structures are essentially the "architecture collection" in a museum that has been accurately described as a "collection of collections." Above all, the Shelburne Museum is a "collection of enthusiasms." Saturated with the personality and taste of its owner from its overall concept to its smallest detail, it has a rare and engaging vitality.

Even its few "period houses" are often somewhat unorthodox. Several dedicated antiquarians have turned in embarrassment from the anachronisms of objects earlier and later than the date of the particular house they furnish. Electra Webb listens politely to their tactful disapproval. When they have departed, she continues her brisk and merry way. What family, she asks ingenuously, ever lived with furnishings, clothes and objects of use all rigidly and exactly contemporaneous with the architecture? What house, in which successive generations have lived, has remained architecturally intact? She puts together things which look well together and make sense together. For her, historical accuracy is often less convincing than human instinct.

Then, with a flair for the amusing and telling detail, she animates a static display into a stage-set which, like any good stage-set, communicates an atmosphere, a mood and the personalities of its inhabitants.

In the schoolhouse, a dunce cap made out of a newspaper of 1868 is set rakishly on the corner of an instruction board, and the blackboard bears, in the painstaking penmanship of the nineteenth century, the terse reminders that "People who are wrapped up in themselves make small packages" and "Nothing is work unless you would rather be doing something else."

Attuned more to people than abstractions, she thinks of places in terms of personalities. The "Vermont House" is conceived as having been built by a sea captain who retired in the late 1700's. "A man of some wealth," she explains, "who has ranged the seven seas and gathered his possessions—Queen Anne furniture, Chippendale, Salem chairs, Delft tobacco jars—over the decades of his travels." The dining room has a maritime theme, including the wallpaper that once upset Mrs. Havemeyer's digestion. In the captain's study, the walls are lined with some of the oldest known maps of New England and paintings of steamboats. By the well-worn chair in which he presumably sat out his landlocked existence, his spectacles mark his place in a Bible and his slippers and pipe seem only momentarily laid aside.

Mrs. Webb shops for these life-giving "props" in the giant super market of her personal collections. She decided that the S.S. *Ticonderoga* should have a bride-and-groom's room. Her memory leaped to a brass bed, originally exhibited in a manufacturer's display at the Chicago Exposition of 1893, which she had purchased five years before for the simple reason that she liked it. Then ("How do I think of these things?") she recalled a Victorian bureau and heavily embroidered prayer chair that had long stood among dozens of chairs and cabinets and tables in a corner of the attic that looks like a heterogeneous auction-room exhibition.

When the big pieces were in place, she set out one morning with a small clothes hamper. The trunks in the attic are labeled according to Mrs. Havemeyer's meticulous housekeeping techniques, but the labels are superfluous. Mrs. Webb's encyclopedic memory is her collection's inventory. She could dart unhesitatingly to one of the big steamer trunks to extract a particular bureau cover, to another for nightclothes, male and female. She swept up a pin cushion from a bureau in a guest room, took from her bedroom a Victorian bridal bouquet that one of her grandchildren had given her for Christmas. En route to the boat, she plucked out of an enormous collection of maritime paintings and prints in the Lighthouse a specific Currier & Ives which she remembered showed the S.S. *Ticonderoga* in the distance. When she unpacked her hamper, everything fitted as she had visualized it.

If, by some astonishing chance, cupboards, attic and house are bare of what she wants, she sets out on a relentless crusade to find or commission it. For bedspreads for the *Ticonderoga,* she spent an exorbitant amount to have a quality house weave cloth with the ship's insigne of two jaunty blue-clad sailors. "It cost a lot to get them to make it look like something turned out to be sold wholesale," she explains blandly.

Mrs. Havemeyer's ineffable joy in personally contrived artistic effects bubbled up again in her daughter Electra. If the Shelburne Museum provides her with "places" for her "pieces," it also supplies her with fine, unsullied spaces in which to indulge her decorator's zest. Old pine pickets of the original Shelburne Farm fences could be made into mosaic paneling for the Hat and Fragrance Unit. A large cache of seasoned wood, the stock of a defunct box factory which she came upon while deer hunting in the Adirondacks, could make veneers for the Rug Room. Uninhibited, she could contrive somewhat quaint effects in the Hat and Fragrance Unit or achieve so handsome an installation of quilts and rugs that several museums have admired it to the point of imitation.

Since Mrs. Havemeyer had only one major house in which to arrange her treasures, most of the vast numbers of objects—like 450 of the 475 Japanese tea jars—had to be kept in the attic. Mrs. Webb's zeal for arrangement has met no such drastic frustration since the formation of her museum. When her sons expanded her own excellent collection of duck decoys by giving her the Joel Barber collection ("the only 'ready-made' collection I have"), she simply had a stately, symmetrical house of about 1840 moved from East Dorset, Vermont, to the museum grounds. Then, with a single helper, she installed over five hundred decoys. In a stunning, uncluttered display that would seem sparse and empty to the patron of Louis Comfort Tiffany, the suave beauty of this one original (and continuing) American art form is revealed.

"It takes nerve as well as taste to be a collector," Henry Havemeyer told his daughter. She took his lesson to heart. Only a somewhat hardy spirit would have decided to "collect" the Colchester Lighthouse when the Coast Guard announced that the old structure of 1871 must give way to an automatic beacon. It meant moving the twenty-five-foot-square, two-story, heavily constructed building from its gale-swept, rocky reef near the middle of Lake Champlain twenty miles inland to a hill at the Shelburne Museum.

But it took superabundant nerve, plus a small fortune, to "collect" the S.S. *Ticonderoga,* a steamboat 220 feet long, three decks high, with a displacement of 892 tons.

The *"Ti"* was the last survivor in a long line of sidewheeler steamboats that had plied Lake Champlain since 1809. Though launched in 1906, the *"Ti,"* with its picturesque "walking beam" reaching proudly through three decks, and its plush interiors with cherry and butternut paneling and gold stenciling, preserved the grand, uniquely American steamboat tradition that inspired Charles Dickens to write of a similar boat, the *Burlington,* ". . . a perfect curiosity of graceful comfort and contrivance."

The *"Ti,"* serving in her time as passenger, freight and excursion boat, had kindled a good deal of sentiment in generations of rock-ribbed Vermonters. But increasingly dwindling revenues kept nibbling at the owner's sentiment. In 1950, the Junior Chamber of Commerce of Burlington, Vermont, stayed the *"Ti's"* sentence and ran her for a year as an excursion boat. Faith may move mountains, but sentiment cannot run a sidewheeler. The operation required cold cash. J. Watson Webb—the great-grandson of Cornelius Vanderbilt, who had built an empire with sidewheelers—bought this last of her kind for the Shelburne Museum.

For two more years the *"Ti"* ran on borrowed time as an excursion boat. The captain and the chief engineer were nearly eighty. They had no successors: young men today do not learn navigation by reciprocating engine. In 1953, Electra Havemeyer Webb made the inevitable decision to move the boat to the museum.

Resolutely she faced innumerable obstacles. There were the derisive comments of the community: a landlocked lighthouse was somewhat peculiar, a landlocked steamboat seemed down-right crazy. There was the skepticism of museum trustees and her own family: surely the huge boat would dwarf the other buildings of the museum. There was the necessity of deciding on its final position, since, once arrived, it would be an ungainly object to nudge hither and yon. There was the enormous cost of the operation. And, hardheadedly, the question of whether the boat could be moved at all. Who else had ever tried to transport a 220-foot-long sidewheeler 9,000 feet overland?

The moving operation was, indeed, ingenious, costly and hazardous. A huge berthing basin was dug in Shelburne Bay. The boat was led into it by tugs and imprisoned by a high clay dike. Then, by a system of locks, she was floated up twenty-five feet onto a steel cradle which straddled flat cars on two sets of railroad tracks. The 400-foot lengths of track were picked up and laid down over and over again as the *"Ti"* inched over her two-mile journey.

There were tense moments. Would she flop over on her side? Would she tangle with high-tension wires? Would the spring thaw set in and bog her down as she crossed a large swamp near the museum grounds? It was a situation in which one of Mrs. Webb's most reliable precepts—"The effort is worth the accomplishment"—gave but cold comfort.

But her luck held. After sixty-five days, twenty hours and twenty-eight minutes en route, the *"Ti"* reached her final port. With her pennants flying and her whistle tooting, she is at home on the museum grounds. Vermonters have already made her a beloved landmark glimpsed from distant hills. Mrs. Webb's family was temporarily relieved. But as the triumphant lady departed for a hunting trip in Alaska, one of her sons cautioned her, "Please, Mother, if someone offers you Mount McKinley as a gift for the museum, don't try to move it."

Mrs. Webb has undoubtedly not moved mountains simply because her ungovernable passion for collecting runs to man-made objects and North American game animals. (Inevitably, a hunting lodge will be constructed to display a collection of the latter.) In the last few years she has added a blacksmith shop, an up-and-down sawmill, the last steam locomotive of the Central Vermont Railway and the deserted, charmingly Victorian station of Shelburne at which Dr. Webb's private railroad cars once deposited his guests. Still to come is a building to house a complete steam-driven carrousel. Forty prancing animals, bejeweled and polychromed, along with the carnival-bright gondolas, will spin once more to the lilting melodies of the calliope as they did in their original appearance at the Philadelphia Exposition of 1873, at which Electra Havemeyer Webb's father first became a collector. "The merry-go-round is the one thing I don't have to worry about," Mrs. Webb confides. "The parts are all in the attic of the Stagecoach Inn. If I don't get it up, my children or my grandchildren will. It's these other things I must do . . ."

Among these "other things" there will be, perhaps, a building to house American paintings. For a long time Electra Havemeyer Webb, who would stack a piece of American folk-art sculpture against any of her parents' Degas bronzes, had an uneasy reluctance about American primitives and paintings. Even she had to admit that the European paintings to which she had been exposed in the Havemeyer house had a slight edge over the home-grown variety. But when she saw the American paintings collected by Maxim Karolik and Colonel Garbisch (large portions of which are now in the Boston Museum and the National Gallery, respectively), she was cured of this one inherited artistic prejudice.

Mrs. Havemeyer had exactly one piece of Americana—a mirror—in her house on East Sixty-sixth Street. Mrs. Webb, more broad-mindedly, will devote an entire building of her museum to her mother's non-Americana. Into it will go the great Havemeyer treasures which she inherited, along with any other objects from that magnificent accumulation which other Havemeyer heirs, including her own children, may choose to give. For Mrs. Webb, like her mother before her, has given her offspring a generous amount of art. ("To give when you're healthy is golden, to give when you're dead is lead.")

Her children occasionally warn her that even with the little hop-on, hop-off bus to transport visitors to and from the twenty-nine buildings, the museum will become too large and lose its pleasantly intimate scale. But tolerantly and affectionately, they understand that it is as impossible for her to stop collecting as to declare the museum finished. And Electra Webb herself, born collector, knows too that she will not stop. Thinking of how certain other people with an addiction less constructive, but no less urgent, have banded together to cure themselves, she says cheerily, "Thank goodness there is no Collectors Anonymous."

She runs the Shelburne Museum with an astonishingly small, able and devoted staff ("My very best collection"). At one meeting she presented them with a toy monkey that bobbed up and down, clashing a pair of cymbals in aimless agitation. "A trustee talking to the staff," she explained. But they would not accept such a caricature of this normal, efficient, enthusiastic woman. She sets a project in motion with the kind of organizational clarity and swift attention to detail that once enabled her father to command the sugar trust and herself to do a spectacular job running the New York Blood Bank during World War II. She is modest and unpretentious; her family and her museum are her prides. She beams visibly when she hears a report that in addition to over 160,000 Americans, visitors from sixty foreign countries have come to see what her mother once deprecated as "American trash."

The Shelburne Museum is as much the expression of one woman's taste and personality—simple, honest, very American— as Fenway Court is of another's. It preserves an extraordinary record of our American heritage and presents it with freshness and light-heartedness as well as with historic significance and discriminating taste. In 1956, in recognition of the "discernment and affection" with which the collections were assembled and displayed, Electra Havemeyer Webb received (only one of five women ever so honored) an honorary degree of Master of Arts from Yale University. She was told, "You have brought the American past into its own for the delight and edification of the present."

Cowboys and Indians

THOMAS GILCREASE

"A man must leave some sort of track." That is the credo of Thomas Gilcrease, a shy, sparse, sixty-eight-year-old Oklahoman who "struck it rich" in oil. Thomas Gilcrease is resolutely proud of being one-sixteenth Creek Indian, No. 1505 on the Final Roll of Creek Citizens by Blood. He is so proud, in fact, that he does nothing to correct the repeatedly published fraction of one-eighth. For the benefit of European friends who are naïvely and romantically excited at meeting an American Indian, he will even obligingly pose as a full-blooded Creek.

The Indian blood comes from his mother; his father was of French-Scotch-Irish descent. Although Thomas Gilcrease's bearing is ramrod straight as any chief's and he is given to Indian-like withdrawn moods, his soft speech and silent steps, his small, gray-brown eyes behind gold-rimmed glasses, his thin lips, his other moods of loquacious reminiscences and the frugal way in which he lives make the Scotch-Irish strain more apparent than the Indian one. He dresses in the neat, anonymously conservative style of a bank teller.

The old-master market is drying up. Those of the oil-rich who would like to out-Morgan Morgan must be content with lesser hauls. Even oil man J. Paul Getty, probably the world's richest private citizen, who likes to buy old masters for "investment" as well as beauty, has had to be content with a mere $4,000,000 worth—with a fairly low density of masterpieces—picked up since he began collecting in 1931. Or, like the Charles B. Wrightsmans, the rich collectors must venture into the field of the eighteenth century, which, although exceedingly expensive and popular in Europe and South America, has never been quite as fashionable in America. The Wrightsmans have bought such out-of-period items as a marvelous Vermeer for, allegedly, $350,000, along with about a dozen other paintings including a Tiepolo ceiling. But their main effort and income have gone into making their home into a Rococo stage-set with superlatively beautiful objects. It is so exquisitely perfect that any visitor short of Voltaire must seem an impostor, and talk of prorated oil a vulgar anachronism.

These rare worlds of splendor and elegance are not the worlds of oil man Thomas Gilcrease. The "track" that Thomas Gilcrease will leave—and to whose making he has devoted some of thirty-three years and all of the last twenty—is a mountainous, heterogeneous collection of documents, rare books, artifacts, paintings and sculptures valued at $12,000,000. Now owned by the city of Tulsa, it is known as the Thomas Gilcrease Institute of American History and Art. (Why it is "Institute" instead of "Museum" is a somewhat baffling question which Tulsans brush impatiently aside.)

That history overwhelms art in this collection is not accidental. Thomas Gilcrease set out to tell the story of America from prehistoric times to the present, with special emphasis on the story of the American Indian and the development of southwestern

United States. He would tell the narrative in documents, objects and pictures.

If Rembrandt or Renoir had painted American Indians, Gilcrease would have been after their canvases like a bloodhound. Sir Joshua Reynolds and his contemporary, the English painter Francis Parsons, *did* paint Indians. They painted portraits, respectively, of Syacost Ukeah and Cunne Shote, Cherokee warriors who went to England after a treaty with the British in 1762, to receive shining silver "peace medals" from George III. (Cunne Shote amiably posed with his scalping knife as well as his medals and a gorget inscribed G.R.III.) Gilcrease bought these paintings more for their meaning than their esthetic excellence, just as he purchased a handsome full-length portrait by Thomas Eakins because it represented Frank Hamilton Cushing, a painter who had ventured into the Dakota Badlands.

Some other rather good painters have painted the kinds of things that Gilcrease was after. In 1883, John Jarvis did a portrait of the Sauk and Fox Chief, Black Hawk, and his son, when Black Hawk, who liked white men's clothes, put them on for a tour of the United States in which he was exhibited as a trophy of war. Gilcrease owned that painting, too. So, too, he owned such handsome illustrations of American fauna as Audubon's magnificent oil of "The Wild Turkey"; intimate and panoramic views of the American landscape by such talented artists as Thomas Moran and Albert Bierstadt; and large holdings of work by the best of the documentary artists who began making their animated records of the land beyond the wide Missouri in the precamera days.

If a painting Thomas Gilcrease wants has esthetic quality as well as meaning, he is very pleased. If it has none—as is true of hundreds out of a total four thousand—he is not the least bothered. He is the first to admit that the one hundred and twenty-six Indian chiefs, warriors, medicine men and army scouts by Henry H. Cross, with their brash color and waxwork realism, are not the greatest art in the world.

All but thirteen of them were commissioned around 1909, by T. B. Walker, a self-made lumber baron who lived in Minneapolis, and he once owned all of them. According to the State Historical Society of Wisconsin, T. B. Walker's attitude toward Indians was somewhat more patronizing than Thomas Gilcrease's. "However deplorable he thought their way of life," we are told, "he was genuinely interested in them as human beings. He even entertained in his Minneapolis home some of the tribal delegations that journeyed periodically to Washington to visit the Great Father." In that home, the tribal delegations had a chance to gaze upon a collection of paintings and sculptures which John G. Johnson would have dismissed as "Names." T. B. Walker was, indeed, on surer grounds of authenticity with his Cross collection of Indian portraits than he was with his old masters.

To Gilcrease, the Cross series, regardless of artistic merit, is an essential link in his narrative. Buffalo Bill Cody himself certified to the "striking likenesses" of the portraits and they are faithful in detail down to the last feather and piece of wampum.

Even if the documentary value is not in question, Gilcrease still likes paintings to "tell a story" or "have meaning" or "capture realism." Thus he represents, without the slightest equivocation or false embarrassment, popular, mass taste in America—the taste which likes Norman Rockwell's pictorial soap-opera scenes, praises the three-dimensional bronze version of the photograph of "Raising the Flag on Iwo Jima" and thrills to "Silver Threads Among the Gold" played on the *vox humana*. No matter what the fluctuations of sophisticated taste, this mass taste remains solid as bedrock below. It prevailed at the exhibition of the Philadelphia Centennial in 1876 and it determines all "popular" exhibitions today, as it will tomorrow.

Thomas Gilcrease had arrived at his criteria at the age of twenty-two, when he bought his first painting. But he has never fooled himself about these criteria having anything very much to do with esthetics.

Certain dealers from New York and Chicago made regular traveling-salesman trips to the Southwest in the years just before and after World War I. They did a brisk, not always ethical business with the unsophisticated, eager *nouveaux riches* of the youngest states in the Union, as their predecessors had done several generations before on the Eastern seaboard. There still exists in Texas one of the collections that dates from these art-carpetbagging days. It consists of paintings purportedly by such old masters as Rembrandt and Hals and Gainsborough. Under each painting, a brochure in a tooled Florentine leather cover explains that *this* is an original of which a copy is in the Rijksmuseum in Amsterdam or the Louvre or the Metropolitan. It is a collection still proudly displayed by its either very innocent or very stubborn owners.

Thomas Gilcrease, who had no pretensions and no predilection for million-dollar masters, fell into better hands. In 1912 he wandered into the Hotel Tulsa, where a New York dealer was showing anecdotal paintings by conservative contemporary artists. Gilcrease fell for a picture by Ridgeway Knight called "Rural Courtship," in which a girl with apple cheeks and wooden shoes leans on a gate toying with her apron while an apple-cheeked boy, also with wooden shoes, courts her in his shy and tongue-tied way. Thomas Gilcrease was entranced by the sweet depiction of wholesome puppy love—and he was reminded of it many years later on a hunting trip in Alaska when he spent a day following softly behind a herd of three hundred moose and watched the young cows and bulls clumsily and affectionately nudge each other in the play of early courtship.

Such sentimental storytelling pictures still appeal to Thomas Gilcrease. Not so long ago he commissioned Howard Chandler Christy to paint an enormous picture called "Hiawatha's Wooing," which takes place in a green-blue landscape of Technicolor intensity. Never has Minnehaha had so much the glamorized sweetness of an early Hollywood starlet.

But pictures with sentimental associations appeal to Gilcrease less than those with historic interest or documentary validity. History is his consuming interest (on peripatetic trips with his daughter to Europe and to forty-seven of the forty-eight states, he reacted to a historical marker like a bird dog who has sniffed his quarry). The clue to the man is his inquiring mind. He wants to know What, How, When, Where so that he can ponder the important question: Why. To stimulate others toward similar speculation, especially about the history of our own land and its peoples, by showing them the What, How, When and Where, seems to him "something worthwhile." He is a serious, simple man, who, in his philosophic way, has taken on the conscience of one race, the griefs of the other. The only kind of track that Thomas Gilcrease would want to leave would be a "worthwhile" one.

On February 8, 1890, Thomas Gilcrease, the eldest of fourteen children, was born to William and Elizabeth Vowell Gilcrease in Robilene, Louisiana, a small town about a hundred miles from Shreveport. The father was an energetic, restless, pioneering soul who kept trying his hand at one thing after another in the uphill battle of feeding his brood. Farming was the most constant occupation, but there were supplementary ones. Shortly after the birth of his first son, William Gilcrease decided to take advantage of his wife's rights as a Creek. They moved across the river into the Creek nation, where any Creek citizen could live where he wished on the tribal lands.

Stopping first at Eufala, the family settled in a place now known as Twin Mounds. When Thomas Gilcrease was five and a half, his father put on him a pair of black boots with brass toes and took him to the father of the Creek poet, Alex Posey, to learn to read and write. Fortunately, he learned quickly. The shoes were thrown away before they were outgrown. Thomas Gilcrease went to work helping his father farm, run the cotton gin and work the grist mill.

"The time to begin plowing or picking cotton is when the sun rises and the time to stop is when it sets," his father told him. Before the sun rose, he had to feed the hogs, turn the cattle to pasture, harness the horses and start the fire in the kitchen. After it set, he had to feed the stock again, milk the cows, unharness the horses, bring in the wood for the morning. "When all that is done, you can do what you want," his father said. What he wanted to do was to read. He still handles a book reverentially and caressingly. When his daughter was small, one of the first things he taught her was how to open a book and lay its pages flat so that it would not be damaged.

He was a sensitive boy, isolated from other children both by the responsibilities of being the eldest son and by a rather bad limp from a crippled leg (that was later completely cured by surgery). His habits of introspection and observation started early.

On the way to feed the cattle, he would stop in wonderment at the dew-speckled, magically intricate spider's webs that blocked his path and run his hands gently over the fronds of ferns to see them curl up protectively. "These things show a kind of intelligence," he concluded. He noticed the tall grass in June that made his bare feet white, "white as the sugar in the breakfast bowl"; listened to the gobble of wild turkeys close at hand send up a chain reaction of gobbling along the Frio River; heard the Indians call longhorn steer "white man's buffalo" and sneer at its skinniness; watched the Indians play "stick-ball" (lacrosse) and learned from them to kill small game with stones and shoot fish with a homemade bow and arrow. When the white families met in successive houses on Saturday nights for dancing, poker and drinking, he fled and hid under the porches to escape being witness to the brawling, the knifings, the gunplay with which the evenings always ended. He vowed at the age of six never to gamble or to touch liquor, and he never has.

"There were things to make a boy think," he says. Not the least of the things that made Thomas Gilcrease think was what was happening to the Indians. Back in the eighteen thirties, yielding to the pressures of white settlers in an expanding economy, Andrew Jackson had forced the Five Civilized Tribes (the Cherokee, the Choctaw, the Chickasaw, the Seminole and the Creek) from Georgia and Alabama to the desolate, uninhabited lands of the "Indian Territory," including what is now Oklahoma. Driven like cattle, mistreated and neglected by the United States soldiers, the Indians suffered terribly during their difficult winter journey. Only a quarter of them survived "The Trail of Tears."

They had been promised that the new land would be theirs "as long as the grasses grew and the water ran." They had barely established their nations and their civilizations before the white man's troubles pressed upon them. They were reluctantly drawn into the Civil War on the side of the Confederacy, then punished by the Union with loss of a large part of their western territory. White cattlemen driving their stock westward and frontiersmen traveling on the first railroad of the seventies began looking greedily at the great fertile ranges. Neither laws nor covenants nor treaties could keep the land-hungry settlers out.

In the eighties, the settlers grabbed so-called unassigned lands which had been taken in various ways from the Indians. At high noon on April 22, 1889, the year before Thomas Gilcrease was born, prospective settlers were allowed to "run" from the Kansas border to claim more land. The "run" was not played according to Marquis of Queensberry rules: many settlers jumped the gun. Known as "sooners," these overanxious settlers were once despised, but now the word has taken on connotations of "enterprise" and "ingenuity." Still, the whites were not satisfied. In 1893, the Dawes Commission, brushing aside Indian resistance, simply did away with tribal land titles by making allotments to individual Indians. It was a nastily ingenious device: alloting a 160-acre tract to each Indian, left a large surplus for white settlers.

Young Thomas Gilcrease knew of this perfidy. He knew, too, the tales of treachery to other tribes: the way French and English fur trappers disarmed the Indians for their own purposes; treaties with the government made but not ratified or deliberately misinterpreted; the mishandling of funds for the Indians; the ravages of the white man's alcohol and tuberculosis; the hypocrisy of many of the itinerant preachers (he was himself first baptized by a "preacher" who was later unmasked as a horse thief). He saw white settlers shooting Indians on sight, because it was keener sport than shooting deer, and justifying their fun on the grounds that their targets were "uncivilized savages." In 1904, the Gilcrease family moved to nearby Weakala and Thomas Gilcrease helped his father run a general store. He flinched when the settlers, putting their hands on his shoulders, paid him their greatest compliment: "Son, when you grow up you'll be a real good Indian shooter."

In 1899, William Gilcrease received 160-acre tracts for the Creek citizens of his family: his wife and each of their children. That same year, a farmer showed Thomas Gilcrease an oil seep. It did not mean very much to the nine-year-old boy or to his parents. They used the oil to grease harnesses. They found it effective, too, for saturating sacks which could be wound around logs for the hogs to rub against, as the oil killed hog lice.

Six years later, in 1905, the first oil well in the Oklahoma Territory was brought in at Glen Pool. Thomas Gilcrease could hear its roaring gush four miles away. Soon he would hear the reassuring sound at closer range. His own 160 acres lay in that rich oil region. In 1910, he procured drilling tools and was "in oil." By 1917, the 160-acre tract had thirty-two producing wells. He used his royalties to have his game leg fixed, pay his tuition at Bacone Indian College and then briefly at a teacher's college in Kansas, and to buy more farm land. Soon he was trading in oil leases and drilling wells in a line southwest from Tulsa. In one area he found oil in hitherto unknown sand at a depth of 3,150 feet, a formation since known as Gilcrease sand.

By 1925, at thirty-five, Thomas Gilcrease had been married, had produced two sons, had been divorced, and had founded the

Gilcrease Oil Company. He was a prosperous man. He began to think about "leaving a track."

He went off on a hunting trip to Canada and Alaska, where he could "think out what would be worthwhile." He flirted briefly with the Utopian notion of turning four hundred acres of farm land into a self-supporting writers' colony, because writers "had a way of getting a message to the people." It was a brief flirtation. Restless, uncertain, aware of how limited were the horizons of Oklahoma and Texas, he decided to go around the world and look before he made up his mind.

Impulsively he took a train to New York, arriving on a Saturday. The next morning, sitting in his room in the Hotel Astor, he was overwhelmed by the Sunday edition of the *New York Times,* whose bulk even in 1925 was somewhat surprising to a man accustomed to four-page Oklahoma newspapers. Conscientiously he read through every column—as he habitually did with newspapers at home—and then started resolutely on the ads. A big announcement that the S.S. *Leviathan,* "the world's largest ship," was sailing for Cherbourg the following Tuesday morning snared him. Accustomed to days that began at 4:30 A.M., he dallied a bit on Monday morning to suit himself to "city ways"—but he still arrived at the steamship office an hour and a half before it opened.

The office hours in New York were no more strange than the Folies Bergères in Paris. "It wasn't in keeping with my thinking. Oklahoma was never like that," he told a reporter later. Even such inadvertent frivolities were exceptions. He was an assiduous, dedicated sightseer, who boned up each night on what he would see the next day. He clocked off not only the three-star items in the guidebooks, but those in the small print, too. He made detours in the interests of history. He followed Jeanne d'Arc's route from her birthplace to the stake at Rouen to try to understand her motivations. He lingered a month at Carcassone. He taught himself French and Spanish. He had decided, romantically, to follow the sun around the world. In fourteen months, he had gotten as far as the Holy Land when his partners cabled him to come home because of his attorney's grave illness.

Before the European trip, his collecting had been confined to huge trophy heads of moose, bear and Dall sheep. They leered from the walls of the large, unpretentious, rather gloomy house on former Indian territory which he had bought in 1912 to help out the recently widowed lawyer who built it. After the European trip, most of the trophy heads were relegated to storage.

Thomas Gilcrease, who felt squeamish about the Folies Bergères, was apparently not averse to beautiful American girls. In 1928, he married barely-twenty-year-old Norma Des Cygne Smallwood, who had been Miss America of 1926. The house was redecorated in her honor with souvenirs, paintings and *objets d'art* from the first trip abroad and added to from subsequent ones. The marriage ended in a bitter divorce in 1934. Gilcrease, who never liked anything unwholesome, was further hurt when the tabloids played up each detail of the messy case. It left him stand-offish about the press for many years. Custody of the six-year-old daughter, Des Cygne L'Amour Gilcrease, was awarded him.

He had observed in Europe that the knowledge of civilizations is reconstructed from the things they have left. Oklahoma had no museum, no library, nothing which showed anything about the old civilizations of the Americas before Columbus or the development of the new, raw Southwest, nothing that told the story of Indian civilization. As he explained later, he had "no tomahawk to grind," but he wanted to preserve and tell that story. He had found something worthwhile to do.

Along with the indiscriminate souvenirs, the Brussels lace, the Rococo clocks, the Delft china and other objects which filled not only the Oklahoma house but also an apartment-office he had taken on the Champs-Elysées in Paris, he had begun buying the documents and rare books that would implement his collecting plan. That buying was a secret operation, partly because of his own uncertainties, partly because he wanted to avoid preying dealers and inflated prices. Even his sons were unaware of what he was doing. "Why does your father have all that storage space and what's he putting in it?" people asked them. "We don't know. Probably things he likes to buy," they answered.

The outbreak of World War II made him more than ever aware that things outlast people and that evidences of cultures and civilizations must be safeguarded. He decided to devote his full time to acquiring those informative things, and to come out in the open.

In the forties, he became a familiar figure to certain London dealers. Large quantities of American Indian material were available in England. Some of it had been brought back by the English fur traders and British officers in Colonial times. British interest in the subject remained keen well into the nineteenth century.

Much as documentary photographers today would accompany such expeditions, a number of artists had gone West with prospective fur traders and such romantic European adventurers as Maximilian of Wied-Neuwied. They had accompanied military expeditions and traveled with the railroad surveyors. George Catlin was, in 1832, one of the first to record Indian life; Albert Jacob Miller set out in 1837; Charles Bodmer, Albert Bierstadt, Thomas Moran were among others of the best of these recorders. Their pictorial documents were enormously interesting to European audiences, who had both romantic and economic curiosity about the new lands of the New World. George Catlin had huge success when he exhibited his "Indian Gallery" in London in 1836 and he procured British financing for his North American Indian portfolio. One of Gilcrease's paintings, called "Contested Game," by a rather mediocre artist, William Carey, was exhibited in London in 1885. This thrill-packed canvas, showing a bear and three Indians fighting over a dead buffalo, was one of the popular hits of the show.

It was not until the twentieth century that Americans began to interest themselves very much in the artistic records of the West, although they had been buying American landscapes from the mid-nineteenth century on. Now, thrilled by Owen Wister's best seller, *The Virginian,* which was published in 1902, or goggle-eyed at Buffalo Bill's Wild West Show, or hero-worshiping Teddy Roosevelt's rough-and-ready concepts of manliness, East-erners went West and brought back paintings as romantic testi-money to their adventures. Others, like Ogden Mills, who gave a large group of Catlins to the American Museum of Natural His-tory, were interested in the West historically. A little later, men like Copley Amory of Boston, who went to Montana to visit the family's copper mines, bought art as souvenirs.

As the century wore on, the most popular of the recorders were two of the late ones: Charles Russell, who became a Montana cowboy himself and died only in 1924, and Frederic Reming-ton, who died in 1909. Russell, whose paintings bear such reveal-ing titles as "Meat's Not Meat 'Til It's in the Pan," "Where Guns Were Their Passports," "The Strenuous Life" and "Where Tracks Spell War or Meat," had what Thomas Gilcrease calls "the hu-man touch." He also had a photographic eye so precise that, as one of his admirers remarked, he could get exactly "the nostril dilation of a buffalo bull."

Remington had a sense of fact, too, that was both enthusias-tic and conscientious, as well as a facile draftsmanship that later made him a superb illustrator of the Spanish-American War for the Hearst press. His paintings of Indian warfare and buffalo hunts had both an excitement and authenticity far greater than those of the very popular contemporary one-reel "Westerns," which fea-tured city-bred "Bronco Billy" Anderson. Even Remington's horses had personalities, and his cowboys, scouts, soldiers and In-dians never looked like "extras" miscast in their roles. In addition to paintings and drawings, Remington started, around 1895, mak-ing bronzes of extraordinary virtuosity that showed cowboys and Indians in such exuberant action as "Coming Through the Rye" or such spine-tingling episodes as that in which an Indian reins his horse and lifts aloft a recently captured scalp. His art supplied all the blood and thunder, danger and adventure and rugged manliness of life on the range. It was life in the raw with, as he put it, "men with the bark on." Women played an even lesser role in his paintings than in the Western movies: they are almost never in evidence.

This sort of thing rarely appealed to the collectors of Great Art or even the collectors of Modern Art. (Henry Walters was a rare exception, with a taste so catholic and an interest in artists so strong that he bought quantities of Western scenes by his fellow Baltimorean, Albert Jacob Miller). But this he-man art began to have an increasingly wide audience in America. The elegant firm of Knoedler, supplying high-priced old masters to Henry Clay Frick and Andrew Mellon, did a brisk side-line business in supplying landscapes of the American scene and in catering to the taste for cowboy-and-Indian art.

In recent years, there have been a few "specialists," such as the big, breezy, colorfully cussing Texan president of American Airlines, C. R. Smith, and the even breezier, more colorful publisher of the *Fort Worth Star-Telegram,* the late Amon Carter. Known as "Mr. Texas," Carter was a brash, swashbuckling showman, booster of Fort Worth and Texas, who handed out silver dollars, jeweled Western belts, pearl-handled six-shooters and ten-gallon Texas hats to acquaintances around the world and entertained his visitors in a room where, above the mantel, the head of a longhorn steer puffed smoke from its nostrils and blinked its eyelids over red electric-light bulbs. Inspired by C. R. Smith, Carter became interested in Remington and Russell as faithful depicters of cowboy life. He ultimately acquired a large group of their work, including the entire Mint Saloon from Great Falls, Montana, which had been filled with Russell's work. He paid $250,000 for it.

Gilcrease's interest extended far beyond the paintings of Indians and the West. He bought anything and everything that had any possible connection with his theme. He gathered hundreds of Indian pipes, blankets, ceremonial objects, pieces of beadwork and jewelry. He purchased pre-Columbian material of all kinds. He got hold of 85,000 books, letters and manuscripts. One of the letters, from General George Custer, ends, "You will next hear from me . . . not from the plains of Philippi . . . but from those of Dakota, the home of S.B.," referring, of course, to the Sioux Chief, Sitting Bull, before whom Custer made his "last stand." Gilcrease's enormous library includes the first letter sent from the New World, signed by Columbus' son Diego, written in Santo Domingo in 1512; the only certified copies of the articles of Confederation and Declaration of Independence outside the Library of Congress; five suitcases full of Cortez material, which cost $130,000 and tells in detail of the boats which Cortez used in conquering the Aztecs; and the original document of April 29, 1775, appointing Paul Revere to make his much-touted midnight ride.

Tirelessly, diligently, Gilcrease bought and bought, unnerving dealers with an inscrutable, Indian-like silence as they displayed their wares. He bought single objects and such ready-made collections as Sir Thomas Phillipp's Catlin group in England and the extensive Grant Foreman collection of War Department and Indian Office material.

When the Dr. Philip Cole collection of Remington bronzes was going to be sold, one of Gilcrease's strong competitors was oil man Frank Phillips of Phillips-66 renown. Phillips presumably wanted them for *his* estate-cum-museum, Woolaroc (Wood + Lake + Rock), near Bartlesville, Oklahoma. Although Phillips' Woolaroc driveway is only 2.5 miles as compared to the 5.4 miles of Hearst's San Simeon driveway, it rivals the California one with wandering deer, elk and moose, cages of such wild animals as gnus, over-life-sized painted plaster Indians saying "How" and a grove of bleached white ox skulls hanging from trees. The very popular museum, which seems to be dedicated to showing objects from "the dawn of history" to the present, is one of the most bizarre and, to sophisticated critics, one of the most unsettling, in the world.

Tulsans tell the story that Phillips offered $350,000 for the bronzes and then telephoned to ask Mrs. Cole a question about one of the sculptures. He was, they say, told not to bother, since a bid had been received, accompanied by a blank check, offering $10,000 more than any other bid. Gilcrease got the Remington bronzes.

The wholesale buying of whole collections often means, as Gilcrease knows, that "you have to take the bad to get the good." He is inured to that circumstance from his extensive operations in buying land for oil-well drilling. If one well comes in, the purchase has been worthwhile.

In 1942, Gilcrease formed the Thomas Gilcrease Foundation, a part of whose funds were permanently allocated for education of Indians. He put a part of his collection on public view in temporary quarters until, in 1949, the Thomas Gilcrease Museum of American History and Art opened. It is a building shaped like an Indian long-house, built by Indian workmen out of sandstone quarried in the adjacent Osage hills. With ten ample galleries, it still provided space for the display of only about four percent of the collection. Visitors would see the quiet man lurking unobtrusively and reflectively in the galleries, seeming in his silent rounds more like a trusted caretaker than the owner of these millions of dollars' worth of documentary art and artifacts.

The museum had been open only four years when, in 1953, Thomas Gilcrease found himself in a tough financial spot. Oil production had been sharply prorated because of overproduction here and abroad, and underconsumption when the fighting in Korea ceased. "You don't starve, but it makes a difference in your calculations," Gilcrease confided in 1953. It made a particular difference as far as his bills for art and artifacts were concerned. His oil income was not sufficient to meet outstanding bills of

$2,200,000 for which he was being hard pressed by the dealers.

To sell a part of the collection to meet the obligation seemed to him unthinkable. "It has value only when held intact for the people," he maintained with stony dignity. What would happen to the Gilcrease collection became a public issue. It was said that universities in Texas and North Carolina were after it; that Amon Carter would buy it lock, stock and barrel; that the state of Oklahoma would purchase it and move it to the University at Norman or construct a new building for it near the Will Rogers Memorial at Claremore.

At the last minute, a group of Tulsa citizens formed a "Keep the Gilcrease Museum in Tulsa" Committee. Headed by oil man Alfred E. Aaronson, it proposed voting a bond issue of $2,500,000 to pay off the Gilcrease Foundation's debts, in return for which Gilcrease would give his collection to the city of Tulsa, assign it one-half interest in five East Texas oil leases (which average a little under $4,000 a month) and lease the building for five years at one dollar a year. The committee whooped up enthusiasm. Even Brownie Troop 209 in the third grade at a local public school contributed two dollars toward the $10,700 that had to be raised to defray the cost of a special election.

On August 24, 1954, the citizens braved a scorching sun to vote three to one in favor of the bond issue that would save the Gilcrease Museum for Tulsa. It now operates under the Tulsa Park Board with a Citizens Advisory Committee.

Having made these new commitments, and provisions for his children and grandchildren, Thomas Gilcrease is no longer a very rich man. He lives alone in the big house, whose only staff is a few-hours-a-day cleaning woman. He drives himself, not in a Cadillac, but in a Buick, and he eats all his meals, including breakfast, in Tulsa's unpretentious restaurants. All his money goes into art and artifacts for a new private collection, intended, of course, ultimately as a gift to the museum. He could no more stop collecting than he could stop reading.

Some of the money is being spent for paintings by the best American painters chosen for their quality as *art,* but, naturally, Gilcrease is happiest when that circumstance coincides with the kind of subject matter that fits his big theme.

His new collecting enthusiasm is "digging." Thomas Gilcrease got into archeology obliquely. For several years he had been interested in the Indian cultures of two and three thousand years ago that are being increasingly revealed and studied from the burial materials found in the mounds of the Southwest. A trusting, honest man, who can "never believe that people like to gyp you," Gilcrease was aghast when he discovered that certain persons were selling him fake pots and pipes. "If you dig yourself, you know the things are right," he concluded.

He has undertaken several excavations and acquired a vast amount of material from them in the last few years. His informal method of working is somewhat nerve-racking to professional archeologists, who work at slow tempo, photographing, measuring and rushing samples off to laboratories for carbon readings at almost every turn of the shovel. Their systematic, molasses-slow speed is equally unsettling to Gilcrease, who insists they are, "like preachers, 'sot in their ways.'" His staff on the site is headed by a man familiar with early Indian cultures by long interest and reading and by a young archeologist so recently graduated that he has not yet had a chance to "get set." Whenever possible, he is out digging with them.

Even the most "set" archeologists admit, however, that Gilcrease is doing an inestimably valuable service with his blitz rescue operations. He goes in to mounds which, but for his action, would be destroyed by bulldozers making way for housing developments or by the plows of farmers seeking richer loam below the surface. Such projects can be held off—even with cash—for a minimum amount of time only. Gilcrease has preserved thousands of objects. Although they may not be recorded to the last jot of scientific detail, they have nevertheless been saved from destruction.

Of all Gilcrease's collecting activities, this "do-it-yourself" operation has been most rewarding. When he uncovers a tomb with all the evidence of 2,000 years ago intact, looks at the way the skeleton faces, examines the marvelous animal-figure pipes, the neatly stacked spoons, the wonderful little pots, he is confronting the What and How and When and Where that help answer Why. With his own money, by his own labor, with his own hands he is finding and saving things that tell the story of America. These things are dear to him. He spends hours examining the infinite variations in the pots. Even in the handsomely stylized animal-figure pipes he admires the realistic detail of a beaver's buck teeth or a raven's feathers.

When the museum was his, he used to fuss with its arrangements. Now he is satisfied with a smaller space, a little gallery adjacent to the Gilcrease Foundation office. Here he hangs and re-hangs his paintings, new and old, of the West; places on the shelves below them an inventory of pots beyond count; and lays out on the center tables a whole arsenal of arrowheads.

The city's dollar-a-year lease on the museum building will expire in 1959. Gilcrease has made the city another proposition. If Tulsa will pledge to build a fireproof, air-conditioned museum of 50,000 square feet (as compared to the present 15,000) and keep the collection there, he will give it the twenty-five acres on which the museum stands, plus his house and other buildings, for a public park, and will also leave as a gift his new private collection, valued at $750,000. The prognosis is that the citizens of Tulsa will accept his proposition and vote another bond issue for its fulfillment.

Thomas Gilcrease will have left a worthwhile track.

Appassionata of the Avant-Garde

PEGGY GUGGENHEIM

In 1937, Peggy Guggenheim, at the age of thirty-nine, found herself temporarily without a man. Having made a frantic career of men for the past twenty years, she could easily have acquired another, but she was momentarily surfeited.

According to her autobiography, she had loved, brawled, drunk her way through one marriage (her husband, who was a writer and later a decorator of bottles, was the father of her two children) and through several love affairs. The carefully annotated roster includes an Englishman working in an avant-garde publishing house who later became a Communist, and a man whom many describe as a genius—a writer who did not write and died tragically young—who was her one real love. Later, she was to acquire a gloomy young Irish writer who *did* write, although he eventually preferred to do so in French, and many other more or less talented companions.

A tormented, undisciplined, lonely child, she had become a member not of the Lost, but of the Mislaid Generation. She had been riding the expatriate merry-go-round from the south of France to England to the Tyrol, careening from the twenties into the thirties. In 1937, examining her coffers, she found them full of brass rings.

Restless, bored, satiated, she wanted something to do. Her lot had been cast with a world of wandering intellectuals. Starting a publishing house or opening an art gallery seemed the logical possibility for a woman in her position.

In cold fact, her position was much less gilt-and-copper-edged than was generally assumed. Her father, Benjamin, was indeed one of the seven Guggenheim brothers who made a spectacular fortune in the American Smelting and Refining Company, and consequently, the press has inevitably referred to Peggy Guggenheim as a fabulously rich woman (in 1957, carried away by Latin exuberance, one Italian newspaper even called her "the richest woman in the world"). But shortly before he was drowned on the *Titanic* in 1912, when Peggy was fourteen, Benjamin Guggenheim had left his family's business and gone on his own. Solitariness proved less lucrative than solidarity. At his death Peggy Guggenheim inherited $450,000, and when her mother died in 1939 she came into a like amount. Relatively speaking, Peggy Guggenheim was indisputably a poor relation.

She was a tall, slim woman with a squarish face, remarkable blue eyes, a somewhat bulbous nose and a roguish smile. She had very pretty legs and long arms which, frequently twisted into awkward schoolgirl gestures, gave her a touching look of helplessness. It was not wholly deceptive. For all the sophistication of her gold sheath dresses and teeteringly long cigarette holders and her flamboyant Bohemianism, she was astonishingly naïve and entirely without malice. Hungry for affection and admiration, she would dash impetuously and with trusting ingenuousness into situations which were bound to leave her injured or abandoned.

Undisciplined and self-indulgent about her emotions, she never pampered herself with money. Occasionally she lapsed into the cautious suspiciousness common to the rich and tightly closed her fist, but usually she handed out money with impulsive and warm-hearted generosity. She is so generous, in fact, that it is probably only the hampering restrictions of trust funds that have saved her from becoming a dependent instead of a poor relation.

When the coal miners went on strike in England in the early thirties, she was so moved by their plight that she gave them the last $10,000 that remained from her grandfather's inheritance. At one point she was contributing to the support of one of her ex-husbands, her children, and the wife of one of her lovers, signing checks regularly for a talented woman writer and helping out various other authors and artists. Her respect for creative people is reverent. One suspects that she often became mistress in the hope of becoming muse.

At the moment of decision in 1937, the well-meaning friends who warned her that she would lose her chemise in the publishing business were innocent of the equally certain outcome of running a gallery for avant-garde art. So, it was to be the art gallery.

There was one slight obstacle. At the time, she knew very little about modern art. In Munich, in 1902, at the age of four, she had been painted as a little princess by Lenbach, the fashionable portraitist who epitomized her parents' taste. (This painting is now confined to the privacy of the ironing room.) Later she had been introduced to Italian Renaissance painting by Armand Lowengard, a nephew of Joseph Duveen. It can be surmised that Uncle Joe knew she was a poor Guggenheim or he obviously would have bent his efforts on changing the introduction into a permanent liaison.

Young Lowengard challenged her to read Berenson's art criti-

cism. Years later she generously acknowledged that she owed her
career as a collector to Berenson's influence, but that exquisite
gentleman, surveying her abstract and surrealist art, recoiled
from the responsibility. Powerful as Berenson's influence may
have been, his writings on Florentine and Venetian painters were
hardly handy guides to contemporary art.

She turned for help in that direction to Marcel Duchamp, who
had already been an amiable mentor to that far more formidable
lady, Katherine Dreier. The curriculum included both abstraction
and surrealism. The year before, in London, Peggy Guggenheim
had abjured the huge international exhibition of surrealism at the
New Burlington Galleries, dismissing surrealism as "old hat." But,
receptive always to the strong convictions of those in whose grasp
she placed herself, she now followed Duchamp diligently
through the haunted landscape and architecture of the surrealist
dream world. Katherine Dreier had conscientiously included the
surrealists in her documentary survey, but it was not her dish of
tea. Duchamp found his new pupil more responsive to these paintings of irrational fantasies, delicate enigmas, shocking juxtaposi-
tions and weird incongruities.

Duchamp introduced her to the surrealists in the flesh. She met
André Breton, who had been a founder of the preceding antira-
tional dada movement and who was to become a kind of boss of
surrealism's most enduring faction. Among others, she met the
sculptor Jean Arp, from whom she bought her first piece of modern
sculpture, and the surrealist writer Jean Cocteau, who had gone
into such ecstasies over Rousseau's "Sleeping Gypsy." She honored
Cocteau with the first exhibition at the gallery in London which
opened on January 24, 1938, under the name of "Guggenheim
Jeune."

The Cocteau show raised a rumpus with the English customs.
Along with drawings, furniture and plates, Cocteau had sent two
sheets. On one of these he had portrayed arch, slithering creatures
with pubic hair. The customs officers were not the least mollified

by the fact that this hirsute display was conspicuously covered with fig leaves. They permitted Miss Guggenheim to remove the object from the dock only on the condition that she confine it to intimate showings in her private office.

A few months later, another row with the British customs produced a more lasting and beneficial result. Under Duchamp's aegis, she had arranged for a contemporary sculpture show with the work of such recognized masters as Brancusi, Arp, Gabo, Pevsner and Calder. The issue was the old one. Were the objects art, and therefore free of duty, or simply so much stone- and wood-carving, and therefore dutiable? In America, Uncle Sam's agents acted as art experts, but in England the director of the Tate Gallery made the esthetic decisions. At the time, this post was occupied by James Bolivar Manson, a man fifty-eight years old, with a cherubic face, a somewhat jaundiced view of modern art and apparently total ignorance of the fact that the United States Customs Court had accepted Brancusi's sculpture as art back in 1928.

Manson's rejection of two sculptures by Brancusi and Arp inspired so many lengthy protests in the press and so many comments by liberal members of Parliament that he rescinded his decision. Peggy Guggenheim has made a forceful impact on many men's lives, but none more decisive than her indirect effect on Mr. Manson. He resigned from his job, explaining that his nerves could stand no further strain and that he had become subject to recurrent blackouts, one "of which had occurred recently at an official luncheon in Paris" at which he "startled the guests by suddenly crowing like a cock. . . ."

The spirited exhibitions at Guggenheim Jeune, during the two years of its existence, were inspired by a constellation of reasons. Duchamp was responsible for several, such as the show for the Russian painter Kandinsky. There were exhibitions, too, of *collages,* children's art, abstract art. The Dutch painter Van Velde was given a show because one of Peggy Guggenheim's lovers admired him and for the same reason she kept buying his paintings "under different names and as gifts for my friends." The English abstract painter John Tunnard got a show because when he walked into the gallery with his paintings, she liked them. With the surrealist Yves Tanguy there was a happy coincidence: she liked both the man and his art.

If the relationship with Tanguy was an amorous success, Tanguy's paintings were an artistic success. Surrealism was having a limited vogue in London at the time. But the other exhibitions had not done so well. Peggy Guggenheim herself bought one or two things from each show, but this Peter-Paul arrangement did not disguise the fact that the money came and went from the same till. By March of the second year, realizing that she would continue to lose about $3,000 annually on the gallery, she decided she might "just as well lose a lot more and do something worthwhile," like opening a museum of modern art in London.

It was a notion which gratified Peggy Guggenheim. However free she felt from her bourgeois Jewish background, it had chronically infected her with a strong sense of moral responsibility about wealth. The admiration accruing to her from the performance of "good works" has, in the long run, given her far more satisfaction than the notoriety she achieved by being a "bad girl." The founding of a modern museum was also a gratifying notion to Herbert Read, to whom she turned for aid in the projected enterprise. Despite his looks, docile as a blue-eyed sheep's, this literary and art critic had been one of England's most forceful champions of modern art. Pinning down her somewhat flighty and idealistic financial notions into a firm legal contract that guaranteed him $5,000 annually for five years, he quit his job at the *Burlington Magazine,* took a far pleasanter one as a partner in a publishing house and agreed to act as the director of her museum. He found a location for it in a beautiful Regency house on Portman Square, spacious enough for gallery and living quarters. Peggy Guggenheim grew a little cool toward the idea when she discovered that

Mrs. Herbert Read would also be living on the premises, but she went gamely off to the Continent to round up pictures for the opening exhibition in the fall. The outbreak of the war solved all such problems. She temporarily shelved the notion of starting the museum and settled amicably with Herbert Read by paying him half of his contracted salary.

She flirted for a while with the idea of forming an artists' colony where surrealists and abstractionists would live together in happy fraternity as her guests during the war. Each would receive a small allowance in return for pictures to go into her future museum. It was perhaps the most naïve idea of the century. Artists are notoriously nonfraternal: surrealist artists are perhaps the least brotherly of the lot. They not only continually split into opposing factions, but even got into brawls at their social gatherings (at one of these, a bottle being hurled through the air neatly cut out the painter Victor Brauner's right eye).

She soon realized the wisdom of abandoning this scheme. She settled in Paris (the Germans were so far only in Poland) and set out on a proud new crusade of buying a picture a day.

A legacy of her relationship with Herbert Read was a list that he had concocted for the projected opening exhibition of the museum—a systematic historic survey of all the major movements of modern art from about 1910 to the present. Peggy Guggenheim deplored the inclusion of a few such old-fashioned predecessors as Cézanne and Rousseau and such a maverick from any strict "ism" as Matisse. With Marcel Duchamp and Nellie van Doesburg, the impassioned widow of the Dutch constructivist painter, she revised the list.

The new list became the basis of her collection and the essence of her diurnal crusade. She visited artists' studios and, like a lesser and vastly more informal Morgan, was besieged by dealers in her bedroom as well as her salon. Howard Putzel, a pudgy blond with acute, courageous taste, who had tried running a gallery of avant-garde art in California, lent his services. She acquired all manner of things, including a Dali, a Man Ray painting, a Giacometti sculpture, a Pevsner construction. While the Germans bombarded Paris, she bought a "Bird in Space" from Brancusi, who was now asking $4,000 for this sculpture. Then, as she remarks in one of the most blandly balanced sentences of all times, "The day Hitler walked into Norway, I walked into Léger's studio and bought a wonderful 1919 painting from him."

As the Germans approached Paris, she tried to persuade the Louvre to sequester her paintings in its secret country refuge, but the Louvre decided the art was too modern to be worth saving. She finally lodged it temporarily in a friend's barn at Vichy.

The pictures were gone, but Peggy Guggenheim lingered awhile in Paris drinking champagne with a new friend. At the last moment, with Nellie van Doesburg and two Persian cats, she fled south to unoccupied France and took a house with the Arps, near her ex-husband and her children.

She wiled away the time by indulging in a few casual affairs and by having her hair dyed a succession of colors, ending with the jet black she still favors. But she interrupted these absorbing activities to make a trip to Marseilles to see Varian Fry. Head of the Emergency Rescue Committee, Fry was doing a dangerous and heroic job raising money for stranded refugees and members of the Resistance and helping those who wished them to get American visas. Having already sent money generously to several artists who were in danger of being put in concentration camps, Peggy Guggenheim signed another large check for Fry to enable others to flee to safety. She kept in her own hands, however, the problem of the evacuation of the German surrealist painter Max Ernst, who had long been interned. The arrival of her paintings broke the tedium of hair-dyeing. The director of the Musée de Grenoble gave them shelter in the basement. For a while, until she shipped them to America as household goods, she busied herself cataloguing them.

Then the months dragged on in Mégève, in Marseilles, in Portugal, as the macabre tangle of intertwined relationships among herself, her current lover Max Ernst, his ex-mistress and *her* lover, as well as between her own ex-husband and *his* about-to-be-ex-wife, grew ever tighter. Finally, on July 13, 1941, Peggy Guggenheim, her ex-husband and his wife, Max Ernst and seven miscellaneous children left on a Pan-American clipper for America.

After a while, Peggy Guggenheim pulled her spectacular house-coat, which was made entirely of peach-colored feathers, around her and came to roost by the East River in a splendid mansion that stood on the spot where the British hanged Nathan Hale as a spy. She became Mrs. Max Ernst. The house, with Max Ernst enthroned on a ten-foot-high Victorian chair, became the hangout for the many surrealists who were living in exile in New York.

Peggy Guggenheim found nothing astonishing in a life larded with blood-splattering parties, gatherings with public confessions and public disrobings, flagrant infidelities and hysterical rows. All this seemed as normal and *de rigueur* in this small surrealist world as discretion, gentility and good manners were to Mrs. Potter Palmer's Edwardian one. She took it all as a matter of course and proceeded to get on with her good works.

She unpacked her paintings and sculptures. Then, with the list in hand and the added counsel of André Breton and Max Ernst and the objective advice of Alfred H. Barr, Jr., and the art critic James Johnson Sweeney, she set about expanding her collection. She also worked earnestly on its catalogue. That volume, which includes prefaces by Breton, Mondrian and Arp and statements (and a silhouetted eye) of each of the artists, became a valuable document of modern art, as has the collection itself, which is later, smaller, more careful and systematic than Katherine Dreier's.

Neither abstract nor surrealist art—the one born around 1910, the other around 1924—was any longer new to America. After all, Katherine Dreier's Société Anonyme had circulated exhibitions of abstract art in the twenties. America's first exclusively surrealist show was held in 1931 at the Wadsworth Atheneum in Hartford,

Connecticut, where four years later Gertrude Stein's *Four Saints in Three Acts* would make its debut. Certain small commercial galleries, like Julien Levy's, had regularly been giving one-man shows to abstract and surrealist artists. But this art was still caviar.

The turning point was 1936. In April and December of that year, Alfred Barr, in the two most brilliantly lucid exhibitions ever produced at the Museum of Modern Art, gave these movements full-dress retrospective showings. They took on a sort of respectability for America's newly growing art public, to a large portion of which they seemed "the last word." Even the man on the street knew of the painting accurately entitled "White on White" in the one exhibition and of the literally "Fur-Lined Teacup" in the other, for these objects became symbols and *causes célèbres* in the press as "Nude Descending a Staircase" had done twenty-three years before.

By 1942, when Peggy Guggenheim opened the museum and gallery she called "Art of This Century," Madison Avenue was already borrowing from Fifty-seventh Street. The influence of abstract and surrealist art was beginning insidiously to confront the housewife in the packages on the grocery-store shelves, in the advertising pages of her magazine and in Fifth Avenue store windows. But in its undiluted form, this art was still controversial stuff. To the unabashed glee of the surrealist group in New York, it was also still good newspaper copy. Sagaciously, they kept it so.

On October 14, 1942, they staged an exhibition with deliberate incongruity in the gilt-encrusted ballroom of the staid Whitelaw Reid mansion in New York. Marcel Duchamp stretched a mile-long maze of string in front of all the pictures, crossing and recrossing it as if it had been spun by a drunken giant spider.

The exhibition, given respectably for the benefit of the Coordinating Council of French Relief Societies, made surrealism chic and newsworthy. Its opening-night auction (during which little boys played football in Duchamp's cat's cradle) attracted those glittering and white-tied socialites who were already creating the new aristocracy known as café society, whose goal, as Cleveland Amory cogently pointed out, is the public eye.

But the opening of Peggy Guggenheim's "Art of This Century" a week later, given equally respectably for the benefit of the American Red Cross, was no anticlimax. Putzel had said to her one day, "Why don't you get Kiesler to give you a few little ideas about decorating your gallery?" Frederick J. Kiesler, who was then director of the laboratory of the Columbia School of Architecture, is a diminutive man, five feet high, with a tiny pale face and a grandiose, large-scale imagination. The "few little ideas" he contrived for Peggy Guggenheim's gallery cost her $7,000, but they created a sensation.

The Cubist Gallery had a tent-like dark blue canvas wall. Unframed, the paintings were suspended in mid-air on strings. Even the sculpture seemed floating, since its pedestals were suspended, too. In the Surrealist Gallery, things were slightly more stable but no less ambiguous. The paintings, each individually spotlighted, projected from the concave walls. Every two minutes the lights went on on one side of the tunnel; then, after a three-and-a-half-second interval, accompanied by a roar like the sound of an oncoming subway train, they went on on the other side. "Like the pulsing of your blood," Kiesler explained calmly. What the press specifically described as Coney Island was a corridor where revolving wheels exposed paintings by Klee and, seen through a peephole, the total *oeuvre* of Marcel Duchamp.

At the opening, Peggy Guggenheim wore one abstract earring (a wire and metal mobile by Alexander Calder) and one surrealist earring (a tiny oval painting of a bone-strewn pink desert by Tanguy). Fortunately, lest her balanced impartiality between the two movements be upset, she had lost in Paris the silver cigarette lighter on which Tanguy had had Dunhill engrave a phallic drawing.

But "Art of This Century" became more than a Fun House display of modern art. For all her restless impatience with the war that was keeping her in America, Peggy Guggenheim had arrived in the right place at the right time. The American avant-garde artists needed an impresario. And Peggy Guggenheim, exactly wise enough and naïve enough, exactly brave enough and vain enough, and almost rich enough, became one. "Art of This Century" had one conventional gallery for changing exhibitions: it became the center in New York for discovery and opportunity.

A so-called Spring Salon in May of 1943 precipitated the activity. Having heard of the event through the grapevine, the young and eager and experimental trudged uptown with dozens and dozens of their canvases. The improbable jury included Marcel Duchamp, who wanted to include everything that seemed at all peculiar and quaint; Piet Mondrian, who favored anything which inspired a theoretical esthetic defense; and the art critics James Johnson Sweeney and James Thrall Soby, who, with Putzel, took a somewhat more discriminating attitude. The first salon was followed by two others with other juries in May and October of the next year.

The salons introduced the press and a small public to the work of most of the men who were later to be part of the influential group known as "The New York School," or, even more loosely, as "The Abstract Expressionists." Peggy Guggenheim immediately began showing and buying their work. She committed herself to them. She was goaded, encouraged and guided by Putzel. But, whereas she depended heavily on advice in choosing "old masters" of modern art for her collection, she acted largely on her own in choosing the new.

"Her taste," says the critic Clement Greenberg, who effectively championed her artists in the columns of the *Nation,* "was often erratic and unsure. But she had a flair for life, a sort of smell for life that made her recognize vitality and conviction in a picture. It was surer ground in selecting the new than taste."

Standing on this sure ground, she smelled very well, indeed. Robert Motherwell, William Baziotes, Ad Reinhardt, Jimmy

Ernst, Mark Rothko, Adolph Gottlieb, Clifford Styll, Pousette-Dart and Jackson Pollock were given their first one-man shows and their first promotion in "Art of This Century."

Her personal life with Max Ernst had fallen violently to pieces and she was unsuccessfully seeking solace in other arrangements, but she worked in the gallery with the tireless seriousness of a convert to a cause. Out of both conviction and necessity, she became a persuasive saleswoman. An avant-garde gallery in New York was no more lucrative than in London. And marriage to Max Ernst, with his penchant for elegant clothes and his insatiable appetite for primitive art, Kachina dolls and totem poles, had not been a penny-saving undertaking.

Jackson Pollock, who had been the star of the first salon, became her special concern. This king of the abstract movement had not yet arrived at his paroxysmal creations, where the very act of painting became the heroic theme in the swirling labyrinth of paint dripped on the canvas. But what was to come was inherent in the exuberant early paintings that Peggy Guggenheim took enthusiastically off his hands in return for a generous annual income.

Almost single-handedly, she made him a success. She sold one of his canvases to the Museum of Modern Art, and that gave him a seal of approval. She showed his work to everyone who entered the gallery. A Detroit collector who came in looking for a Masson walked out happily with a Pollock. Edward Root and Joseph Hirshhorn both bought his paintings. She even bought his work herself to give as gifts. One such recipient was her stepson Jimmy Ernst, to whom she gave a very small painting by Pollock as a wedding present. The young bride was in despair. "Oh, Jimmy," she said to her artist husband, "we don't need paintings. We need a can opener." One morning in 1957, eleven years later, Jimmy Ernst sold the little Pollock. Handing his wife $3,000, he said, "Here is your can opener, my dear."

With the disappearance of Max Ernst into the arms of a surrealist lady painter, Peggy Guggenheim's house and gallery became less parochially surrealist. Mondrian would drop by the gallery for a martini. Clement Greenberg would come in to chat and look. The gatherings in the house on the East River were less *outré*. Arshile Gorky (whose paintings she bought very early) would end a discussion on painting by going out on the terrace and singing old Georgian songs. Virgil Thomson would come in with musician friends. Mary McCarthy and the young writers would appear. The Barrs, the Sweeneys, the Sobys were frequent visitors. Peggy Guggenheim gave her corner of New York the color of Montparnasse. Since Stieglitz, there had been no one who had given modern American art so vital a shot in the arm.

Many of her friends made their confessions on the analyst's couch. Peggy Guggenheim apparently craved a wider audience. In 1946, her autobiography, *Out of This Century,* appeared.

It is a tale frank to the point of total naïveté or brashness, with the names of auld acquaintances either spelled out or thinly veiled and a play-by-play chronicle of abuses, rebuffs and triumphs recounted with methodical detail. There was a rumor that the Guggenheim family—already embarrassed by and disapproving of her behavior—bought up as much of the edition as possible. The review copies were obviously beyond their control. The book was mercilessly panned. Philip Wylie, commenting in the *Saturday Review of Literature* on what he called the "confession-travelogue in sixth-grade English," took a typically sizzling tone. "However much Miss Guggenheim and her dazed associates may have contributed to the emancipation of art," he wrote, "it has not been enough to let me print what I really think of the book, anywhere on earth."

Peggy Guggenheim, keeping her avant-garde up, was not shaken by the reviews. Sportingly, she pasted every one of them in her scrapbook and, bolstered by numerous private letters of applause, continued to regard her recital as a brave banner of personal and artistic freedom. She is still ingenuously surprised that her autobiography has kept many people from taking as seriously as she would like what she calls her "serious side." And indeed, this side has been underestimated.

She had always thought of her stay in America as an enforced exile. In 1947, when Europe became possible again for the eternal expatriates, she closed the gallery, conscientiously—and not without exceeding difficulty—found new galleries for her "stable" of advanced artists, packed up her belongings and her collection and was off. For her new life, she chose an old city, Venice.

Every second year there, on the banks of the Adriatic, a huge international exhibition is held, in which various countries display, each in its own special pavilion, their newest art. In 1948, Greece was too troubled with matters of other moment to bother with this event and its pavilion was empty.

Peggy Guggenheim was invited to take her collection from storage and exhibit it here. Among the signs on the exhibition grounds reading POLONIA, AUSTRIA, BULGARIA, was GUGGENHEIM. With this temporary national status, Peggy Guggenheim chose the earrings for *this* opening to commemorate herself: she wore huge marguerites in honor of her given name. The collection was a success and was subsequently invited to museums in Brussels, Zurich, Amsterdam, Florence and Milan, where it was enthusiastically received. Peggy Guggenheim was a success, too, and decided to stay on in Venice.

She found herself an eighteenth-century palazzo on the Grand Canal. It was a truncated structure whose construction never proceeded beyond the first pilastered story (some say the money ran out, others that jealous city officials stopped building lest the palazzo dwarf the city hall directly opposite). Long and low, it stands like some ambiguous surrealist statement between its tall, completed neighbors.

Peggy Guggenheim is neither the most flamboyant nor the most spectacular of the palazzo's successive occupants. The original owner, Giralomo Fratelli Venier, kept lions in the garden, a circumstance commemorated in the six lions' heads that look broodingly out about four feet above the Grand Canal and in its name, Palazzo Venier dei' Leoni. The Marchese Casati, who moved in next, had a leopard for a pet. Both she and the next owner, Lady Castelrosse, gave famous parties.

Peggy Guggenheim has not betrayed the palazzo's traditions. She has not gone as far as the Casatis, who, for the Leonardesque décor of one of their revels, had a young boy completely painted with gilt (he subsequently died from it), but she *does* paint her finger- and toe-nails silver. With outsize earrings—pre-Columbian or Egyptian or Renaissance or modern—hanging down beneath her jet hair, flamboyantly rimmed dark glasses shielding her blue eyes, and sandals on her pretty feet, she is a familiar figure in her zooming speedboat or her gondola propelled by two gondoliers who wear blue sashes to match her eyes. From Harry's Bar to the Piazza San Marco, she is known as *"L'Ultima Dogaressa"* or *"Principessa."*

Neither lions nor leopards, but seven Lhasa terriers roam through the garden or make a shaggy blanket as she lies on her wide bed, under a headboard arabesque of flora and fauna which Calder made for her (in silver, since other metals were unobtainable during the war). These little creatures, who look the same coming and going, answer to such names as Emily (economically honoring Emilys Spreckles, Coleman, Brontë and Dickinson) and Sir Herbert (whereby Peggy Guggenheim anticipated by two years Herbert Read's knighthood). An equestrian bronze statue by Marino Marini stands on the gondola landing, confronting the city hall. Peggy Guggenheim had it cast so that the rider's erect phallus would be detachable. Most often *in situ,* it is respectfully removed on such special occasions as the festival days when the nuns come to Venice and the Patriarch floats by to bless the city. In a second, less confessional memoir she tells the story that is current in Venice: that the horse has different-sized parts.

She installed the paintings in the spacious rooms and down the spine-like corridor. The garden, with some of the loftiest and most beautiful trees in Venice, became a God-given exhibition space for sculpture. She took advantage of it in 1949 when she held there a handsome loan exhibition of contemporary sculpture.

The role of impresario was not abandoned. When she arrived back in Europe, she touted for Pollock there as she had in New York, peddling his paintings out of her hotel room. She countered the attractions of the 1950 Biennale exhibition by holding a Pollock exhibition that fall in a gallery on the Piazza San Marco.

With perhaps less objectivity, but no less enthusiasm than in New York, she picked young Italians for discovery. In 1954 she turned the basement laundry area of the palazzo into fluorescent-lit public galleries, making a stunning Jackson Pollock room and exhibition space for the new young men, of whom the abstract painters Tancredi and Bacci have been her favorites. She takes her role of impresario as seriously as the postman completing his appointed rounds: no insult, no involvement, no personal crisis is allowed to interfere with her promised monthly payments or her promotion of the artists.

Her collection has become not only one of the sights of Venice, but also one of the sights of Europe. Nowhere else in Europe is there a similar historic survey of modern art, nor one that exhibits the Americans—like Pollock and Rothko—who are major figures in the international world of art. Visitors of all kinds have crowded the palazzo since she opened the collection to the public in 1951. The cognoscenti and the curious, artists and writers and students and even the sailors from the United States Sixth Fleet come to call. Unpredictable, sometimes gay and gregarious, sometimes painfully shy and uncomfortable, she may be on hand to act as courier or flee to the palazzo roof for a sun bath. Especially during the Biennales, the Palazzo Venier dei' Leoni, with Peggy Guggenheim as hostess, is a brilliant international salon.

Peggy Guggenheim could have played cat-and-mouse, in the acceptable manner of many collectors, with the museum directors, both American and European, who were after a whole or a part of her collection. She chose instead to declare her hand. In 1957, she set up a foundation permanently to preserve her palazzo collection: it is, thus, a gift to Venice.

A half-century ago, the vanity of one woman was gratified by re-creating a Venetian palace for old masters on the Fenway in Boston as her monument. In what a great arc American taste has swung, to the moment when another woman fills a ready-made Venetian palace on the Grand Canal with surrealist and abstract art for her monument.

Yet it is perhaps even more as an impresario than as a collector that Peggy Guggenheim will be uniquely remembered in the history of twentieth-century art. The Steins were catalysts and publicists; Katherine Dreier was a forceful crusader; but Peggy Guggenheim created and managed a unique art center not only of discovery but also of opportunity. A group of American artists who benefited by the discovery and the opportunity, speak of holding an "Homage to Peggy" when next she visits America. The group includes almost every significant modern American artist who was producing in the forties. Almost all of them are fashionable in the fifties. The "good works" linger longer in memory than the self-publicized escapades of the Scott Fitzgerald-type girl.

The One Luxury

THE ROCKEFELLERS

Art is almost the only luxury the Rockefellers can afford. Not in terms of dollars and cents, of course. The astronomic total of the family's fortune has never been accurately computed, although ambitious amateur statisticians in 1906 figured out that if John D. Rockefeller, Sr.'s, wealth were left to accumulate at the current rate of interest, in approximately thirty years it would amount to ninety million million dollars ($90,000,000,000,000).

The money was accumulating so rapidly, in fact, that Mr. Rockefeller's friend Frederick T. Gates, a former Baptist minister, warned him to distribute it as fast as it rolled in, lest it crush him and his children and his children's children. Distribute it he did. The benefactions of John D. Rockefeller, Sr., and John D. Rockefeller, Jr., alone are placed at more than two and a half billion dollars, and the "Brothers" (and one sister) of the third generation have been distributing it, too. Thus none of the family has been crushed. But they are still well-heeled enough, so to speak, to own yachts and palaces and the Hope diamond—if they so wished.

They have not so wished. John D. Rockefeller, Jr.'s, sister Edith, who married Harold McCormick and tried to unseat Mrs. Potter Palmer from Chicago's social throne, sported Catherine the Great's emeralds and a Russian ermine cape of 275 skins from Ishim at the Chicago opera. But the main line of the family has kept rather more closely to the stern, Puritanical attitudes of the elder Rockefellers. They have a strict sense of stewardship, rather than mere ownership, of wealth—and a rigid abhorrence of the showy.

When, in 1915, the late J. Pierpont Morgan's Chinese porcelains were in Duveen's hands, John D. Rockefeller, Jr., wanted to buy a large number of them. As his excellent biographer, Raymond Fosdick, relates, he was not at the moment in a position to produce the slightly more than a million dollars necessary for their purchase. His credit was good, of course, but Duveen was so craftily playing Frick and Widener (who were also after the porcelains) off against each other and against Rockefeller, that John D. Rockefeller, Jr., grew panicky at the thought of losing his chance. He appealed to his father for a loan, was rejected and tried again:

"I have never squandered money on horses, yachts, automobiles or other foolish extravagances," he wrote. "A fondness for these porcelains is my only hobby—the only thing on which I have cared to spend money. I have found in their study a great recreation and diversion, and I have become very fond of them. This hobby, while a costly one, is quiet and unostentatious and not sensational. I am sure that if I had the actual cash on hand, you would encourage rather than discourage my development of so innocent and educative an interest. The money put into these porcelains is not lost or squandered. It is all there, and while not income-producing, I have every reason to believe that even at a forced sale, I could get within ten percent of what these things would cost, while a sale under ordinary circumstances would certainly realize their full cost value, and, as the years go by, more . . .

"Is it unwise for me to gratify a desire for beautiful things, which will be a constant joy to my friends, and to my children as they grow to appreciate them, as well as to myself, when it is done in so quiet and unostentatious a manner?"

In this well-tempered plea (which, incidentally, so persuaded the elder Rockefeller that he made his forty-one-year-old son not a loan but a gift of the necessary amount) lies the crux of the matter. Art is the one luxury the Rockefellers can *morally* afford.

Art is conveniently endowed with exactly the right characteristics to make its pursuit not only pleasurable, but also wise and virtuous. According to his biographer, S. N. Behrman, Duveen used to point out to his prospective clients that a picture was the only thing on which you can spend $100,000 without incurring an obligation to spend a great deal more for its upkeep. In addition, wisely chosen, art has again and again proved in the long run to be a sound, often an extraordinarily profitable, investment. Waste is a sin: but the purshase of art can be rationalized as a prudent, rather than a reckless, act.

Art has other less mundane and less practical merits. It stands for beauty, which, like truth, is on the high plateau of the good. It can be considered educational. And its personal accumulation can be justified in terms of its future public benefit. Art, as we have seen, can be used as the most conspicuous of objects consumed, but, as Mr. Rockefeller pointed out to his father, it need not necessarily be so employed.

Thus, happily, the craving to be intimate with and surrounded by lovely objects can—like few other desires of the senses—be gratified without loss of virtue. And several Rockefellers, taking advantage of this fortuitous circumstance, have allowed themselves the luxury of collecting art.

The Rockefeller family's public united front is impregnable. Almost all very rich families—isolated by their wealth and mutually interdependent—function as clans. The Rockefellers' particular solidarity is further cemented by the uniformity of strict upbringing and common convictions about stewardship of wealth. But as if to compensate for having so often to think and act as group entities, the various Rockefellers have carefully cultivated their individualities. Nowhere are their distinct personalities better revealed than in their diverse tastes for art—tastes which, however, taken collectively, become a microcosm of American art collecting.

John D. Rockefeller, Jr., born in 1874, had the distinction and the stigma of being the only son of the richest man in the world. "Money," says the wag, "can't buy everything. It can't buy poverty." "But," counters his colleague, "rich or poor, money is a nice thing to have."

Raymond Fosdick takes a more original and braver attitude toward great wealth. It can, he asserts in his sympathetic biography, *John D. Rockefeller, Jr.,* be a kind of adversity, tending to stifle energy and to nourish frustration, cynicism and purposelessness. It encouraged none of these qualities, however, in John D. Rockefeller, Jr.

He came of age in 1913, in the violent days of the so-called Ludlow Massacre, which grew out of a strike in Rockefeller-controlled mines in Colorado. In the public mind and the public press, his father represented the ruthless "Mr. Moneybags," the arch monopolist of Standard Oil, embodying every evil of the capitalist world. In time, helped by Ivy Lee, the original public-relations expert, the name of Rockefeller took on sweeter connotations, associated with gifts to universities and the end of hookworm and yellow fever made possible by a yarn-spilling old man.

John D. Rockefeller, Jr., a modest, simple man, emerged from his background dedicated to a life of public service, in which, with Frederick T. Gates, he evolved a new creative kind of philanthropy. In its practical achievements and its philosophic implications, this concept of philanthropy is one of America's great—and surely unique—contributions to twentieth-century life and thought.

The young man's rearing had been strict and strait-laced. When, as a student at Brown University, after long and respectful deliberation, he decided to disregard his parents' ban on social dancing, he must have felt like a libertine. Abby Aldrich, daughter of Senator Nelson Aldrich, whom he married in 1901, was a joyous, gregarious girl. She brightened his attitudes and loosened some of the constricting rigidity. Accustomed to beaux, parties, books and travel, Miss Aldrich was also accustomed to "nice things," like the sculptures from Egypt and Mesopotamia and the Persian miniatures which her father collected on their trips (and in whose interest he had been instrumental in changing the tariff laws). She introduced many amenities into the Rockefeller household, even persuading her parents-in-law, who were living in correct Moorish-Turkish furnishings on West Fifty-fourth Street, to block the glare from their uncovered windows with curtains.

In 1911, the young John D. Rockefeller, Jrs., moved into a new house at 10 West Fifty-fourth Street. Like anybody else's new house, it provided an excuse for buying decorative objects, but whereas somebody else might have gone to a lesser emporium to pick up a few odds and ends, Abby Aldrich Rockefeller, abetted by her sister Lucy Aldrich, went shopping at Duveen's for Italian primitives.

They picked up an exquisite lot of pictures—including, eventually, not only such primitives as Duccio and Piero della Francesca, but also a Goya and a Chardin. However, all these old masters were intended merely as decorative adjuncts to the house, along with the pianola-type organ that played semi-demi-classical music and carillons slightly louder than the pitch of conversation during mealtimes. The exuberant ladies procured John D. Rockefeller,

Jr.'s, courteous acceptance of the pictures, but though he had a warm affection for Sir Thomas Lawrence's full-length portrait of the beautiful Lady Dysart, which he had chosen himself, he never really liked paintings.

His own predilections led him to quite other areas. He is an exceedingly methodical and meticulous man, who, like his father before him, has an almost superhuman zeal for painstaking detail, an absorbing passion for exactitude and precision. He has always liked measuring things and almost all his life has carried a four-foot rule in his hip pocket.

"One of Father's favorite expressions," his son Nelson recalls, "is 'The last five percent is what counts.' His whole feeling is that if the last five percent—the finish and the detail—are taken care of, everything else will come out all right." Obviously the siren lure for such a man is beautiful craftsmanship, the kind of exquisitely detailed artifice one finds in Gothic tapestries and seventeenth-century Polonaise rugs, in medieval jeweled chalices and Chinese K'ang Hsi porcelains.

But craftsmanship was not their only enticement. Hidden in this Puritanical and abstemious man, with his solemn, square face, is a warm response to the pure sensual delights of color and texture. He has always liked jewels. "He can spot the difference between a cultured pearl and a real pearl across a room or recognize the quality of an emerald," says another of his sons. "The best time I have ever had in my life was when he took me jewelry shopping for my engagement present," a daughter-in-law recalls, adding with ingenuous surprise, "The salesmen fell flat on their faces for us wherever we went."

Happily, John D. Rockefeller, Jr., did not have to depend, for the gratification of his desire for radiant color, on the jewelry appropriate for the Rockefeller women's adornment. Those discreet, conservative pieces would have left his longings sadly thwarted. Instead, he could find color far more lustrous in the Chinese porcelains, entertain splendor in the Persian rugs woven with gold and silver thread, enter an enveloping world of enchanting, springtime hues with the tapestries of "The Hunt of the Unicorn."

But fortunately, objects of virtue, these, objects of use and, even more important, objects formal, restrained and impersonal. Such qualities would be *a priori* for a man himself reticent and reserved, coldly disapproving of any form of excess, self-expression or lack of discipline. "By and large," he told Mr. Fosdick, "I do not find beauty in modern art. I find instead a desire for self-expression, as if the artist were saying, 'I'm free, bound by no form, and art is what flows out of me.' " Not so with his beloved objects of the past.

Thus art became John D. Rockfeller, Jr.'s, sole Lucullan adventure, his closest brush with self-indulgence. It began innocently enough in 1913, when, searching for decorations for the mantelpiece in his new home, he was shown some Chinese Black Hawthorn porcelains. It was love at first sight. But it was an overflowing love that not only embraced these initial objects of ardor but extended to more and more porcelains of the same period. It was, however, not blind love. Even in matters of the heart, Mr. Rockefeller was a perfectionist. Each object of affection was subjected, before its acquisition, to Mr. Rockefeller's tidy scrutiny. "Sitting on the floor," says Mr. Fosdick, "he would roll the vase about—they were frequently as high as thirty inches—looking for marks of repair, noting any signs of repainting or of camouflaging of cracks."

By 1915, when the Morgan porcelains came on the market, Rockefeller's private passion had become public knowledge. In a letter to a friend abroad, John G. Johnson, in his customary tone, prophesied the future of the Morgan vases. "I presume that Frick, whose new home needs filling, and Rockefeller, who has come into the market recently, will take some of the valuable things. With his father's fortune of over one and a quarter billion dollars to draw upon and an excited desire to secure expensive porcelains, the ability to secure high prices is not entirely gone. Thus far, however," he adds, "Rockefeller seems to buy nothing but porcelains and rugs. The other day he competed at an auction for a blue Chinese rug, worth about $2,500 . . . and got it for $15,400. It will take a long time to exhaust his fortune and it is hoped that the dealers will keep up the excitement."

One of the dealers who did keep up the excitement was, of course, Duveen. It broke his heart to have Mr. Rockefeller paying too high prices at public auction and it upset him that this prince of wealth should be buying blue Chinese rugs. He had something far more appropriate: the famous, resplendent Persian rugs known as Polonaise, which had belonged to royal families in Poland and other European countries. Since the Rockefellers were expanding into the house next door—12 West Fifty-fourth Street—whose floors, after all, needed covering, Mr. Rockefeller felt justified in buying Duveen's rugs. Duveen felt so bad at seeing those beautiful rugs in rooms with barren walls that he talked to Mr. Rockefeller about getting some tapestries to keep the rugs company. Since the rugs deserved the best company, Duveen found a set of ten exquisite eighteenth-century Gobelins tapestries, "The Months of Lucas." Predisposed already toward tapestries by his architect friend, Welles Bosworth, Mr. Rockefeller agreed to the liaison.

Shortly thereafter, Mr. Rockefeller acquired (through a French dealer) an even more beautiful and festive set of tapestries, the Gothic "The Hunt of the Unicorn" series, which are among the very greatest in the world. They were installed so that, reaching from floor to ceiling, they completely lined a room in the new house. They even hid the door, so that Mr. Rockefeller could joyously and completely escape into the medieval world. He examined minutely every detail of the hunt as it wound through the *milles-fleurs* landscape of periwinkles, cowslips, holly, rosebushes and delicately green trees in the quest of the wild, uncontrollable white unicorn, who could be caught only by a virgin. An allegory of the Incarnation of Christ and of marriage consummation, this incredibly lovely set of tapestries was woven to celebrate the marriage in 1499 of Anne of Brittany to Louis XII, King of France.

Years later, when The Cloisters, the Metropolitan Museum's medieval branch in Fort Tryon Park, was built, Mr. Rockefeller generously parted with the six tapestries. Although they had survived without damage rather hazardous employment as coverings to protect potatoes from frost during the French Revolution, he fussed like a doting mother over their care and treatment at The Cloisters. His concern was in areas both practical and esthetic. He asked for—and was given—reassurance that the window glass would block harmful sun rays and he was responsible for their happy installation as the only hangings in a small room. No matter what his mission to The Cloisters, he always makes a pilgrimage to the Unicorn Room.

Conscience, however, kept pricking his pleasure in these earlier days. He worried lest he was letting his art expenditures jeopardize other causes. He was uneasy about his enjoyment of these objects. Should a simple Puritan allow himself such sybaritic indulgence? But he found his justification: The beautiful objects would "in time probably come into public possession through their ownership by museums. In the end, beauty would be preserved for a wider audience."

Mr. Rockefeller has kept his beloved porcelains and he still, in the words of a dealer who has profited from this passion, "likes to nose around for them." Most of the rugs and tapestries are already in the Metropolitan. In 1922 he became involved with a new, reassuring adventure—a kind of "public-collecting"—The Cloisters.

Taste in America for medieval architecture and sculpture was a fairly late phenomenon. The Bostonians were among the first to be romantically aware of the art of the Middle Ages. Charles Herbert Moore, the first director of the Fogg Museum, wrote on Gothic architecture in 1890. Henry Adams' brilliant idealization of the thirteenth century, *Mont St. Michel and Chartres*, was published privately in 1904 (it appeared publicly in 1913). And Isabella Stewart Gardner, with her intellectual ear to the ground, had, indeed, acquired some Romanesque capitals and Gothic sculpture as early as 1892.

But it was the sculptor George Grey Barnard who really introduced medieval architecture and sculpture to America. In 1914 he opened on Fort Washington Avenue and 190th Street a museum he called "The Cloisters." In a dramatic, highly romanticized setting he installed the superb miscellany—including the major part of four arcaded cloisters which he had been patiently discovering and collecting in France for the last ten years.

Just about this time, John D. Rockefeller, Jr., was working closely with the architect Welles Bosworth, who had designed his father's house on the 3,000-acre estate at Pocantico, N.Y. Bosworth introduced Rockefeller to George Grey Barnard, an introduction that was decidedly pleasant to the sculptor, for one hundred objects, totaling $100,000 (as well as some of Barnard's own muscularly overdeveloped sculpture), were immediately ordered for the Westchester estate. In 1922, Mr. Rockefeller indirectly made an even larger purchase. He gave the Metropolitan Museum funds to buy Barnard's entire Cloisters. Rearranged and augmented with gifts from Mr. and Mrs. Rockefeller, the old Barnard Museum opened as a branch of the Metropolitan in September, 1926.

Mr. Rockefeller had a grander idea for these treasures. He saw them housed in a new structure on the crowning summit of the Fort Tryon property which he had bought and had offered to the city as a park. In 1930 the property was accepted and four wonderfully commanding acres, high above the Hudson, were set aside for The Cloisters. Mr. Rockefeller also purchased eleven and a half miles of Palisades opposite, so that the neon lights and factories of the twentieth century would not intrude on the medieval world.

The final design and the pervading spirit of The Cloisters is owed to the architect Charles Collens and, especially, to James J.

Rorimer, then curator of medieval art and since 1954 director of the Metropolitan Musuem. They decided against either a didactic reconstruction or a stark exhibition stage. Instead, they created a serene modern setting in which, sometimes architecturally incorporated, sometimes freely displayed, the art and architecture of the Middle Ages harmoniously assert themselves. The total is a living, lovely evocation.

John D. Rockefeller, Jr., found craftsmanship in small-scale objects good; the craftsmanship involved in large-scale operations like building was even better. The painstaking historic reconstruction of Williamsburg engaged his minutest attention and his financial support to the extent of $60,000,000. The building of The Cloisters, with its four courts, its chapels, ramparts and commanding tower, captivated him completely.

He scrutinized every detail of the plans. He agreed to the building of a full-size mock-up of the first story, so that there would be no guesswork. On hot spring days, carrying his coat over his arm, he trudged up the hill to the wood and burlap structure. With blueprints in hand, he paced off the spaces of the Gothic chapel and the Cuxa Cloister; he indicated which trees would block a view; he approved the decision to use huge, hand-hewn granite blocks for the exterior. He gave eagle-eyed, inquiring attention to each stage of the construction.

Opened to the public in 1938, The Cloisters continued to exert its fascination for him. Unembarrassed by the implications of private acquisition, he could enjoy without any feelings of guilt the resplendent beauty of these objects gathered for the public. His funds are responsible for ninety-five percent of the contents of The Cloisters. But The Cloisters has been no private play-toy. Available to Rorimer at any moment, his characteristic remark is "The decision is yours."

In 1935, a dealer in France showed him a portfolio of photographs of a fabulous twelfth-century Spanish Romanesque apse. He brought them back, handed them to Rorimer and said, "I'm just acting as your errand boy, but if you want the apse, we might be able to find the funds." (His one injunction was that Rorimer return the shoelaced portfolio cover to the French dealer, but since it cost only ten francs that gentleman allowed Rorimer to keep it.)

It turned out that the dealer's offer was somewhat in the nature of a man selling the Brooklyn Bridge: the lofty apse from the Church of San Martin in Fuentidueña, a little town near Segovia, was a national monument. But both Rockefeller and Rorimer, with the construction of The Cloisters just under way, had their hearts set on getting it.

Talks went on for several years, until the Spanish War intervened. Negotiations were resumed in 1952. Like an eager Dr. Watson, John D. Rockefeller followed step by step as Rorimer tried to find a way to procure the apse. Rorimer finally hit on the scheme of offering in exchange six Spanish medieval frescoes, which he knew were on the New York market, and financial aid in the reconstruction of the Church of San Martin. Mr. Rockefeller concerned himself with each maneuver as approval had to be obtained from the Spanish Government, the Foreign Office, the Ministry of Education and its Department of Fine Arts, the Academy of History, the Academy of San Fernando, the Bishop of Segovia, the Mayor of Fuentidueña and the Holy See. The apse arrived in New York in February, 1958, and will become a new wing at The Cloisters. John D. Rockefeller, Jr., aged eighty-four, wintering in Tucson, hung on every detail of the arrival of the apse in which he had been interested for twenty-three years.

When he was purchasing for himself, John D. Rockefeller, Jr., was cautious and often guilt-ridden about price. A dealer recalls that many years ago, when Mr. Rockefeller came to buy a Renaissance marble head that Bosworth had recommended, he left his dogcart parked a few blocks away lest the merchant take advantage of a man driven in a private vehicle. He paid three visits before he made the $850 expenditure. Later, he often paid enormous prices, but never without a twinge of conscience. It took Duveen a whole year to sell him two busts by the Renaissance sculptor Laurana, because their price was $1,000,000. But when he was purchasing for the public, the necessity of getting the object overrode all other considerations.

One Thursday in 1919, Kelekian wrote him about the great Assyrian winged bulls and relief sculptures from the palace of Ashur-nasir-apal which, lacking a buyer, he was about to take back to Europe. The following Saturday the dealer met Mr. Rockefeller on Fifty-sixth Street and Madison Avenue on his way to the gallery. The transaction was concluded on the spot, though the sum involved was greater than that for the Laurana ladies, and the splendid monuments were given to the Metropolitan.

Concerned about the future of The Cloisters, in the early 1950's John D. Rockefeller, Jr., asked Rorimer to make a report on what might be done with a special gift of $1,000,000. Before the report was submitted he raised the amount to $2,000,000 and then to "$5,000,000, more or less."

One day in 1952 he telephoned Rorimer and asked him what progress he had made on the report. "I have a twenty-page document, prepared with your lawyers, in an envelope on my desk ready to be mailed," Rorimer told him. "We haven't time for that," Mr. Rockefeller said. "Come right over."

At the apartment, Mr. Rockefeller informed Rorimer that the gift was more rather than less, twice more, in fact. He wrote out a simple statement giving the $10,000,000 "for the enrichment of The Cloisters in the broadest sense of the term and for the preservation, housing and presentation of its collection" and phoned his office to get it typed. Then he looked inquiringly at the two three-cent stamps clipped to the envelope Mr. Rorimer had brought. "To whom do these stamps belong? You, me, or the museum?" The philanthropist nodded pleased agreement when Rorimer decided they should be returned to the museum.

"Just about the time that Mother got Father to accept the Italian primitives and to feel a little enthusiastic about them," Nelson Rockefeller recalls, "she switched to modern art."

The young always tend to oversimplify their parents. John D. Rockefeller, Jr., had approved, of course, not only the Italian primitives, but also the Persian miniatures, the Japanese prints, the Chinese bronzes (including two superb gilt-bronze altarpieces), the Georgian silver and the English porcelains which Abby Aldrich Rockefeller had been acquiring for—and 'way beyond—the furnishing of their house. "In a well-rounded life," he had said, "beauty plays a real part."

Nor, of course, was Mrs. Rockefeller's switch dramatic and sudden. Miss Lillie P. Bliss and Mrs. Cornelius J. Sullivan were good friends who took her to tea with their artistic mentor, Arthur B. Davies. Mrs. Rockefeller, too, was impressed by the soft-spoken esthete in his tormentingly high stiff collar, and began to be interested in modern art. She and Mrs. Sullivan took to dropping in to Kraushaar's gallery, which, like Duveen's grander palace, was conveniently around the corner from Mrs. Rockefeller's Fifty-fourth Street house. Mrs. Rockefeller made occasional purchases, including some of Maurice Prendergast's most compact and charming watercolors. But it was in early 1927 that another counselor was to appear whose encouragement spurred her to become a collector.

The role of adviser on art, as we have seen in these successive profiles, has fallen to many diverse souls: artists, dealers, fellow collectors, experts, professors, museum personnel and even those curious parasites that merchandise of intangibly priced objects attracts.

The mantle has even descended on such unsuspecting persons as domestics. With perhaps some atavistic Rousseauian respect for the Noble Savage and the Innocent Eye (or perhaps some deep suspicion of anyone with an overt mercenary motive), such a collector as Mrs. Lewis Larned Coburn of Chicago depended upon the esthetic reactions of the chambermaids, waiters and other personnel who served her in Chicago's Blackstone Hotel.

This commodiously shaped lady loved two things: to eat and to live in her pictures. Usually she was as definite in choosing her Renoirs, Monets, Degas and Cézannes as she was in selecting a filet mignon or a marron glacé from the Blackstone's menu. But in occasional moments of hesitation, she sought, not exactly advice, but corroboration. She decided in favor of a Van Gogh because a chambermaid, who found it reminiscent of Ireland, indicated her approval. Another time she made what she always felt was a grievous error. She refused a Daumier because the plumber who came to fix her bathtub found the painting too dark.

But though museum men today have moved into the front as advisers—as men like Berenson were in the past—architects have been among the most consistently acceptable counselors. The architect falls into a category which is particularly congenial to Americans, who are congenitally suspicious of artists. Architects are artists who, *ipso facto,* have to understand money and be practical. The divine spark of genius is a lot more trustworthy and palatable when it has been tempered by budgets, structural necessities, codes and zoning laws. Moreover, by the very nature of their clients, architects are artists who *have* to be gentlemen.

The Rockefellers have been particularly well disposed toward architects as artistic advisers. Welles Bosworth, the architect of the Pocantico house, not only counseled Mr. Rockefeller about tapestries and guided him to George Grey Barnard, but also undertook Mr. Rockefeller's researches when the latter gave funds for the restoration of Rheims Cathedral and for the rehabilitation of palaces and gardens at Versailles and Fontainebleau. Duncan Candler, who designed the $500,000 playhouse at Pocantico in a grandiose version of a French medieval town house, was the architect who encouraged Mrs. Rockefeller's leanings toward modern American art.

Wandering about Greenwich Village one night in 1926, Candler saw some lights on in a little house on West Thirteenth Street. Thinking it was a speakeasy, he knocked on the door. He entered instead the newly opened Downtown Gallery, which was run by Edith Gregor Halpert, who had an impudent and fighting faith in American art, especially in such young Americans as Burlin, Kuniyoshi, Weber and Zorach. Candler bought a portfolio of etchings of Washington Square by John Sloan. Within a week he returned and bought a second one. He kept buying other things for himself—woodcuts by Max Weber, Arthur B. Davies' prints —and each time he returned for duplicates or equivalents.

In 1927, the young dealer decided to give an exhibition of landscapes by American artists, contrasting the older generation of Inness, Ryder, Homer, Hassam (whose work she would borrow) with her "boys," the younger generation (whose work she wanted desperately to sell). When she had difficulty locating a borrowable Winslow Homer, Candler said he could get her one to be loaned anonymously. Homer's Nassau scene was duly hung between seascapes by John Marin and William Zorach.

When visitors to the show asked about buying the Homer, the dealer replied that it was not for sale—and neither, she added indignantly, were the Marin and the Zorach, except "to the idiot who owns the Homer and doesn't have these descendants to go with it." Just before the show ended, a friendly woman with a sharp, prominent nose, alert eyes and an elaborate hat came in. She asked the prices of the two modern seascapes (they were $750 and $250, respectively), said, "I am the idiot," and bought both paintings.

Abby Aldrich Rockefeller was a warm, buoyant woman. She found delight in all sorts of things, from buying a new hat to arranging flowers for the parties she loved to give, from seeking out a Persian manuscript at the Bibliothèque Nationale to reading aloud to her six children. She was, of course, temperamentally opposite to her husband. Where he was shy and withdrawn, she was outgoing and charmingly gregarious. Once when they were on a trip together, she wrote to one of her children, "Your father is afraid that I shall become intimate with too many people and will want to talk to them, so generally we eat in what I call the old people's dining-room where he feels I am safer."

His wit was dry and sparse; she had an easy humor that delighted especially in the absurd. He trusted logic, she was intuitive. He was devoted to detail and accuracy; she was gaily indifferent to both. When he suggested early in their marriage that she keep accounts, she replied flatly, "I won't." His interest in philanthropy was on the broad level of idea and principle; hers was expressed in acutely personal terms. He preferred to participate in life from the wings. She, who liked being actively involved with the living, enjoyed the excitement of stage center.

She was intrigued with the Downtown Gallery—its touch of Greenwich Village, its forthright, blue-eyed director, its art. Easily moved, she always commiserated over the mishaps to her children's pets ("I'm terribly sorry over the death of your mother rabbit. Do you suppose she could have died from eating your shoestrings?"). Now she listened sympathetically to Edith Halpert's lurid tales of the plight of the American artists. She shook her head in horror at the thought of Zorach living above a bakery where the rats ran over his children at night. She deplored the long period between creation and appreciation—and later, when she got interested in founding the Museum of Modern Art, her major hope was that the museum would close that tragic gap.

Her patronage was impelled by both interest and philanthropy. She continuously gave commissions in order to help artists. Marguerite Zorach was set to making a tapestry portrait of the Rockefeller family outside the house at Seal Harbor, Maine. Ben Shahn, very young and unknown in the depths of the depression, was given the job of painting portraits of the Rockefellers' horses at $250 apiece (it was not his forte). Stefan Hirsch was commissioned to paint a view from her window, Charles Sheeler to depict buildings at Colonial Williamsburg. Her gestures were many. She gave money to an artist to go abroad to see Italian primitives; money to a Negro artist who was stranded in Europe; seventy-five dollars so that fifty artists could buy tickets to a New Year's Eve party.

And she bought and bought. For many reasons, she eschewed large, "museum-piece" pictures in favor of small, modest ones. Temperamentally she preferred the spontaneous, informal work, with which she could have an intimate feeling, to the formal, imposing one. (And it is especially in the watercolors and drawings, by such men as Demuth, Burchfield, Marin, Hart, Prendergast, Weber, that her collection had its greatest distinction.) Her choice of small pictures was also influenced by problems of money and space.

"We never lack material for lively arguments," her husband once remarked. "Modern art and the King James Version can forever keep us young." She respected his aversion to modern art by financing her hobby with "Aldrich money" and by avoiding extravagance. Her most expensive purchase was the Zorach tapestry, which cost $20,000. Her outside limit was usually $1,000. (It was said that she thought what Lillie Bliss paid for a single modern picture was a little sinful.) Her total purchasing was probably less than the $1,200,000 which her husband allegedly spent on the Unicorn Tapestries.

She also respected her husband's antipathy to modern art by keeping it tactfully out of his sight. On the ninth floor of the house, the Rockefeller children had had a playroom ("It was there I first saw a crystal set with cat's whiskers," Nelson Rockefeller recalls). Early in 1928, Abby Aldrich Rockefeller had this room converted into a gallery. Candler and the young designer Donald Deskey lined it with light wood-paneled walls and installed polished metal strips to hold the prints. These—there were so many that their single-spaced typewritten listings cover thirty-one pages—were kept in boxes in cabinets underneath the racks. At teatime, when the children and their wives gathered in the gallery or friends came to call, she would pull out a box and go over the work of an artist. On the walls, she hung paintings in ever changing groups.

Even in the mid-twenties, it was rare to find a collector willing to support the young Americans so grandly. Only a few intrepid souls like Ferdinand Howald, Edward Root, Mrs. Gertrude Vanderbilt Whitney (herself an artist buying the work of fellow artists) and Mrs. Rockefeller were, as Dorothy Miller, the curator of the Museum of Modern Art's collection, says, "majoring in American art."

The fact that a representative of so conservative a family was acquiring this art gave it a reassuring respectability for other potential buyers. The collection was not, of course, open to the public. Mr. Rockefeller would have been appalled at strangers trooping and snooping through his privacy. But dealers, notoriously garrulous about who buys what, made her activity a significant part of their sales talks. Many of Mrs. Rockefeller's friends, making their acquaintance with modern art in her gallery, spread the news. A few times, Mrs. Rockefeller did put on special shows for an artist, his friends and the critics.

The first such occasion—and the first time she was publicly revealed as a collector of American art—was in December, 1928. The guest of honor was a somewhat incongruous character, George Overbury Hart. "Pop" Hart, as he is better known, was a vagabond, a stumblebum, a creature who looked more like "Bathless Groggins" in the Abbie and Slats comic strip than the kind of artist the wealthy usually entertain. He had wandered the earth recording his vivid impressions in fluent watercolors, but only a few people had taken them very seriously. Mrs. Rockefeller was one. Now sixty years old, he was confronted with her collection of his work—over three dozen watercolors and drawings and a complete set of prints. With her exhibition, "Pop" Hart's reputation as an artist was established.

The next year, Mrs. Rockefeller began venturing seriously into another field. Edith Halpert pointed out to her that the modern American artists needed "ancestors." Mrs. Halpert, who had herself begun acquiring the weathervanes, cigar store Indians and eagles that had been intriguing Mrs. Webb, had also been gathering a group of American "primitive" or folk-art paintings. These, she maintained, were the "ancestors." Mrs. Rockefeller enthusiastically gave her $500 to spend on this earlier branch of the family tree. That was the beginning of the splendid American folk-art collection, which was subsequently expanded, with the help of Holger Cahill, to about 400 objects and is now in a special museum outside the historic reconstruction of Williamsburg.

Its arrival at this resting place was fraught with problems. After Mrs. Rockefeller's death, some of the folk art had been installed in a house *within* the restoration. Almost all of the paintings were made about a century later than the Williamsburg period and were at variance with its elegance. They were an embarrassing aggravation to those who felt reverent about the rigid historical accuracy of the project.

Finally, Mr. Rockefeller, Jr., decided to remove these untouchables. He gave money for a new museum *outside* the sacred precincts, where all of his late wife's folk art could be brought together. At this point there was another embarrassment. Mrs. Rockefeller had given many of her choicest pieces to the Museum of Modern Art. But that institution, in a fancy arrangement with the Metropolitan, had sold them to the older museum and had long since spent the money on some newer art. The Rockefeller sons came to the rescue and bought the folk art from the Metropolitan. Everybody is now completely happy.

At the same time that she was acquiring these ancestors in 1929, Mrs. Rockefeller was worrying about their descendants. A respectable genealogy has never helped much to fill a stomach. The necessity of founding a museum of modern art, over which Mrs. Sullivan and Miss Bliss had been fretting since the dispersal of the Quinn collection, seemed even more pressing after the death of Arthur B. Davies and the sale of *his* collection. Mrs. Rockefeller and Miss Bliss talked about it when they met in Egypt, wealthy ladies being apparently more loquacious in the desert sands than wealthy gentlemen like Morgan and Frick. When Mrs. Rockefeller met Mrs. Sullivan on the boat coming back from Europe, they talked about it, too.

Back in New York, the three ladies invited a gentleman called A. Conger Goodyear to join them for lunch at Mrs. Rockefeller's. Several things interested them in this round, blunt-faced gentleman from Buffalo, who had made his money in lumber. He was a collector of modern art, whose possessions ranged from Matisse drawings to a group of seventeen Maillol sculptures, nudes and torsos, with peasant-like proportions and carefully coiffured hair. Mr. Goodyear had also been director of the Albright Gallery of Art in Buffalo. Fighting step by step on the side of modernism (in 1926, he had arranged for the Société Anonyme's international show to be exhibited there), in 1927 he went too far for his conservative Buffalo trustees. Outraged at his spending $5,000 of museum funds for Picasso's "La Toilette," they gathered forces and ousted him.

He was somewhat nonplused by Mrs. Rockefeller's invitation, since he had never met her. He went out and bought "a very dignified gray suit, which," he recalls, "my Buffalo friends thereafter always called the Rockefeller suit, and appeared at 10 West Fifty-fourth Street at the appointed time feeling rather like Aloysius in Wonderland."

This was no Mad Hatter's luncheon. The ladies made perfectly clear what they wanted. Mr. Goodyear agreed to be president of an organizing committee of the new museum. He recruited the urbane editor of *Vanity Fair,* Frank Crowninshield; Mrs. W.

Murray Crane, widow of the paper manufacturer; and Paul Sachs of the Fogg Museum at Harvard. Sachs proposed for the museum's director "a very young man," a former student who was then teaching art at Wellesley. Alfred H. Barr, Jr., was a tall, thin, ascetic-looking man even at twenty-seven. He brought to his job a Calvinist integrity, a capacity for painstaking scholarship that he had probably acquired in early undergraduate days when he thought he might be a paleontologist, and a broadly imaginative understanding of modern art as architecture, design and films as well as painting and sculpture. The program was established: the museum would be an educational institution, would arrange exhibitions, dispatch shows on the road and have a collection "permanent as a stream is permanent—with a changing content." Soon fourteen trustees and a small, inspired staff were working with the zeal of pioneers carving out a homestead in the wilderness.

In October, 1929, as *Variety* declared in its immortal headline, "Wall Street Laid an Egg." Notwithstanding, in November— just five months after the founding luncheon—the Museum of Modern Art opened in improvised galleries in an office building at 730 Fifth Avenue. The gentlemen involved had plugged for an opening exhibition of American art, but they yielded to what they called "the adamantine ladies." The première consisted of work by Cézanne, Gauguin, Seurat and Van Gogh.

This quartet was hardly avant-garde. These men had, after all, provided a historic background for the young moderns in the Armory Show sixteen years before, and Katherine Dreier had been circulating exhibitions far more advanced in character during the twenties. But they were still controversial to the many whom Alfred Barr described as "the recalcitrant few," and they were successful drawing cards for 47,000 people who jammed into the small rooms in the first month and for those who subscribed $115,000 annually for the next two years. The Museum of Modern Art continued to be such a success that the other occupants of the office building complained they could never get into the elevators.

Miss Lillie Bliss was so pleased with its success that when she died in 1931 she left her collection, with its twenty-seven superb Cézannes, to the museum on the condition that money be raised to care for it. Mrs. Rockefeller took the lead, and $600,000 was obtained. In 1932 the Museum of Modern Art moved into a private, Rockefeller-owned house on West Fifty-third Street, and in 1939—ten years after its founding—into its own shining glass, marble and steel building on erstwhile Rockefeller land. The museum's arteries have hardened slightly with age: in 1958 it gave Seurat—by now almost an "old master"—a one-man show (three of whose most significant paintings were bought by John Quinn over thirty years before). Yet the Museum of Modern Art has been and continues to be the most ardent champion of modern art and the most important taste-making institution in the world. No single adviser, including Berenson, has ever played so influential—or often so dictatorial—a role for so many collectors. Its role in the artistic lives of the Rockefellers has been dominant.

With the founding of the museum, Abby Aldrich Rockefeller, as her son Nelson says, began "stretching her collection from at home to the museum." Her personal taste ran to realism, straightforward, as in Sheeler's Ford plant, or romanticized, as in Burchfield. She cared little for the social-consciousness paintings that intrigued Joseph Hirshhorn during the thirties, or for abstraction and surrealism. Yet, turning more and more to Alfred Barr for advice and with the museum's needs in mind, she included some of these in her orbit. She bought Ben Shahn's documentary Sacco and Vanzetti series and Peter Blume's somewhat surrealist "Parade" from the 1930 Carnegie International in Pittsburgh, thereby, as the *Literary Digest* reported, leading a crowd to it. She disliked Picasso's biting comment on war, the great "Minotauromachy" etching, but she gave the museum money to buy it with the suggestion, "Let's

label this: purchased with a fund for prints which Mrs. Rockefeller doesn't like."

But by 1935, she was more or less through with personal collecting. Some people said she had decided to mollify her husband's resentment of this consuming interest. Once John D. Rockefeller, Jr., told Matisse that although he might seem to be as stone
in his dislike for modern art, "Mrs. Rockefeller, thanks to her very
special gifts of persuasion, would eventually wear him down to
the consistency of jelly." But in this instance, he overestimated her
very special gifts.

The respect he showed for her concern for the museum was,
to say the least, substantial. He gave the land for its buildings
and gardens and his total gifts were to exceed $5,000,000. But his
dislike for modern art had not been mitigated. In 1952, when he
made a generous contribution to the museum's endowment
fund, he wrote to his son Nelson, "I am writing to you as President of the Museum of Modern Art. Because Mama and a small
group founded the museum in 1927 [*sic*], I was naturally interested in it, although, as you know, modern art has never greatly
appealed to me."

Nelson Rockefeller has another explanation for the fact that by
1938 over half of Abby Aldrich Rockefeller's collection had
gone to museums and colleges (among them Dartmouth, Fisk
University, the Newark Museum, Rhode Island School of Design,
Williamsburg and, particularly, the Museum of Modern Art).
"It's just what happens to all collectors," Nelson Rockefeller explains. "You begin buying for yourself and then you just get too
much. At that point, you get out of collecting on a personal basis."

The same thing was to happen later to Nelson Rockefeller himself. Meanwhile, as his mother became less active in the Museum
of Modern Art, he became more active—although on a higher ad-
ministrative level. After his mother's death in 1948, he decided
that her personal artistic mantle should descend on his sister-in-

law, Blanchette Hooker Rockefeller, the wife of the eldest brother, John D. Rockefeller III.

Blanchette Rockefeller, a cool, pale beauty with a regally poised head that gives her the look of a Despiau sculpture, was hardly prepared for her role as Abby Aldrich Rockefeller's successor. Her own interest was music, in which she had majored at Vassar, and her only early skirmish with art was posing as a teen-ager for her elder sister's sculpture. Her first extracurricular activities, as a Rockefeller wife with four children, were the conventional and expected ones of philanthropy and education.

But Nelson Rockefeller tapped her for art. In 1949 he persuaded her to set up a Junior Council for the Museum of Modern Art, a sort of greenhouse in which future trustees might be cultivated. Soon the young garden was flourishing. Like Gaul, Blanchette Rockefeller's interests were now divided in three parts: the Community Service Organization, Vassar College and the Museum of Modern Art. But, encouraged by Nelson Rockefeller's infectious enthusiasm and Alfred Barr's persistent crusading, she found herself more and more engaged by modern art.

Abby Aldrich Rockefeller had enjoyed art at first hand and had helped the cause by her patronage: Blanchette Rockefeller began toying with the idea of acquiring some herself. At exactly this pregnant moment, Alfred Barr showed her some photographs of a bronze horse (without rider) by Marini. On an impulse, she ordered one. A few months later, she was startled to see two brawny men pushing a horse's head into the foyer of her Beekman Place apartment. "Where shall we put this, madam?" they asked.

It was a good question. The large horse looked as improbable in the conventional English setting as Thurber's seal in the bedroom. However much she wished to study modern art at close range, she knew from her mother-in-law's experience that it might be prudent if that range was not too close to a husband who, like his father, took a somewhat dim view of modern art and would certainly prefer Black Angus cattle in the pasture to a Marini horse in the drawing room.

She needed a stable. Using "Hooker money" for this project, as Mrs. Rockefeller, Jr., had used "Aldrich money" for hers, she found a house on East Fifty-second Street which could be remodeled into a gallery-guest house.

The architect to whom *she* turned was Philip C. Johnson. As first director of the Museum of Modern Art's Department of Architecture, in 1932 he had staged an exhibition which introduced the American public to the new European architecture of Le Corbusier, Gropius, Oud and Mies van der Rohe. "The International Style," Barr called it. Exhibited and propagandized by the Museum of Modern Art over the years (to the annoyance of the supreme American architect, Frank Lloyd Wright, whom the museum has also shown but not propagandized), this is the style which has become the basis of most modern architecture in America.

Unlike the fashionable architecture of the Stanford White period, which encouraged its owners to buy mountains of art and objects for its furnishings, in its early purist stages this glass-and-steel architecture did everything possible to discourage *its* owners from cluttering it with anything at all except some tubular or bent-plywood furniture. Pictures, it was said, "destroyed the walls," although there was often so much glass that there were hardly any walls to be destroyed. Not many collectors commissioned these modern mansions. But gradually the architects and their architecture relaxed into more amiable attitudes. After all, Le Corbusier had been willing to include not only the Michael Steins' Matisses but also Italian Renaissance furniture in the house he designed in 1927.

The proving ground that Philip Johnson provided for Blanchette Rockefeller's experimental art presented a characteristically unostentatious Rockefeller façade to the street. Its interior was

serene and elegant, with white-painted brick walls, a granite fireplace and a charming Japanese-influenced reflecting pool in its
middle, separating the living room and downstairs bedroom.

With the guest house under construction, it was time to go
shopping for art. The Rockefeller children had been brought up
to be as unself-conscious and unaware as possible of their great
wealth. A favorite story is that when John D. Rockefeller III was
a little boy, sailing a modest boat on the pond in Central Park, a
playmate taunted him because his father had not gotten him a bigger and better one. "Who do you think we are," the little Rockefeller asked earnestly, "the Vanderbilts?" It is, of course, an apocryphal tale, but its spirit is true. Yet as the Rockefellers became
adults they could not avoid the curiosity, incredulity and fawning
which their name evoked. Shy, therefore, about shopping for art
herself, Blanchette Rockefeller made the gallery rounds as the
anonymous companion of her architect and Barr. She was also dependent on their guidance, though her dislikes and likes were
spiritedly definite.

The word got around anyway, of course. The fact that Mrs.
John D. Rockefeller III was buying avant-garde art had the same
electrifying and reassuring effect on other collectors that her
mother-in-law's purchasing had had twenty-five years before. What
she was buying was still avant-garde, although most of the paintings she chose were by the very artists whom Peggy Guggenheim
had launched in "Art of This Century" a decade earlier. But men
like Rothko, now painting floating squares of colored mist;
Motherwell, suavely placing ovals against vertical forms; Pollock;
Willem de Kooning, hacking forceful imagery out of angry
strokes (who had also been asked to exhibit at Peggy Guggenheim's); and dozens of others younger and newer all needed this
touch of respectability to make them *à la mode*.

The Nelson Rockefellers, pleased at her pleasure, gave her a
Lipchitz bronze to go over the fireplace. She bought lots of sculptures to keep it and the Marini horse company. Standing where

he eternally pointed an accusing spectral finger at committee meetings, was Giacometti's super-skinny, six-foot-tall "Thin Man," whom the Rockefeller children nicknamed "No Dessert."

Blanchette Rockefeller's mother-in-law could usually keep both her collection of modern art and her participation in the Museum of Modern Art from infringing on her life with her husband. It was not always easy, however. Her biographer, Mary Ellen Chase, quotes a letter to one of the children: "Your father gave me a lecture previous to my going to the dinner about my talking to Mr. [Stephen] Clark all evening about the Museum, so I went very much chastened, but nevertheless with a small list concealed in my purse of things I really wanted to talk to him about."

For Blanchette Rockefeller the separation of museum and home was more difficult. The Museum of Modern Art, as Russell Lynes points out in *The Tastemakers,* has made modern art chic. The Rockefellers, Whitneys, Clarks and Blisses give prestige as well as money. The museum's evening openings have something of the glittering quality of Mrs. Potter Palmer's Charity Balls. Museum trustees, expected to play their part in making these openings social successes, patiently give pre-opening dinner parties for those whose presence is determined by the museum's discerning "social director." The mixed bag of guests ranges from artists to wealthy collectors (usually potential donors), with a sprinkling of architects, critics and museum personnel to act as a buffer between Bohemia and Wall Street.

The Rockefeller guest house, with its ample space, its modern architecture and its art-oriented atmosphere was so ideal a setting for museum dinners and receptions that it was in almost constant use, the more desirably so from the museum's point of view if Mr. and Mrs. John D. Rockefeller III were present to act as host and hostess. John D. Rockefeller III gamely turned up on several of these occasions. Shy, reticent, gazing dubiously above the piano at the calligraphic web by Bradley Walker Tomlin entitled "Homage to Gertrude Stein," he would circulate among the guests, modestly introducing himself. Then president of the Japan Society, responsible for the building of the Japanese house in the museum's garden and devoutly interested in bringing about closer Asian-American understanding, he was touchingly grateful to a dinner partner who talked with him about Asia instead of abstract art.

Not only museum social obligations, but also museum committee responsibilities began to press like an octopus upon the Rockefellers' private life. At one point, Blanchette Rockefeller was on the museum's board of trustees, its executive committee, its collection committee, its exhibition committee, honorary chairman of its Junior Council and chairman of its International Council, which she had helped found, to say nothing of committees for the C.S.O. and Vassar.

Something had to be done. She extricated herself from some of the committees. In the summer of 1955, she turned the guest house and most of its contents over to the museum and gave an annual purchase fund of about the same amount as she had been spending herself. Switching her activities in the direction of her husband's interests, she began boning up on Asian history and art.

But the collector had not died. She kept making forays into Fifty-seventh Street and to the museum's "New Talent" shows, arriving at one of these ahead of brother-in-law Nelson and getting a sculpture he tried to buy from her. On frequent trips to the East, she began seeking out Asian art, both old and new, woodblock prints in Tokyo, a wood-temple carving in Bali, pottery, paintings, bronzes.

Finally, she called on Philip Johnson to convert the basement of the Pocantico house into a little gallery. With incisive tact, she celebrated its completion by arranging a little display of "some of the Japanese things we had, ancient and modern." The many Japanese guests who came that summer were pleased by the pretty compliment. So was John D. Rockefeller III.

So pleased was he, in fact, that she dared the new, fascinating pastime of raiding her brimming storage closets to make changing installations in which old and new and East and West confront each other. A handsome, voluptuous Gupta torso looks at the ferocious black slashes of a Soulages abstraction; a lovely Shinto wood carving of a humble monk faces a Brancusi "Kiss"; the poetic calligraphy of Japan faces the swirling web of a Pollock. In endless variations, she plays with old possessions and new acquisitions. The Asian visitors continue to be amazed and delighted with these displays, as they are with the suave, contained Shaker furniture in another wing of the house.

Blanchette Rockefeller, like her brother-in-law Nelson, has thus discovered a new reason why the Rockefellers can morally afford the luxury of collecting art. It is a reason as pertinent to the thinking of the mid-twentieth century as the uplifting Victorian idea of beauty for the masses was to the earlier generation: art is an instrument of international good will.

John D. Rockefeller III, seeing the validity of this thinking, has started himself to enjoy the search for Asian art. Like his father in his reserve and reticence, he seems more at ease with the discipline, formality and understatement of Eastern art than with the "self-expression" of modern Western art. A Khmer head, bronze Buddhas from Thailand, silver boxes from Cambodia, now punctuate the Beekman Place apartment.

A magnificent, nearly four-foot-high stone Lobpuri Buddha is a temporary resident. Fifty years ago, Mr. Freer would simply have ordered this sculpture to be shipped home with dozens of other objects. But the lessons of Americans like himself and Fenollosa have finally been learned. Asians now protect their treasures with stringent export licensing. Only because this handsome piece is destined for exhibition in Asia House (the headquarters, now under construction, of the Asia Society) was it allowed to come to America. John D. Rockefeller III is as pleased as his wife to have this serene house guest. This act of public-collecting for international good will has left its mark. "We'd better leave time for shopping for art in Delhi," he remarked as they were planning their next Asian trip.

David Rockefeller, John D. Rockefeller, Jr.'s, youngest son, and his wife insist that they are not collectors. The art and artifacts which are so amiably disposed behind the Georgian façades of their New York and Pocantico houses are there, they say, because they like them and because they want to educate their children to appreciate beautiful things. These six young Rockefellers need have no complaint whatsoever about the quality of their education.

Their curriculum includes marvelous English porcelains (many of them inherited from Aunt Lucy Aldrich), superb eighteenth-century Chinese export wallpapers, T'ang female polo players, Louis XV chairs, handsome English furniture, shimmering Queen Anne crystal chandeliers and paintings of choicest quality by such masters as Cézanne, Manet, Corot, Pissarro and Seurat, with a portrait of George Washington by Gilbert Stuart, to boot.

As the youngsters run up the broadly sweeping staircase from the first floor to the second, their passage is lined with entrancing watercolor views of Paris by Arthur B. Davies, which once belonged to their paternal grandmother. As they climb to the third floor, their journey is marked by her arresting Japanese prints. An eight-year-old son shooting his atom-ray gun in the foyer does so in the shadow of an early Degas.

There is nothing self-conscious or stilted about this environment. Periods and styles are mixed in pleasant, informal harmony. George Washington shares the walls of the morning room with eight Oudry-like paintings of birds and flowers by an unknown French eighteenth-century master. Georgian silver and Chinese bronzes are neighbors in the library with a Sir Thomas Lawrence and a superb Corot.

The Sully portrait of a self-possessed English gentleman at one end of the living room looks without rancor at the introspective, slightly sullen Cézanne "Boy in a Red Waistcoat" at the other. The pale Seurat seems perfectly at home above a crimson-damask-covered English sofa, and the Manet still-life—at once savage and succulent—is strangely not jarred by the flowered chintz nearby.

The post-impressionists seem, indeed, so at ease and so assimilated in these surroundings that it comes as a shock to remember that work by these men was really "the last word" a half-century ago when collectors like the Havemeyers bought some of it, and that it even seemed outrageous to a large public when the Metropolitan showed it in 1921. These French nineteenth- and early-twentieth-century painters have become old masters.

The David Rockefellers truly are not "art collectors." They buy only "for the walls," and collecting art, as such, engages neither of them. (David Rockefeller's obsession for collecting runs instead to beetles—he has over 40,000 of them, ranging from the size of mites to that of mice, one of the finest collections in the country.) But the David Rockefellers' few exquisite paintings reflect the taste which has been increasingly prevalent in American collecting since the Armory Show—the taste for the French impressionists and post-impressionists, a taste which includes the post-fauve Matisse and stops short at cubism, a taste which is, on the whole, far less adventuresome than that of John Quinn and the other pioneer collectors of modern art.

This predilection began shortly after the Armory Show—Miss Lillie Bliss after all, bought Cézannes and Redons from that exhibition. Some of America's most illustrious collectors—Stephen Clark, Robert Clark, Sam A. Lewisohn, Maud and Chester Dale, Carroll Tyson, Duncan Phillips—began their discriminating and still intrepid buying then. The demand for this art gained increasing momentum in the twenties, the thirties, the forties—and, among others, Edward G. Robinson, Mrs. David Levy, Maurice Wertheim, the Leigh Blocks, John Hay Whitney, entered the field.

French nineteenth- and early-twentieth-century paintings were soon indisputably *comme il faut*. It was inevitable. The old-master market was dwindling. Their prices were high. The French "modern" paintings were plentiful, and just expensive enough to be trustworthy, and they had been around long enough so that they had stopped looking "crazy." But there were other cogent reasons.

The dwelling units of the Collector Class had changed. The exodus from mansions to town houses and to apartments meant smaller rooms and lower ceilings, a shift from ponderous English furniture to lighter French furniture, from Persian rugs to gray wall-to-wall carpeting, from dark, wood-paneled walls to pale, painted ones. In these new living quarters, English eighteenth-century portraits, such as those with which Huntington filled his California palace, were too large; tapestries ridiculous; and most old masters too dark. The French paintings—right in scale, light in hue and charming in Louis XV gold frames—seemed appropriate. Later, Greek shipowners were to find that they even made agreeable little $150,000 decorative accents on the walls of sea-going yachts.

The titans and tycoons were gone. The "lords" of industry had given way to the "captains" of industry. The new generation of socially secure bourgeoisie no longer felt any necessity for adopting British ancestors or equating themselves on cultural levels with condottieri and princes of the past. It would even have been a little unbecoming in the decades of the new social democracy instituted by "that man in the White House." Far more desirable were paintings that presented a joyous, reassuring material world. Here were light-filled landscapes and blithe women, handsome Tahitian natives and luscious flowers and fruits (even apples so beautiful as to obscure the memory of those the unemployed were selling on the streets). Here were ever so comfortably remote backstage views of ballet dancers rehearsing, prostitutes undressing or café singers performing. Even the visions of Van Gogh were painted in color so dazzling and eye-filling as to remove their sting of torment.

Once established and made respectable by those who bought

them in the twenties and thirties, these paintings had another distinct advantage to attract those new collectors of the booming postwar forties and fifties who would collect art for its "prestige value," and for those indiscriminates who would make the Correct Collection of Names, whose recipe of one Renoir, one Manet, one Degas, one Van Gogh, etc., is as standard as that for bran muffins. These French impressionist and post-impressionist paintings are easily recognizable. A Renoir or a Van Gogh or a Gauguin is as identifiable as the Cadillac fin.

Moreover, as their vogue has increased and their five- and six-figure prices have become international news, their value is as plainly visible as if they wore price tags on their elaborate frames. Like the Cadillac, they have become—regardless of quality—"success symbols."

As such, their prices have skyrocketed and the auction sales at which they change hands have recently attracted international buyers and made international headlines. The frenzied climate of these sales recalls that of the 1910 Yerkes sale, whose runaway prices so amused Mr. Johnson.

The art world gaped in 1952 when a Cézanne still-life with fourteen apples in the Cognacq sale in Paris went for $82,500—approximately $6,000 per apple. But five years later in Paris (at the Margaret Thompson Biddle sale), the Greek shipowners Basil Goulandris and Stavros Niarchos, competing against each other, bid a Gauguin "Still-Life with Apples" up to an unprecedented $297,000. No single bid reached this incredible amount at the London sale of the Weinberg pictures two months later, but the level of bidding for not particularly extraordinary pictures was so high that many observers were staggered.

When the sale of sixty-five French paintings from the collection of Georges Lurcy was announced for November, 1957, at the Parke-Bernet Galleries in New York, excitement ran high. On the night of the sale, 850 privileged persons holding coveted first-class cards crowded into the velvet-shrouded main auction room. Seven hundred, of presumably less importance—but as it turned out no less funds—were herded into the purdah-like isolation of side rooms, where they could view the proceedings over closed circuit black-and-white television and have their bids transmitted by loudspeaker to the main room.

As the auctioneer in his pulpit began ritualistically intoning the amounts and banging his hammer with decisive accents, the tension mounted. The understated gestures characteristic of the auction-room habitué—an abrupt nod of the head, a catalogue lifted in a quick arc—began shoving prices far above optimistically anticipated levels. Everyone knew that the popularity of Pierre Bonnard and Edouard Vuillard, later impressionists with intimate, personal expressions, had increased mightily since the Museum of Modern Art exhibited them in full dress in 1948 and 1954. But no one expected that in two minutes and fifteen seconds, Vuillard's view of the Tuileries—appraised at $25,000—would rocket from a $15,000 opening bid to make a world-record Vuillard price of $70,000. Dozens of other United States price records for various French artists toppled, too, as the evening wore on. The climax came when a Renoir landscape, "La Serre," expected to sell at $120,000 to $140,000, went under the hammer at $200,000. Mrs. Henry Ford II leaned over to say, "Thank you," to her husband.

The David Rockefellers are unconcerned about the fact that the paintings they happen to like are so fashionable. If they are annoyed when a friend of the family says, "Remember, David is the banker of the family [he is vice-president of Chase Bank and has been called "the keenest, steadiest, most precise" of the brothers]. Of course, his taste is conservative," they show no displeasure. Neither do they reveal any elation when they are congratulated by perceptive observers for having chosen superbly good paintings and having perhaps the most beautiful dining room in New York. The paintings, like the rest of the house, seem to them a personal, private matter.

It happened that a Signac landscape which they both liked was in the Lurcy collection, so Mrs. Rockefeller went to the sale on the night of November 7. In Parke-Bernet's confidential book, $20,000 was noted as the Signac's expected price. Mrs. David Rockefeller, the former Margaret McGrath, is an amiable young woman without an ounce of pretension. A friend asked her if it had not been an extraordinary experience bidding in that excitement-packed auction. "Not at all," Mrs. David Rockefeller remarked blandly, "I just raised my hand and kept it up until I reached my top price. Fortunately, the other bidding had stopped and the painting was mine." The children's curriculum now includes a $31,000 Signac.

Nelson Aldrich Rockefeller has a habit, like the United States Marines, of dramatically arriving in the nick of time and saving a situation. It was he who precipitated the $8,500,000 gift of land by John D. Rockefeller, Jr., to the United Nations and thus at the last minute kept the United Nations headquarters in America.

Informed that the U.N. Headquarters Committee was caught in deadlock and indecision, Nelson Rockefeller flew back from Mexico. He arrived twenty-two hours before the committee's deadline for decision at eleven A.M. on December 11, 1946. He worked frantically through that last pressing day, exploring every possibility (including the surrender of the Rockefeller brothers' land at Pocantico, but the delegates preferred the city to the suburbs).

Just before dinner, he spoke again with his father on the telephone. The seventeen-acre property along the East River, which William Zeckendorf owned and was planning to redevelop, came into the conversation. It might be available, Nelson told his father, relaying the information from his architect friend Wallace K. Harrison, for $8,500,000. Suddenly Harrison heard Nelson say, "Why, Pa!" and saw him smile broadly.

The fifteen remaining hours were grueling ones. That night, city approval had to be obtained; federal acceptance of the tax-free status of the gift assured; Zeckendorf located in a night club and persuaded to sell the land; and a legal deed of gift written.

After breakfasting at his father's apartment the next morning, Nelson Rockefeller called upon Senator Warren Austin and presented him with all the necessary assurances, approvals and documents. At three minutes past ten, the Senator was on his way to the U.N. Committee meeting at Lake Success.

Exhausted, Harrison and Rockefeller got into a taxi. As they stopped for a light on Third Avenue, Nelson Rockefeller grabbed the architect's arm. "Wally," he said, "we've got to celebrate." The way another man would have nipped into a corner saloon for a few quick shots of whiskey, Nelson Rockefeller ran into an antique store and bought five carrousel figures he had glimpsed in the window.

It was not an eccentric act for Nelson Rockefeller. Art collecting for him is a matter of urgency and necessity. It is a means, almost, of saving and protecting himself.

He is an energetic, ebullient man, whose life consists of chronic, excited work. He is the organizer, the politician, the "cosmic catalyst" of the brothers, a man resilient, optimistic, interested in large-scale ideas, quick, restless, assertive, unembarrassed by his wealth. His easygoing, boyish charm is reinforced by slangy, punchy talk, a broad smile and thick, wavy hair with one irrepressibly forward-falling lock. He has served under three presidents, been the brilliant landlord of Rockefeller Center, is the best known American in Latin and South America, a high power in the Museum of Modern Art, the founder and president of some of the Rockefeller brothers' most adventuresome economic and philanthropic undertakings, and in recent years has kept an alert eye cocked on a political career.

He throws himself into every activity on his crowded agenda with concentration and seething enthusiasm. Strangers are so convinced of his sincere, intense involvement with their problems during a fifteen-minute interview that they are incredulous at finding later that their problems have not necessarily continued as priority concerns for him.

He keeps running his nerves and energy at their highest gear. Then, having arrived at a pitch of tension, he has two outlets: driving a sports car at breakneck speed and collecting and rearranging objects of art.

In 1954, he served in Washington as President Eisenhower's special assistant (so unhappily out of sympathy with our vacillating foreign policy that he resigned after a year). During this taxing period, he frequently telephoned René d'Harnoncourt, the director of the Museum of Modern Art and his mentor in collecting primitive art, and asked him to bring down "some stuff." D'Harnoncourt, who comes from a titled Austrian family of French origin, is an oversize man of six feet six, who wears 14-½ shoes and speaks with a richly romantic Esperantesque accent. He would arrive in Washington with a suitcase full of paper-thin Peruvian gold pendants, little bowlegged Tarascan dogs, a suavely curving ceremonial paddle from Easter Island. Green and exhausted, Nelson Rockefeller became visibly refreshed and revitalized during a half-hour spent selecting the "stuff" he wanted to buy.

He is as exhilarated by the purchase of a work of art as if he had taken a dose of Benzedrine, and a half-hour spent leading an interested observer through his collection leaves him stimulated —and late for his next appointment.

But the excitements of buying and looking at art are rivaled by the pleasures of fussing with his possessions. Very often, Nelson Rockefeller escapes in New York from the pressures of the day's work at about six-thirty. He dashes home to his Fifth Avenue penthouse triplex, takes off his jacket, kicks off his shoes and, busy with nails, hammer and stepladder, spends thirty minutes or so rehanging his pictures. On a Saturday, he will suddenly decide to change all the furniture and fixings in the guest house at Pocantico or transform the dining room thirty minutes before guests are expected. His wife, the former Mary Todhunter Clark, a tall, forthright woman, blessed with intelligence and a Homeric sense

of humor, accepts with indulgent good nature the somewhat unsettling experience of never knowing at what she will look or on
what she will sit. The only area in all of their dwellings whose
transformations are in the hands of God and herself rather than
Nelson Rockefeller is the small greenhouse on the roof of their
New York apartment, which, in deference to *her* hobby, Nelson
Rockefeller gave her a few Christmases ago.

The business of moving heavy sculptures around outdoors is a
somewhat more strenuous activity than rehanging pictures (and
requires the assistance of children or gardeners), but Nelson
Rockefeller finds it correspondingly more gratifying. Had he not
been a Rockefeller, with a father, a grandfather and a group of
family lawyers to point out the obligations and responsibilities of
wealth, he would have been an architect. Having sculpture outdoors is a quite different, less sensual, less personal delight for him
than sculpture in a garden is for the Philadelphia collector
R. Sturgis Ingersoll. It is, rather, an architectural challenge. As if
he were designing huge city squares and intimate living spaces, he
spends hours of his few free weekends at Pocantico building stone
wall after stone wall to make new areas and new enclosures. An
over-life-size Lachaise bronze of a striding male nude will be set
on a hilltop for a while, so that it seems even more monumental
for having a sweep of the Hudson River and distant mountains as
its backdrop. Two delightful dowagers by Elie Nadelman will be
moved into a covert spot appropriate to their secret gossiping. Female torsos by Maillol, Kolbe girls, a huge Calder mobile will be
moved to make new accents in a circular space or to interrupt an
axial view. In the New York apartment, where opportunities are
more limited, he will pause while dressing to open a shallow
drawer in his dressing room, from which socks and handkerchiefs
have been removed to allow dozens of little four-inch pre-Columbian figures to lie in serried ranks. He will take a few out and set
them in groupings, like the actors in a toy theatre.

Nelson Rockefeller's explanation of his passion for hanging and rehanging, arranging and rearranging is that it is a vicarious way of being a creative artist and architect. He is a good one: he has a flair for making all sorts of things look well together. All this is an activity—and a therapy—which he apparently inherited from his mother. Abby Aldrich Rockefeller also liked rearranging objects and she often remarked that she was going upstairs to rehang her pictures because she felt sure nothing would raise her spirits more.

It is not the only quality Nelson Rockefeller inherited from her. Of all the sons, he is most like her in temperament (and like his grandfather, Nelson Aldrich, for whom he was named). He inherited her exuberance for collecting and her love of art: but he carried the exuberance to a higher power and he has combined love of art with uncannily good and daring taste.

Nelson Rockefeller, John D. Rockefeller, Jr.'s, second son, born in 1908, cannot remember when he was not aware of the art that was "always around the house." When he was at Dartmouth, besides playing soccer, skiing, teaching a Sunday school class for girls and making Phi Beta Kappa (intensely competitive, he was spurred to this effort because his roommate had done so), he arranged a few exhibitions, edited a magazine called *Five Lively Arts* and began scouring the countryside for Americana.

In 1930, during his senior year, he became engaged. Mary Clark, a Philadelphia girl who had been, since childhood, a summer neighbor of the Rockefellers' at Seal Harbor, Maine, liked Americana, too. Since Nelson had a running start in the field, they decided to furnish their house with Early American furniture. John D. Rockefeller, Jr., schooled, after all, in the Duveen tradition of proper furnishings, said it was ridiculous to spend money on antiques of *that* kind. He pointedly handed his son a furniture catalogue of Early American reproductions. Nelson Rockefeller went through it and checked every item needed for the house. Catalogue in hand, he approached his father again, announced the total sum and asked whether, if he could buy the originals for the same amount, he could have the money. Disapprovingly, his father agreed. Nelson Rockefeller is still proud of his accomplishment. Some of the Early American furniture is in the minuscule pre-Revolutionary house at Pocantico in which the Nelson Rockefellers live. The rest make a handsome pendant to the glass-and-steel guest house designed by Wallace K. Harrison. "You see that clock?" Nelson Rockefeller will ask. "It cost $12."

There is a difference between a weakness for collecting, which is an obsessive pack-rat operation, and a passion for collecting particular things, which implies an involvement with the coveted objects. Nelson Rockefeller is subject to both. What he calls his "weakness for collecting" had its first big chance on his honeymoon trip around the world. He bought the same kind of handsome "souvenirs"—Japanese, Chinese and Siamese sculptures, paintings and prints, textiles and jars—that had caught the discriminating fancy of Grandfather Aldrich, his mother and his Aunt Lucy on their travels. Journeys, ever since, have furnished a happy opportunity for this sort of wholesale shopping. Long after the Rockefellers have flown home, crates and boxes continue to arrive from wherever they have been, disgorging dozens of Japanese baskets and whatnots, Indian brasses, Spanish textiles, bits of Sicilian carts. "There wasn't very much to buy in Iran," one of his friends remarked. "After all, you can't collect mosques. But he took hundreds of photographs and had them blown up into prints, and those are his Iranian mosque collection."

But if his "weakness" for collecting expresses itself in wholesale acquisition of anything that he finds beautiful, his "passion" for collecting was bound to take a specific direction. Nelson Rockefeller is a man temperamentally impatient with the status quo, idealistically interested in change, and so ambitious to be a part of the forces that shape the twentieth century that it was inevitable his imagination would be captured by the new art of the new world.

His inclinations in that direction were first nudged along—true to Rockefeller form—by an architect. In 1933, Nelson Rockefeller went with his father to a meeting at which the seven architects who were designing Rockefeller Center were discussing the façade. "Father was accustomed to buildings that had fluted columns or Gothic arches marching up their sides," Nelson Rockefeller said later, "and he was outlining his ideas on that subject. The architects all listened until Father had finished and then Wally exploded. 'Goddam it, Mr. Rockefeller, you can't do that!' he said. 'You'll ruin the building if you cover up its lines with that classical gingerbread.'" Although they had known each other before, that explosion marked the beginning of a beautiful friendship between the two very junior members of both architect and management teams and the beginning of Wallace Harrison's position as "court architect" to the Rockefellers.

From the beginning, the Rockefeller Center planners accepted art as part of the project. By the time the Center was completed, over thirty artists had contributed over one hundred major works in the largest private program of public patronage in our time. The art ranges from Lee Lawrie's "Atlas," the most photographed statue in America, to the abstract artist Stuart Davis' mural for the men's room off the main lounge of the Radio City Music Hall, explicitly titled "Men without Women," from works as humdrum as the worst of W.P.A. projects to some excellent creations.

Harrison and Nelson Rockefeller were allies with Abby Aldrich Rockefeller to get as much really modern art commissioned as possible. Lined against them in favor of conservative work, of course, were Mr. Rockefeller and John R. Todd, the engineer in charge of the development. In the foreign field, the Harrison group were stumping hard for Picasso, Matisse, Despiau, Maillol, and Diego Rivera. Ironically, the only one of their candidates to make the grade was the Mexican Rivera, and they were all to wish devoutly that their score had been completely negative.

For the 1,071 square feet at his disposal, Rivera made sketches showing "the emancipation of mankind through technology." In these sketches, the mankind as well as the technology was anonymous. But as soon as he began working on the wall, Rivera apparently decided to bite the capitalist hand that was feeding him $21,500. One prominent member of mankind took on the unmistakable features of Vladimir Ilich Lenin. Nelson Rockefeller tactfully pointed out that this visage might offend quite a few people using this public building and requested that it be removed. Rivera, of course, remained adamant. The Rockefeller Center management paid him in full and halted the commission (acts about which the press was sympathetic), and then destroyed the work (for which they were editorially scolded even by the usually restained *New York Times*). It was an act for which, unfairly, for a long time Nelson Rockefeller had to bear the brunt.

Although Nelson Rockefeller could not maneuver a commission for Matisse on the public project, he could give the French artist a private one. Soon rubber-jointed nude ladies by Matisse were cavorting and bending all over the wall surrounding the fireplace in the living room of Rockefeller's Harrison-designed triplex apartment on Fifth Avenue. They were soon joined by carpets and tapestried chairs designed by Bérard and lighting fixtures by the sculptor Giacometti in an ensemble that has a very Paris-nineteen-thirties look. Later Léger was to do bold, abstract murals for the staircase walls.

From 1930 on, Nelson Rockefeller had been on the Board of Trustees of the Metropolitan Museum, futilely arguing in favor of the Metropolitan's buying the new art of the new world and equally futilely urging that it conduct archeological expeditions for old art of the new world. He obviously felt more at home at the Museum of Modern Art, where he was also a trustee. He became its president when it moved into its new building in 1939, and on and off, between Washington jobs, ever since has been president, chairman or trustee, the most dynamic and influential member of management regardless of title.

His pursuit of art, which had been going on all the while, accelerated with his post as president of the institution which Franklin D. Roosevelt hailed at its 1939 celebration as "the citadel of civilization." Soon Alfred Barr and Dorothy Miller were acting as his scouts and spotters in the exhilarating chase.

The pace kept gaining momentum. According to Carol Kinzel Uht, who works as Nelson Rockefeller's art cataloguer, excluding the primitive arts, he had 249 items in the collection at the end of 1950. Now it far exceeds 1,000. None of his modern art dates before 1900—and only a few things are pre-cubist. There is a vast sculpture collection, of which, as a frustrated architect interested in three-dimensional forms, he is particularly fond. It ranges from classic Maillols to Henry Moore's handsomely knit "Family Group" and to metal abstractions by Seymour Lipton and those other of the modern sculptors who use acetylene torches as their ancestors used the chisel.

Picasso is the one dominant artist in the varied group. Besides a spectacular group of Picasso paintings of various periods, he has Picasso prints and rare books with original Picasso drawings, two Picasso tapestries (including one of "Guernica"), Picasso sculptures (he is particularly fond of Picasso's owls and vultures), and in 1956 he paid $98,000—the highest price ever paid for a cubist picture—for Picasso's "Girl with a Mandolin," which Alfred Barr calls "the Venus of Cubism." Alfred Barr, who naturally hoped sometime to have public custody of this expensive music-making girl, kept urging Rockefeller to make the purchase. Even though Nelson Rockefeller agreed that someday she would belong to what his father called "a wider audience," he hesitated at the price. He finally rationalized the purchase by asking Barr to pick out some things that might be sold. Barr did. Like most other collectors who make similar rationalizations, Nelson Rockefeller bought the painting he wanted and kept delaying the decision to sell anything.

When he is traveling, Nelson Rockefeller manages ingeniously to tuck his art activities into his urgent schedule of more important commitments. In 1955, he flew to Germany expressly to confer with four German cabinet ministers, but he was anxious to be at the opening of an exhibition of American art that the Museum of Modern Art had sent to Frankfurt. He accomplished both missions by persuading the German ministers to ride with him on the train between Bonn and Frankfurt. Then, by accepting an invitation to a dinner which his uncle Nelson Aldrich (then the United States Ambassador to the Court of St. James's) was giving—where he could see certain strategic British political figures without consuming a day in successive appointments—he was able to spend a few hours with D'Harnoncourt looking over a collection of primitive art that was about to be dispersed.

But in New York, in recent years, there is apparently less time. He does most of his shopping for the newest of the new art in the Museum of Modern Art itself, buying regularly from its "New Talent" shows and from those larger exhibitions, constellations of little one-man shows of Americans, which Dorothy Miller selects and arranges. He makes up his mind immediately; besides knowing all about art, he knows very definitely what he likes and what he does not like. But since almost all the preliminary "screening" is done by Barr and Miller, his collection recently represents a super-selective Museum of Modern Art taste (just as, during his ardent involvement with Latin America, the museum reflected *his* taste).

The Fifth Avenue apartment is the headquarters for the collection and its receiving and distribution point. With a retentive memory for inventory, Nelson Rockefeller decides what shall go where. Fortunately, there are a goodly number of places. Besides New York, there is a house in Washington, the main house and several guest houses at Pocantico and a large house in Seal Harbor. Recently he had Philip Johnson remodel part of the inside of a huge coal-storage house on a wharf there into a handsome, pandanus-lined 60-by-20-foot gallery. This new space, with thirteen-foot-high ceilings, has solved a rather ticklish problem. Avant-garde modern artists like painting enormous pictures. It is hard enough for New York apartment dwellers to get them placed once and for all in low-ceilinged rooms, but they present even more of a problem to a collector like Nelson Rockefeller who likes moving them around. The huge paintings by Franz Kline, Grace Hartigan and Ernest Briggs can be shifted in the Maine gallery with the greatest of ease. Besides interior spaces, there are, happily, acres and acres of the great outdoors in which he can dispose his holdings.

Neither spaces nor projects will ever run dry. Imaginative, enthusiastic and energetic, Nelson Rockefeller continually promotes new ones, which reach fulfillment because of his persuasive charm and his capacity to sweep others along in his buoyant belief.

Like his mother, he has been unable to reduce his father's stony dislike of modern art "to the consistency of jelly." But to the incredulous astonishment of his brothers and sisters-in-law, he has been able to persuade his father to sanction improbable acts. His father allowed him to commission Wally Harrison to build a modernistic swimming pool in front of Candler's French medieval playhouse; to move to the Pocantico grounds from the Modern Museum's garden the exhibition house that Marcel Breuer had designed for a hypothetical family of rather less than Rockefeller income; and to agree to commissioning Matisse to design a rose window in memory of Abby Aldrich Rockefeller in the Union Church of Pocantico Hills (it was Matisse's last work before his death).

Nelson Rockefeller's passion for collecting art reaches its ultima Thule, however, with the "primitive arts"—those artistically very *un*-primitive objects which peoples of ancient and tribal civilizations have been creating over the past twenty-two thousand years. As if they were created to suit his particular temperament, these handsomely synthesized three-dimensional forms have directness, vitality and energy.

They have another quality that—perhaps surprisingly—appeals to Nelson Rockefeller. Though he has none of his father's devotion to detail and finish as such, he does have an acute awareness of craftsmanship and an inquiringly keen eye for detail. One day in his office on the fifty-sixth floor of Rockefeller Center, he telephoned to Victor Borella, general manager of the Center, to ask why the pools on the tenth-floor roofs of the International Building were being painted a shade of blue different from the original one. Borella, explaining that the pools were being repainted simply as a part of maintenance, said he did not think that the color was being changed. "Oh, no," Nelson Rockefeller replied, "I've been looking out of my window and they are making them a slightly purplish blue." His forty-six-story scrutiny proved correct. Another day, he and Borella were walking along Fifth Avenue where honey locust trees were being set out along the street in front of the buildings. Nelson Rockefeller remarked that one tree was out of line. Borella insisted that since the trees all had different diameters it was impossible to tell the accuracy of alignment without measuring. He had them checked. The tree was four inches out.

Nelson Rockefeller first encountered "primitive" art on his honeymoon trip in 1930. In Sumatra, he saw a knife whose handle was a sculptured head with human hair. He found it irresistible. A few years later, in Mexico, he fell for some pre-Columbian objects, at once less gruesome and more beautiful. At exactly this ripe moment of enthusiasm in 1934, he met René d'Harnoncourt, who was to play so fruitful a part in this area of his collecting.

The handiwork of most of the races of man was hardly known before the Victorian age began systematically to explore them. Until very recently, these artifacts of ancient and tribal peoples found their place—as fetishes and oddities—in the curiosity cabinets of the inquiring, souvenir-hoarding collectors of the nineteenth century or were accepted as proper material for natural history museums. They belonged to Archeology, Ethnography and Curiosity.

It remained primarily for the artists of the twentieth century to recognize in these objects directness, vitality, abstraction and distortion which linked them to their own art. Expression, not naturalism, was their common intention. Modern artists began to endow these objects, group by group, with esthetic respectability.

The cubists paid this compliment to African art in the first decade of the twentieth century. The surrealists in the twenties discovered the arts of Oceania, intrigued particularly by their vivid sexual symbolism and fetishistic properties. In Mexico, in the thirties, artists like Miguel Covarrubias were gathering collections of the art that preceded the arrival of the Europeans in the new world, while simultaneously in the United States, the writer Oliver La Farge, the painter John Sloan and the archeologist Joseph Spinden, were recognizing as art the handicrafts of the American Indian.

Some of the pioneer collectors, buying art created in the twentieth century, also began buying the things first appreciated as works of art in the twentieth century. Gertrude Stein and John Quinn had African masks. Walter and Louise Arensberg, purchasing their first pre-Columbian piece in 1915, amassed finally a large collection of primitive art, particularly of the art of the Americas, as discriminating as their collection of moderns. Others specialized in the "primitive" arts for their own sake. Such a collector is Robert Woods Bliss, who limits himself primarily to pre-Columbian art and, with the taste of a Morgan, cares particularly for objects of gold and jade, acting almost apologetic about what he refers to as his few "clay pieces."

By the time Nelson Rockefeller met him in 1934, René d'Harnoncourt had spent eleven years becoming an authority on primitive and contemporary Mexican folk art. He has been seeking it out, first for tourists and private collectors, then for the Mexican

Government and finally for the American Federation of Arts, for whom he brought a show to fifteen American cities. Then he moved on into the arts and crafts of the American Indian. In 1946, when Nelson Rockefeller became president of the Museum of Modern Art for the second time, he found D'Harnoncourt there (with the fancy title of Vice-President in Charge of Foreign Activities and Director of the Department of Manual Industries) ready to put on the spectacular exhibition of "Art of the South Seas."

Two years later, just before D'Harnoncourt moved into the museum's directorship, they joined forces in the pursuit of the primitive arts. D'Harnoncourt began looking around for those African masks, Alaskan totem poles and huge impassive stone carvings from Easter Island which would presumably stir Rockefeller's affections. Like any good marriage broker, he knew the financial arrangement proper to each liaison—no mean trick, since the price of these objects was rising rapidly. A Tarascan dog which could have been picked up for about $2 in the market place in Mexico in 1927 (and bought at the same time for $25 in New York), was bringing between $250 and $400 in 1948. (In 1957, a first-class example—if available—cost about $1,500.) D'Harnoncourt also acted as chaperon, charged with marking as undesirable any object which might not be genuine—no mean trick again, for this market was beginning to attract a large number of competent fakes.

Nelson Rockefeller, buying only for his own pleasure, had very definite likes and dislikes. The bronze plaques from Benin pleased his fancy, but the heads from the same area of Africa did not. But so many more of the primitive objects pleased him than displeased him that after four years the New York apartment— which, after all, contained fifty percent of the other art plus a wife and five children—had reached a crucially crowded state. Even the patient Mrs. Rockefeller occasionally inquired whether saturation had not been passed. It was time, as Nelson Rockefeller said of his mother's collecting, "to move from the private thing to the public thing."

He looked at his accumulations with a critical, Rockefeller eye. "Look here, René," he said, "maybe all this is too good to be a private collection, but is it good enough to be a public one?" From that point on, their buying became systematic. D'Harnoncourt made a series of little loose-leaf notebooks with drawings of the supreme examples in the world of each kind of art. Then, when a piece was located which was as good or better than, say, the one in the Louvre or the British Museum, the drawing would come out and a photograph of the Rockefeller object would take its place. Nelson Rockefeller carried these little books in his pockets until 1954, when there were more photographs than drawings. The collection was good enough for the public.

The problems of finding a location (a Rockefeller-owned brownstone on West Fifty-fourth Street), a director (the gifted art historian, Robert Goldwater) and trustees for the new museum were all comparatively simple compared to the problem of finding a name. For a while, during its settling-in period, it was known as the "Museum of Indigenous Art." That led to a good bit of bewilderment, because, as D'Harnoncourt says, some people thought the new institution had something to do with art from the poorhouse. Another group, somewhat more literate but also more chauvinistic, decided that indigenous referred, of course, to art native to America. Since Mrs. Vanderbilt Webb (Mrs. J. Watson Webb's sister-in-law) was opening a museum just down the street which would feature American crafts, there was additional confusion. Reluctantly the trustees settled on the inadequate title, "Museum of Primitive Arts." Opened early in 1957, it is the first museum in the world to be devoted exclusively to showing as capital "A" art the best examples of the handicrafts of all ancient and tribal peoples.

If Nelson Rockefeller's conscience were to nag him for indulging his urgent necessity for collecting, he would have ample,

Rockefeller-approved justification for salving it. Although on a vastly more modest financial scale, he stands in the same relation to the Museum of Primitive Arts as his father does to The Cloisters. He is responsible for about ninety-five percent of its objects and is most significantly responsible for its endowment. He is also one of the Museum of Modern Art's most staunch and generous supporters and, among other gifts, is the donor of Henri Rousseau's "The Dream," which, allegedly costing $750,000, is the most expensive painting in that institution. He not only buys avidly, but he lends generously, and the words "Lent by Nelson A. Rockefeller" are blue-chip assets to young artists.

In the summer months of 1958, there was speculation about whether some of Nelson Rockefeller's art might not soon have another influential setting. He announced that he would run for governor of the state of New York on the Republican ticket against Averell Harriman on the Democratic ticket. The art world chuckled: either way, there would be modern art in the Executive Mansion at Albany, where Harriman arrived in 1954 with handsome twentieth-century pictures that, gathered by him and his wife, the discerning erstwhile dealer, Marie Harriman, are testaments to the rare phenomenon of sophisticated and discriminating taste in a public-officeholder.

But for Nelson Rockefeller, as for his sister-in-law Blanchette, a far more cogent justification for private art collecting than the benefits it brings to a "wider audience" is its importance in international good will. He castigates America for allowing itself to be considered the only uncultured country in the world. He berates American businessmen for their sinful unawareness of the significance of art and culture. He zealously insists that his interest in art has been his best ambassadorial asset around the globe. He is at his evangelical best on the congenial theme of the international implications of a respect for art and culture. No one could accuse Nelson Rockefeller of failing to practice what he preaches.

Thus, each of the Rockefellers has a sincere moral justification for his one luxury. These were ethical considerations that hardly bothered a J. Pierpont Morgan, for whom the act of *noblesse oblige* was simply the casually correct gesture of a patrician, or tugged at the conscience of an Isabella Stewart Gardner, who was concerned with contriving immortality, like mortality, to suit her fancy.

Strangely, it all becomes the same in the end. "Private vices, public virtues," wrote Sir John Mandeville in the fourteenth century. In the story of art collecting in America, private possessions have become public pleasures.

Sources and Obligations

It would be tedious, for both the reader and myself, certainly fruitless and surely pretentious to append here an exhaustive bibliography of all the material I have read. Of necessity, I have consulted hundreds of newspaper and magazine articles, books, catalogues, sales catalogues and, wherever they were available, correspondence, diaries, memoirs and bills.

I had planned originally, however, to include here specific sources for all my data. For instance, in support of my statement that Charles Lang Freer raised his chefs' salaries over the years from sixty to one hundred dollars and could not countenance one who knew nothing of pastry work, I had listed over twenty references to his correspondence with managers of hotels, employment agencies and employees' families. To support my interpretation of Mrs. Potter Palmer as a social leader and of the social position of Middle Westerners in France, I had listed, in addition to society notes in newspapers, articles in such now forgotten periodicals as *Munsey's Magazine,* October, 1900, and *Hampton's Magazine,* October, 1911, and a gossipy piece by Walter G. Robinson, "The American Colony in Paris," *Cosmopolitan,* October, 1900. It soon became apparent that the tail would wag the dog.

Therefore, it seemed more appropriate to indicate only in general terms the primary sources on which I drew for my portraits and to list only those published works which were important sources for data or those from which quotations appear in the text. I have done so, chapter by chapter.

I would like first, however, to call the reader's attention to five books of special merit which make an excellent background for my biographical "close-ups."

The first is René Brimo's *L'evolution du goût aux Etats-Unis d'apres l'histoire des collections.* The astonishing fact is that although private art collections form a significant part of American social and cultural history, only one person has attempted to record all the important ones, and it is even odder that he should be a Frenchman. His book was published in Paris in 1938. It remains the basic and only comprehensive compilation. Yet it has never been translated or brought up to date by the addition of the many important collections of the forties and fifties.

Douglas and Elizabeth Rigby's *Lock, Stock and Barrel,* New York, 1944, is a delightful and ambitious book on the whole subject of collecting. Russell Lynes' *The Tastemakers,* New York, 1954, is an invaluable, perceptive and entertaining book on taste in America. Wayne Andrews' *Architecture, Ambition and Americans,* New York, 1955, gracefully and informatively tells the story of architecture as a cultural-social phenomenon as well as an artistic one. S. N. Behrman's *Duveen,* New York, 1952, is a scintillating biography of the world's most spectacular art dealer. I am gratefully indebted to these last three books for data.

As I said in my Foreword, I have listed below, under each chapter heading, the people who generously aided me in this research. If I have inadvertently forgotten any, my gratitude is not lessened by my carelessness, and though my phrasing may sound repetitive, my appreciation is always specific and personal. None of the men and women who discussed the collectors with me should be held responsible for what I have written. The interpretations and evaluations are my own.

Provincial Princess: Mrs. Potter Palmer

I am grateful to Daniel Catton Rich, now director of the Worcester Museum of Art, but at the time of my research, director of the Art Institute of Chicago, and to Margaret F. Bush, registrar, for general assistance; to Bernard Berenson; to the staffs of the Ryerson Library, where I consulted photographs, the Newberry Library and the Chicago Historical Society, in both of which I consulted photographs, contemporary newspapers (especially the *Chicago Tribune* and the *Chicago Inter-Ocean*) and miscellaneous material; and to the staff of the *Chicago Tribune* morgue.

Aside from these sources, major sources for this chapter were: Wayne Andrews' *Battle for Chicago,* New York, 1946 (invaluable for background material on Chicago and Mr. Potter Palmer) and his *Architecture, Ambition and Americans,* cited above; Daniel Catton Rich's "O Pioneers," *Town and Country,* January, 1951 (for relations of Chicago and Paris); Henry B. Fuller's *With the Procession,* New York, 1894; Frank L. Davis' "An Architect Describes the Palmer Castle," *Illinois Society of Architecture Bulletin,* February, 1956; *Arts and Handicrafts in the Woman's Building of the World's Columbian Exposition,* edited by Maude Howe Elliott, New York, 1893; *Addresses of Mrs. Potter Palmer,* Chicago, 1894; World's Columbian Exposition, *Official Catalogue, Part X, Dept. K, Fine Arts,* Chicago, 1893; Hubert Howe Bancroft's *The Book of the Fair,* 1893 (fascinating to the point of distraction); Thomas B. Hess' "The Degas-Cassatt Story," *Art News,* November, 1947; Jefferson Williamson's *The American Hotel,* New York, 1930. The Kipling quotation is from Rudyard Kipling's *From Sea to Sea,* Vol. II, New York, 1899.

C'est Mon Plaisir: Isabella Stewart Gardner

My gratitude to Morris Carter, Mrs. Joseph Lindon Smith, George Peabody Gardner, Arthur Pope, James Hazen Hyde, George L. Watson (author of a forthcoming biography of the fascinating lady),

Emily C. Woodruff and, most especially, to Bernard Berenson for talking with me about Mrs. Gardner and to Mr. Berenson for permission to quote from his correspondence to Mrs. Gardner and myself.

I am deeply grateful to George L. Stout, director, and to the trustees of the Isabella Stewart Gardner Museum for their permission to consult and quote from material in the archives. It is primarily on this material that my portrait of Mrs. Gardner is based. Special warm thanks to Mr. Stout, who, sympathetically understanding the pressures of time, allowed me to work at Fenway Court far into the nights.

Mrs. Gardner was colorful copy and the contemporary Boston newspapers, the *New York Times* and contemporary periodicals record most of the by now famous anecdotes.

Aside from the sources mentioned above, major sources for data were: John La Farge and August F. Jacacci's *Noteworthy Paintings in American Collections,* 1907; Philip Hendy's *Catalogue of the Exhibited Paintings and Drawings, The Isabella Stewart Gardner Museum,* Boston, 1931; Morris Carter's *Isabella Stewart Gardner and Fenway Court,* Boston, 2nd ed., 1940 (the basic and indispensable biography); Van Wyck Brooks' *New England: Indian Summer,* 1865-1915, New York, 1940 (I used material from pages 251, 420, 435, but feel respect and debt far greater than such page references indicate); Bernard Berenson's "Les peintures italiennes de New York et de Boston," *Gazette des Beaux-Arts,* I, 1896.

The information on the tapestries is from Ella S. Siple's "Some Recently Identified Tapestries in the Gardner Museum," *Burlington Magazine,* November, 1930, and Berenson's remarks about being an art expert are from his *Sketch for a Self-Portrait,* New York, 1949.

The Grandiose Gesture: J. Pierpont Morgan

I am indebted to Frederick C. Adams, director, and the trustees of the Pierpont Morgan Library for permission to use and quote from material in the archives (and to the assistance of Marian Kenway, librarian), because this portrait of Morgan as a collector is based primarily on the letters, bills, notations, newspaper clippings and photographs in these files. I also thank Albert Ten Eyck Gardner of the Metropolitan Museum for allowing me to consult files and the invaluable volumes of early clippings in that museum. Bernard Berenson, Edward Fowles, Geoffrey Agnew, Alfred M. Frankfurter, John Goldsmith Phillips and Captain Edward Steichen kindly gave me interviews about Mr. Morgan.

Aside from the above sources, major sources for this chapter were: *Guide to the Loan Exhibition of the J. Pierpont Morgan Collection,* Metropolitan Museum of Art, New York, 1914, with an introduction by Edward Robinson; Frederick Lewis Allen's *The Great Pierpont Morgan,* New York, 1949 (unquestionably the best of the many Morgan biographies; I drew for data on pages 49-50, 60, 114, 117, 145, 216-218 of the 1956 Bantam Book edition); and Herbert L. Saterlee's *J. Pierpont Morgan: An Intimate Portrait,* New York, 1939 (written by Morgan's son-in-law; I drew for data on pages 353, 412, 434, 495, 505, 535-537, 564).

Other important sources for data in this chapter were: Wayne Andrews' *Architecture, Ambition and Americans,* cited above (for general architectural background and the almost verbatim Stanford White-Mackay house story); F. H. Taylor's *Pierpont Morgan as Collector and Patron, 1837-1913,* New York, 1957; Wayne Andrews' *Mr. Morgan and His Architect,* New York, 1957; Virginia Woolf's *Roger Fry: A Biography,* New York, 1940; Winifred E. Howe's *A History of the Metropolitan Museum of Art,* New York, 1913; *Report of the Committee on the Export of Works of Art, Etc.* Her Majesty's Stationery Office, London, 1952.

Gamesmanship: John G. Johnson

This chapter is based largely on the voluminous letters from John G. Johnson to Bernard Berenson. My deep gratitude, obviously, is to Mr. Berenson for making these available to me; to the First Pennsylvania Banking and Trust Company, executor and trustees under the will of John G. Johnson, for permission to quote from this correspondence; and to counsel for the estate, Saul, Ewing, Remick and Saul.

My thanks also to Henri Marceau, director of the Philadelphia Museum of Art, and Barbara Sweeney, curator of the John G. Johnson Collection, who patiently and helpfully allowed me to consult the archives of the Johnson Collection, which were my other main source. Mr. Marceau, sensitive to the problems of out-of-town research, kindly made other requested material conveniently available and Miss Sweeney answered questions patiently. My thanks, too, to R. Sturgis Ingersoll for his summary of newspaper clippings about the building of the Philadelphia Museum (dating from 1893) and to the staff of the morgue of the *Philadelphia Bulletin.*

Aside from these sources, major sources for this chapter were: John G. Johnson's *Sightseeing in Berlin and Holland Among Pictures,* Philadelphia, 1892 (reprinted from articles in the *Philadelphia Press*); *Catalogue of a Collection of Paintings Belonging to John G. Johnson,* Philadelphia, 1892; *John G. Johnson Collection, Catalogue of Paintings,* Philadelphia, 1941; *John G. Johnson Collection, Book of Illustrations,* Philadelphia, 1953; Barnie F. Winkleman's *John G. Johnson, Lawyer and Art Collector,* Philadelphia, 1942 (a conscientious and comprehensive biography which was an indispensable source for factual biographical data and for several anecdotes); the obituary in the *New York Times,* April 15, 1917 (so extraordinarily full an account that I make an exception in citing a specific newspaper article here); Frank Jewett Mather, Jr.'s, "John G. Johnson," *The Nation,* April 19, 1917; Arthur Hoeber's "Art Collector: John G. Johnson's Old and Modern Works," *New York Commercial Advertiser,* May 31, 1902 (interesting because of its date).

Other important sources for specific data in this chapter were: Henri Marceau's "A Salute to the Past—A View of the Future," *75th Annual Report of the Fairmount Park Art Association* (and other reports of this organization); *The Hudson-Fulton Celebration, Catalogue of an Exhibition,* Metropolitan Museum of Art, New York, 1909; *Catalogue of the Sale of the Charles T. Yerkes Collection,* American Art Association, New York, 1910; and, for data on Andrew Mellon, Roger Butterfield's "The Millionaire's Friend," *Saturday Evening Post,* March 8, 1947 (an excellent profile) and Harvey O'Connor's *Mellon's Millions, the Biography of a Fortune,* New York, 1933.

Tea and Champagne: Charles Lang Freer

My gratitude to Arthur G. Wenley, director, John A. Pope, assistant director, and to the trustees of the Freer Gallery of Art, Smithsonian Institution, for permission to consult and quote from material in the archives of the Freer Gallery (including Whistler's letter, March 24, 1897, to Mr. Freer). Mr. Freer's daybooks with their miscellaneous correspondence and accounts, his diaries, the letters to him, the photographs and many large scrapbooks of newspaper clippings were the basis for my portrait. My thanks also to Bertha M. Usilton, librarian, for her patient assistance.

Agnes E. Meyer (with her keen reportorial eye and insight), Katharine N. Rhoades, Louise Hecker Fletcher, Grace E. Guest all kindly allowed me interviews, and the staff of the Merrill-Palmer School allowed me to inspect Freer's house.

Primary publications on the Freer Collection are those published by the Smithsonian Institution, Freer Gallery of Art, under the groupings of *Occasional Papers, Oriental Studies* and *Ars Orientalis.*

In addition to the sources mentioned above, others of significance for data in this chapter were: Agnes E. Meyer's "The Charles L. Freer Collection," *The Arts,* August, 1927; Katharine N. Rhoades' "An Appreciation of Charles Lang Freer" (typescript for *Ars Orientalis*) and her chronology of Freer's career; Louisine E. Havemeyer's "The Freer Collection," *Scribner's,* May, 1923 (most other periodical articles are based on earlier and often inaccurate newspaper accounts, especially that in the *Logansport Journal,* September 10, 1904); Ernest Fenollosa's "The Collection of Mr. Charles Lang Freer," *Pacific Era,* November, 1907, and Leila Mechlin's "The Freer Collection of Art," *Century,* January, 1907 (the two best early accounts of the collection and the terms of the gift); Van Wyck Brooks' *New England: Indian Summer,* cited above (indispensable for discussion of New Englanders' yearning for the East, with specific information taken from pages 358-360, 362-365, as well as the quotation from Edward S. Morse's *Japan Day by Day*); Mary Fenollosa's introduction to Ernest Fenollosa's *Epochs of Chinese and Japanese Art,* London, 1913; *The Whistler Peacock*

Room, Smithsonian Publication, Pub. 4024, Washington, D.C., 1951.

   In addition, small quotations or specific data come from Hesketh Pearson's *The Man Whistler,* London, 1952; Henry C. White's *The Life and Art of Dwight D. Tryon,* Boston, 1930; David Fairchild's *The World Was My Garden,* London, 1938; John La Farge's *An Artist's Letters from Japan,* New York, 1890; Hawkins Ferry's "Representative Detroit Buildings: A Cross-Section of Architecture, 1823-1946," *Detroit Institute of Arts Bulletin,* March, 1953. Under the pseudonym of "Rusticus," Freer's sporting Capri companion, Thomas Jerome, wrote a charming and well-illustrated article on their villa, "A Letter to Pliny the Younger Relating to the Villa Castello on Capri," *House and Garden,* August, 1902.

The Last Word: The Henry O. Havemeyers

I profoundly thank Mrs. Havemeyer's daughters, Mrs. P. H. B. Frelinghuysen and, especially, Mrs. J. Watson Webb, for their magnificent generosity and courtesy. They shared with me recollections and anecdotes; allowed me to see family photograph albums, correspondence, privately printed biographies, genealogies and catalogues, and gave me permission to quote from these. My portrait would have been impossible without this material and I am particularly indebted to Mrs. Havemeyer's delightful and invaluably informative, privately printed *Memoirs.* My thanks also to George Frelinghuysen; and to Albert Ten Eyck Gardner, who allowed me to consult files in the Metropolitan Museum.

   Aside from these sources, the major sources for data were as follows: *Catalogue of a Loan Exhibition, The H. O. Havemeyer Collection,* the Metropolitan Museum of Art, 1910 (*The H. O. Havemeyer Collection,* a revised catalogue with introduction by James J. Rorimer, had not yet appeared when my manuscript was completed); *The Art Work of Louis C. Tiffany,* New York, 1914; Gertrude Speenburgh's *The Arts of the Tiffanys,* Chicago, 1956 (especially pages 81-82); and Montgomery Schuyler's *A Review of the Work of Charles Haight, The Architectural Record,* New York, 1899 (which disproved the family's belief that Richard Morris Hunt had been the architect of the Have-meyer house).

Data on Mr. Havemeyer as a businessman and on the sugar trust came primarily from Franklin Clarken's "The So-called Sugar Trust," *Century,* January, 1903; Robert N. Burnett's "Henry Osborne Have-meyer," *Cosmopolitan,* April, 1903; David G. Phillips' "The Treason of the Senate," *Cosmopolitan,* May, 1906. Data and quotations concern-ing Mrs. Havemeyer's suffragette activities are from her own "Mem-ories of a Militant: I. The Suffrage Torch, II. The Prison Special," *Scribner's,* May and June, 1922.

Americans in Paris: Gertrude, Leo, Michael and Sarah Stein

My gratitude to Bernard Berenson, Walter Pach, Alice B. Toklas, Henri-Pierre Roché, Captain Edward Steichen, Henry McBride, Richard Offner for allowing me interviews about the four Steins; and particularly to Gabrielle Osorio, Elise Haas, Dr. Jeffrey Smith, Dr. John W. Dodds and Dr. Grace McCann Morley for their information on the much less known Michael and Sarah Stein.

Essential sources for this chapter were Leo's and Gertrude's own writings, especially these: By Leo Stein—*Journey Into the Self,* New York, 1950, edited by Edmund Fuller, with foreword by Mabel Weeks and introduction by Van Wyck Brooks (the remark about discoverers of modern art and Homer's birthplace is from the latter); *The A.B.C. of Aesthetics,* New York, 1927; *Appreciation: Painting, Poetry and Prose,* New York, 1947. By Gertrude Stein—*The Autobiography of Alice B. Toklas,* New York, 1933; *Everybody's Autobiography,* New York, 1937; *Lectures in America,* New York, 1935; *Portraits and Prayers,* New York, 1934; *Picasso,* London, 1938; *Two: Gertrude Stein and Her Brother,* with a foreword by Janet Flanner, New Haven, Conn., 1951; *Selected Writings of Gertrude Stein,* edited and with an introduction by Carl van Vechten, New York, 1946; *The Flowers of Friendship: Letters Written to Gertrude Stein,* New York, 1953, edited by Donald C. Gallup.

Other important sources for data in this chapter were as follows:

Elizabeth Sprigge's *Gertrude Stein: Her Life and Work,* New York, 1957 (especially useful for factual biographical detail on the Steins' background and childhood); *Pictures for a Picture of Gertrude Stein,* Catalogue of an Exhibition, Yale University Art Gallery, New Haven, Conn., 1951; Alfred H. Barr's *Matisse,* New York, 1951 (a monumental work); Ambrose Vollard's *Recollections of a Picture Dealer,* Boston, 1936. Small quotations are from James T. Soby's "Gertrude Stein and the Artists," *Saturday Review of Literature,* May 24, 1947; Carl W. McCardle's "The Terrible Tempered Dr. Barnes," *Saturday Evening Post,* April 4, 1942; Fiske Kimball's "Discovery from America," *Art News,* April, 1948; "Le Corbusier," *Architecture and Building News,* March 17, 1929.

The list of the nineteen Matisses sent to Berlin from the Michael and Sarah Stein collection is in the archives of the Cone Collection, Baltimore Museum of Art. For the subsequent adventures of these pictures, I have followed the version of the story told by Sarah Stein to Gabrielle Osorio, Elise Haas and Dr. Jeffrey Smith. I remain skeptical of this version because Alfred H. Barr's version (told in his *Matisse,* pages 177-178)—that the Steins recovered the pictures and *then* sold them to the Scandinavians—is supported by letters to him from Hans Purrmann and Leo Swane. Despite my leaning toward this well-documented version, however, I have used in my text Sarah Stein's version because in her reliable years she clung unequivocally to it.

I am grateful to Adelyn Breeskin, director of the Baltimore Museum of Art; Gertrude Rosenthal, curator; Mrs. Joseph N. Ulman; Edna Long Lichtenfels; Alice B. Toklas; and Walter Pach for granting me interviews about the Cone sisters. My thanks also to the staff of the *Baltimore News Post* and the *Evening Sun* for giving me access to their morgues, whose clippings proved useful for background and for straightening out misinformation about Dr. Claribel's medical career.

Other important sources for data on the Cones were: *The Cone Collection of Baltimore, Maryland,* Baltimore, 1934, with an introduction by George Boas; *The Handbook of the Cone Collection,* the Baltimore Museum of Art, 1955, with articles by George Boas and Gertrude Rosenthal; Adelyn Breeskin's "Early Picasso Drawings in the

Cone Collection," *Magazine of Art,* March, 1952; Adele Nathan's "The Cone Collection of Baltimore," *Vogue,* March 1, 1949.

Patron: John Quinn

My warm thanks to Jeanne Robert Foster, who gave me access to the invaluable Quinn correspondence, diaries, photographs, legal arguments and memorabilia which she has devotedly preserved; to Henri-Pierre Roché who also shared essential material with me; to John Quinn's niece, who drew aside the "silken curtain of silence" to help me with material and give me permission to quote from her uncle's letters. I thank Walter Pach, Marcel Duchamp, Ezra Pound and the late Constantin Brancusi for helpful interviews. I acknowledge the courtesy of the Manuscript Division of the New York Public Library in allowing me to consult the copies of the letters to Quinn preserved there.

In addition to these basic sources, major sources on Quinn and his collection were: *Complete Catalogue of the Library of John Quinn,* 2 vols., the Anderson Galleries, New York, 1924; *John Quinn Catalogue of Paintings, Watercolors, Drawings and Sculptures,* with foreword by Forbes Watson, Huntington, N.Y., 1926 (the most nearly complete record); *Catalogue of Paintings from the John Quinn Collection,* the American Art Association, February 9-11, 1927; *Catalogue des Tableaux Modernes provenant de la collection John Quinn,* with foreword by Jean Cocteau, Hôtel Drouot, Paris, October 28, 1926; *Catalogue of John Quinn Memorial Exhibition at Art Center,* with foreword by Maurice Leon, January 7-30, 1926; John Quinn's *Memorandum against the Imposition of Any Duty on Original Works of Art,* privately printed; Walter Pach's *Queer Thing, Painting,* New York, 1938; James J. Walsh's "John Quinn: Lawyer, Book-Lover, Art Amateur," *Catholic World,* November, 1924; Jeanne Robert Foster's "Preface" to the Quinn correspondence in the New York Public Library; Henri-Pierre Roché's "Homage à John Quinn, Collectionneur," *La Parisienne,* August-September, 1954 (excellent on Quinn's personality, unreliable on facts of purchasing, etc.); and F. J. Gregg's "Quinn Collection," *The Independent,* February 27, 1926.

Important sources for other aspects of this chapter were as follows: Walt Kuhn's *Twenty-five Years After: The Story of the Armory Show,* New York, 1938; Daniel Catton Rich's *The Arthur Jerome Eddy Collection,* the Art Institute of Chicago; Milton Brown's *American Painting from the Armory Show to the Depression,* Princeton, N.J., 1955; and, for the story of the Brancusi trial, the Stenographic Minutes, U. S. Customs Court, C. Brancusi vs. U. S., New York, 1927.

My thanks to A. L. Chanin, R. Sturgis Ingersoll, Anna Ingersoll, the late Edward Root, Walter Pach, Henri-Pierre Roché and Bernard Berenson for granting me interviews about Dr. Barnes. A. L. Chanin's "The House that Barnes Built," *Harper's Bazaar,* July, 1952, was helpful, but I am most grateful to Carl McCardle's excellent and courageous four-part biography, "The Terrible-Tempered Dr. Barnes," *Saturday Evening Post,* March 21, 28, April 4, 11, 1942, for facts and anecdotes. My thanks to the staff of the *Philadelphia Bulletin* for giving me access to its morgue.

Propagandist: Katherine S. Dreier

My sincere gratitude to Mary E. Dreier, Katherine Dreier's sister and author of *Margaret Dreier Robins,* New York, 1950, for talking with me and putting at my disposal privately printed family books and boxes of informative photographs; to Marcel Duchamp, primary and essential source on Miss Dreier as a collector and the collection; to George Heard Hamilton of Yale University; and to Henri-Pierre Roché, Naum Gabo, Henry McBride, James Johnson Sweeney for adding to my knowledge of the collector.

Aside from these sources, major sources were as follows: *The Catalogue of the Collection of the Société Anonyme: Museum of Modern Art, 1920,* New Haven, Conn., 1950; George Heard Hamilton's "Anonyme No Longer," *Art News,* January, 1953; Katherine S. Dreier's "Intrinsic Significance of Modern Art," *Three Lectures on Modern Art,* New York, 1948; Katherine S. Dreier's *Burliuk,* New York, 1944;

Rudi Blesh's *Modern Art USA,* New York, 1956 (which contains spirited accounts of the Society of Independents, Duchamp, Arensberg and Dreier); Milton Brown's *American Painting,* cited above, to whose analysis of Walter Arensberg I am indebted.

The Quiet World: Edward Wales Root

I was fortunate in knowing Edward Root before his death and in having a chance to talk with him several times about his collecting. My unqualified thanks to Grace Cogswell Root, his wife, who generously gave me access to her late husband's correspondence, diaries, notes, photographs, notebooks and all sorts of memorabilia, including her "secret Boswell" volumes, all vastly enhanced by her organization and annotations. My thanks also to Robert Beverly Hale, curator of American painting at the Metropolitan Museum, and to all the artists and dealers and members of the staffs of Hamilton College and Munson-Williams-Proctor Institute who talked with me of Edward Root.

Major sources for other aspects of this chapter were as follows: Aline Bernstein's *An Actor's Daughter,* New York, 1941; *The Private Collection of Thomas B. Clarke in New York Exhibited at the American Art Gallery,* New York, December 28, 1883-January 12, 1884, with notes by Thomas B. Clarke and introduction by S. R. Koehler; the various sale catalogues of the Thomas B. Clarke collections; Ralph Seymour and Arthur Stanley Rigg's "The Gellatly Collection," *Art and Archeology,* May, 1924; Karl J. Bolander's "Ferdinand Howald and His Collection," *Bulletin of the Columbus Gallery of Fine Arts,* January, 1931.

Little Man in a Big Hurry: Joseph H. Hirshhorn

Joseph H. Hirshhorn's own frank and colorful testimony, in person and, inevitably, on the long-distance telephone, is the major source of the material in this chapter. I thank him heartily. I am also indebted for informative interviews to Abram Lerner, Stephen Kay, Edward

Parker, Theodore Heinrich, Allen Jarves, Henry Moore, Philip C. Johnson and many artists and dealers.

My major source for data on Hirshhorn's childhood and financial career was Emmett Hughes, "Joe Hirshhorn, the Brooklyn Uranium King," *Fortune,* November, 1956. Of many newspaper and periodical articles, "Big Spender," *Time,* July 25, 1955, and "A Town's New Life," *Life,* August 1, 1955, were most useful. The article by Albert Dorne on Hirshhorn as a collector in the summer 1958 issue of *Art in America* did not appear until after my manuscript was completed.

Americana: Electra Havemeyer Webb

My deep gratitude to Electra Havemeyer Webb for sparing many hours out of a busy life for me, for answering streams of questions and putting private material at my disposal and for acting as a charming and informative guide to the Shelburne Museum. I am also grateful for illuminating anecdotes and affectionate insights to her five children: Samuel B. Webb (my main and wholly delightful source on the hunting episodes, whom I hope I have not betrayed by my own ignorance of Dall sheep and brown bear), J. Watson Webb, Jr., Mrs. John Wilmerding, Mrs. Dunbar Bostwick, and Harry Webb; to Ralph Nading Hill, trustee of the Shelburne Museum, Lilian Baker Carlisle, curator, Sterling D. Emerson, director; and to Mrs. P. H. B. Frelinghuysen.

Aside from those mentioned above, major sources for this chapter were: two articles by Mrs. Webb, "Folk Art in the Shelburne Museum," *Art in America,* May, 1955, and "Americana at Shelburne," *Winter Antiques Show, 65th Street Armory,* January 7-12, 1957; Ralph Nading Hill and Lilian Baker Carlisle's *The Story of the Shelburne Museum,* Shelburne, Vt., 1955; Ralph Nading Hill's *Shelburne Museum,* Newcomen Society in North America, New York, 1955; Lilian Baker Carlisle's *The Carriages at the Shelburne Museum;* Allene Tallmey's "The New Shelburne Museum," *Vogue,* February 1, 1953; *Art in America,* May, 1955 (an issue devoted to reconstruction villages, with an especially useful article by Abbot Lowell Cummings). Alice Winchester, writing in *Antiques,* August, 1954, is responsible for the astute, often-quoted comment that the Shelburne Museum is "a collection of collections."

Cowboys and Indians: Thomas Gilcrease

Thomas Gilcrease himself is the major source of my data in this chapter. I sincerely thank him for his friendly and outspoken cooperation. I am grateful also to Mr. Gilcrease's daughter, Mrs. Mack Phillips, James T. Forrest, director of the Thomas Gilcrease Institute of American History and Art, Roger Devlin, Mrs. Devlin, and E. Teenor for talking with me about Mr. Gilcrease and his collection; to C. R. Smith and William Davidson, as guides to art of the West; and to the staff of the morgues of the *Tulsa Tribune* and the *Tulsa World,* in which I used extensive and invaluable clippings. Aside from these my major source for data was "Saving a Vanishing Frontier," *Life,* March 8, 1954 (and the quotation about the "conscience of one race, etc.," comes from this article). James T. Forrest's article on the Gilcrease collection in the summer of 1958 issue of *Art in America* appeared after my manuscript was completed.

Important sources for other aspects of this chapter were: Alva Johnston's "Colonel Carter of Cartersville, Texas," *Saturday Evening Post,* November 26, 1938; and *The T. B. Walker Collection of Indian Portraits,* the State Historical Society of Wisconsin, Madison, Wis., 1948.

Appassionata of the Avant-Garde: Peggy Guggenheim

Peggy Guggenheim, in person and in print, is the primary source of the material in this chapter. I thank her warmly for her frankness, patience and kindness and for giving me access to her well-organized scrapbooks of clippings and catalogues, to family photograph albums and to other pertinent material.

Major sources for data were: Peggy Guggenheim's *Out of This Century,* New York, 1946, and her later, *Una Collezionista Ricorda,* Venice, 1956, with an introduction by Alfred H. Barr, Jr.; *Art of This*

Century: objects, drawings, photographs, paintings, 1910-42, edited by Peggy Guggenheim with introductory remarks by André Breton, Piet Mondrian, Jean Arp and statements by the artists, New York, 1942; *La Collezione Peggy Guggenheim,* with introductory notes by W. J. H. B. Sandberg, Sir Herbert Read and Alfred H. Barr, Jr., Florence, n.d. (this catalogue documents some of the post-1942 acquisitions, including those by the young Americans whom she sponsored).

Peggy Guggenheim's art activities have been extensively covered in the press. *Time,* April 25, 1938, and December 16, 1957, and *Newsweek,* November 2, 1942, were of special value.

I thank Sir Herbert Read, Clement Greenberg, James Johnson Sweeney, Alfred H. Barr, Jr., Margaret Scolari, Jimmy Ernst, Marcel Duchamp, Julien Levy and Harry and Lydia Winston for granting me interviews about Peggy Guggenheim.

The One Luxury: The Rockefellers

JOHN D. ROCKEFELLER, JR. My major source for data was Raymond B. Fosdick's *John D. Rockefeller, Jr., A Portrait,* New York, 1956 (an excellent and fascinating biography, indispensable for an understanding of both its central subject and the Rockefeller family). I am beholden to Mr. Fosdick (and through him also to John D. Rockefeller, Jr.) for permission to use direct quotations from pages 334, 329, 336, 330 and to use factual material from pages 335, 330, 333, 337). My thanks also to James J. Rorimer, Edward Fowles, Mitchell Samuels, Bernard Berenson, Kenneth Chorley and several of Mr. Rockefeller's children for talking with me about the collector.

The computation of the astronomical possibility of the Rockefeller fortune is quoted in Joe Alex Morris' "The Rockefellers," *Saturday Evening Post,* December 30, 1950, and the figure of the Rockefeller benefactions was ingeniously arrived at by Victor H. Lawn in the *New York Times,* August 7, 1955. The data on Mrs. Harold McCormick is from Wayne Andrews' *Battle for Chicago,* cited above, and the Dirkan Kelekian incident is from that dealer's article in *Art News Annual,* February 25, 1939.

ABBY ALDRICH ROCKEFELLER. Two major sources for data on Mrs.

Rockefeller were: Mary Ellen Chase's *Abby Aldrich Rockefeller,* New York, 1950 (the basic and indispensable biography and one to which I am indebted) and Dorothy C. Miller's "Contemporary American Painting in the Collection of Mrs. John D. Rockefeller, Jr.," *Art News,* March 26, 1938. I thank Edith Halpert, Dorothy Miller, Alfred H. Barr, Jr., Antoinette Kraushaar, Edward Fowles and several of Mrs. Rockefeller's children for granting me interviews.

Important sources for other aspects of this chapter were: Daniel Catton Rich's "O Pioneers," cited above (for data on Mrs. Coburn); A. Conger Goodyear's *The Museum of Modern Art: The First Ten Years,* New York, 1943; and Rudi Blesh's *Modern Art USA,* cited above.

"THE BROTHERS." Naturally, I consulted many, many magazine and newspaper articles about the members of "The Third Generation." Aside from particular sources noted below under each name, the two major articles for my data were Joe Alex Morris' "The Rockefellers," *Saturday Evening Post,* December 30, 1950, January 6 and 13, 1951, and Richard Austin Smith's "The Rockefeller Brothers," *Fortune,* February and March, 1955.

BLANCHETTE ROCKEFELLER. Blanchette Rockefeller charmingly and agreeably subjected herself to interviews and acted as guide and mentor for me in several situations. I am deeply in her debt. I am also grateful to John D. Rockefeller III, for his patience and good humor about this project; to Nelson A. Rockefeller, Alfred H. Barr, Jr., Philip C. Johnson and several dealers who talked with me about Mrs. Rockefeller's collecting.

DAVID ROCKEFELLER. I am appreciative of the courtesy and assistance of David Rockefeller and "Mrs. David" and thank them also for permission to reproduce a detail of their living room. Other members of the family and Alfred H. Barr, Jr., were helpful in supplying data. "Living with the Great," *Vogue,* February, 1956, splendidly illustrates the interiors of the New York residence.

NELSON A. ROCKEFELLER. With his usual capacity for enthusiasm and single-minded concentration, Nelson A. Rockefeller talked with me about his art collecting, and this section is based largely on his testimony. My thanks also to "Mrs. Nelson," Wallace K. Harrison, Alfred H. Barr, Jr., René d'Harnoncourt, Dorothy C. Miller, Carol Kinzel

Uht, Victor Borella, Frank Jamieson, Philip C. Johnson and members of the Rockefeller family.

I wish to make special recognition of two articles from which I drew data: Geoffrey Hellman's "Best Neighbor," *The New Yorker,* April 11 and 18, 1942, and Herbert Warren Wind's "Architect," *The New Yorker,* November 20 and 27, December 4, 1954.

Special thanks to Martha Dalrymple, associate director of public relations for the Rockefeller brothers, for her cheerful perseverance in answering many requests for information, photographs and permissions.

Other Acknowledgments

In addition to the people mentioned in the Foreword and those specifically acknowledged in connection with various chapters, there are others to whom I would like to express sincere gratitude:

To my son Hal Louchheim, for setting up a work routine for me; to the staff of the *New York Times* morgue, which I used extensively, and to the bureau chiefs and "stringers" of the *New York Times,* who arranged for me to use local newspaper morgues; to Janet E. Smith, who added long-term enthusiasm to long-term secretarial assistance; to Ruth Weigmann, who rallied magnificently for the "charette"; to Lily Lampi, especially, and the intermittent others who relieved me of household responsibilities at necessary moments; to the Bell Telephone long-distance operators, who helped me track down innumerable people strategic to my research; to the patient Mrs. Constance Barnes of the Cranbrook Academy of Art Library; to the friendly staff of the library of the Detroit Institute of Arts; and to the hard-working staffs of the General Information, Microfilm and Fine Arts Departments of the Detroit Public Library, where—because of its extraordinarily good collection of books and periodicals—I was able to do a large part of my research. The Chase Manhattan Bank Money Museum kindly supplied currency conversion figures. Elizabeth Shaw, director of public relations at the Museum of Modern Art, supplied factual information with efficiency and friendliness.

Index

ABOUT THE AUTHOR

ALINE B. SAARINEN was born in 1914, in Manhattan. Although she now lives in Bloomfield Hills, Michigan, with her husband, the architect Eero Saarinen, and their three-year-old son, Eames—and has at other times lived in Pittsburgh and Washington, D.C.—she remains loyally a New Yorker. Her two older sons, Donald Louchheim and Hal Louchheim, are, respectively, a senior at Yale and a sophomore at Harvard.

Her interest in writing stems from the childhood free-verse period when her ambition was to be a great poetess with the pen name of Emily Isabelle Amber. Her interest in art began when she was taken, at the age of nine, through French Romanesque and Gothic churches. In 1935 she graduated from Vassar College. She received an M.A. from the Institute of Fine Arts, New York University, in 1941. From 1944 to 1948 she was on the staff of *Art News;* from 1948 until 1954 she was Associate Art Editor and Critic of the *New York Times.* Since then, except for a year's leave of absence, she has continued as Associate Art Critic, commuting once a month to New York.

Her articles have appeared in *Vogue, Atlantic Monthly, Reader's Digest, Cosmopolitan,* etc. She received the international award for the best foreign art criticism of the Venice Biennale in 1951; the Frank Jewett Mather award and the American Federation of Arts award, both for best newspaper art criticism, in 1953; and a Guggenheim fellowship in 1957 for the completion of THE PROUD POSSESSORS.